TEMAGAMI LAKES ASSOCIATION

The Life and Times of a Cottage Community

TEMAGAMI LAKES ASSOCIATION

THE LIFE AND TIMES OF A COTTAGE COMMUNITY

Pamela (Glenn) Sinclair

Temagami Lakes Association

Temagami, Ontario

TRAFFORD PUBLISHING

Editor: Patricia Healy
Publisher Liaison: Vince Hovanec
Cover photographs by (clockwise from upper left) Lookout: Autumn splendour from the North
Arm's Beaver Island Lookout. Photo by Harold Keevil; Loon family. Photo: Adam Keevil;
Centre Falls above the Golden Staircase in the Lady Evelyn-Smoothwater Wilderness Park.
Photo: Harold Keevil; Joan Peninsula west of Rabbitnose Island shows its autumn colours.
Photo: Harold Keevil; Dancing Loon. Photo: Adam Keevil; February at the mouth of the
Obabika River. Photo: Harold Keevil.

Printed in the United States of America.

ISBN: 978-1-4269-6762-7 (sc)
ISBN: 978-1-4269-6763-4 (e)

Trafford rev. 06/21/2011

 www.trafford.com

North America & international
toll-free: 1 888 232 4444 (USA & Canada)
phone: 250 383 6864 ♦ fax: 812 355 4082

Temagami Lakes Association: The Life and Times of a Cottage Community is dedicated to the TLA membership – past, present and future. Without their support, this organization would not be celebrating 80 years of existence and there would be no vibrant history to recount in these pages. It is dedicated in particular to my father Jack Glenn who wrote "the white paper" in 1991, which led to the adoption of the Tenets for Temagami.

TABLE OF CONTENTS

PREFACE

Shore Lines

I blame/thank Fred. I've never met him but the evolution of this book is his fault/credit. Fred Hunt to be precise, an enlightened gent who likes to keep himself informed. It all began on July 10, 2008, when Fred guilelessly emailed TLA Executive Secretary Peter Healy: "I have been coming to Temagami since 1960 as a camper and mostly guest at Ojibway of Keewaydin, so I have long known of the good work of TLA."

This is where Fred sprinkles a little sugar dust: "In "surfing" your site today in preparation for coming up, I read the history article. I have known and heard bits and pieces of many of the issues described, but the written description was incredibly fair and candid. Nice job. Thanks for all TLA does."

Fred's words, dripping with honey, stuck to Peter. He forwarded Fred's message to me on July 13. Peter added: "Any interest in updating the file or your Historical Perspective?" The "file" referred to the history section of the TLA's website, which I wrote sometime around the computer hysteria of the New Millennium. It's the tab Fred had pointed and clicked on. The "Historical Perspective" was the book *Temagami Lakes Association: An Historical Perspective,* which I (literally) penned from 1991 to '92.

Peter's lines were met with a sourpuss response from me on July 14: "Please recall that the original book had a limited readership base." Read: Who's going to buy it? "I write about curling rock hounds for three newspapers and I'm also the news hound for my curling club's monthly newsletter." Read: Who's got the time to write it? The icing on the cake: "I don't want to write a book that collects dust bunnies instead of dog ears."

Nothing much from Peter landed in my inbox for a time. Then he followed up with this candy-coated communiqué: "I really think we should do this regardless of the immediate market. It is important to get the story right while the players are still with us and more important for an organization to respect its past if it hopes to be effective in the future."

While I waffled, the board of directors greenlit a revision. An update would await another day when the board decided the time was right for a new book. I breathed a sigh of relief. Writing more about the lake's trailblazers and characters held a lot of appeal, Temagami's Official Plan and the MNR's Comprehensive Plan – not so much. Not that either was unimportant; it just seemed that getting them up and running took an eternity. And their production was not immune to the one constant that Temagami planning is notorious for – controversy. My relief was short-lived; upon my submission of some book revisions in June 2009 the board committed to an updated volume.

The learning curve was steep. I know more than I ever wanted about Ontario's municipal, public lands and corporations acts, and the best and worst of cedar versus plastic canoes...I'm still unsure what a PAC acronym signifies. Is it a municipal planning, a forest advisory or a land claim consulting committee? All of the above, it turns out. Did you know the TLA has a Shoreline Reserve, the MNR has shoreline reserves and the Anishnabai want their own reserve? Then there's Shiningwood Bay's David Taylor and Island 847's David Taylor, and Bear Island contractor John Turner and former Prime Minister John Turner.

The publication of the original book set off a series of significant events, some more significant than others. In the mid to late-1990s a memorial plaque, dedicated in 1934 to founding president Robert Newcomb, up and vanished from the lawn of the Bear Island store. The large boulder to which the tablet was affixed has four clean bolt holes. It was recently moved by Temagami First Nation (TFN) forklifts.

The rock bore silent witness to raucous regattas, the heralded arrivals and departures of the *Belle* and the *Aubrey*, nefarious break-ins, hopeful and hopeless land claim settlement offers, square dance revellers, fires, drownings, parched canoe trippers downing copious amounts of pop and ice cream and, finally,

the theft of its bronzed jewel. The elements and vegetation had conspired against the plaque, rendering its inscribed message difficult to decipher and the boulder hard to find. By the 1980s a majority of TLA members and Bear Islanders were unaware of the tablet's existence and its historical significance.

My retelling the story of the plaque prompted an idea from a relative who inherited the Newcomb island in the mid-1990s. He suggested the tablet be relocated to the TLA building, subject to TFN sanction, to spare it further deterioration and neglect. Will the mystery ever be solved? Probably not. My theory is that a souvenir hunter became intrigued after reading about the tablet and viewing a photo of it in the 1992 book.

In the book's aftermath, a burgeoning fictional crime writer began hatching new plots. Michael and Shelley Bloomfield of Chagrin Falls, Ohio, purchased South Arm Island 950 about 1999. Michael's family had a substantial connection to the lake. His parents met as Camp Wabikon counsellors in the late 1940s. His sisters attended Metagami and Michael went to Northwoods. Michael and Shelley accordingly sent their daughters to Wabikon.

Shelley has a PhD in English and teaches writing and literature. She writes under her maiden name Shelley Costa. She became interested in the Newcomb chronicles, recounted in the book and the *Temagami Times*, especially the part where Robert and his wife Faith meet a grisly end. Shelley fictionalized their demise in one of her capers, a short story titled "Black Heart and Cabin Girl." It was published in *Blood On Their Hands*, a 2004 crime fiction anthology, and earned her an Edgar Award nomination from the Mystery Writers of America.

"The Newcomb story was creatively stimulating," Shelley affirmed. Among her published prose, three others are either set on or inspired by the lake. She was working on a mystery novel in 2010, again borrowing the lake as a venue. "Mind you, I invent whole new arms of the lake in order to keep things clearly fictional," she said.

Still another tie-in emerged in the late 1990s. Donald Smith has taught Canadian history at the University of Calgary since 1974. He authored a trilogy of biographies about three prominent historic figures – Honoré Jaxon, Long Lance and Grey Owl – who all faked aboriginal ancestry. Grey Owl, whose real name was Archie Belaney, adopted aboriginal ways he learned on Bear Island more than one hundred years ago. Donald sought and received my and the board's permission to use the book for teaching non-computer-based research skills. You could say that the earlier book motivated a thief, let an author's creative juices run wild and set an unusual standard as an academic tool.

I wrote *Temagami Lakes Association: An Historical Perspective* at my dining room table. I had to move to the kitchen table for this project so I could plug in my laptop. Once again, a dog rested and often snored at my feet, my third Japanese chin since I authored the original book. Last time, a cat purred

and rubbed her ears against the corners of old TLA directories. Her loafing replacement padded across the keyboard and pounced on the mouse. My two-year-old daughter Bethie insisted on frequent "kiss and hug" breaks back in 1991. Now I insist on infrequent "kiss and hug" breaks the rare times when my 21-year-old Liz is home.

Upon re-examining personal material I drew on for the initial book, I was delighted to discover early efforts to make a mark on her tiny world – ripped and ragged papers bearing tooth indentations, crayon scribbles and chicken noodle soup stains. It is my hope that this book reanimates some good memories for readers.

Pamela (Glenn) Sinclair 2011

CHAPTER 1

WANDERLUST

What kind of place would draw well-bred city folk to venture hundreds, even thousands of kilometres north into the unknown, at the turn of the 20th century? The land of Temagami is such a place. Other beautiful places have lakes, rivers, forests and ancient rock. Temagami transcends these. Here, the unique combination of pure crystal waters, diverse forests, high granite outcrops, big skies and exciting wildlife lends a primeval quality to its wildness.

Temagami pulled in those with wanderlust. It drew those yearning for adventure, for the soul-nurturing peace of wild nature and for some, wealth. Early adventure seekers called it a "paddler's paradise," while the Anishnabai have called it home for centuries.

Within the region's 10,000 square kilometres of water, forests and rocky hills lies Lake Temagami. On a map, the island-studded lake appears like some multi-armed creature. Bear Island, located at the heart, became a central meeting place for the slow stream of turn of the century canoeists who traversed the region's interconnected waterways.

Coming hard on the heels of land and mineral surveyors, timber cruisers, federal Indian agents and Oblate priests were poets and artists. These included Ottawa's Archibald Lampman who penned the renowned poem "Timagami." Archibald tripped in the area in autumn 1896. Already weakened by childhood rheumatic fever, he suffered a cardiac relapse due to exertion, leading to an early death in 1899 at the age of 37.

> *Timagami*
>
> *Far in the grim Northwest*
> *beyond the lines*
> *That turn the rivers eastward*
> *there to the sea,*
> *Set with a thousand islands,*
> *crowded with pines,*
> *Lies deep water, wild Timagami:*
> *Wild for the hunter's roving, and the use*
> *Of trappers in its dark*
> *and trackless vales,*
>
> *Wild with the trampling*
> *of the giant moose,*
> *And the weird magic of old Indian tales,*
> *All day with steady paddles*
> *toward the west*
> *Our heavy-laden long canoe we pressed:*
> *All day we saw the thunder-travelled sky*
> *Purple with storm in many a trailing tress,*
> *And saw at eve the broken sunset die*
> *In crimson on the silent wilderness.*
> Archibald Lampman, 1896

Following in Archibald's wake, American George Marsh canoed Temagami country about 1905. His poem "The Old Canoe" was published in *Scribner's Magazine* in 1908. It is oft-recited in song by campers around the fire at Temagami's youth camps, past and present.

The duplicitous Duncan Campbell Scott arrived in Temagami as a gentle, sensitive poet of note. As the head of the Department of Indian Affairs in later years, he was a notoriously tyrannical champion of repressive assimilation policies, including native residential schools where communicable diseases and sexual abuse ran rampant.

After experiencing early Temagami, United Church Minister Charles William Gordon, who wrote under the pen name Ralph Connor, became a prolific writer of best-selling novels portraying frontier adventures. Artist C.W. Jefferys, whose central passion was portraying early Canadiana in order to preserve it, must have filled many sketch books during his time in Temagami. Celebrated painters, novelists and poets would return en masse in the 1980s, not to explore Temagami but to save it.

Postcard Passages

Other less professional writers have painted a vivid picture of life on the lake. Images on old Temagami postcards are a trove of historical interest. Haileybury photographer Alex MacLean, who was fond of Temagami, took photos of the area from 1909 to '59. Many of his images became postcards that are popular today with collectors. The writing on the back often tells a tale of torment or terrific times. Between 1905 and 1965, bad weather was often the main topic. It ranged from "raining cats and dogs" and "we haven't had an overdose of sun" to "I had 3 wool blankets over me last night and my feet are still cold."

Regardless of the climes, most writers reported a "swell," "dandy" or "grand" time, fishing being the main pursuit. "Being 30 miles from any town has its advantage which is proven by the fact we all feel so much better," one wrote in 1935. "We've been having a grand time. Just as nice as Paradise [Iowa] and much cheaper," another wrote in 1933. "Extraordinary sunsets and northern lights. Ice 52 inches thick here in winter," a scribe observed in 1943.

A tourist at Camp Wabi-Kon wrote home in 1922 saying, "The fried fish is best I ever had. Have not seen big game yet. Rabbits and squirrels running all over my tent on top playing tag I guess." Electricity was on the mind of this writer in 1937: "Well here we are at the hopping off point but we have a fine log cabin but this time with an oil lamp instead of G.E. bulbs."

A Keewaydin staffman wrote in 1933, "Big square dance in our honour last night with canuck musicians and callers. Much hilarity." The following summer, Claire Rannie's father Bob Rannie, 18, worked as a Keewaydin kitchen boy. He penned these words to his mother: "An awful 10 hour train trip. The camp is swell. We have started work and I think I will like it." The card was postmarked at camp July 9 and arrived at Bob's home in Chesley, Ontario, July 10. The stamp cost two cents.

Some interesting cards were postmarked at Bear Island. "This is some wild place," one visitor wrote in 1922. "No place for eats as there are almost 400 wild huskie dogs here and they all yowl at once." A nurse bound for a tent hospital at the Cobalt silver camp in 1909 wrote of her experience: "We had to call the police twice, one for drunks beside the tents swearing and for another one with a revolver."

A *Belle of Temagami* passenger wrote in 1927: "Am on the "Bell of Temagami" about headed for Bear Island where we will get an 18 foot canoe and go on 11 miles to a portage and then about 2 miles to Lake Obabika where we expect to be for about a week."

Perhaps these lines best sum up the Temagami experience for postcard scribes: "It is our ideal spot – wild but beautiful. We are having the time of our lives." An October 1905 visitor had trouble recording his impressions: "There are only 3 post cards here so those who do not get one will know the reasons."

A Settlers' Paradise?

One notable early camper was Father Charles Paradis who visited in 1890, calling himself Temiskaming's first tourist. He established a mission at Sandy Inlet a year later, where Camp Wanapitei is now located. After clearing some acreage, he put orphaned Franco-Ontarian boys to work planting vegetables. Following the construction of the

Tall-tale postcards were all the rage prior to World War Two. *Photo: Reg Sinclair*

Temiskaming and Northern Ontario Railway (TNOR) to Temagami, Charles began selling his produce to central-area cottagers.

C.C. Farr, the founder of Haileybury, wrote of Lake Temagami in an 1894 pamphlet: "When this lake is opened up for the public, nearly every man of leisure can become, for a few months in each year, an inhabitant of his own island – an amateur Robinson Crusoe. It

A year-round log home and office built in 1905 on Forestry Island near the village employed 59 summer rangers. This grew to 137 by 1912, nearly half the provincial contingent. *Postcard photo: Reg Sinclair*

is not, nor will it be, a settlers' paradise; but summer tourists will rejoice in it, and be glad for a greater than Muskoka is there. Thirteen hundred islands studding an immense lake where water is as clear as crystal and abounding in fish will make such a resort for city-choked, sun-scorched, dust-laden tourists as Canada never saw before."

The Keiths – Deep Roots

Toronto's George Keith learned the truth of C.C.'s prognostication. The Keiths of South Arm Island 956 are believed to be the cottaging family with the deepest roots on Lake Temagami, stretching back to 1893. That's the year George, a business partner in Keith Seeds, set out for the lake after canoeing extensively in southern Ontario. He was accompanied by five others, including Henry and Harry Mason of the Mason and Risch piano company. They crossed Lake Nipissing in their birchbark canoes, went up the Sturgeon River to the Temagami River, then through Cross Lake and into Lake Temagami.

They ventured to the backcountry again in summer 1894, this time from Lake Wanapitei in Sudbury District, eventually through Gull Lake and into the Southwest Arm. One of the highlights was a stop at Bear Island for a chat with Hudson's Bay Company (HBC) post Factor Fraser and a slice of Mary Turner's blueberry pie, even though the Turners' Lakeview House would not open for a few more years.

Needing a break after working as soldiers of the soil during the First World War on

Scarborough and Essex county farms, George Keith returned to Temagami in 1919 with his son Bill. While on Obabika Lake, they spotted a raging forest fire. They paddled back to the Bear Island forest rangers' building, which had opened in 1901 with 15 rangers, and alerted Chief Ranger Clarence Hindson.

The chief ranger later sold fishing guide licences for $5 each to the Keiths who guided tourists picked up at Bear Island. Father and son returned in 1920 and bought a canoe from A.L. Cochrane who told George Aulabaugh about the pair. George had recently opened Camp Acouchiching, a rustic fishing camp on the South Arm. Soon Bill and several young Toronto friends, mostly University of Toronto (U of T) students, had summer jobs guiding tourists at Couch for $5 per day.

Bill Keith's cousin John Keith also guided at Couch from 1926 until '31. John met his future wife Mary Carson at her nearby family cottage on Island 956. Mary's father Herbert Carson was a superintendent of the Pennsylvania Railway. He ventured north about 1908 and camped at Shiningwood Bay. In later years he stayed at Couch with his family. Herbert leased Island 956 in the mid-1920s.

Bill became Canada's chief neurosurgeon at the Hospital for Sick Children and Toronto Western Hospital. John also took a medical path and graduated from the U of T medical school in 1932, having earned tuition money from his guiding days. He went on to become a world pioneer in children's heart disorders. He founded the cardiology department at Toronto's Hospital for Sick Children and what

is now the Heart and Stroke Foundation. John died in 1989 and Island 956 is now owned by John and Mary's three children – Nancy Smith, and Greg and Christina Keith. Their grandchildren are the fifth generation of Keiths on the lake.

The Keiths' ties to the lake were tested and nearly severed. Actor Jimmy Stewart's father Alexander Stewart, owner of a Pennsylvania hardware store, took a summer break at Couch in 1940. The Carson island was just a stone's throw away from Couch islands 938 and 939. Alexander likely passed it during fishing excursions. He decided he wanted the Carson place, lock, stock and barrel. Both Herbert Carson and Alexander Stewart were of Scottish extraction and the haggling went on for hours. In the end they were a mere $50 apart, but neither would budge and the deal got scuttled. Had the transaction proceeded, we could have expected Tinseltown to produce such classics as *Mr. Smith Goes to Wasaksina* and *The Spirit of St. Ursula*.

Cassels, Kelley and a Cast of Characters

Just a year after George Keith first dipped his paddle into Lake Temagami, Toronto's Richard Scougall Cassels and George Mortimer Kelley discovered "a noble lake that lies forest-hidden in the northern wilds of Canada; in unknown country, unapproachable save by canoe, it is, in its island-dowered loveliness, a divinity well worthy of the paddler's worship," as Richard described the lake in an 1896 *Massey's Magazine* article. Richard and George made canoe excursions through the Lady Evelyn-Temagami routes, and the Mattawa and Montreal rivers, among others, in the years 1892 through 1901. They came specifically to the Temagami area in 1894, '95 and '96.

Richard Cassels was born in 1859 and acquired a law degree from the U of T's Osgoode Hall. He was admitted to the bar in 1882 and became a partner in a Toronto law firm, which became known as Cassels, Brock and Kelley. He was appointed King's Counsel in 1910.

In his younger days Richard served as a lieutenant with the Queen's Own Rifles of the North West Field Force. He was involved in the Northwest Campaign and fought in the battle of Cut Knife Hill, Saskatchewan, in 1885. This encounter was prevented from turning into a slaughter of the Canadian militia by the intervention of Cree Chief Poundmaker. The action ended with the defeat and retreat of the militia, and was one of several engagements intended to suppress the Métis rebellion led by Louis Riel. The Métis are one of Canada's aboriginal peoples. Originally descendants of aboriginal women and European men, they have evolved into a distinct people with a collective identity. The uprising ended at Batoche where, as all Canadian students are taught, Riel was captured, tried and hanged.

Cassels Lake, originally known as White Bear Lake for the Whitebear family who hunted and farmed there, was renamed in honour of Sir Walter Cassels, Richard's older brother. Walter was a lawyer, Queen's Counsel and Judge of the

Exchequer Court of Canada from 1908 until '23.

George Kelley, born in 1871, joined the Cassels law firm in 1888 as a teenager and worked his way up to a senior partnership. He remained active at the firm until his death

George Kelley in 1896.
Courtesy: Robert Wilson

in 1963, following 75 years of service. The prestigious law firm, now known as Cassels Brock and Blackwell LLP, had on retainer two former Ontario premiers in 2011 – David Peterson and Mike Harris – whose Queen's Park decisions resonated heavily on the lake.

Richard and George's trips often lasted a month and they were usually accompanied by a cast of characters, including some of George's relatives. One paddling partner was William "Billy" Ridout Wadsworth, a Toronto lawyer and Queen's Counsel. He was a close friend of George and likely the youngest tripper, born in 1875. All those summers spent building his upper body strength in a canoe later paid dividends. As a rower, Billy competed in the 1904 St. Louis, Missouri, Summer Olympics and garnered a silver medal in the eight-man race. The rowing team captured Canada's sole second place hardware at those games.

Temagamamingue

Richard Cassels and George Kelley collaborated on an 1896 article titled "A Paddler's Paradise" for the U of T's *Massey's Magazine*. Richard wrote in detail of the "four approaches" to Lake Temagami. He noted that the Ottawa River-Lake Temiscamingue route was the least difficult, though the least pleasing, due to log booms delaying passage in waters where "Lumber is King." He recommended making the preliminary stage from Mattawa to Haileybury via steamer, thereby bypassing this "annoyance."

George provided a pictorial glimpse of the Temagami wildlands for the article through photographs he took of Lake "Temagamamingue," the "Tamagami" River, the "Nemaybinagasbishing" (Lady Evelyn) River and others. Most geographic features had not yet been anglicized to reflect European

colonization. George was the 'official' photographer during these early backcountry treks. Richard also took photos. Some of their photos can be found in the National Archives of Canada Cassels Collection.

George's connection with the lake was not severed as this group of professional men

HBC freight canoe at the post in 1896. From l-r: Richard Cassels, W. Rein Wadsworth, Billy Ridout Wadsworth, Joe Turner, unknown, John Turner and Charlie Moore.
Photo: George Kelley, courtesy of Robert Wilson

married, had families and no longer wished to rough it in the bush. He and his wife Evelyn were married in 1903 and spent vacations in their latter years at Camp Acouchiching with their children. Fond memories led the Kelleys' son-in-law Donald Wilson to purchase Island 958 in 1950 from the Crown for $200. Donald had married George and Evelyn's daughter Marion in 1934. The Wilsons' son Robert, a retired Toronto insurance consultant, and his wife Mary-Louise have three grandchildren who are the fifth generation on the lake.

Writing to a friend in the 1950s, George painted a vivid picture of the lake pre-1900. The letter recapped one of his experiences before railways were built north from North Bay and from Mattawa to where the Ottawa River flows out of Lake Temiskaming. "You would have enjoyed the week's journey, paddling and portaging, it took then to get into Temagami from the end of steel. I and my three companions were the first of the amateur courier de bois, to find our way in and explore the lake, which had no buildings on it whatever except the three small buildings, log and frame, that housed the half dozen half breeds in charge of the Hudson's Bay depot that housed the furs, the supplies – flour, pork, meal, sugar, gunpowder, fish lines, traps, calico [to sew dresses], needles and thread that the people at the post and the Indians who traded there required."

The as yet unregulated lake exuded pure, unfettered, heady wilderness in every sense: "It was rather agreeable, as we fished and shot, to think that no rangers, police magistrates, or tax gatherers were within a hundred miles of the lake, and that we were monarchs of all we surveyed," George wrote. A similar expression of liberation and mastery of domain would lead TLA founding president

Robert Newcomb to be figuratively crowned "King of Temagami" a few years later.

John Gibson and White Pine Forests

In spring 1899 John Morrison Gibson canoed through the Lady Evelyn-Lake Temagami wilderness. "The trip is one of the most enjoyable I ever took part in," he wrote. He wasn't troubled by black flies or mosquitoes as he had been forewarned and arrived back home to Hamilton, Ontario, about three pounds heavier.

"Old Blacknose" at Bear Island in 1896. Claiming to be 110 years old, he was a member of the Rattlesnake (Katt) Clan. His name was Pikudjick, meaning pile of mud, referring to a mole on his nose. He died soon after.
Photo: George Kelley, courtesy of Robert Wilson

John's adventure wasn't all play and no work. As Ontario's commissioner of Crown lands, he assessed the quality of timber stands, noting plenty of white pine and three outlets for transporting logs off Lake Temagami. He favoured the concept of turning the area into a forest reserve. The Temagami Forest Reserve was set aside in 1901 to assure a future wood supply. It included the mainland as well as the islands.

According to John, when logging was permitted inside the reserve, conditions would be imposed to ensure on-site regeneration. This was the beginning of the government's reforestation program and sustainable-yield cutting. However, the province's forest management record has not lived up to John's ideals, witnessed by the vast clear cutting which occurred until 1990.

John was a military man as well as a politician. He was a lieutenant in the 13th Battalion in 1866 and fought at the Battle of Ridgeway, Ontario, defending against the Fenian Invasion. The Fenian Brotherhood, based in the U.S., mounted attacks on British forts, customs posts and other targets to bring pressure on Britain to withdraw from Ireland.

John's political portfolio was extensive. As a Member of Provincial Parliament (MPP) he was Hamilton's most prominent Liberal. He was parliamentary secretary (1889-1896), attorney general (1899-1904) and lieutenant-governor (1908-1914). For his work with the Red Cross, he was knighted by King George V in 1914 and became Sir John.

His fondness for the lake drew him back as a cottager. He occupied 7.5-acre Island 99 in the Northeast Arm and then leased it in 1906, the first year leasing was allowed by the province. Ontario did not permit cottagers to patent, or own, their islands until the 1940s,

but John circumvented Crown land regulations and purchased his island in 1909. The original deed bore two signatures, that of the minister of lands and forests and that of John Gibson who signed it on his own behalf as lieutenant-governor.

John's son Colin Gibson acquired the island following his father's death in 1929. He was a lawyer and like his father, delved into politics. Some of the federal positions he held were minister of national revenue, minister of northern development and secretary of state. Colin died in 1974.

Colin's son James Kerr Gibson acquired Island 99. He is a retired Toronto chartered accountant who now lives in Ancaster, Ontario. The island is held in a land trust for his four children. The family cabins are rustic, or as James put it, "primitive." They don't have hydro and they don't allow modern amenities to ruin a good thing. The Gibsons have earned the distinction of being the cottaging family occupying the same island the longest.

Getting There

When John Gibson, the two Georges – Keith and Kelley, and other hardy souls began exploring the northern hinterland, travel was accomplished by paddle power. There were no steamboats or launches on the lake. The first steamer, the 33.5-foot *Marie*, was shipped by rail from Toronto and then hauled by a 16-horse team and sleigh over a canoe and portage route from Lake Temiskaming in 1903 by prospector and entrepreneur Dan O'Connor. She was single-decked and weighed 3.74 tons. Trees had to be removed to widen portages and allow her passage. Dan's daring feat was recorded by Ripley's *Believe It or Not*, believe it or not.

Three years later the *Belle of Temagami* became the flagship of the Temagami fleet. Her advent would be via railway flat car right to Temagami. Lodgings were sparse. The Ronnoco Hotel wasn't built by village pioneer Dan O'Connor until 1905, to accommodate travellers on the TNOR, constructed through Temagami in 1904. It conveyed passengers by the 1905 summer season to the top of the Northeast Arm. The train and hotel became jumping off points for tourists who leased islands or visited one of the many resorts that would spring to life.

The original townsite was located slightly south of Temagami and included a post office. After the Ronnoco Hotel was constructed, the post office was relocated there. A swamp ran through the new village. Access to a home and store where Northland Traders is now located was via a raised boardwalk. The swamp was later filled in with gravel by the TNOR.

Grey Owl

The Temagami wilderness experience was as close as a non-native could come to emulating indigenous ways. In the early 1900s Archie Belaney fulfilled his boyhood fantasies of living amongst the "red Indians." He learned practical trapping skills, ancient ways of the wild and canoeing techniques on lakes Temiskaming and Temagami from Bill Guppy, Bear Island's native community, and through guiding for Keewaydin Camp in 1910 and '11.

As the bogus Indian Grey Owl, he tilted sooty England on its axel, as the citizenry romanticized an ideal beyond its reach. His fakery may have been exposed, but his message of conservation lives on in this age of climate change.

It was during his first summer guiding at Keewaydin that Archie, 22, wed 20-year-old Temagami native Angele Egwuna. He met Angele at Temagami Inn where he worked as a chore boy and she was a kitchen hand. The witnesses to the Bear Island forestry building ceremony were Tommy Saville, Archie's best Bear Island friend and fellow English immigrant, and John Turner who ran Lakeview House with his wife Mary. Guests included A.L. and Gib Cochrane of Cochrane's Camp. A vacationing Protestant minister from Chicago officiated. A dance at Lakeview House followed the wedding.

Although he asked her to accompany him, Archie left Angele shortly after the birth of daughter Agnes in 1911. Angele was an excellent trapper and provided for her small family. She built a log cabin on Fasken's Point, near the south end of the Northeast Arm, and sold fish to cottagers and camps. Mother and daughter worked in resort kitchens. Agnes had a long career as an outstanding cook and boarding house operator in Temagami. She had four children and numerous grandchildren. She died in 1998 at age 89.

CHAPTER 2

THE KING OF TEMAGAMI

Robert Burton Newcomb first ventured to Lake Temagami in 1902 at the age of 29. He sought high elevation to relieve his hay fever. So smitten was he with the area's pristine wilderness that his love affair would last until death. He canoed the Temagami-Lady Evelyn routes year after year. Whether he found relief from his allergy is unknown and he probably didn't care.

Alfred Horr (l) and Robert Newcomb on a James Bay canoe trip in 1908. Note the mosquito netting. *Photo: Dora Young*

Robert was born in 1872 in New York City. After earning a medical degree, he graduated from law school in 1899 and became a prominent Cleveland lawyer. He married Faith Warner in 1898. Faith's father was president of an Ohio college where she majored in religion. An aunt of Faith was a medical school graduate. In an era when most women stayed in the shadows, the Warner women were well-educated.

Robert practised law with Frank M. Cobb and Benjamen P. Bole. They forged a close bond under the clear blue skies and shimmering northern lights of Temagami. They were joined about 1904 by Alfred R. Horr. He was an officer of the Cleveland Trust Bank who later became president of the city's chamber of commerce. They and other like-minded adventurers styled themselves the Canadian Camp Fire Club of Cleveland.

Robert was accompanied by Alfred on his longest canoe trip. For five weeks in 1908 they travelled 1,516 kilometres to and from James Bay. They set out on the Canadian Pacific Railway (CPR) to a station northwest of Sudbury. Taking an all-water route home, they reached Matachewan and the Montreal River, and then headed south to Temagami. Accompanied by sternmen Presque Petrant and William Peshabo, they were likely the first adventurers to complete this trek. Early youth camps on Lake Temagami waited until after the TNOR had opened to Cochrane at the end of 1908 and the trip was shorter.

The campfire club kept a journal of its canoe trips; it was a polished magazine celebrating the club's journeys, starting from the time members boarded the train in Cleveland. Although some hardships were surely encountered along the trail, life was a jolly jaunt while these professional men were on holiday. Robert was the self-proclaimed "King of Temagami." His throne, as depicted in journal photos, was an old wooden crate and his crown was mosquito netting. Their kingdom was the vast, sparsely populated Temagami wilderness.

Club members did not lack a sense of whimsy. A campfire-cooked repast was prepared in August 1904 by "chef francais Pierre Beaucage of North Bay." The menu included gherkins a là Tincanne, tomato ptomaines, chow chow au Bill, grass pike au Pescah, tin can roast of beef au portage and peaches garnished with twigs and insects.

Nor did the lads lack appetites. For a Sturgeon River trip in 1905 they packed for five guides and four men: 45 pounds of flour; 20 pounds of self-rising flour; 15 pounds of corn meal; 44 pounds of bread; 20 pounds of butter; 240 pounds of potatoes; 42 pounds of Highlands (powdered) cream; 60 pounds of bacon; 30 pounds of ham; and 12 pounds of milk chocolate. If the pork happened to spoil, they simply wiped off the mould with vinegar.

For Robert's earliest travels, supplies and a head guide were provided by a Haileybury merchant. The head guide obtained the services of several native and non-native guides. Provisions that could not be procured

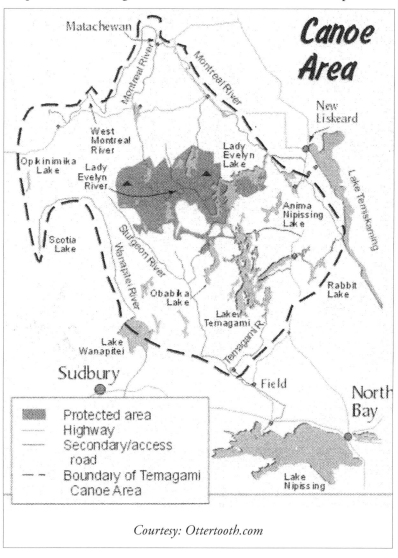

Courtesy: Ottertooth.com

in Haileybury were purchased at New York City's Abercrombie and Fitch Company, an elite sporting goods outfitter, or in Toronto during a train stop-over and carted north.

A ratio of one guide per man and a cook were usually hired. The men would carry their personal gear but left the more unpleasant tasks, such as portaging canoes and scouring cast iron frying pans, to the guides and cook. They engendered little physical danger or exertion. Earlier explorers, such as George Keith, Richard Cassels and George Kelley, hired no guides or cooks to accompany them and did their own grunt work.

Robert's first visit to Lake Temagami occurred one year after the Temagami Forest Reserve was set aside to protect the pine stands for future logging and from forest fires started by tourists. The Ontario government enlarged the reserve in 1904 to 15,000 square kilometres. No land disposition was permitted but that didn't stop tourists from exploring the wonders of Temagami – nor did the lack of a rail line.

The main route in 1902 began where the Ottawa River meets the lower end of Lake Temiskaming. By 1894 a branch line called the Temiskaming Colonization Railway was laid northward from Mattawa to Lake Temiskaming. Once the steel highway ended, adventure canoeists were transported by steamer to a small settlement on a sand beach called the Montreal River landing. A canoe trip lasting a few days ensued. Paddlers went southwest along the Matabitchuan River against the current, eventually reaching the top of the Northeast

Arm through a series of lakes and portages. The final portage crossing now lies beneath the Ontario Northland Railway tracks and Highway 11.

Surveying the Scene

In 1887 Mattawa prospector Peter Ferguson was issued a mining patent for a 16-acre Northeast Arm island designated "Island C." Ontario used an alphabetical character registry to track the rare island properties. The province had miscalculated North Americans' hunger to experience a place untouched by civilization and the industrial age. When islands were surveyed in 1904, the province switched to an open-ended numbering system. It meant that when

A Survey of Sorts

In 1899 the province conducted an incomplete survey. No numbers were assigned. The only islands addressed were west of Bear Island where settlement was expected to occur close to the Hudson's Bay Company post. Islands surveyed included: 974 Atlantis (now owned by Wendy Mitchell and Ian and Geordie Walker); 976 Fairview (Allyne S. Portmann); 977 Ruby (Marilyn Corl Brinkman); 992 Carthew (Don Fraser, Tanya Steinberg and others); 993 George (Sheila Bonapace); 995 William (Barb Olmsted and Heather Windrem); 997 Peter (Killius family); and 989-990 Ewa-Yea (Boyd and Rose Matchett and Lynn Hinds).

the lake was opened up to island leasing, more than 26 leases could be granted. Ontario also halted island freeholds, more or less.

In 1904 the director of surveys for the Ministry of Lands and Mines sent surveyors scurrying to assess the lake's "approximately 1600 islands for their suitability for settlement as summer resorts" and to assign numbers to those deemed inhabitable. The province reasoned that if settlers could be contained on islands, any fires they might start would also be contained, preventing damage to the highly valued mainland pine preserve. This is the origin of the government's islands-only development policy, which has been maintained with few lapses to the present day.

T.B. Speight, the first surveyor, set off in March 1904 with instructions to mark numbers on posts or trees, to be painted on island rock faces once the snow melted. "Your better way will be to work from the south to the north as I understand the best class of islands are in the southern portion and it may be possible that the ice may go out before you have completed the survey," the survey director advised.

"There is a post office at Lake Temagami and the Hudson Bay Company has a post on Bear Island and as a number of Indians are living there, as I understand horses may be available, it may be possible that you can hire one with a sleigh to facilitate your movements," he added.

In June T.B. Speight reported that he had surveyed islands 1 through 343, starting on the Northeast Arm instead of taking the director's preferred southern approach. Peter Ferguson's Island C was renamed Island 6. T.B. made it down Shiningwood Bay, around High Rock Island and partially around Temagami Island. The arrival of break-up ended his travels on April 12.

"All islands within the scope of the survey were given consecutive numbers from 0 to 343, with the exclusion of No. 202, which was inadvertently omitted," he noted. So instead of 1,259 surveyed and numbered islands, there are 1,258. Not all of these are large enough for cottages, even though promotional railway brochures would declare just a few years later that there were 1,259 surveyed and numbered islands ready for settlement. T.B. and his successor Alexander Niven surveyed and numbered some tiny, uninhabitable islets. For example, an islet off Chimo Island 665 was counted and surveyed as Island 666, even though it is too small for a cottage. It has in modern times been listed as Tim Gooderham's property in the TLA directory.

T.B. Speight was accompanied by an L. Loughrin. His task was to assess timber values on the surveyed islands. T.B. reported that Bear Island, High Rock Island and Temagami Island should not be made available for summer resorts until the pine timber was harvested. However, Bear Island was already a summer or permanent home to many Temagami Indian Band members. Dan O'Connor and his Temagami Hotel and Steamboat Company were soon building the Temagami Inn on Temagami Island.

Alexander Niven of Haliburton was sent forth to finish the numbering system in May

1904. In his report and field notes, dated 1905, he described one and a half acres on the south end of Bear Island as cultivated in hay, oats, potatoes and vegetables. The gardens were just north of the forestry building, now the Bear Island Public Library.

Aboriginals also grew spuds on Tamar Island 856 in the 1800s, calling it Potato Island after a forest fire left behind ideal soils. On Garden Island 981, where Camp Wabun is now located, the land was cleared and planted with vegetables. In even earlier times, Island 981 was known as Wabun-No-Min-Nis-Si or "Coming Daylight Island." It was used for summer ceremonial gatherings, according to Gary Potts. Cattle

Island also borrows its name from a traditional practice. After the HBC relocated its post to Bear Island from Temagami Island in 1876, the native community drove livestock across the ice to Cattle Island to protect them from predation. According to oral tradition, a bear attacked and killed the entire herd one year.

Alexander Niven discovered that many islands within a five-kilometre radius of Bear Island were already occupied. Robert Newcomb had claimed Island 969 in 1904. Island 970 was claimed by W.C. Boyle, a Cleveland attorney and friend of Robert. These lawyers would later try to convince Nisi Prius, a Cleveland legal association, to lease Island 972. Island 971 had

---

An Early Map

In 1905 the Ministry of Lands and Mines produced a map called "Plan of Islands in Lake Temagami in the Temagami Forest Reserve District of Nipissing," based on the 1904 surveys. It is the earliest official lake map featuring island numbers. Printed by the Copp Clark Company of Toronto on white linen, the map measures five by four feet and features a chain scale. The only colours used are two shades of green to delineate lake water.

Latitude and longitude coordinates are indicated on the plan. It shows the Bear Island and Garden Island agricultural clearings, and "William Friday's clearing." Near the bottom of the South Arm, there are three mainland clearings and one on the north end of Island 855. Another clearing is shown at the centre

of Island 856. The mainland clearings were the ancestral homes of some Temagami Indian Band members while the nearby island clearings were planting grounds. The only permanent structures shown are Bear Island's HBC post and forestry building, and Temagami Inn.

Many Anishnabek features are translated into English, including "Shining Wood" Bay and "Rabbit Nose" Island. Some features, for example "Ko-Ko-Ko" Bay, are not anglicized. A few are named for non-native explorers and settlers, including O'Connor Island and Ferguson bay, mountain, point and island. Others were renamed at a later date; Matagama Point became Fasken's Point where David Fasken had a cottage and Loon Lake became Spitzig Lake for 1920s Temagami Inn owner Joe Spitzig.

been taken by Frank Cobb. Three other islands, 968, 972 and 1073, were claimed by Robert's associates. Island 1005 was taken by Harry Woods who was the post manager until 1918.

Living off the Land

By 1908 the Cleveland coterie and other non-Ontarians were required by the province to purchase fishing permits, costing $2 per person or $5 for a family. They could legally leave the province with a two-day catch. Non-residents could hunt big game – moose, woodland caribou and deer – after purchasing a $50 licence. A small game licence for ruffed grouse, ducks, marten and mink could be had for $25. A ban on trapping beaver and otter was in place for several years to allow populations to recover from the pressures of the fur trade. Canadian residents were charged $2 to track deer and $5 to hunt moose and caribou. The limit was two deer, one caribou and one moose per season per person. The caribou population dwindled and vanished by 1930. Logging is a likely culprit as they require large, undisturbed areas of mature coniferous forest. Caribou hunting by non-natives was banned in Ontario in 1929.

What did you do on the lake at the turn of the 20th century once the fish had been filleted or the moose dressed and the firewood gathered? You might have paddled over to the post to chew the fat with Factor Harry Woods as you topped up your supplies from the post's meager offerings. The post was a rough and tumble assembly of mostly wood frame buildings. Its main commerce was the native fur trade, not tourism.

"Dignified with the name of Fort, is but a small collection of peaceful looking dwellings, alone faintly reminds the wandering nature-lover that such a thing as civilization exists," wrote Richard Cassels in 1896.

Within the context of time immemorial– the more than 6,000 years the Temagami region is believed to have supported human life–the arrival of these adventurers is akin to a single spruce falling in the vast boreal forest. Nastawgan travel ways, weaving through rugged terrain and crystal clear waters carved by glacial

Bear Island forestry building circa 1905. *Photo: W.G. Gillespie, reprinted by the Highway Book Shop in Cobalt the Silver City.*

ice, bear ancient testament to past occupations. The aboriginal inhabitants used this interconnected network of trails, portages and water routes in winter and summer. Healed axe blazes on old-growth trees and smoothly-worn rock faces bear silent witness to their seasonal travels.

In spring 1902, the year of Robert Newcomb's first appearance, some 14 Temagami Indian Band families rendezvoused at Bear Island, sheltered in balsam-scented teepees and a smattering of wood frame or log homes. Come fall, extended families would return to widespread trapping territories where some lived in permanent log homes on patches of cleared land. They hunted and trapped for their livelihood, just like their forebears. They sold pelts to the post factor, one of few regular contacts they had with non-native folk.

Every summer they met federal Indian agents conducting inspections and Oblate missionaries confirming that the recent conversion of most of the populace to Catholicism wasn't unravelling. Traditional dances, such as the feast and bear, were still performed at Petrant's Hall through the 1920s, to the chagrin of the priests. Powwows ceased in 1929, not to be revived until 1994 when traditional practices experienced a rebirth.

Post interior in 1899. Lanterns, footwear, ladles, smoking products and a few tinned goods were part of a limited line.
Photo: Richard Cassels, courtesy of Robert Wilson

Modern day politicking occupied much of Chief Ignace Tonene's time. As second chief in 1868 he approached an Indian agent with his concerns over lumbermen encroaching on traditional lands. He also told the agent that the band had never signed a treaty ceding its land but desired a reserve and treaty annuities. The band was promised a reserve by the federal government in 1885, acting upon a tribal council proposal for a 259-square kilometre tract around Austin Bay a year earlier.

The Department of Indian Affairs urged the province to provide Crown land for a reserve but the government balked due to the value of the pine stands. It was now a new century and the reserve had yet to materialize. Band leaders were stepping up demands for a land base as accelerating commercial pressures threatened the old ways.

The Browns

On his first trip to the Temagami forest, Robert Newcomb might have bumped into A.S. Gregg Clarke, a teacher at the Gunnery, a private boys' school in Connecticut. With three Mattawa guides including Peter Brown, A.S., the son of a Republican congressman, was scoping a suitable site for a canoe camp. Keewaydin Camp, meaning "northwest wind" in Anishnabek, set up a permanent base on 47-acre Devil's Island 1147 in the North Arm in 1904. There were 66 in the original group at Devil's Island.

For Peter Brown it was the start of a lifelong attachment to Keewaydin and Lake Temagami. He was born in 1874 in Quebec. He married Bear Island-born Caroline McLean in 1908. They leased Brown's Island 1186 in the early 1930s. Caroline was a daughter of Malcolm McLean (1828-1905). He was from Stornoway in Scotland's Outer Hebrides. He worked for the HBC and then became an independent fur trader. His oldest daughter was Mary Turner (1851-1943).

Caroline's half brother William Peshabo was the Temagami band chief in the 1930s. Caroline cooked for Keewaydin for four decades. She baked 70 loaves of bread every other day in a dutch oven, manipulating the pans with a long paddle. Islanders were steady customers. After he retired from guiding, Peter stayed busy with caretaking and canoe repairs. He died in the mid-1940s, followed by Caroline in 1956.

The Cochranes

In his second year on the lake, Robert Newcomb might have met up with Arthur Lewis "A.L." Cochrane on a portage. Born in 1870, A.L. arrived in Canada from England in 1894 and became a physical education instructor at Upper Canada College, a private boys' school in Toronto. He was an expert boxer who taught boys that victory and defeat are less important than modesty and courage. A.L. founded organized camping in Canada, assembling canoe groups in Muskoka in 1900. Disillusioned with Muskoka, he headed further north in 1903, selecting a cluster of South Arm islands as a base for Cochrane's Camp (officially known as Camp Temagami).

"It's the last northern summer resort that can serve

The Bear Island cemetery in winter. *Photo: Harold Keevil*

Murder Most Foul

Caroline's mother was Manian "Marie Anne" Kanintcic, a daughter of Konatinj, meaning "tomtit" in Anishnabek, a small blue bird. Band chief in the 1860s, Konatinj was killed by his brother Syagquasay in 1877. Post Factor Arthur Ryder sent him to Mattawa to stand trial in district court. A local family had witnessed the slaying and to spare them the stress of testifying, Arthur sent a written report. The factor had taken action because the priests' policy of non-intervention might have resulted in "a longer list of deaths and a far shorter one of Fur here now," Arthur said in a letter. The evidence was ruled insufficient and the case was dismissed. Meanwhile, the Temagami band meted out its own traditional justice, by putting Syagquasay in a barrel and tossing it into the lake. If the accused was innocent, the barrel would float to the surface. It didn't.

Konatinj's remains are said to lie beneath the original Keewaydin lodge. His rotting birchbark canoe, laid on top of the grave to help convey him to the Spirit Land, was purportedly discovered by Keewaydinites in 1911 while they were digging a hole to build a fireplace. It is an apt resting place considering that many Konatinj descendants have ties to Keewaydin. Although the original lodge is gone, a commemorative plaque remains.

Malcolm and Marie Anne McLean, Peter and Caroline Brown and Annie Whitebear, another McLean daughter who married Frank Whitebear, Temagami band chief from 1910 to '25, are all interred at the Bear Island cemetery.

Toronto," A.L. told the *Toronto Star* in 1932. "We built up Lake Simcoe, Georgian Bay, Muskoka, then the Lake of Bays. After that we entered Algonquin Park. When we reached Timagami we went as far as it is practicable for a summer resort to be from a large city if it is to be a weekend resort…If we ruin Timagami we destroy the last great summer playground."

"It was a revelation to me," A.L. said of his first sighting of the lake. "It was utterly unlike Muskoka or the Lake of Bays or any northern lake I had, until then, seen. The tall white pines came down to the water's edge. It had never been lumbered. There were no burnings and no welter of drift wood and brush to foul the clear rock shore. It had about it a primeval quality which it still retains."

The *Star* described A.L.'s first encounter on the lake: "Suddenly, he was back in the days of La Verendrye and the North West fur trade. He heard a chorus of voices, the nipple of paddles. Around an island swept a leviathan. It was the Hudson's Bay factor coming out in state in an eighteen-foot birchbark canoe manned by a dozen Indian paddlers swinging to the rhythms of a chant."

Cochrane's was the first private camp established in Ontario. "Early Cochrane canoe trips were taken in unsurveyed areas for which government maps were not yet available," A.L.'s granddaughter Carol Cochrane reminisced in the *Temagami Times*. Paul Whitebear, who guided for Keewaydin in the early years, assisted A.L. by charting the course of the lakes, rivers and portages on various routes. A.L. and his son Gib also drew maps. Food supplies were cached at portages in case a group had to backtrack, she added.

Scarcely another human would be encountered for weeks at a time. A.L.'s campers took the English Royal Life Saving Society course and were tutored in old world gentlemanly conduct. A.L. co-founded the Ontario Camping Association in 1933. Four generations of Cochranes have enjoyed the Temagami experience and all have played TLA roles.

The Gooderhams

Other TLA players include Bill Gooderham and his nephew Gordon "Tim" Gooderham, whose family's presence on the lake extends back to 1903. Bill's father Gordon Stuart Gooderham accompanied A.L. on the 1903 trip that led to the founding of Cochrane's Camp. Gordon opened Camp Chimo in 1926, a family fishing resort on Island 665 near the top of the South Arm.

The Gooderham family stamped an indelible mark on the Temagami landscape, though it pales in comparison to their contribution to the industrial, commercial and cultural heritage of Toronto. It all started when a farmer named James Worts emigrated from Yorkshire, England, in 1831 and settled in Muddy York where he opened a flour mill.

William Gooderham, his brother-in-law, arrived in 1832 and went into business with James. Distraught over his wife's death during childbirth in 1834, James took his own life by throwing himself down a well.

James Worts' son James Jr. went into partnership with his uncle William. They built a distillery in 1837 to process surplus grain from the flour mill. So successful was the enterprise that in 1859 they built a larger 13-acre distillery on Mill Street. The partners were soon producing one-third of all proof spirits distilled in Canada. The Gooderham and Worts industrial complex expanded to encompass railways, livestock yards, retailing and woolen mills. William's contributions to Toronto's cityscape include Little Trinity Church on King Street. The Gooderhams' Victorian mansion, built in 1882, is now the Clarion Hotel and Suites.

George Gooderham, William's eldest son, inherited the company in the early 1880s. He parlayed family interests into railways, life insurance, newspapers (Southam) and philanthropy. George constructed the Gooderham "Flatiron" Building at Front and Wellington streets in 1892. Once company headquarters, the uniquely triangular-shaped structure was designated a heritage site in 1975. He also built the upscale King Edward Hotel on the corner of King and Victoria streets in 1903.

The prohibition era brought hard times to the distillery industry. The Gooderhams sold their controlling interest in 1924 and merged with the Hiram Walker Company. Small amounts of Gooderham and Worts whiskey and rum, as well as antifreeze, were produced at the Mill Street factory until it closed in 1990.

Today the former Gooderham property is known as the Distillery District, a trendy pedestrian-friendly village within a city, replete with 19th-century limestone and red brick industrial buildings. Restoration of some of the derelict buildings began in 2001. They are leased by theatre companies, galleries and merchants. The old pumphouse is a coffee shop, and the boiler and barrel-shipping rooms are restaurants. *The Gooderham* is a 35-storey condominium tower slated for completion in 2012. The Distillery District has been the location for more than 800 film and television productions, including *Chicago* and *X-Men*. It is Toronto's sole national historic site.

Known as Toronto's richest man at the time, George Gooderham fathered a dozen children, one of whom was Chimo founder Gordon Stuart Gooderham, Bill Gooderham's father and Tim's grandfather. George's brother William was a philanthropist and a financial backer of Dan O'Connor's Temagami Steamboat and Hotel Company when it was formed in 1904. Brothers and law partners David and Alexander Fasken also lent a financial hand. They practised with the Toronto firm doing legal work for Gooderham and Worts. The company soon built the Ronnoco Hotel (Dan's surname spelled backwards) in Temagami, the Temagami Inn on Temagami Island and the Lady Evelyn Hotel on Deer Island in the North Arm.

Boom Times

David Fasken and other investors founded the Nipissing Mining Company Limited in 1904 and acquired substantial claims at the centre of the Cobalt silver camp. He became one of the 17 Canadians and eight Americans whom Cobalt had turned into millionaires by 1909.

David bought one and a half acres of mainland property at the south end of the Northeast Arm. It became known as Fasken's Point. Political connections may have permitted him to circumvent normal channels. Most cottagers were only able to acquire 21-year leases on islands, not mainland, when the lake was opened to development in 1906. According to historical researcher Brian Back, David built a double boathouse and two cabins. Following

Chimo canoe dock and dining hall. *Photo: TLA Archives*

Belle of Temagami at back, *Bobs* at centre
and *Temagami* at front, circa 1907. *Postcard photo: Reg Sinclair*

his death in 1929, the family inherited the freehold cottage. The property was rundown by the late 1930s. The Ontario Northland Boat Lines (ONBL) owned it by the end of World War Two and tore down the buildings. The point was used as a passenger boat transfer depot until the early 1960s.

Between 1891 and 1911 the population of northern Ontario rose from four per cent to 11 per cent of Ontario's total population. Royalties from the north's forests and mines accounted for nearly 25 per cent of the province's total revenues. Northern boom times fuelled southern Ontario industry and turned Toronto into a financial zenith.

Through a Child's Eyes

A trip to Temagami was an eye-opener for a youth from a small Connecticut town. Standish Hall, father of Bradford Hall of Island 1067, took his first trip to the lake in 1908 as a Keewaydin rookie. From his diary, we learn that he stopped in New York City en route, where he visited the aquarium and a Broadway soda fountain, picked up Winchester cartridges and film, and had a "bully time" at the Astor House Roof Garden. He caught the Grand Trunk overnighter and finished reading *A War Time Wooing*. Arriving in Temagami with a Keewaydin-bound group of campers, he boarded the *Bobs* steamboat.

Standish's first canoe trip, a short circuit of Kokoko Lake, wasn't a hardship. His section got towed by a launch on Lake Temagami, ate supper at Temagami Inn, slept in the post factor's office and ate breakfast at "Mrs. Turner's" Lakeview House.

During his second lengthier trip, the campers amused themselves one rainy afternoon by building a pond and stocking it with 13 fish. Another day they caught 40 pounds of fish and gave some to prospectors. Besides fish dinners, their menu consisted of corned beef hash, potatoes, apple sauce and cocoa one evening, and pancakes, baked beans, rice pudding and coffee another night. They took turns setting the birchbark table and being "dish-wallopers." At night they slept on balsam bough beds.

The boys spotted some 20 moose, and innumerable black bears, loons and ducks. In a display of bravado they once chased a swimming cow moose and calf. One lad jumped on the cow's back and went "moose-back riding." She dove and surfaced beside a canoe, nearly upsetting it. The "cowboy" got off as the moose neared shore and she disappeared into the bush. Another boy lassoed the calf and towed it to shore. A photo session ensued before the calf was set free to rejoin its mother. Moose-back riding was outlawed by the camp in the 1960s.

In his second and final summer at Keewaydin in 1913, Standish took the challenging James Bay-Moosonee trip. Capricious Mother Nature turned the tables and provided some hair-raising moments. Caught in rapids near Matachewan, canoes were upset, canvas was torn and the boys lost their hats, shoes, pots and reflector oven. The next day they deprived a prospector's empty shack of a frying pan, salt (the most missed item) and dilapidated tin pails. They left a note instructing the prospector to send his bill to camp.

Chessman Kittredge Sr. first trekked to the lake in 1908 with some university buddies and was soon on staff at Keewaydin. Richard "Mal" Scovil and Brooks Shepard were introduced to the Keewaydin way in 1908. Russell Cleminshaw was initiated into its ranks the following year. In a few years Mal and then Russell would be involved in the Association, serving long terms as treasurer and secretary, respectively. Brad Hall and Chess's son Chess Jr. would also serve the Association. Brooks' son Jack would help put the TLA's VHF marine radio service on the air in 1987.

CHAPTER 3

THE WELCOME MAT GOES OUT

The Newcombs had the zeal of crusaders and the conviction of recruiters when introducing friends to Lake Temagami. By 1907 Robert had finished building a two-storey log cabin on three-acre Island 969, dubbed Red Pines. It became his canoe-tripping headquarters. Friends were royally entertained by Robert and Faith and then outfitted for their guided travels.

Next door on vacant Island 1002, the Newcombs raised chickens to add variety to the dinner fare. The late Ted and Margaret Brady, whose family later owned the island until 2008, used to sweep the odd wind-blown chicken feather off the porch – even though no fowl have roosted there since at least 1923 when Dana Latimer leased the island.

The Ontario government began allowing campers to lease islands within the Temagami Forest Reserve in January 1906. There was one lease per person, renewable after 21 years and a structure of no less than $300 in value had to be built. Annual fees were $20 for the first half acre or less and $3 for every additional acre or part acre. Thirty-four leases were issued in 1906, 20 to Americans. Robert's law partners Frank Cobb and Ben Bole leased islands 971 and 680, respectively.

Some early cottagers didn't take out a lease because they preferred living in tents.

Others did build, including the Tretheweys of Island 1003, who put up the lake's first water boathouse in 1907. They didn't lease the island until 1909. Trethewey grandson Jack Glenn would become TLA president in the 1980s. In effect the Tretheweys and others were illegal squatters, though nobody would have challenged them as most islands were still available. Some cottagers seeking a hearth and home didn't wait for the province to permit island leasing. Frank Newton built a cabin on Island 977 in 1905.

A shoreline sketch by one of A.L. Cochrane's children. *Photo: Carol Cochrane*

Clevelander David Knight Ford, Frank Cobb's brother-in-law, visited the Cobb and Newcomb islands in 1909, staying in a canvas tent on Island 971. He returned for his honeymoon in 1920. David was the founder of Lubrizol Corporation, a producer of lubricants for the auto industry. He worked there for 65 years until two weeks before his death at age 99. Over the years he took numerous canoe trips, including one with Robert Newcomb to the Albany River in 1916.

David's son David Kingsley Ford met his future wife Ann Garretson in Cleveland. Both had family ties to Temagami. Ann was a granddaughter of Dr. George Washington Crile, a leading Cleveland surgeon who leased Island 1167 in 1921. He became interested in Temagami when his son George Jr. went to Keewaydin as a camper and staffman from 1919 to '24.

Cleveland's High Society

George Crile Sr. was one of the founders of the American College of Surgeons in 1912 and a co-founder of the renowned Cleveland Clinic. He performed more than 25,000 thyroidectomies to treat cancer and other thyroid diseases.

The Criles lived in a mansion on Derbyshire Road in Cleveland Heights, a tony Cleveland suburb. Their three-storey palazzo featured a massive ballroom and a dining room that could elegantly seat two dozen. Guests staying the night had 12 bedrooms to choose from, not including the six servant chambers. Derbyshire

is the same street on which Robert and Faith Newcomb resided in a stately red brick colonial. The extravagant Crile home was torn down in the 1940s to make way for a church. The Newcomb home still stands as a family residence.

"Barney," as George Crile Jr. was known, followed in dad's footsteps and became a Cleveland surgeon. He was an object of ridicule in the 1960s amongst his peers for campaigning against radical mastectomy. It had been routinely performed on breast cancer patients for a century. Instead, Barney preferred a simple mastectomy or, in the early stages, a lumpectomy. He believed that radical, intrusive procedures were often unnecessary and met the surgeon's needs rather than the patient's.

Jane, Barney's first wife, ironically succumbed to breast cancer in 1963. His second wife was Helga Sandburg, a daughter of the distinguished Carl Sandburg who won two Pulitzer Prizes. *The Way It Was: Sex, Surgery, Treasure, and Travel, 1907-1987* is Barney's published autobiography. It includes reminiscences of good times spent on the lake.

Barney's son, journalist George Crile III, produced ground-breaking documentaries for CBS. He worked on the current affairs program *60 Minutes*, covering international events. His 2003 best-selling book *Charlie Wilson's War: The Extraordinary Story of the Largest Covert Operation in History* recounts the CIA's secret war in Afghanistan during the Reagan administration. The book formed the basis of a 2007 movie starring Tom Hanks.

Island 1167 was subsequently passed to Ann Ford and her brother Richard Garretson in the late 1950s through their mother. That is where David Knight Ford stayed during a

Diamond Lake looking north from the Sharp Rock portage. *Photo: Harold Keevil*

nostalgic return to the lake in 1983 at the age of 89. Frank Cobb's Island 971 is now owned by Jeffrey Simmons of Arizona. Ann Ford died in 1998.

Richard Garretson spent every summer on the lake except the Second World War years. The elderly Richard decided his final summer at Island 1167 would be 2008. The current island owners are the children of Richard and Prue Garretson – Rick Garretson and Emily Garretson Little, and the children of Ann and David Kingsley Ford – David, John and Susan Ford.

One Property Per Person

Robert Newcomb acquired other properties, leased under the names of friends or family due to the stipulation of one property per person. Island 680, southwest of Temagami Island, was leased by campfire club member Ben Bole. It was dubbed Sixatee when the Newcombs dotted it with tents. During the 1920s the camp was in the hands of Roscoe C. Skiles, another Newcomb peer. It was eventually acquired by Robert's brother Adrian Newcomb when he married. Robert had by then formed a law partnership with Adrian.

When Adrian died in the early 1950s, William G. Pace Jr. bought Island 680 from Adrian's widow Helen. It was later purchased by Ed and Joan Loving. Ed died in 2005. The Lovings still own the island. Robert is believed to have also built on nearby Island 741, owned by Michael N. McGrew. Robert built several outpost camps, including one on an island in Sharp Rock Inlet, from where he could readily reach the portage into Diamond Lake – gateway to the Lady Evelyn wilderness.

Best Ever Wedding Gift

Keller Sheeler, a Pennsylvania Railroad lawyer, was Adrian Newcomb's best friend. They canoed together in the 1920s and once came upon a lake east of Kokoko Lake that enchanted them. It's now called Chambers Lake. The following year Robert and Adrian asked Keller to portage back with them to the same spot to stake a claim and build on an island. However, the men couldn't find the lake.

Sometime later they rediscovered this special place, appropriately calling it Lost Lake. The first cabin on Island 2034 in Chambers Lake was built in the 1930s. Adrian gave Keller free reign over Lost Lake Camp and he went on to build five log sleeping cabins, three docks and a large "cook" cabin replete with propane stoves, refrigerators and lights.

When Keller's son William married in 1948, Adrian bestowed the island on the stockbroker and his wife Mildred as a wedding present. In 1978 William and Mildred passed the island on to their three daughters – Lynn, Dana and Anne – who have loved and cared for it ever since. William died in 1992 and is interred at Lost Lake Camp. The Sheelers appear to be one of only two property-owning TLA member families whose main cottage is not located on Lake Temagami. Gord and Doreen Lak are the other. They own the only cottage on Cross Lake.

Cabin Falls

Robert and Adrian Newcomb built a small cabin in the 1920s at one of the most scenic vistas on the Lady Evelyn River overlooking Cabin Falls, upstream from Bridal Veil Falls. Howard and Katharine Hyde were friends of Adrian and Helen. A deal was struck during the 1940s whereby the Hydes would restore the cabin and acquire a one-half interest. The Hydes' son Alan recalled helping to haul a load of 2 by 12s and a four-ton jack over the three-kilometre portage from Diamond Lake up to Willow Island Lake on his way to rebuild the porch. All the blood, sweat and tears prompted an elderly Adrian to sell his remaining interest in the cabin to the Hydes in 1949, prior to his final visit in 1951. The property was transferred to the Lathrop family of New York state in 1957 for $600 – plus six bucks for the deed. The deal was brokered on the front deck in 1951 by Adrian who was terminally ill.

The property has earned the distinction of being the only patent ever registered within Lady Evelyn-Smoothwater Wilderness Park. When the park was proposed in 1981, David "Hap" Wilson persuaded the Lathrop family to transfer a one-third interest in Cabin Falls to him. At the time, he was working for the Ministry of Natural Resources (MNR), cleaning and clearing campsites, portages and routes. Instead of expropriating private property, the province allowed Hap to become its local caretaker. He was expected to maintain low-impact standards of stewardship within the wilderness park. Hap replaced the old Newcomb outpost with a new lodge in 2000, where he ran eco-friendly canoe trips and retreats as Sunrise Adventures.

Hap has worn many hats, including wildlife artist, canoe route cartographer, park ranger, wilderness guide, trip outfitter and author. His 1978 *Temagami Canoe Routes*, written for the MNR, became a staple in most canoeists' packs. Perhaps Hap's most eye-catching role was his hiring as former Agent 007 Pierce Brosnan's personal canoeing and knife/hatchet-throwing trainer for the Richard Attenborough film *Grey Owl*, released in 2000. Lindsay Coté, Teme-Augama Anishnabai chief in the mid-2000s, helped teach Pierce how to dance and also appeared in the movie.

Ooshke

Alfred Horr leased Island 672 southwest of Temagami Island on July 12, 1905, six months before leasing was permitted. How he managed this feat is unknown. The island had just been surveyed and numbered by Alexander Niven. Alfred was to pay $38 per year for his 21-year lease. All standing trees, and gold, silver, copper, lead, iron and "other mines and minerals" on or under the island were reserved to the Crown. The lease was not registered with the lands title office as it was likely deemed invalid. Alfred re-leased the island in 1916. He also had an island on Hansen Lake, east of Chambers Lake. Robert and Alfred built an outpost camp on Eagle Rock Lake, west of Gull Lake.

Alfred built on the south end of Island 672 in the 1900s and then put up cabins on the north end in 1925, which he called Ooshke, simply meaning north end. Ooshke is the call sign used today by the owners to call the TLA's VHF marine radio service. There are now some 14 buildings on the seven-acre island, the newest being a winterized 1984 Viceroy. He invited Harlan S. Yenne, a young Cleveland Trust employee, to take possession of the south end of the island in a 1928 letter. It was hoped that the elevation and pure air would cure Harlan's wife Harriet of hay fever.

"Of course, if your lady would prefer a place where she would be free from housekeeping cares this isn't the place," Alfred wrote. "Everybody on this island works with his hands but not with his head." Harlan was assured of a well-equipped cabin. "All you need to bring is your old clothes and your eats and the latter you can get in Toronto," he advised. The Yennes settled in nicely but were disconcerted upon reading some temperature records kept by the Horrs. The temperature dipped to -30 F in May 1920 while it soared to +90 F in May of 1927.

Alfred and his wife Charlotte had no children. When Alfred died, the Yennes bought the north end and thus had the entire island. Yenne daughters Dora Young and Mary Soper obtained the north and south ends, respectively, in the early 1970s. Dora and her husband Hilton went on to serve the TLA in sundry ways, starting in the late 1980s. They began enjoying all four seasons on the lake in the 1990s, following Hilton's retirement from a Cleveland trust company.

Word of Mouth

Marquette "Bill" Lane and his wife Betty used to get together with the Yennes in their hometown of Lakewood, Ohio, to play cards. They got to talking about the lake and the Yennes invited the Lanes up for a two-week stay in summer 1948. Temagami fever gripped three new victims, including the Lanes' daughter Nancy who had to be "dragged" up north. They bought three acres on Cattle Island 849 the following summer, the Lanes' granddaughter Linda Cain wrote in the *Temagami Times*. Nancy and her husband Richard Walker later acquired the Lane property where Nancy spent 55 happy summers. It now belongs to the Walkers' daughter Linda and her husband David Cain.

The Newcombs also introduced Dr. George Follansbee to the lake. He leased Island 664 in 1918, which he called Crescent Island, and Island 663 in 1928. The main cabin on Crescent Island was unique in design – the second storey was larger than the first. There was a dumb waiter to the kitchen from the upper dining room. George, one of Cleveland's foremost surgeons, tried to talk his wife into spending September 1928 on the lake. "Her consent to this arrangement will probably be contingent upon the obtaining of a satisfactory cook to feed the Indian [guide] while we are up there. The family itself is no trouble to feed, but the Indian is a task," he wrote in a community newsletter. He was referring to the mainly wild food diet of First Nations people, in contrast to the mainly canned or powdered (and far less healthful) food consumed by cottagers.

Both islands were later occupied by Ohio lawyer John Bricker. He served as the state's attorney general, then governor before becoming the Republican nominee for vice president of the United States in 1944, sharing a ticket with presidential hopeful Thomas Dewey. He lost to Franklin D. Roosevelt. John served as a U.S. senator from 1946 to '58.

The top-heavy cabin on Island 664 burned down about 1950. The fire was caused by a kerosene floor heater. Dr. Ross Flett, a southern Ontario urologist who had first experienced Temagami in 1928, bought the island soon after the blaze. It was inherited by his son Dr. Norm Flett in the early 1970s. Norm worked for the TLA in various capacities and earned its Member of the Year award in 1979.

The Brickers sold Island 663 in 1983 to Michael and Nicole Brooker, former Torontonians now residing in Guelph, Ontario. Nicole is Raymond Delarosbel's sister. Ray, of Ogama Island 843 and North Bay, was the TLA's president from 2002 to '04.

Robert Newcomb was also indirectly responsible for the Wychgel family's arrival on the lake. Dr. James N. Wychgel, an attending physician at a Cleveland steel plant, was an associate of Dr. George Follansbee. James began exploring the Temagami region about 1918. Following two train trips and two hotel stays, he took a steamer from Temagami, fondly known by cottagers as T-Station. His destination was Bear Island where he met up with his friend and guide John Turner, wrote James' grandson James "Jim" Wychgel Norton, referencing a journal James kept.

Fast Friends

James and John, grandson of the original John Turner, explored the lake for an island James could lease. They settled on Island 1066 near the entrance to the Northwest Arm, which he leased in 1927 for $100. James enlisted John and a crew to construct a one-bedroom cottage and boathouse costing $750.

James N. Wychgel with
a nice mess of fish in the 1920s.
Photo: J.N. Wychgel

A small sleeping cabin was added in 1941 for $150. John built for dozens of cottagers. His namesake grandson has renovated some of the cabins his grandfather built. He is a fifth generation Turner on the lake.

James and his wife Ruth spent their honeymoon canoeing the Temagami area. They travelled in style from Cleveland in James' new car, a fancy Packard roadster, up the newly completed Ferguson Highway. Refinement and polish vanished once they parked in Temagami.

"Once again, John Turner was their guide and it was just the three of them in the wilderness. There are many family stories about this adventure," Jim Norton wrote. "Ruth couldn't swim so it must have been traumatic for her to be in the middle of the canoe, crossing open stretches of water. To make matters worse she was told to bring only warm wool clothes and it turned out that she was allergic to wool and the temperatures reached into the 80s. The tent was set up at one campsite on an anthill and near a stinky dead duck in the bushes at another."

John and James spent hours exploring and fishing. They canoed to Hudson Bay in the 1920s. A paddle, tent post and water cup on the cottage mantle commemorate the journey. The Peterborough canvas canoe that they paddled and portaged is still owned by the Wychgels and has been rebuilt twice. When James wasn't in his canoe, he drove what the family called "that ridiculous pointer," a 26-foot Norwegian flat-bottom boat that sprayed so much water passengers wore raincoats even when there was barely a ripple.

James was the first seasonal resident to bring propane to the lake. He loaded two 20-pound propane tanks into the car along with the tubing needed to connect a propane stove. After Marty Taylor set up shop in Temagami a lot of car space was freed up.

"Delivered Larry's wife's 7 ½ lb girl. Fished and caught 10 ½ lb trout." This is James' journal entry for July 13, 1925. Although he came to the lake to shed professional duties, he often attended to boating accidents and stitched up cuts. John and his wife Maggie, née Quill, named their son Adam Edward James after he delivered the infant.

On their annual excursion to a sportsmen's show in Cleveland, John and Maggie often

A publicity shot from a 1938 New York City sportsmen's show. John Turner stands at far left and Madeline Katt Theriault is at far right.
Photo: Madeline's Moose to Moccasins

visited the Wychgel home. "Unfamiliar with the city streets, he once was stopped by the police for driving the wrong way down Shaker Heights Boulevard. John was a charismatic man with a broad smile, warm disposition and a loud belly laugh. Before long he was escorted by police cars with sirens blaring to Gramps house for their stay in the city," Jim related.

"John and other Temagami natives regaled the city folk with stories of hunting, fishing and canoeing along with demonstrations of wilderness techniques, such as log rolling in the swimming pool at the Cleveland Athletic Club. After seeing and hearing these presentations, many a young boy was bitten by the wilderness bug and couldn't wait to attend a canoe camp on Lake Temagami. Undoubtedly there are many families enjoying Temagami today who owe their first experiences to these winter promotions in large cities to the south."

James Wychgel was one of the "settlers" who joined the Timagami Association in 1931. He went on to serve on the membership committee from 1961 to '71, the year of his death. James and Ruth's son James Follansbee (honouring James' mentor George Follansbee), Jim Norton's uncle, was cottage custodian for many decades and recently turned that responsibility over to Jim and his cousin Anne White. The family has never allowed hydro or telephones to invade their space. "Unlike the suburbs of cities which are constantly changing, the island doesn't and that's the special part. My grandfather would recognize the island and would be pleased with how it looks," Jim said. James and Ruth's great-grandchildren are the fifth generation to love life on Island 1066.

Friendships Point North

Annie Fenn and her sister Jane Macdonald owe their love affair with the lake to Robert Newcomb's friendship with Alfred Horr. Their grandfather Hugh Allyn worked with Alfred as vice president at Cleveland Trust. Alfred introduced Hugh to the lake in the early 1920s. He settled on Island 661 about 1925 and coined it Sunset Rock Camp. Annie met her husband Don Fenn in the early 1960s when he was a counsellor at Camp White Bear. Don and Annie both went on to serve the TLA in myriad ways. Their greatest claim to fame is the *Temagami Times*, "the Voice of the TLA," a newspaper they started in 1971.

Isaac Denton, a Cleveland steel industrialist, and his wife Christine accompanied Robert to the lake in 1915. They returned the following summer and leased Island 1007 near Bear Island. Isaac died in 1923 but Christine kept coming to Temagami with her niece Virginia. Christine had a flair for entertaining and her guests included Dr. Allan Roy DaFoe. He achieved notoriety after he delivered and went on to exploit the Dionne quintuplets of Corbeil. Another visitor was George Lee, chair of the TNOR from 1920 to '34. Politicians were also on the guest list, including four Ontario premiers.

Virginia Coltrin inherited Island 1007 from Christine in 1961. Harold and Betty Lou Hiner, their daughter Holly and her husband John Robbins became the proprietors in 1997 and called their piece of paradise Heaven. The Hiners were friends of Everett and Jean Myers in their hometown of Ashland, Ohio. They first visited the Myers' Island 1128 in 1970 and later rented the Island 1123 Woodman cottage. The Hiner-Robbins family sold Island 1007 in 2008 to Judi and Dieter Maier.

CHAPTER 4

SETTLERS UNITE

A group of about 100 "settlers" met at Lakeview House on Bear Island in August 1931 and the Timagami Association, as the Temagami Lakes Association was originally known, was born. "Some one had to be president, and the job was passed on to me," Robert Newcomb modestly remarked afterwards.

The Association was "organized for the mutual benefit and protection of the permanent residents of Lake Timagami and the Timagami Forest Reserve." Robert's definition of a permanent resident seemed to be someone with a permanent intention of residing seasonally. "Already the investment in public and private camps on Lake Timagami exceeds half a million dollars. That large investment justifies an Association to protect the property and to further the interests of the owners," he stated during the first membership drive.

There were 198 cottage, camp and resort leases on the lake in 1931, more than enough to present a strong and unified front in dealing with government and industry, Robert reasoned. His thinking was not far off the TLA of today. "It is important," wrote the founding executive in a 1932 letter, "that the property owners on Lake Timagami be properly organized to meet any commercial invasion of the Reserve that may arise in the future. That invasion would sweep like a forest fire and leave nothing but wreckage behind it. Few would even care to return again. The best way to avoid that calamity is to be properly organized against it."

Forest fire prevention and refuse disposal were other prime concerns, going hand in hand with increased tourism. Cottagers were urged to burn or bury garbage. Private family dumps proliferated until the 1960s when Ontario began providing controlled dumping sites. The Association also desired cooperation with forest rangers, and praised Chief Ranger Clarence Hindson and staff for keeping the forests "well protected" and portages and trails in good condition.

Anishnabai and Cottagers

For the Bear Island people, the lake's prosperity was a mixed blessing. Temagami canoeist Richard Cassels was eerily prescient when he wrote this passage in an 1896 article published in the U of T's *Massey's Magazine*: "About one hundred Indians live in this district…Hunting and fishing are their chief occupations and means of livelihood. When the chance offers they are very glad to act as guides or carriers, being from their knowledge of the country and great strength, most useful in either capacity; and very soon it will be necessary for them to depend upon work of these kinds, for though game is still plentiful, so that a good trapper can make $400 in a season, if the threatened invasion of the locomotive becomes an accomplished calamity, this region will no longer be the great centre of the fur-trade that it is now."

since "time immemorial," and could locate the most obscure portage on the darkest night.

Many aboriginal women worked as housekeepers, waitresses and cooks. Using skills passed through generations, they also crafted birchbark baskets, and stitched moose hide moccasins, jackets and mitts with intricate beadwork. They sold these directly to tourists and for a lesser profit margin to the post. The post paid $3 for large footwear and 75 cents for wee wear. The post's best sellers during the 1930s, save for staples, were HBC blankets, imported Inuit carvings and model birchbark canoes, Temagami beadwork apparel and dew worms.

The William Petrant family in 1896. He was second-in-command at the post, under Factor John Turner. *Photo: Robert Wilson*

The men did indeed secure work as fish and hunt guides, as well as handymen, drivers for the boat lines, caretakers and builders. In the quiet of winter, there was firewood to chop and ice blocks to cut for summer refrigeration. About one member of each of the approximately 40 Bear Island households worked as a guide by 1931. They were highly recommended because they knew every nook and cranny of the homeland they had occupied

While seasonal residents and tourists brought their money and dreams, hard on their heels came disturbing controls and checks on the native lifestyle and culture. Some Anishnabai were allowed to hunt, fish and trap only specific numbers, at certain times of year, in particular areas and in a prescribed manner. They complained about harassment by game wardens, and they were being asked in 1929 to pay rent for use of the land their homes were on. Some had been banned from cutting timber to build homes in 1910.

Formal schooling arrived in 1915 under the auspices of Catholic priests. Classes were held for six weeks in the summer, allowing families to pursue a livelihood on their hunting territories the rest of the year. The curriculum consisted of moral education and the three R's, taught at the church. A school was built in the 1930s to manage increasing enrolment and the post factor's wife often assumed teaching duties. It wasn't until 1950 when Ontario took responsibility for education that the school year was lengthened to 10 months.

The band's grievances weren't directed at seasonal residents but at the province and its "neo-colonial institutions," which was disposing of their ancestral lands and trying to control nearly every aspect of their lives – from education, religion, hunting, trapping, to where they lived and how high or low the water level should be. Dam construction had flooded some families' traditional homes. To add insult to injury, Ontario was doing it all without a negotiated land trade in exchange for a reserve.

Federal Indian agents were "telling people who can and who can't be Indian people," as they added some names to and struck others from their status registration lists, said Gary Potts (chief from 1972 to '95) in 1997. "People were feeling a lot of pressure," he added. Ironically, as aboriginals were being labelled status or non-status on Ottawa's band lists, they continued to protest that they had not

signed the 1850 Robinson-Huron Treaty, nor ceded title to their lands.

One of the Association's early objectives was to sustain the good relationship existing between seasonal and Bear Island residents. "Your president has lived among these folks for thirty years. They are simple, honest, friendly people. They are the natural guardians of our property," Robert Newcomb wrote in 1932. "In return, we should be interested in their welfare and help them when the opportunity offers. In the early days they lived largely by trapping, but the trapping is now gone [in temporary decline] and they must depend on such work as we can give them to keep from want and suffering. Any spare shoes or clothing for men, women or children, should be brought to the Annual Meeting for distribution."

Members were urged not to bury surplus fish, but to give them instead to Bear Island residents. While cottagers may have been burying excess catch, one resort went a step further. According to Island 970's Gaye Smith, Temagami Inn had a large fire pit in its early days. After the black and white photos of stringers were snapped, the fish were thrown into the pit and cremated.

Seventy-five years have passed since Robert and Faith's deaths, yet a handful of Bear Islanders are still cognizant of the Newcomb generosity and interest in their wellbeing. Gary Potts said in 1991, "We always felt comfortable dealing with the TLA going back to the Newcomb time. It's been like a union between the people who use the lake – the indigenous people, Americans and Canadians. We've always gotten along."

Robert and Faith visited family trapping grounds in the winter by hired dog team, travelling the frozen northland for about three weeks. They were frequently guided by John Turner or Presque Petrant and often stayed at Lakeview House. Presque, the descendant of a French Canadian Bear Island post packeteer, was the Newcomb caretaker until the late 1950s. He was also a master craftsman of fine log furniture. His wife Kathleen, née Wabi, was the Newcomb housekeeper. Some of her hand-braided rag rugs still adorn floors around the lake.

In return for their hospitality the Newcombs invited Bear Islanders, including the Peshabos, Turners and Petrants, back

to Cleveland to see the sights. John Turner trekked south to Cleveland, New York and Boston to promote northern Ontario tourism at sportsmen's shows. In 1948, long after the Newcomb era, the boat line's *Grey Owl* driver Tom Potts, number one fan of the Cleveland Indians, fulfilled a dream by venturing south to see his team play in the World Series. The Indians beat the Boston Braves.

The Newcombs introduced the children of Bear Island to jolly St. Nick. One Christmas they sent up a parcel brimming with tree ornaments, a Santa Claus suit, and a toy and candy for every child. A tree was set up at Lakeview House so everyone could enjoy the festive season. Until then Christmas had been mainly a religious occasion, celebrated with a feast of roast beaver and raisin pudding. From a list supplied by Mary Turner, gift-giving became a tradition. Dorothy Ames, whose husband George Cecil Ames would become the Association's third president, also pitched in to buy gifts. After Robert and Faith died in 1934, Bear Island families continued to celebrate the Yuletide but moved festivities to their own homes.

The Newcombs, their contemporaries and most Bear Islanders

William Petrant's wife (l), Mary Turner and Faith Newcomb (seated in sleigh) at Bear Island during a 1920s winter. *Photo: TLA Archives*

genuinely believed the actions of seasonal residents helped without harming the indigenous community. They would have been loath to recognize that the recent surge in tourism had contributed to a loss of independence and pride, just as logging, mining, and religious and government interventions had done. Prior to the 20th century, exploitation of the fur trade by Europeans had wrought an aboriginal reliance on non-native goods. Instead, Robert guilelessly cited a scarcity of fur-bearing animals for their plight. This attitude of pity carried into the 1940s with the establishment of a welfare fund.

Gone Fishing

In the early 1900s two fishermen landed 35 lake trout in two days with a combined weight of 110 pounds. Canoeists routinely jumped into the "birch-bark" 30 minutes before their next meal and returned with "a beautiful mess of small-mouthed bass." Temagami resident George Guppy was guiding an American in 1924 who hauled in a 42-pound laker. Another 42-pound trout was hooked at Sandy Inlet the following year. A.L. Cochrane spoke of seeing a 60-pound lake trout. Ten to 20 rabbits could be had in a day's hunt. Ruffed grouse were seen in the hundreds and moose were found in every bay.

A favourite pastime of the hundreds of cottagers and tourists flocking to the lake was angling. Pressure on the fishery was potentially degrading native stock. The Association initiated a restocking program in 1932 with

over three million walleye and 300,000 lake trout supplied by the province. The Perron and Marsh Navigation Company voluntarily distributed the fish in local waterways. The stocking program probably lured more new members in the early years than any other accomplishment.

The importance of fishing in the daily lives of cottagers is brought into focus in *Those Were the Days: The Temagami Journal of Clarence Seaman*. Clarence "Sam" of Island 977, dubbed Happy Isle, wrote a fishing log covering a period from 1927 to '37. In 1931, the same year the Association was spawned, Sam and family members went fishing on July 25th, the same day they arrived from Ohio. Until Sam's departure on August 15th, the family fished on all but two days when it rained too heavily. They cast lines off Garden Island, the Newcomb Island 969, Cattle Island, the Southwest Arm, the Haserot Island 1128, Gull Lake, Rabbitnose Island and Skunk Lake.

Often aided by ace guide Tom Potts, Sam and kin also took a three-day fishing trip to Wasaksina Lake and a four-day outing to the Trout Streams. Sam still had time to fish for two hours the day he went back stateside. He kept a tally of the family's annual catch. This is their record for 1935: 121 lake trout, 20 bass, 27 walleye and 31 speckled trout. Sam and many others lived to fish and fished to live.

Fishing also underpinned the success or otherwise of area resorts. No matter how pretty the scenery, how comfy the beds and how hearty the chow, the end game for guests was to weigh the success of their vacation by

A Chimo fishing certificate. *Photo: TLA Archives*

the weight of their catch. Chimo issued signed certificates to guests, attesting to their angling prowess. Photos of the beaming faces of fishers alongside their conquests were published in Chimo's annual brochure in a section dubbed "Fish of Distinction." Underpinning the success of fishing were the Bear Island guides who could locate the hot spots.

Aboriginal guides were also invaluable at the early youth camps for their navigational and canoeing skills. Alongside the fishing gear, guides often packed firearms to fell the occasional deer that crossed their path. The organs were roasted straight away, being quick to spoil, and enjoyed by the entire fishing party. The rest of the meat would be

smoked and cured once the guide returned home.

Original Association Officers

The founding Association executive consisted of President Robert Newcomb, Secretary Gilbert "Gib" Cochrane and Treasurer Sherman Thorpe. The installation of an American president was the origin of a trend continuing to this day – assigning the person most willing and able to fulfill the demands of the post, regardless of nationality. At the time the lake's seasonal population was an equal balance of Canadians and Americans. This was mainly the result of many islanders' affiliation with the tourist and youth camps, particularly American Keewaydin Camp and Cochrane's Canadian camp.

Between 1931 and 2011 there have been 18 known Canadian (all Ontarians) and nine known American helmsmen. Canucks have wielded the gavel over 57 years while U.S. citizens have steered the course over 23 years. Curiously, from 1944 until 1984, all known presidents were Canadian.

Gib Cochrane, A.L.'s son, had spent his summers at Cochrane's Camp since he was a tot. He was the director of athletics at the University of Toronto schools. During the First World War he was a fighter pilot. A.L. turned over the camp's administration to him in 1948. Gib was on the founding executive for only one year, but returned to serve in various capacities. In the 1940s and '50s both A.L. and Gib were involved in the investigation of illegal timber cutting in the skyline and shoreline reserves, some right to the water's edge of Aileen Lake just east of the South Arm.

The Mentholatum Hydes

Founding Treasurer Sherman Thorpe was the post manager from 1922 until '37. He was widely respected in the north by business associates and summer residents – and by one young boy. Ted Hyde was always surprised when Sherman took the time to talk to him, personally. "A nice gentleman," he recalled. He even invited Ted to his birthday party in his quarters above the post. He attended but his mother didn't approve of

her son gadding about the lake in his small flat-bottom boat.

Ted's father Charles Hyde and his uncle George Hyde discovered the lake in 1924. Charles and George were sons of Albert Alexander "A.A." Hyde. He founded the Mentholatum Company in Wichita, Kansas. Charles worked for the company out of Buffalo, N.Y., and leased Island 1076 across from Camp Wabun in 1933.

Temagami resident Dorothy Zimmerman's late husband Elly lived in Fort Erie, Ontario, just across the border from Buffalo. He worked as a handyman for Charles in the 1930s. Charles urged him to honeymoon with Dorothy on Island 1076 in exchange for some cottage repairs. The young couple was smitten and returned the following year to take up permanent residency in the village. Dorothy turned 97 in 2010.

Ted Hyde was a spry 85-year-old in 2009. Finding Island 1076 a bit too much to handle, he began spending his summers on Lake Erie. Fourth and fifth generations of Hydes enjoy Island 1076, including Charles' grandchildren Allan Eustis and Annette Jarman. Allan spent 10 years with the National Oceanic and Atmospheric Administration (NOAA). He began supplying NASA/NOAA satellite images of break-up and freeze-up, snow cover and fall colours to Brian Back's Ottertooth. com and the TLA website. He previously worked as a science and weather reporter at NBC, ABC and other network affiliates across the U.S. He won an Emmy Award in 1979 for his coverage of Hurricane David.

Cabinet Minister Joins Executive

Another important player on the original Association roster was Conservative MPP William Finlayson, Ontario's minister of lands and forests from 1926 to '34. A South Arm Island 857 cottager, he assured the Association of his "earnest support" at the 1931 founding meeting. In the wake of his assistance, the fish stocking schedule was adopted in 1932.

Snagging William to pull strings at Queen's Park was a huge bonus for the fledgling and politically unknown Association. He was named honourary president in 1932. The Association had by then obtained year-round Ontario Provincial Police (OPP) representation, partly due to William's clout. The OPP was then a relatively novice and rural force, having been formed to deal with violence in the Cobalt silver mining camp. The first seasonally-present officer was assigned to Temagami in 1926.

The Association produced its first reward notice about this time, to be nailed on the cottage or boathouse door as a warning. The reward for information leading to the arrest and conviction of trespassers was $50. Today it is $1,000. Through the reward system the first intruder was nabbed by 1936.

Night time navigation and the lake's infamous shoals were significant concerns, though the federal government had mitigated the risk by installing buoys and signal lights on some main channels. "This work should be further encouraged by the Association so that the hazards of lake travel will be reduced to a minimum," wrote the founding executive.

William Finlayson pledged in 1931 that "no harm will be done to the forest. Selective timbering may be undertaken, but it will not be noticed from the shore, and will not offend the settlers." There were five companies holding logging berths in 1930, including William Milne and Sons. Milne rail-hauled logs to its North Bay sawmill until it relocated to Temagami in 1936. Very little logging had been permitted until the mid-1920s when some pine stands were considered mature and approaching decadence. Logging activity had almost come to a standstill by 1931 due to the Great Depression.

There were two types of memberships. Owners of camps, cottages and homes on the

Robert Newcomb in his later years.
Photo: TLA Archives

lake, Bear Island and Temagami were called active members. Associate members were non-property owners. No salaries would be paid and dues would be kept "as nominal as possible." Annual dues were set at $5 in 1932 for active members.

Association Day

Annual meetings came to be called "Association Day" and were held at Lakeview House for the next 30 years. Robert Newcomb styled the yearly get-together "a regular powwow with all the frills." He arranged to have the Army Band and Boy Scout Choir entertain the crowd at the 1933 meeting and free refreshments were served.

Gib Cochrane was replaced as secretary by James Ross Sproat. He ran the Timagami Boat Company from 1936 until '44 when he was bought out by the TNOR. The railway ran the service for the next 20 years as part of the Ontario Northland Boat Lines (ONBL). Ted Guppy was head skipper of the *Belle* for the

company. Captain Ted was already a familiar face on the lake, having formed the Temagami Navigation Company back in 1924.

A new position was created in 1932 for Frank H. Todd who became the first vice president. Frank had emigrated from Yorkshire, England, to Toronto about 1900 at the age of 20. He worked for an insurance company and was sent north to Cochrane in 1912 to do a fire insurance adjustment. On the southbound train, passengers spoke of the silver boom town of Cobalt. He decided to see it for himself. Cobalt's prosperity convinced him that the bustling community was the place to be. With some Toronto insurance companies sponsoring him, he pulled up stakes and established the Todd Insurance Agency.

Frank discovered the lake in 1912 when he paddled a canoe down the Northeast Arm. He and his wife Ella settled on Island 159 the following year. Ella's first cousin was Captain Fred Marsh of the Perron and Marsh Navigation Company.

CHAPTER 5

THE STEEL HIGHWAY DRAWS TOURISTS

In the 30 years leading up to the Association's founding, some dramatic changes occurred. The TNOR opened to Temagami in 1904, bringing passengers to the top of the Northeast Arm. Ontario built the rail line from North Bay due, to a large degree, to the agricultural potential of the Little Clay Belt surrounding New Liskeard. Silver was discovered in 1903 by two contractors searching for suitable railway tie timber, precipitating one of the largest mining rushes in Canadian history, centred at Cobalt.

A steam locomotive pulls into T-Station. *Photo: Reg Sinclair*

The province consulted with George Kelley in 1900 as to the best route for a planned James Bay Railway, because of his first-hand knowledge of Temagami territory. "From a consideration of all the conditions it seems clear that so far as the Southern Belt or South Ontario is concerned the present railway to North Bay [the Grand Trunk from Toronto] answers every purpose as a link in the proposed James Bay Railway," George stated in a railway memo. He noted that a second belt, extending 322 kilometres north from North Bay, was "still the primitive wilderness."

George believed that a railway route surveyed in 1893 "through a rocky and difficult country" was the wrong way to go. This route, skirting the Northeast Arm, is the same one the government chose to build a few years later. He argued that it didn't take in the Sudbury area where nickel ore had been discovered. The CPR had rendered the surveyed line redundant, according to George, by building the Temiskaming Colonization Railway from a main line at Mattawa to Lake Temiskaming.

"Why the present proposed line should run so far east, avoiding the mineral deposits [of Sudbury] and encountering the competition of a [CPR] line designed to carry traffic to Montreal and the sea, it is hard to explain," he said. "From the standpoint of Toronto's interests there are no arguments peculiarly favorable to this route and it may well be dismissed from consideration."

George preferred running the line through the Sturgeon and Montreal river valley, offering agricultural potential and costing much less to build than the "rocky" surveyed course. It would open up Lake Temagami as "a region for summer resorts without an equal on this side of the continent."

The route advocated by George would have taken passengers further from the lake than the surveyed and later constructed route. Had the province been swayed by his memo, there would have been no silver rush at Cobalt and Temagami Station would never have sprung to life. A difficult canoe trip up the Temagami River would have been the way in.

In 2009 Island 958's Robert Wilson, George Kelley's grandson, put forward a tentative explanation for George's seemingly contradictory stance: "I don't know the answer to that unless he envisioned some sort of spur line east from the Sturgeon River to the lake...His intent I guess was to address the best overall route to James Bay, not just Temagami."

The route would have kowtowed to corporate Toronto's bottom line where generating revenue transcended all other considerations. Did George have an ulterior motive – discouraging tourism so Temagami

would remain the rail-free and unspoiled virgin territory he had first encountered, accessible to others only if they were willing to sustain a litany of blisters, scratches and bug bites?

Another route under consideration would have run east of Rabbit and White Bear (Cassels) lakes. Temagami founder Dan O'Connor envisioned the lake's tourism potential and lobbied Queen's Park to stay the surveyed course, even giving several MPPs a tour of Lake Temagami aboard the *Marie* in 1903.

"Forest Primeval"

Soon after the steel highway reached Temagami, the Grand Trunk Railway began publishing an annual promotional brochure floridly touting the area's virtues as wilderness's last stand: "The white man, in his ceaseless search for the earth's endowments, is now wiping out the wilderness. A little while and the "forest primeval" shall be no more," warned the 1908 pamphlet. "In all probability we of this generation will be the last to relate to our grandchildren the stirring stories of the hunt in the wilderness forests of Canada...Therefore, it behooves you, O mighty hunter, to go forth and capture your caribou or moose while you may. The scenes are shifting. Civilization is shoving the wild things farther and farther to the North."

Cover of the 1908 Grand Trunk Railway brochure.
Courtesy: Reg Sinclair

passenger *Belle of Temagami,* which was built for $18,000. She was coal-burning while the earliest steamers were wood-burning. The *Temagami* and the *Bobs* were obtained from the Temagami Navigation Company when this short-lived boat line was bought out by the larger company. The *Temagami* was a former Muskoka pleasure yacht purchased from the Eaton family of department store fame. The steamboat and hotel company also ran three hotels – Temagami Island's Temagami Inn, Deer Island's Lady Evelyn and the village's Ronnoco. The Ronnoco originally accommodated 50 guests, while the Temagami Inn had room for 75 tourists. Both would expand.

The Lady Evelyn was the largest, accommodating 150 adventurers. It burned to the ground in summer 1912. The resort must have been quite full at the time and the wooden structure would have burned like tinder. According to Brian Back, there are no extant newspaper records of cause, injuries or fatalities.

An ornately-worded 1931 TNOR brochure painted the lake as a haven for fishermen to catch "toothsome and gamey" specimens. Speckled trout were described as the "living arrow of the white-waters" and lake trout as "the Lancelot among the fishes."

Six years after the TNOR reached Temagami, the Temagami Steamboat and Hotel Company was operating ten steamers, according to Ottertooth.com. They included the 300-

Lady Evelyn Hotel in 1910. *Postcard photo: Reg Sinclair*

Remnants

An old blurry postcard photographed soon after the Lady Evelyn Hotel fire shows hotel guests sifting through blackened rubble for possessions. The North Arm site still holds a scattering of picked-over artifacts, including iron headboards, bed frames and bathtubs, a wood stove door and a corner pillar. The root cellar is still discernible. A nearby dump is a receptacle of medicine bottle relics and the rusted remains of tin cans.

The strangest find at the dump, recounted by Brian Back in The Keewaydin Way (2004), was the skeleton of an E.M. White & Company wood-canvas canoe crafted in Old Town, Maine. The Kittredge family recognized the remains in 1993, five years after the canoe was recovered, at John Kilbridge's Temagami Canoe Company where it was taken for restoration. It had been purchased jointly by Keewaydin and Chess Kittredge Sr. before 1930.

Don't Forget the Purgative

Canada's current food guide would blacklist a 1908 Temagami Steamboat and Hotel Company outfitting list for setting out on a canoe trip. It recommended staples like: salt pork lard; orange meat-force (likely pemmican); grape nuts (a spoilage-resistant cereal produced by Post); jars of dried beef (jerky); Underwood devilled ham (a canned meat spread); lunch tongue; HBC smoking tobacco; and chewing tobacco plugs.

William Edward Aitken, a participant in some of the 1892-1901 Cassels-Kelley northern expeditions, authored a 1901 article titled "Where the Loon Laughs" for *Forest and Stream* magazine. It is an account of one of their Temagami canoe trips and featured an inventory of supplies needed by four men for one month.

Requisite foodstuffs included: 40 pounds of shanty biscuit (tea biscuits originating at lumber camps); five pounds of clear pork; three pounds of Edwards' English desiccated soup ("suitable for gravies, hashes and stews," according to the label); five pounds of hard cheese; and three pounds of sweet stick chocolate. All food was to be stored in "separate drill bags made to fit. Tea, soup and salt to be covered in addition with oilcloth. All bags have tie strings at mouth."

William wrote that a first-aid kit should incorporate carbolated and plain petrolatum (petroleum jelly to protect skin against sun and wind); Pond's Extract (a cut-healing tea extract from witch hazel); Purgative (a laxative); Carminative (to prevent or relieve flatulence, especially among bowmen); and Quinine pills (no longer sold over-the-counter due to side effects including death) to reduce fever, pain and inflammation.

To make canoe repairs, a combination tool holder containing a screwdriver, file, awl, copper wire, pincers, a strip of tin, white lead mixed with putty, riveting nails, stout canvas, wood screws, wire nails and oil stone should be packed.

Personal gear was described in fine detail, right down to the number of socks required (at least four). Hockey boots with rubber soles would grip the rocky terrain. Skates were then two-piece affairs with the blades self-fastening onto the soles of the boots. Slouch hats, wide-brimmed felt chapeaus with chinstraps, kept the hot sun off. Seaman's long oilskin coats kept the rain off. Two heavy blankets could be sewn together to form a sleeping bag.

William Aitken pegged the total cost to outfit a month-long Temagami canoe trip for four at less than $15 per person. The rental of two all-wood William English canoes cost $10. The canoe maker was based in Peterborough, Ontario, from 1861 until the early 1920s when its moulds and patterns were purchased by the Peterborough Canoe Company. The price tag to rent a seven by seven-foot tent was $4. Five dunnage bags to carry supplies cost $10. The same number of leather tumplines with head bands could be had for $3.75, while three waterproof sheets cost $3.

William advised recreational canoeists to get outfitted at Mitchie and Company in Toronto. This merchant could tell them where to rent canoes, tents and dunnage bags. The total weight of the outfit, excluding canoes, shouldn't exceed 300 pounds.

Amenities

A sojourn at the Ronnoco in 1913 cost $2.50 to $3 per day or $15 to $18 per week including meals. An all-inclusive night at the Temagami Inn set one back $3 to $3.50 daily or $16 to $18 per week. Round-trip steamer fares from T-Station to Temagami Inn and Bear Island were $1.50. Travellers to Keewaydin were out of pocket $2.25. The Temagami Steamboat and Hotel Company's canoe and skiff rental rates were identical to the post, at 60 cents and 75 cents per day, respectively. The post's canoe fleet consisted of canvas-covered cedar New Brunswick Chestnuts.

Those wanting to travel the lake in style could be outfitted in Temagami with a launch.

Ronnoco Hotel circa 1905. *Photo by W.G. Gillespie, reprinted by the Highway Book Shop in Cobalt the Silver City*

Rates varied from $5 to $25, depending on its size and how finely it was appointed. At the post, the hiring of a guide in 1913 would leave a fisher's billfold $2.50 to $3 lighter.

Fruit and vegetable orders, to round out trout and pickerel feasts, could be placed with Factor Harry Woods and shipped from Toronto. The post carried moose and caribou moccasins and other native handiwork, imported from the Hudson Bay region. It would take a few more years for the post to shop locally. Bear Island-made apparel would become best sellers in the 1930s.

Dan O'Connor, a managing partner and part owner of the Temagami Steamboat and Hotel Company, departed Temagami for new prospects in Timmins in 1909. The business was sold to part owner David Fasken. He, in turn, sold to a Cobalt syndicate including Ed Holland. Ed was Cobalt's postmaster, an Island 49 cottager and a Victoria Cross recipient, Canada's highest military honour. Arthur Stevens, who had opened a train station restaurant in 1905, bought the Ronnoco and a general store from the syndicate in 1926. Arthur and his wife Frances ran the hotel until 1945.

The First World War brought some hard times to the tourism industry. Temagami Inn was as deserted as, well, a desert. The 100-foot *Belle*, the longest vessel ever to cruise the lake, was left moored in the harbour in favour of using smaller, less costly boats in the fleet. The *Kokomis*, commonly called the Old Koke, was a converted sailboat, as was the *Winonia*. Both were normally used to haul freight, but

The Great Temagami Mining Swindle

Julian Hawthorne, the son of heralded 19th-century Scarlet Letter author Nathaniel Hawthorne, was implicated in a 1908-10 mining scam centred at Cassels Lake. Julian was invited by an old university pal to join two others in promoting a new mining company. The scammers wanted the Hawthorne name attached to their fake venture to make it easier to sell stock to unsuspecting Americans. They sold $3.5-million worth of hollow shares. The company was known as the Hawthorne Silver and Iron Mines. All told, 21 worthless claims were staked. Following complaints from shareholders, the men were arrested and charged with mail fraud.

The New York Times covered the trial and their reporter had trouble keeping up with technical mining jargon. Temagami Chief Ranger Clarence Hindson was called as a witness for the prosecution and testified that the nearest operating mine was in the Cobalt camp. Julian Hawthorne was convicted in 1913 and served one year in the Atlanta federal slammer.

the Old Koke became the main vessel to carry passengers and mail. Others were sold off.

When the war ended in 1918, tourism resumed with a bang. It was common for 300 people to crowd the train station platform. Oderic Perron and Fred Marsh bought the *Belle* and operated the Perron and Marsh Navigation

Company until the mid-1930s. Competition sprang up in 1924 when Ted Guppy brought in the *Iona* from Lake of Bays and formed the Temagami Navigation Company. He was financially backed by, among others, A.L. Cochrane and the Greey family of Island 775.

Both lines shared the central lake, while Perron and Marsh exclusively serviced the North Arm and the Guppy collective worked the South Arm. Just like the lake, Temagami harbour was sectioned. Perron and Marsh staked the north side while the Temagami Navigation Company was headquartered to the south. The two boat lines ferried vacationers, lumber, fuel, ice, groceries and mail. Hotels, restaurants and shops bustled during the summer months, and the attractive stone train station, built in 1907, had a flower bed spelling Temagami.

About the time of the Association's inception, Perron and Marsh was charging return rates of $3 to central points and $4.25 to Keewaydin, its most distant port of call. Passengers on the two rival boat lines could stop at Bear Island, Wabi-Kon, Acouchiching, Eucaroma, Cochrane's, Wigwasati, Friday's Camp (run by William Friday on the mainland near Kokoko Bay), Temagami Inn, Garden Island and Chimo.

A Resort to Fit Any Budget

Resort rates covered all expenses except boat and guide hire. The cheapest places to stay were Wabi-Kon (accommodating 125),

Lakeview House (accommodating 50), Friday's (accommodating 60) and Garden Island's Ka-Kena Inn (accommodating 50). Ka-Kena charged $4 per day and $25 weekly to stay in a log lodge or $21 per week for a double-occupancy tent.

Temagami Inn (accommodating 200) was the most expensive, charging from $4.50 to $7 per day and $28 to $45 per week. Least costly was a cabin-style tent and the dearest was a first-floor room. Chimo was the next steepest, where guests forked over from $30 to $40 a week, followed by Couch (accommodating 75) where weekly rates were from $28 to $35. A week at the Ronnoco could be had for just $10 since it was essentially a staging area for travellers going elsewhere.

It wasn't unusual for Chimo staff to serve 130 dinner guests. The camp consisted of a main lodge, dining lodge, bathhouse, boathouses, 17 guest cabins, plus several more for family and friends. When enough fish had been caught, filleted and fried, the tennis and badminton courts beckoned.

Chimo wasn't outlandish enough to lay out a golf course like Cochrane's Camp and Camp Wabun did. Cochrane's maintained a short six-hole course chock full of naturally-occurring hazards. The golf course happened accidentally after someone tossed a cigarette butt, according to Carol Cochrane. Wooden-shafted mashie niblick clubs were exclusively used, the equivalent of today's 7-iron. Wabun's one-hole, nine-tee, one-club course was the venue for a 75th anniversary memorial golf tournament.

An early image of Temagami Inn. *Photo: Reg Sinclair*

Gordon Alexander Gooderham, Tim Gooderham's father, laid claim to Chimo Cabin One, closest to the main lodge. He had trouble walking because his right leg was three inches shorter than his left, due to a World War I Anson aircraft crash whilst he was training pilots. Cabin 22 was reserved for frequent visitor Sir William Mulock, knighted in 1902 and member of federal parliament for North York from 1882 until 1905. Sir William was Canada's first postmaster general under Prime Minister Sir Wilfrid Laurier. He and others purchased Dan O'Connor's staked claims to the Big Dan mine prior to Dan's departure from Temagami. Decades later the claims became the Sherman Mine.

Chimo owned at least four wooden launches over time, used to transport fishing parties and often trailing a canoe flotilla. The *Chimo I* was the original 1920s launch, replaced in the 1930s by the 28-foot *Chimo II*. The *Chimo III* was brought to the lake as the executive launch

of the Temagami Mining Company. She is a 34-foot 1929 Minett-Shields and the sole vessel of Chimo's woody fleet known to still be plying water, albeit in Muskoka. The *Lenore*, the resort's last wooden craft, sank and is now covered in mud off the north end of Chimo Island.

Cochrane's and Keewaydin camps faced new competition in 1925 from Dr. Frank Wood's Camp Cayuga for Canadian boys and their fathers on Island 1088 at the start of the Northwest Arm, and in 1931 from Canadian Camp Wanapitei. Henry Woodman, a biology teacher at Philadelphia's George School and later the Baltimore Friends College, bought Cayuga in 1940 and converted it to a girls' camp, the first on the lake.

The Brown Bunch

Henry Woodman met his future wife Marjorie Brown, one of Peter and Caroline Brown's four children, aboard the *Belle* in 1938. The Woodmans ran the camp together for 30 years. Henry died in 1968 while in the process of selling the camp and buying a cottage on Island 1123. Marjorie passed away in 2002. Woodman children Clay Woodman and Mary Faith Miller sold the cottage in 2009 to Susan Shane of California.

A fishing trip flotilla departs Chimo in the *Chimo I*. Gordon A. Gooderham is at the helm.
Photo: TLA Archives

Marjorie's sister Phyllis met her husband Alan McMillen through Henry Woodman with whom he taught. The McMillens bought a cabin on Island 1182 that had belonged to Robert Lochead, Keewaydin's bookkeeper-postmaster, after he died in 1946. Alan died in the late 1980s, followed by Phyllis in the mid-1990s. The island is still enjoyed every summer by McMillen sons Peter and Ted, and their families.

The Browns' other daughter Helene Brodie also met her husband through the Woodmans. Helene shared Brown's Island with her brother Hubert after their parents' deaths. She had a fatal stroke in the early 1980s while vacationing on Island 1186.

Hubert was a Keewaydin caretaker in the 1940s and '50s. He also drove the long, narrow *Ojibway* and the *Aubrey Cosens VC* for the boat

line. To get an early start, he moored the *Aubrey* off his sister Phyllis's island the night before Keewaydin campers left the lake. Hubert and his wife Caroline later lived in Temagami and he worked at the Milne sawmill. He died in the early 1980s. Caroline later moved to Thunder Bay, Ontario, to live with her son. She died in 2008.

Wanapitei's proprietor was Ed Archibald, an Ontario prospector and 1908 Olympic pole vaulting bronze medalist. His boys' camp was located on the mainland at Sandy Inlet, the site of Oblate Father Charles Paradis' former retreat-mission-orphanage. Ed managed to obtain a 64-acre lease, despite a ban on mainland development. Charles had squatted there so long – 10 years prior to the establishment of the Temagami Forest Reserve in 1901 and another 23 years thereafter – the land was designated an honourary island, according to Bruce Hodgins.

Wigwasati, an American camp for boys aged 12 to 17, had sprung up in 1930, on Island 583 at the entrance to the Southwest Arm, and was operated by Homer and Eva Grafton of Ann Arbor, Michigan.

Upchuck Alley

Charles Paradis called the changes he had seen by 1924 "a revolution," noting that a trip from North Bay to Temagami in the old days involved five days of canoeing. It now took less than five hours by rail. Had he lived to see it, Charles would have looked on the completion of the Ferguson Highway through Temagami three years later as an incredible feat.

Cobalt resident Norm Abell, whose family owned Island 154, said it all in a *Temagami Talker* tabloid reminiscence: "Most of the roads were equally bad but the Ferguson Highway from Cobalt to North Bay took the cake for switch backs and hair pins, and also sinkholes in stretches of muskeg where you just tried to get your speed up and hoped for the best. If you stalled, you got stuck, especially in wet weather, and then you were in for it...In those days one carried several tires, tubes and patching material, as well as a complete set of tools and an axe. When it was obvious the game was up and no end of rocking or pushing would work, you would go off into the swamp and fell two spruces, about 20-30 feet high. You would then open the windows and push the trees halfway through and run like hell for

---

Untitled Poem

Have you ever watched a campfire
When the wood has burned down low,
And the ashes start to whiten
Round the embers rosy glow?

Have you ever heard the wavelets tapping
At the rocks around the lake,
And the sound of night wings flying
Toward some mystic muskeg brake?

Have you seen the spruce spines pointing
Sharp and black against the moon,
Heard the far-off wailing wind-call
Of a wakeful sentry loon?

Is there any power that holds you
Like those awesome silent places
Any calm that reaches deeper
Than the moon washed open spaces?

With the night sounds all around you
Making silence doubly sweet
With a full moon high above you,
That the spell may be complete?

Tell me, were you ever nearer
To the land of heart's desire
Than when you sat there thinking
With your face turned toward the fire.

Henry Woodman, 1933

help. You often didn't need to go too far as the next car might as well turn around and take you to town since he was not going anywhere that involved passing you until you were towed out and the hole filled with logs."

There was one dissenting voice amongst the Ferguson maligners. When Harlan and Harriet Yenne first visited Island 672 from Ohio in 1928, they were warned by owner Alfred Horr that it was best to abandon all hope at North Bay and take the train. Ignoring Alfred's advice, Harlan braved the Ferguson and came out the other end with nothing but praise: "In any event, the seventy-mile section between North Bay and Timagami is a beautiful panorama and the loveliest part of the entire drive. The road twists and turns in the spruce, birch and pines," he wrote.

To chance the Ferguson, you needed a travel permit, issued by the Department of Lands and Forests from a small guard's station near the North Bay entrance. Frank Goddard opened a service station in Temagami in 1928 and business off the Ferguson Highway was likely brisk. Anticipating that cottagers would need a place to store their Packards in the summer, Arthur Stevens built a 150-car garage after he bought and renovated the Ronnoco Hotel in 1926. Andy Stevens' son Findley is the fifth generation of Stevens on the lake.

Many cottagers avoided "upchuck alley" and stuck with the train. A round-trip ticket between Cleveland and Temagami in 1930, including Pullman berth, cost $40. The highway's reputation improved after it was realigned, widened and paved, and renamed Highway 11 in 1936. Driving to Temagami became the norm by the late 1930s.

Today stretches of the old gravel road comprise a nature trail/bog for wildlife lovers. Nature has done some reclamation work. Red-eyed vireos and ruby-crowned kinglets sing up a storm, while lady's slipper, bunchberry, meadow rue, blue iris and trilliums may get trampled by moose.

A Temagami Outfitting Company postcard of the Ferguson Highway at Jumping Caribou Lake. *Postcard photo: Reg Sinclair*

Cottage Life in the 1930s

The same year the Association was born, cottagers' leases required they erect a building worth not less than $500 within two

1928 Ferguson Highway travel permit. *Photo: Vintage Postcards*

years and have it "painted or stained according to the directions of the Chief Ranger." Lessees were warned about the dangers posed by forest fires to the extensive white and red pine stands within the Temagami forest. While residing in Canada, U.S. citizens were expected to comport themselves with respect for the Dominion: "If and when any National Flag other than the Union Jack is flown on any leased or licensed area, a Union Jack of a larger size than the said other flag shall be flown above it and on the same pole."

A typical cottage consisted of more than one building. The main cabin contained kitchen, dining room, living room and porch. There were separate sleeping cabins, a boathouse, bathhouse and, of course, the outhouse. Until the 1940s when Servel propane refrigerators began popping up, there was also an icehouse supplying the icebox.

The icehouse was stacked with 50-pound blocks of ice, cut from the lake and insulated

The Cottage Guest Book

Many cottagers had coffee table guest books to record the march of visitors through time. The Tretheweys of Island 1003 were no exception. Borrowing from a Persian poem composed by Omar Khayyam in the 11th century, Lloyd Matchett penned this entry in August 1938: "Sunny days – Temagami nights, Ah Wilderness were paradise enow."

Most guests gathered their thoughts to convey the deep impression the lake left. A 1953 entry reads: "If I never get to Temagami again I have seen beauty enough to last the rest of my life." Sometimes company praised meals of trout, sheppard's pie and blueberry pancakes. Others tried their hand at original poetry, some more successfully than others. One guest wrote four pages of well-executed verse.

with sawdust. The ice would be split into smaller chunks and carried to the icebox. There was always some ice remaining in the icehouse at summer's close. Ice was placed in the top of the icebox so the cold air would circulate down to the food inside. It was insulated with rust-free zinc. Most iceboxes around the turn of the 20th century cost $10 to $15. In original condition, they could fetch about $500 in 2011 from collectors.

A heated rivalry between Toronto suppliers for cottagers' grocery orders was in full flush. While King Street's Michie and Company, established in 1835 by George Michie, provided better service according to some cottagers, Yonge Street's T. Eaton Company, established in 1869 by Timothy Eaton, carried superior quality meat, vegetables and fruit. Michie's was first to offer to check groceries as baggage for the train trip. Eaton's didn't provide this service until 1928.

A wood stove was used for heating and cooking. Aladdin lamps fuelled by coal oil were a constant source of worry and added to the heat of a stifling summer night. One arm became muscle-bound from operating the hand water pump. For local gadding about, cottagers jumped into the cedar skiff, powered by an Ole Evinrude or a Johnson brothers' Sea-Horse. If you wanted to impress company, you'd take your heavily-varnished, badly-planing and shower-generating launch out for a spin. For fishing, you were likely to slide the Peterborough cedar strip canoe into the water.

Most first aid for cook stove burns, poison ivy, fish hook mishaps and dock splinters was self-supplied. Broken bones were set at the Misericordia Hospital in Haileybury. A heart attack usually meant a one-way trip to the Pearly Gates.

Post Manager Sherman Thorpe always had the latest news. That's where many cottagers picked up mail and stocked up on non-perishables such as flour, tea and Preston's jam. Though bass and blueberries were the highlights of cabin cuisine, a variety of dry goods could be had, including foul-tasting powdered Klim whole milk and canned Spork mystery meat. You could also pick up one of the HBC's warm wool

Regally Roughing It

Seasonal residents formed an informal social network they called the South Temagami Neighborhood Association. They produced an annual bulletin apprising cottagers of summer plans. Robert and Faith Newcomb are referred to as "the King and Queen" in the 1928 edition while Charlotte Horr gets the royal treatment as "the countess." "Scouting expeditions report that the Algonquin paradise passed through the winter unscathed, although five or six feet of snow in the bush melted simultaneously in the spring and the water rose to unprecedented heights. Outside of a few docks that have a penchant for wandering about the lake, no damage appears to have been done," the unnamed bulletin's author noted.

point blankets. Canoe trippers were completely outfitted and Bear Island guides were available. The post had a change room and free lockers for storing city clothes.

The post also sold fishing permits to non-residents of Ontario. Eight smallmouth bass, five lake trout and 12 pickerel could be plucked per person per day. It's no wonder that some cottagers apparently buried surplus fish. Today the sport fishing limit is six smallmouth bass, two lake trout and four pickerel. A couple of entrepreneurs offered fresh produce during the 1930s. The Guppys sold strawberries, lettuce, eggs, etc., produced in the Little Clay Belt. A southern Ontario poultry farmer visited the islands via the *Winonia* and sold fresh meat and vegetables. Oven-fresh bread could be had from Bear Island and some camps. Many camps offered Sunday dinner when campers were out.

You could get junior out of your hair by sending him to Keewaydin for $300. Cochrane's Camp welcomed 100 boys in 1930, whose parents paid $250 for eight weeks of character building. Cayuga offered an eight-week opportunity for 25 boys to bond with their fathers for $200 per person.

Granny Turner

Mary "Granny" Turner's Lakeview House was just a short walk from the post. It was praised in a 1910 Grand Trunk Railway brochure as a place where "the wants of the inner man can be substantially satisfied with dishes fit for a king, the menu very often

including moose, venison or bear and always the tasty bass or lake trout."

Malcolm McLean's oldest daughter, Mary married John Turner in 1872. Of Scottish, Cree and Inuit ancestry, John came to the Temagami area in the 1860s from the James Bay region. His grandfather Philip Turnor (note the earlier surname spelling) was the first qualified surveyor engaged by the HBC. From Moose Fort on James Bay, he was sent down to lakes Abitibi and Temiskaming in 1781 and '82 to map out the waterways and to ascertain the region's suitability for establishing trading posts. Renowned geographer David Thompson learned the art of map making from Philip.

John Turner built the HBC post on Bear Island in 1876. The structures included a dwelling house, store, warehouse and kitchen. "The houses here are at least in a habitable condition," Factor Arthur Ryder commented. The original post, located on Temagami Island in 1834, was "on its last legs." The move to Bear Island came about when Arthur got wind that Alexander Dokis, an independent trader at Cross Lake and the post's arch rival, was planning to set up shop at Bear Island. The two fur traders lived side by side until Dokis departed for Lake Nipissing in 1883.

John succeeded Arthur Ryder as factor until 1899 when Harry Woods assumed the position. John later operated Lakeview House with Mary. Once he started building on Bear Island, other First Nation families gradually moved there from their ancestral lands, many just seasonally. Those territories extended over a vast area and would comprise the lands covered

Alfred and Charlotte Horr at Ooshke Island 672 in the 1930s.
Photo: Moose to Moccasins by Madeline Katt Theriault

by legal cautions filed by the Temagami Indian Band in 1973. John died in 1926 at the age of 84.

Mary raised cows and chickens to serve guests and to supply cottagers with fresh milk and eggs. She made her own fish nets, salting and smoking her catch. Jean Klingman was one little girl who took high tea with "Granny" Turner, escorted by her grandmother. Mary had a special place in her heart for children and would beckon them to the Lakeview porch or to her small cabin after she retired. Jean's grandfather Samuel F. Haserot had established the Haserot Company in 1889, a wholesale Cleveland grocery.

The Haserots leased high-bluffed Island 1128 on the Northwest Arm in 1908. Sam had owned an island in what is now Algonquin Park. After a fire, it was an easy decision not

to rebuild; he was finding the area too crowded. He took the train north, hired two native guides and paddled for two days. That's how he discovered five-acre Island 1128 where he loved the panoramic views from the cliffs. In the winter of 1911-12, he hired Bear Islanders to build the main lodge, according to Pam Morgan, Jean's daughter. They erected a 20 by 40-foot log cabin and a screened veranda without using a single nail. The original bark remains on the exterior logs. The interior faces were all hand adzed. The builders wrote their names on the exterior end of one log and they are still visible.

The island, called Gibraltar, was passed down to Jean and Everett Myers through her mother Helen Klingman. Jean died in 2002 and the property is now owned by Jean's grandchildren – Elizabeth Morgan, Timothy Morgan and Everett R. Myers – who are fifth generation islanders.

On summertime Tuesday and Saturday nights, cottagers and staff from Keewaydin and Wabun would let their hair down at the "Square Island Bear Dance." After kicking up their heels, revellers gorged on all-you-can-eat cake and sandwiches with coffee for 50 cents. Mary always sat by the door, turning away young people she felt were slovenly attired. Stylish dance dress for men consisted of Levi's blue jeans, a plaid shirt and a red bandana tied around the neck or belt.

If John's namesake grandson John, born in 1897, smelled liquor on anyone's breath, he would grab the suspect by the neck, shout something in Anishnabek and follow through with a quick ejection. A younger generation of Turners assumed ownership of Lakeview House and the dancehall upon Mary's death in 1943. John is best remembered by cottagers for his prolific cabin-building skills. Success at Lakeview bred short-lived competition from Walsh's Hotel on Bear Island, which burned down in 1918. Tom Petrant also ran a dancehall.

John and Mary Turner in 1896. *Photo: Robert Wilson*

CHAPTER 6

THE STARS COME OUT TO PLAY

Lake Temagami was the place to be in the 1920s and '30s if you wanted to bump into stars of the big screen. The CBS television network was founded as the Columbia Broadcasting System in 1927, a joint venture between Columbia Records and New York City talent agent Arthur Judson. He opened Camp White Bear in 1929 on Island 488 in the Southwest Arm. Facilities included a games court, a large two-storey lodge, a gift shop and a hospital.

Some of Arthur's star-studded guests were Cary Grant, Clark Gable, Carole Lombard, Jimmy Stewart, Lucille Ball and Bob Hope. Guests strolled at night on lighted pathways,

had their shoes polished when left on their doorstep overnight, and cabin service was available. Meals were prepared by a cordon bleu chef. Lucy and Bob paid Bear Island a visit.

Jimmy Stewart also vacationed at Camp Acouchiching in 1940 with his parents Alexander and Ruth Stewart, and his two younger sisters. Jimmy became a superstar with his breakout film *Mr. Smith Goes to Washington,* and he received the first of five academy award nominations for best actor. In private moments Alexander was still trying to persuade his son to come home to Indiana, Pennsylvania, and take over the family hardware store. Jimmy also stayed at an island on the South Arm belonging to his uncle.

Another legendary actor to visit the lake, at a later date, was the late Canadian James Doohan, a.k.a. Montgomery "Scotty" Scott, the redoubtable chief engineer of the Starship Enterprise on the *Star Trek* TV series. He went fishing with an Ojibway guide named Ole' Charley who knew where the fish were biting.

Interior of the posh Camp White Bear.
MacLean postcard photo: Reg Sinclair

From Rustic to Nearly Refined

George Aulabaugh of Omaha, Nebraska, opened Camp Acouchiching in the early 1920s on Island 938 near the bottom of the South Arm. He started the Temagami Fur Company in 1920, installing brothers Bill and Ted Guppy as trappers-factors. Couch was a rustic fish camp, operating out of floored tents and a few cabins. Sheep and pigs had the run of the place and, inevitably, landed on the dinner menu by season's close. The Temagami Fur Company bought the steamboat *Keego* presumably to ferry camp guests.

Reg McConnell of Toronto guided Couch guests starting in 1922. He and a partner, whom he soon bought out, purchased the camp in 1927. They put window glass in the cabins, did stone work on the chimneys, built a log lodge and generally spruced things up. While the main lodge and 25 cabins were located on Island 938, the smaller Island 939 was home to four more cabins, featuring fireplaces. Bathrooms were installed after the Second World War.

Angele Belaney and her children Agnes and Benny worked at Couch. Angele had a sideline – selling her husband Grey Owl's

internationally acclaimed books to guests. Captain Ted Guppy also had a Couch sideline. It was his final passenger-boat stop before turning around for the return trip to Temagami. After he ate lunch, he had time to engage in a spirited badminton game, taking on whoever was the resort's reigning champ of the day.

Pat Bonnell, one of Reg and Winnifred McConnell's two children, was a carefree child of Couch in the 1940s. She was particularly transfixed by some of the guests. There was the woman from Dayton, Ohio, who always

The Acouchiching lodge in a 1940s MacLean photo.
Postcard: Robert Wilson

showed up with a trunk filled to bursting with craft projects. She would teach the youngsters shell and bead work or crocheting. Another guest, a kindly doctor, would go out of his way to shake children's hands, always leaving a stick of Doublemint chewing gum in their palms.

Couch had several wooden launches over the years, starting with the *Keego.* Later came the *Couch,* the *Judy* (for Judy Runion, a guest and Island 953 cottager) and the *Denton.*

Couch employed guides from Bear Island, Mattawa, and one from Golden Lake, who was a jack of all trades but a man of few words. Alex Aird, of Ojibway, French and Scottish descent, was a master guide, shore lunch chef, canoe repairman and builder. Alex, often with Reg McConnell, helped build cottages for Couch guests who decided to lease property, including the Ogsburys (Island 888), Grouts (943), Beusts (938), Wilsons (958) and Cooks (884). What really set Alex apart was his wry sense of humour, Pat Bonnell recalled. One of

his oft-repeated jokes was an Ojibway recipe for cooking loon.

The Roaring '20s

At Temagami Inn, the 1920s really did roar. Joe Spitzig and some Cleveland partners bought the resort in 1920. Guests included the high-kicking Rockettes, then known as the Roxyettes, from New York's famous Roxy Theatre and later Radio City Music Hall. There was no shortage of fishing guides when the dancers showed up.

Freddie Martin played tenor saxophone at the inn's summer dances, before he became well-known for his own orchestra. The inn

---

A Life of Conviction

Vera Parsons was a regular at Camp Acouchiching through the 1930s, leasing Island 950 in 1941. She took her meals at Couch, dawdling over in her dispro, or disappearing propeller boat. Vera graduated from Osgoode Hall Law School in 1924, at a time when few women practised law. They were particularly unwelcome in litigation and criminal defence. She confronted that attitude by becoming Ontario's first woman criminal defence lawyer.

Born in 1889 she contracted childhood polio and walked with a cane. Vera obtained an MA in comparative languages at Bryn Mawr College. She applied her language abilities to assist Toronto's Italian immigrants. After being

called to the bar, she brought in substantial clientele from the Toronto Italian community.

Vera became a partner in Horkins Graham and Parsons. She was the first female lawyer to defend a first-degree murder case, settling for a lesser manslaughter verdict. In 1944 she was named King's Counsel, only the third woman so honoured.

"Law is hard work," the single Vera said. "I hardly think the study of law is a particularly good preliminary to marriage." She retired in the 1950s and died in 1973. She is remembered in the Vera L. Parsons prize for criminal procedure in the Ontario bar admission course. Current island owners Michael and Shelley Bloomfield of Chagrin Falls, Ohio, admire the former owner.

boasted 100 canoes and a solid mahogany launch, powered by a 16-cylinder Rolls Royce engine. It was considered the fastest boat on the lake. Twenty-five native guides were employed, plus two boat drivers. Facilities consisted of riding stables, tennis courts, a square and ballroom dancehall, card-playing room, barber shop and marine lounge.

Cochrane's Camp hosted its share of public figures over time, including NHL hockey radio broadcaster Foster Hewitt, Timothy C. Eaton of Canadian department store fame, a son of industrialist E.P. Taylor, distiller J.W. Seagram, Richard Southam Jr. of the Southam newspaper chain, politician John Turner, who became Liberal prime minister of Canada briefly in 1984, and Ontario Attorney General Dana Porter and his son Julian.

John Turner went to Cochrane's Camp almost every summer from the age of seven to 24. A.L. Cochrane became a father figure, teaching him to canoe, draw and follow maps, challenge whitewater and survive in the wilderness, according to Carol Cochrane. Such was his attachment to the camp, he attempted to purchase it in the 1950s when it was experiencing financial hardship. Canada's future prime minister later took his own family on daring adventures on Arctic rivers.

Cochrane alumnus and lawyer Julian Porter acted as counsel for the College of Physicians and Surgeons in a 1991 discipline panel hearing involving Ben Johnson's former doctor. The doctor was suspended from practising medicine in Ontario as a result of the sprinter's steroid disgrace at the 1988 Olympics, for which Ben

A.L. Cochrane feeling at home in a canoe circa 1940s. *Photo: Carol Cochrane*

was stripped of his Canadian gold medal and world record. The chastened athlete made his first public appearance following the scandal at Bear Island in summer 1989, during a drug

Bummer

John Turner once tried to grab a pike he had pulled into his canoe and ended up with a fishing plug deeply imbedded in his backside. All standard removal methods failed. A medical student heated a knife to disinfect it, then had eight youths pin John to a rock. He cut a triangle into his rear end, removed the hook and flooded the wound with iodine. John still has a scar from the impromptu surgery.

Sally and Beelzebub

The Byngs accompanied A.L. on his regular tent inspections one summer morning. Neatly-made beds and belongings carefully stowed were a point of pride for A.L. Entering a row of tents, he was horrified to discover tent flaps, normally tidily tied back, were ripped and hanging. Inside the first tent, blankets were pulled off cots and cases of belongings scattered. His blue-blooded guests were not amused. The scene repeated itself over and over until A.L. and his dignitaries approached the last tent from where slurping sounds emanated. They found two bear cubs sitting on the floor sucking on chunks of watermelon with gusto. A parents' gift ordered in Temagami, the melon had been secured inside a trunk, but the curious bruins had managed to open it and extract their prize. The orphaned cubs were a spring gift bestowed on A.L.

awareness seminar organized by Bear Islander June Twain. He delivered an anti-drug message to about 100 Bear Islanders and cottagers.

British nobility was royally entertained at Cochrane's Camp. Aristocratic company, all serving stints as Canada's governor general between 1916 and '35, included: Sir Victor Cavendish, the ninth Duke of Devonshire; Viscount Julian Byng of Vimy; Vere Ponsonby, the Earl of Bessborough; and Freeman Freeman-Thomas, the Earl of Willingdon. Some were guided by Harry Smith, Presque Petrant, Tommy Saville, William Friday, William

Moore, William Peshabo, Alex Paul and Tom Potts. Lady Byng was attired in voluminous layers of skirts, setting Carol Cochrane to wondering how she managed to get in and out of boats, especially canoes.

Facilities at Cochrane's Camp included a dining hall, assembly hall, tuck shop (where Carol later worked), trip house, post office, infirmary, clubhouse, camp office, adult lodge, craft shop, kitchen, canoe shed, and family and staff cabins. Launderers would decide if a camper's sheets needed changing by throwing them against a wall. If they didn't stick, they could wait another week, Carol said.

While in-camp there was plenty to do. Sailboats, a golf course, baseball diamond, and tennis, volleyball and basketball courts left little time for idling. The volleyball nets served a second purpose – as sleeping bag drying racks. There was a causeway between main Island 758 and 757, maintained by camp foreman Alec Steadman. He was borrowed every summer from a gold mine owned by A.L. Cochrane's next-door Toronto neighbour.

Everyone is Welcome Here

Not all resorts were posh affairs. Herbert "Harry" Smith opened Ka-Kena Inn on the southwest corner of Garden Island in 1924. Loosely translated, the name means "everything needed" in Anishnabek. The atmosphere was informal and the camp motto was "Come to dinner in your fishing clothes." Consequently, not only did the executive officers of the New

Cochrane's Camp section arrives at home base. *Photo: Carol Cochrane*

York Central Railway stay at Ka-Kena, so did the secretaries and brakemen.

Harry kept a horse named Minnie. She was used in winter to haul firewood and ice. The branded western bronco roamed Garden Island in summer. Many a guest was startled in the dark by a sudden crashing through the bush, to discover it was only Minnie and not a bear. Angele Belaney was a cook at Ka-Kena as well as at Couch.

A native of Birmingham, England, Harry laboured in the South African diamond mines after Boer War military service. Owen Funnell of Garden Island and Pointe Claire, Quebec, recalled Harry giving an eye-witness account of how the Cullinan diamond was discovered. It is the largest rough gem-quality diamond ever found, at more than 3,000 carats. It was named for the mine owner.

Harry arrived in Temagami in 1918. He opened a store and billiards room just south of the post. It closed in the mid-1920s. George Hutchings, a Ka-Kena carpenter, opened another store near Harry's former premises. The Hutchings moved to Temagami and established White Top Cabins in the late 1930s. Elsie Groves, a Lakeview House guest, took over the Hutchings' store for several years.

Accommodations at Ka-Kena consisted of sleeping cabins and a two-storey log lodge with a lounge, open stone fireplace, and hot and cold running water in the single bathroom. The island featured two broad sand beaches. The lodge was built of red and white pine sourced from Garden Island, accounting for their scarcity over most of the island, according to Owen Funnell. Red pine posts supported a lofty ceiling. The lounge was appointed with writing desks, bridge tables, a piano, violin and an Edison (a gramophone or early record player).

The Pagoda was a two-storey structure with guest rooms and wrap-around porches on both levels. There were also tents with wooden floors and three-foot walls guaranteed "absolutely dry" due to double roofs, according to a Ka-Kena brochure. Some buildings had electric lights. A steamer called every day at 1 p.m., just in time for a lunch of "all home-cooking and a-plenty." Canoes and rowboats could be had for $1, while motors and gasoline launches were available at "moderate rates."

Harry Smith was sharing space on Garden Island with the founders of Camp Wabun in 1933. He died painfully of a strangulated hernia in 1942 during spring break-up. His widow was left alone with the body for three days before she could summon help. Ka-Kena became a Wabun asset, operated as Wabun Lodge, providing accommodation for parents of campers. It closed in 1965 and the building was demolished.

All but one of Wabun's eight founders were disgruntled Keewaydin staffmen. Dick Lewis, Bill Russell, Bill Anderson, Walter "Whitey" Cannon, Bill Roberts, Harry Munson, Ted Fellows and Walter "Mac" McLellan were fed up with Keewaydin's rigid policy forbidding them from visiting their wives and children, staying at Ojibway Lodge on the north end of the island, after campers arrived.

In its first summer Camp Wabun drew 80 campers, mostly former Keewaydinites, the same number Keewaydin drew that year. The Wabun founders later built cottages, save for Harry Munson and Ted Fellows, on the south and east sides of Garden Island. Former Keewaydin staff member Herbert Stokinger built on the west side. He had been asked to participate in Wabun's inception. Due to other commitments he was unable to join the administration until 1941.

Receipt for partial payment by Bill Russell of the $1,250 each of the Wabun founders paid to establish the camp in 1933.
Courtesy: Russell Tuckerman

Wonderland

The Wabun cottages were a hubbub of activity, teeming with youngsters and dogs in a natural setting ripe for wondrous adventure. Anne Rutzen wrote a memoir of childhood summers spent on Garden Island during the 1940s, titled *Islands and Lakes Where Souls Expand*. Her parents were Mac and Maggie McLellan. Boisterous games of sand beach hop scotch, skipping stones and tip-over in a retired canoe filled many sun-splashed hours. Ecology lessons of a sort ensued when the children set up a temporary terrarium for snakes, toads and snails. Boats were built with wood scraps, nails and twine and toads were enlisted as crew members.

Anne keenly observed the mesmerizing sights surrounding her with a child's eye view: "Nature offered her miracles and oddities constantly. Jelly turned into eggs that turned into tadpoles that turned into toads; Pollywogs turned into frogs; Eggs held snails, baby birds, insects, or snakes; Toadstools suddenly appeared in the woodland, then disappeared; Some birds swam under water; Some fish jumped out of the water; Some spiders walked on water; Crayfish lived under rocks under water; Hummingbirds flew sideways, up, down, forward, backward or flew motionless in the air; Toads and frogs caught insects by flipping out a long sticky tongue; Some birds made a home in tunnels in the sand; Birds caught fish and fish caught ducklings; Snakes ate other snakes or toads wider than they were; Rain turned to ice and bounced onto the porch like marbles;

And the lake changed colors. Surprises were endless."

A chicken pen was built one summer to supply fresh eggs for breakfast and roasts at summer's close, Anne recounted. Clipping one wing prevents birds from flying by skewing their balance but someone clipped both wings, meaning they could still fly but not too far. The free-range Wabun fowl nested in the bush and provided a never-ending Easter egg hunt for the kids. The late Ida Moore of Mattawa was Wabun's cook from 1946 until '67, followed by a few years at Camp Temagami.

Square dances were a twice per season treat. Accompanying a piano player and fiddler

Bedraggled Wabun "ragamuffins" ready to call it a day.
Ricky Stokinger (l), siblings Anne, Robbie and
Mary Alice McLellan, and Mary Jane, a Stokinger niece.
Photo: Islands and Lakes Where Souls Expand by Anne McLellan Rutzen

from Bear Island, Bill Russell played drums and Russell "Rusty" Cleminshaw called. Whitey Cannon thumped and twanged on a contraption he called a "whoodle-doodle," made from a branch, a paddle, an old tin washtub, two pie plates, wire and a shoe. Square dancers raised the roof at Ojibway Lodge as well. The guides played fiddles, drums, spoons and the occasional accordion. Islanders and Ojibway guests ensured a good time was had by all.

The McLellan cottage is now enjoyed by family members, including Anne's sister Mary Alice Foster. Mary Alice's husband Benjamin "Bo" Foster spent five summers as a Wabun camper and waiter. Bill and Grace Russell's cabin went to their daughter Grace Tuckerman and is now owned by Grace's daughter Robin Denninger. Bill and Gubby Roberts' summer

place was left to their daughter Sylvia Clark, a talented artist who died in 2010, and is now in the possession of Bill and Gubby's grandson Martin Johnson.

Whitey and Hazel Cannon's cottage belongs to David and Janet Manning. Christopher and Gail Getch have the Herbert and Esther Stokinger property. Bill and Vera Anderson's cabin was purchased by Patricia Healy and her first husband John Anderson (no relation to the Wabun Andersons). Patricia's husband Peter Healy bought out John's interest in 1979. Richard Lewis III and his wife Margaret succeeded Richard Lewis Jr. and his wife Corinne who had succeeded Richard Lewis Sr. and his wife Violet as Garden Island cottage proprietors. All three generations of Lewis men served as Wabun directors.

A Wabun square dance. Bill Russell is on the drums at far left. Whitey Cannon plays his woodle-doodle at right. *Photo: Russell Tuckerman*

66

Ladies Only

Wabi-Kon Camp opened on Temagami Island near the site of the abandoned HBC post by 1908, operated by the Wabi-Kon Camping Club, a Toronto women's organization. Laura Orr was the secretary-treasurer. "Reputable ladies will be continually at the Camp to chaperon girls coming unaccompanied by older persons," demurely noted a 1908 Grand Trunk Railway brochure. Annual fees of $25 entitled members to a two-week camp outing.

Wabi-Kon converted to an adult resort in 1913 and Laura went on an advertising blitz in Canada and the U.S., including ads in the prestigious *New York Times*. Her gamble paid dividends as the camp's tent city expanded. The Orr proprietorship continued until 1926 when the camp was sold to Herbert and Sarah Wilson. The Wilsons had begun operating a village restaurant in 1910. During the Great Fire of 1922, which burned a huge swath from Charlton to Haileybury, they provided meals non-stop to fleeing victims. Cedric, the Wilsons' son, drowned near Wabi-Kon in 1935.

Archie Belaney returned to the lake in 1920 as a Wabi-Kon guide. There he met Gertrude "Anahareo" Bernard, a young native waitress from Mattawa, and fell in love. She began leading him on his ultimate path toward preservation versus exploitation of the land and its wildlife.

Wabi-Kon, meaning "little white flower" in Anishnabek, boasted a dining tent seating 100 with an open stone fireplace, a large lounge tent, a dance hall, a 60-foot stone verandah,

---

First Outboard Motor on the Lake

Outboard motors have been around since 1907 when Ole Evinrude built the first "detachable" – a 1 ½ hp made of iron weighing 62 pounds. By 1925 motors had lightened up considerably. A Johnson 4 hp weighing 35 pounds cost $160. This speed demon could reach about 13 kph. Johnson introduced the Sea Horse in 1929, followed by the Sea King in 1930.

The 1919 Eaton's catalogue was the first to feature an outboard motor. It was an Evinrude 2 hp for $135. Eaton's had its own brand, the Viking, from 1933 until '64. They were manufactured by the Outboard Motor Corporation (OMC) in Peterborough, Ontario. A 1936 Viking 4 hp could be had (and delivered) for $98.50.

Another company of note is Muncie Gear Works of Indiana. One of the best deals around was a 1933 2-hp Muncie for $44.50. The catch? It arrived as a kit requiring assembly. The company stopped producing outboards in 1941. By the 1950s, a 5-hp motor was common on the lake, followed by a 10 hp in the 1960s. The first 25 hp was built in 1951 followed by the first 60 hp in 1960. Nowadays, the sky's the limit. Outboard motors made their first appearance on Lake Temagami in the 1920s. Local lore has it that the first was an Evinrude, brought to Wabi-Kon by an American.

Gordon McIntosh operates Camp Bigiwe's temperamental Muncie during the 1930s. *Photo: McIntosh family*

of locomotion and transport" in the winter.

The Wabi-Kon brochure cautioned: "We do not pretend to be or want to be a "summer resort," as the term is generally understood. Do not expect the service and accommodation found in the city, or fine resort hotels." Women were advised to pack their older clothes and men, their woods or fishing duds. The brochure listed the names of recent Canadian and American guests. John

and colonies of cabins and floored tents. A 1920s camp brochure touted the "Hudson's Bay Company Indian Village" and its large number of husky sleigh dogs, which were put to work as "wolf-dog teams," Bear Island's "only means

Trethewey, a Cobalt mining man, was a guest in 1924. He likely hadn't opened the family cottage on Island 1003 that summer because his wife Colinette had stayed home in Toronto to help look after their newborn grandson. The

Wabi-Kon's tent city. *Grand Trunk Railway photo postcard: Reg Sinclair*

infant was Jack Glenn and he would lead the Association in middle age.

Big Plans for a Small Space

Another camp operating without pretension was tiny Bigiwe, occupying just 1.69 acres on the northwest corner of 57-acre Island 1091, immediately north of Cayuga Island. On some maps, the camp was misidentified as Bigwee. The misspelling is apropos as the island is huge while the resort was small. Bigiwe means "come back again." In a camp brochure, men were urged to pack "trousers you hate to toss" and knickers were suggested for both genders.

Bigiwe was opened by Torontonian Gordon McIntosh in 1930. He was part of a group of young men belonging to the YMCA who canoed the Temagami area from 1923

until '32. They were called the Tillicum Crews, meaning 'trail partner" in the Siwash native tongue. Four of the canoeists decided to start a camp together. The Depression intervened, forcing the other partners to sell their interests to Gordon for $1 each, though they continued to vacation at Bigiwe.

The camp consisted of a main lodge with three guest bedrooms. Double occupancy cost $24 per week. Ten double-occupancy tents on platforms were offered for $20 a week. George Hutchings, who ran a store on Bear Island, headed up construction. A unique feature was a "Varsity Trail" blazed by a group of guests who were University of Toronto graduates. It extended around the circumference of the isle and encircled the main lodge. Gordon was a retail supervisor with just a two-week vacation. It fell to his wife Dorothy, the mother of four young children, to run the camp, the McIntoshes' daughter Barbara Currie recalled.

Having barely survived the Depression, gas rationing during the Second World War spelled Bigiwe's demise. The family was then residing in Hamilton, Ontario, and could not buy enough gas to get to and from the lake, let alone to run a resort. The McIntosh family returned after the war,

A Camp Bigiwe group prepares to depart Toronto for a late 1920s Temagami canoe trip. Note the wooden spokes. *Photo: McIntosh family*

turning the property into a private cottage. Gordon and Dorothy decided it was time to put up a 'for sale' sign when the long trip and maintenance became issues.

Philadelphians Frank Hartzell Jr., his brother Jeff Hartzell, and close friend Bart Harrison bought the property in the early 1960s and continued to use the Bigiwe name. From age 13 Jeff spent eight summers during the 1940s as a Wabun camper and staff member. He was recruited by Wabun co-founder Bill Anderson who was his basketball coach. The camp and the Temagami area left an indelible impression and Jeff was drawn back as a married man, bringing along his wife Ann, buddy Bart and Bart's wife Renata for canoe trips.

They rented Bigiwe about 1962. "It rained 30 days out of 31," Jeff wryly noted. Upon learning the camp was for sale, the two couples realized, even after splitting the $6,000 asking price, Bigiwe was still beyond their means. They decided to ask Frank to chip in. He had also taken a shine to Temagami tripping, so the three men pooled their resources and bought the old camp.

The three families, Frank's wife Molly included, have expanded over time. Seven children and 12 grandchildren later – plus a bevy of in-laws – means Bigiwe has seen its bushes trampled. New cabins and a waste disposal system have been added. In a nod to times past, propane fuels lights and appliances. Most of the original structures are still standing, according to Frank, though a tool shed/storage building was lost in 2007 to a lightning-caused fire. One beloved item destroyed was an ancient hand-cranked washing machine still in use. TLA Executive Secretary Peter Healy has since been scavenger hunting during his property patrols and the annual flea market for a worthy replacement.

The McIntoshes have maintained contact with the Hartzells. Several years ago 13 family members paid a nostalgic visit to Bigiwe. About 2007 Barbara Currie and two brothers came up for Thanksgiving. They arrived in an open boat in driving snow. Despite the weather, "Barbara was happy to see how much hadn't changed," Jeff noted.

Jeff Hartzell's family is still intimately involved with Wabun. Jeff has done stints as a camp physician. His two sons went to the camp, as did two grandsons and three granddaughters. His youngest grandson was to follow suit as soon as he was old enough. Jeff's daughter had to attend Lorien Wilderness on Cayuga Island because Wabun didn't admit girls until 1977.

CHAPTER 7

A MURDEROUS LEGACY

The Association was shaken to its core by a heinous act of brutal violence on March 19, 1934. Robert Newcomb, its guiding light, committed murder and suicide at the age of 61. In the early morning hours, Robert picked up an axe and killed his wife Faith. He then slashed his throat with a razor. According to the coroner, Robert's son Millard, 32, and Faith's mother were asleep in the house and were lucky to escape with their lives.

The Cleveland newspaper headlines screamed, "OVERCOME BY FRENZY KILLS WIFE AND SELF – R.B. Newcomb, Cleveland Lawyer, Known to Many in Toronto, Timagami." The newspapers noted that Robert was president of the Cleveland Canadian Camp Fire Club and had a camp at Red Pines Island. He did little hunting but took hundreds of wildlife photographs and had been a regular contributor to a Toronto magazine.

Adrian Newcomb said his brother had been suffering from delusions but had never given any indication of violence. Robert's Temagami friends speculated that he had been distraught over financial setbacks brought on by the 1929 stock market crash.

It has been documented that only a handful of investors committed suicide as a result of the market meltdown. The iconic image of executives jumping from Wall Street office tower windows has been debunked. Furthermore, had Robert been despairing over financial woes, he likely wouldn't have waited nearly five years to take his life, and he almost certainly would have spared an innocent life.

It is more plausible that he suffered some

The Newcomb home on Derbyshire Road
in Cleveland Heights in 2009.
Photo: Michael Bloomfield

form of mental illness such as bipolar disorder, formerly known as manic depression. Manic episodes are often associated with creativity, goal striving and positive achievements. These characteristics fit Robert to a tee. Depressive episodes can lead to psychotic symptoms such as delusions, to which Adrian alluded. There is also an elevated risk of suicide and violence.

High society families like the Newcombs would have gone to great lengths to shroud such a condition from an unsympathetic public eye. Besides the loss of family prestige due to the stigma attached to mental illness, treatment in the 1930s was fairly primitive and often entailed an enforced commitment to an 'insane asylum.'

Hap Wilson offers an insightful assessment of Robert's psychiatric health in his memoir *The Cabin*, based on his readings about him in *Temagami Lakes Association: An Historical Perspective* and the *Temagami Times*: "The wilderness can have a deleterious effect on a person's psyche, particularly with those who have an infatuation with a lifestyle they can never attain. An affair with wilderness, to live simply with the denizens of the forest, can be a fool's dream. Newcomb had a foot set in each camp; perennially affixed to Cleveland by profession and responsibility, yet tied inextricably to Temagami through spirit. His convictions eventually became muddled; he became morose and angry; truths lapsed into lies, hope betrayed rational thought, and unrequited love of a simpler life eventually pushed his heart into the depths of despair."

Robert's Temagami friends made sure his life and commitment to the Association would never be forgotten. Some 200 aboriginals, campers and cottagers assembled at the Bear Island post on August 5, 1934, to witness the dedication of the Robert Newcomb Memorial Tablet.

The bronze tablet, measuring approximately two by two and a half feet, was designed by R.H. Shreve, one of the architects of the Empire State Building. Members of the Canadian Campfire Club of Cleveland had bumped into him in the 1900s on a Temagami portage and he remained a friend. The tablet was attached to a six by four-foot pinkish-gray granite boulder. Bear Island men toiled a week to move it to the memorial site.

Memorial committee members included Alfred Horr, Sherman Thorpe, William Finlayson and Temagami Indian Band Chief William Peshabo. Alfred gave the dedication address, saying Robert "bubbled over with optimism, faith in the future and joyous memories of past adventures." It was perhaps an attempt to sweep his mental health issues under the carpet and to spare family members who may have attended. The plaque has since vanished without a trace. More on the story of the tablet's disappearance can be found in the Preface.

The passage of time wasn't kind to the memorial plaque. By 1991 the boulder had partially sunk into the ground. Sulphurization and corrosion had caused uneven black streaking of the tablet inscription, leaching into the boulder below. Grass and weeds had

The Robert Newcomb memorial tablet up and disappeared in the 1990s. *Photo: Pam Sinclair*

her enthusiasm and they began trekking to Red Pines regularly.

Pearl served the Association as a member of the logging committee from 1954 to '57. From available records, she seems to be the first woman to take a serious role. Women had served on the highly social membership committee, but don't appear to have tackled the grittier issues.

to be pushed away to read the darkened and faded inscription:

"IN MEMORY OF ROBERT BURTON
NEWCOMB 1872-1934,
FIRST PRESIDENT OF THE
TEMAGAMI ASSOCIATION.
THIS TABLET HAS BEEN ERECTED BY
A GREAT NUMBER
OF HIS CANADIAN AND AMERICAN
FRIENDS AND ASSOCIATES."

Red Pines Continues

Following Robert's death, Robert Jr., one of his two children, attempted to run a small canoe camp at Red Pines but the venture failed. Millard, the oldest, disliked Temagami as a youth because he felt his father was too bossy. When Millard, nicknamed "Newk," married Pearl DeFrain in 1942 she was eager to see the lake, soon falling for it. Newk came to share

Following a 22-year career with government, Newk became a public defender. He was soon known as the Clarence Darrow of the Bay County Bar Association because of his soft-sell success with juries. Newk and Pearl had passed the bar together in 1951 and opened the firm of Newcomb and Newcomb in Bay City, Michigan, when he was 61 years old.

Newk was up to his ears in court-appointed cases by 1967, defending people who couldn't afford a lawyer, including petty criminal "Shortie" Norlock. He spent most of his time in the county jail, accused of minor offences such as trying to rob and then attempting to abscond with a cigarette machine. He was usually sprung in time to join the Newcombs on their trip to Temagami. He loved his summer stints there, his five-foot frame cutting an elfish figure in cap and lumber jacket as he felled dead trees and painted boathouses.

Newk died in 1975. Pearl continued to visit Red Pines most summers until the early 1990s. She died in the mid-1990s in her 90s. Red Pines was inherited by her nephew Ken DeFrain. During his brief tenure, he did some cosmetic work on the decaying buildings.

TLA Archives Chair Walter Kemball, of Island 960 and the Toronto area, secured a donation of old negatives in 1996. Dating from 1906 to the mid-teens, some had been hand painted by Faith Newcomb. More than 2,350 negatives were stored by the Newcombs in old cigar boxes inside a wooden crate. The images have been preserved on six CDs. Few have been identified and catalogued.

Stan and Marlene Casper of Stone Harbor, New Jersey, bought the Newcomb island in 1997 from Ken DeFrain who died in the late 1990s. They had a tenuous connection to the lake through the late Nora Walker of Island 974. She was the grandmother of the Caspers' daughter-in-law. Stan and Marlene first visited the lake in the early 1990s.

Over at Red Pines, the Caspers were left with 11 buildings, hundreds of tables and thousands of pieces of bric-a-brac. Most of the buildings were in tumbledown shape. Many had leaking roofs, and mice and squirrels were claiming squatters' rights.

The Caspers were aware of the island's rich history, but had to tear down the decrepit cabins for safety's sake. The main lodge was replaced by a modern Caledon home with a matching boathouse topped with living quarters. Some Newcomb artifacts were preserved, including a hand-sewn banner depicting the island's three-pine logo, a birchbark moose horn, a pie cupboard and the cornerstone from the fireplace. In raised red cement, it reads, "R.B.N. 1907." The family purchased nearby Island 1002 in 2008 from John and Jane Brady of Pennsylvania. It's the same island where the Newcombs raised chickens.

A Fall from Grace

The Association lost the political clout of William Finlayson in 1934 when the Tory government was ousted by the Liberals, who focused their election campaign on alleged overspending by the Conservatives. Rumours had surfaced concerning his extravagant Temagami lifestyle. While he was minister of lands and forests, he had his staff build the *Wasp*, a 40-foot mahogany boat powered by a 200-hp Kermath engine. It was for the department's use on Lake Temagami, though William sometimes used it for personal outings.

He became known for the lavish parties he hosted in a large main cabin on Island 857, erected in 1920 before his occupancy. He had a massive birch log dining room suite built by local craftsmen. It takes four men to lift the table. Current owners David and Linda Burgess of London, Ontario, have never tried moving the table because they rarely have enough manpower. Although it's still in great condition, Linda has had refinishing it on her 'to do' list every summer. A couple of rotten birch logs enclosing the support structure underneath need to be replaced. "Otherwise, it continues to perform its role as the "place to be" when dinner is served," David reported.

William received approval from the province in 1933 to have three townships on the lake named after his daughter Phyllis and two of her friends. Cynthia Jaffray and Joan Parmenter, daughters of prominent Torontonians, were Phyllis's guests at Island 857 during summer 1932. Finlayson Point Provincial Park was later named in his honour, whether he deserved it or not.

Sterling G. McNees leased Island 857 in 1937 after the Finlaysons' departure. He was a lawyer from Harrisburg, Pennsylvania, and actor Jimmy Stewart's uncle. Jimmy stayed there on a few occasions. Howard Baker, the president of a Toronto advertising agency, bought the island about 1947 after attending Cochrane's Camp in the 1920s. His son-in-law Dick Grout would helm the Association from 1989 until '92 and later return as a director.

CHAPTER 8

SOME HIGHLIGHTS AND LOW POINTS

Following his grisly death in 1934, Frank Todd succeeded Robert Newcomb as Association president. Frank Cassie, also from Cobalt, was secretary and Mal Scovil, a Keewaydin veteran, stepped in as treasurer. Frank and Mal were both in the insurance business, Frank in Cobalt and Mal in Cleveland.

Frank Todd was well-suited for his role as president. As the only insurance agent in the area, he frequently travelled the lake on business and got to know residents. He had strong links with cottagers on the Northeast Arm, the majority of whom then hailed from either the Tri-Towns or Temagami.

Frank Cassie, a Cobalt mining machinery salesman, leased Northeast Arm Island 152 in 1922 and obtained the patent in 1943. When the mining industry slumped and family illness became an issue, he sold to Carmel Donegan, engineer at Cobalt's O'Brien Mine. The island was owned until about 1996 by Carm's widow Frances.

Mal Scovil's Keewaydin adventures, shared by others, would become the stuff of legend: being in the same canoe from which a staffman jumped on the back of a moose; learning to barn dance in 1910 at a little frontier town; sleeping in a farmer's cow pasture and procuring buckets of fresh milk; and reaching the Grand Lac Victoria HBC post in Northern Quebec just as the Catholic bishop was due for his once-every-ten-years visit. Mal watched as more than 200 aboriginals gathered to welcome the dignitary. At sunset the bishop appeared in a birchbark war canoe paddled by eight natives. After blessing the locals, he wished the dumb-founded boys a pleasant trip.

Mal leased Island 1175 in 1925 but soon moved to the larger 1161. Island 1175 was leased again in 1933 by Brooks Shepard who first came to the lake in 1908 as a Keewaydin camper. Both islands are still owned by their descendents.

Mal's cabin was built by Scotsman Henry McLeod, a Maine lumber jack who worked as a guide for Keewaydin. Sleeping cabins were built by Gilbert "Gib" Carswell. He guided for Keewaydin from 1934 until '49 and was a jack of many trades, including trapping, sled-dog running, deer hunt guiding and cottage caretaking. He was also a fine carpenter and built many cabins for summer residents. Gib's wife Margaret was a cook at Ojibway Lodge. The couple later moved to Bracebridge and cottaged on Horseshoe Island 1197. Gib died in 1999 and the property is still family owned.

Founding Association treasurer Sherman Thorpe, Mal's predecessor, was found dead in seven feet of water in August 1937. He had been granted a month's leave of absence as post

> *A Round-About Way of Discovering the Lake*
>
> *William Bonser's grandfather "Pop," born and raised in Toronto, moved to Toledo, Ohio, to practise medicine. A Keewaydin staffer fell ill more than 80 years ago. By some stroke of fate, he chose Pop's office from the hundreds of doctors he could have consulted in the city. Luckily, the patient's condition was not laryngitis and he was able to make small talk. He rambled on in such glowing terms about Temagami that Pop decided he must have a look. The family initially rented a cottage at Island 1091's Camp Bigiwe and eventually bought property on Island 168 in 1946.*

manager due to weak spells. While inspecting one of his launches, it is believed he suffered a heart attack and fell into the lake. He had recently helped officiate at the opening of a new store, replacing the old post which burned down the previous winter. His successor until 1941 was Scotsman Hugh Mackay Ross.

Regatta Days

One of the most fondly remembered activities of the early Association was the annual regatta, held at the post from 1935 to '39. Regatta Day on Civic Holiday was the highlight of the summer for many and saw the lawn and docks overflowing with spectators and participants.

For the first regatta, Ed Archibald floated his 20-foot diving tower down from Camp Wanapitei. A.L. Cochrane arranged for his trippers to be in-camp and had obtained new canoes for the occasion. It must have been worth all the effort because Cochrane boys were the overall victors. Events included a decorated float parade, swimming, diving, a sailing yacht race, canoeing, tilting, log burling and boat races.

Swimmers could synchronize their strokes to the beat of the 24-member North Bay Collegiate Silver Band during the 1937 regatta. "Officials for the Day" were added to the 1937 program, to relieve harried Association volunteers. Keewaydin staff officiated that year, including Mal Scovil, Gifford Kittredge (son of Chessman Kittredge) and Brenton Creelman (son of Ojibway Lodge Director George Creelman). Wabun's founders were the officials in 1938 and Cochrane's staff officiated in 1939.

Over the years boat racers waged a heated battle. Ted Hyde's eldest brother Alex, who was later killed in the Second World War, entered his speed boat named the *Loon* and beat Colonel Ed Higbee's *Miss Canada* from Rabbitnose Island. *Miss Canada* was the first in a series of racing boats designed and constructed by Greavette Boatworks in Gravenhurst. Ed would later become Association vice president.

Another frequent racer was Ed's son Holden Higbee who had a high-powered boat called the *Barbara*. He vied for top spot in the "bang and go back" race during which the *Belle* blasted her horn when it was time to

TLA regatta circa 1936. *MacLean postcard photo: Reg Sinclair*

turn back. Fierce competition also came from Lionel Todd, the president's son. He owned a hydroplane named the *Alpha*, a sleek double-cockpit launch capable of about 72 kph. The Todds simonized the bottom and tuned the motor to the "nth." Lionel won often until the uppity *Miss Muskoka* started entering.

Lionel's brother H. Arnold Todd kept a small medal given to Lionel for winning the boat race. Both served overseas during the Second World War but Lionel did not return. The *Alpha* was sold to Clifford Lowery of Haileybury in 1943, the same year he acquired property on Temagami Island 234. Clifford's son Biff Lowery now owns the family cottage.

The *Sal-Sam*, named for Mal Scovil's children Sam and Sally, is the only race competitor still plying Lake Temagami waters.

She was assembled by Gravenhurst boat builders in a Temagami shed during a mid-1930s winter and powered by a six-cylinder (about 170-hp) Kermath engine. Her body is cedar with mahogany decks. The *Sal-Sam* conveyed more than 25 merrymakers from the North Arm to square dances at Lakeview House. It was imperative that Mal be on time because he called the dances, accompanied by the lively bow strokes of a fiddler. Lamps were placed at strategic spots on islands so he could find his way back in the dark. Passengers could only recall him going aground once, when he clipped a corner short.

The *Sal-Sam* is still owned by the Scovils. Sam had Bill Kitts of Temagami Marine transport her to a restorer north of Toronto about 2003. Her decks were stripped down to bare wood and the punky floor boards were

Regatta Day 1950 at Cochrane's Camp. Guides ready for the canoe races are front (l-r): Bill Twain, Adam Commanda and Robert "Butch" Turner. Back (l-r): Alex Mathias, John Katt Sr., Sonny Moore, Willie Friday, Gordon Turner, Stanley Roy, Johnny Katt and Bill Katt. *Photo: Carol Cochrane*

The Monte Cristo Sack Feat

One of the most memorable events was A.L. Cochrane's Monte Cristo Sack Feat. Huge crowds gathered as he was placed in a gunny sack with his hands and feet tied. The sack was weighed down with a rock and tied on the outside, then tossed into the lake. The ruse was modelled after an incident depicted in Alexandre Dumas' 1844 novel *The Count of Monte Cristo.*

How A.L. made his great escape was known only to the Cochrane family until Carol revealed his modus operandi, exclusively for this book: "The burlap sack was tied with one end inside the bag and his hands were tied loosely so he could slip them free. As soon as he hit the water, A.L. would yank on the rope to untie himself, quickly release his feet, also loosely tied, and then he would swim to the surface." His sack was tossed into the water near a diving board. A Union Jack was casually draped over the board. When A.L. surfaced, he hid behind it. Tension mounted while he treaded water. He then dove and surfaced in front of the dock to a great round of applause. He performed his classic stunt well into old age.

completely replaced. The old gal spends her winters comfortably ensconced at Temagami Marine.

The 1940 regatta was cancelled due to the Second World War. Prior to the Association's hosting duties, the post had traditionally organized a regatta and resumed doing so soon after the war. The last Bear Island regatta was held in 1972 until the Bear Island Trading Post revived them for a time in 1981.

Other popular regattas were held at Cochrane's Camp and Camp Chimo. Cochrane events ranged from swimming and diving to competitive and fun-filled canoe races. Participants gunwale bobbed and crabbed, wrote Carol Cochrane in the 1970s *Temagami Experience* tabloid. The crab put the canoeist in the bow, facing the bow – and into a tailspin.

The most riveting rush of the day was the four-guide canoe races. Many a paddle cracked in half when the sternman took that first powerful stroke. Swampings were not unheard of when four stocky men got moving, Carol recalled. Medal holders would wear their winnings from previous years to impress

spectators and intimidate the competition. In lighter moments water skits were performed with boats as lavishly costumed as their operators.

Regatta day at Chimo got kick-started in 1959. Events included a beauty contest for men only and more traditional fare such as water skiing, diving, crab races, canoe tilting and log rolling. The day was topped by a square dance featuring locals Sonny Doucette as caller, Phillip Potts on piano and George Peshabo fiddling. "It usually took time to find the fiddle, or to find the strings for it, or to find a bow that wasn't in shredded condition," Nancey Gooderham observed in the *Temagami Experience*.

Trophies were often old Chimo thunder buckets affixed with plaques and mounted on birch logs. Prizes were no big catch – a fish

Chimo in 1961 showing the *Chimo III*, a cabin where Tim Gooderham's parents honeymooned in 1932, the shop, Bill and Nancey Gooderham's cottage and the dining hall. *Photo: John Eberhard*

lure or line. The quality of prizes improved to 57 varieties when Heinz executives were guests or a pint or two when O'Keefe or Labatt bigwigs were in-house. Nancey noted that Chimo regattas were few and far between due to rainy weather in the 1960s. The Chimo Horrible Little Theatre Group would then rise to the occasion, aided by the Chimo Ladies' Knitting and Gin Drinking Society and its members' ability to turn old bedspreads into stage curtains or sheiks' duds.

The Skyline Reserve is Born

Between regattas it was business as usual for the Association. Logging was becoming a headache by 1935. Pine stands were being cut in close proximity to the lake. It marked the start of a struggle in which the Association is still engaged. The beauty of the untouched shoreline and its pine vistas had lured early campers, and the executive was determined to see that it remained pristine.

The Association tried but failed to have some licences revoked. Ontario did agree to restrictions being added to contracts. They included: no land clearing for skidways or rollways along the shore; a Shoreline Reserve where trees within 90 metres of portages and shorelines of inland lakes would be spared; a Skyline Reserve where trees would not be cut from the shore of Lake Temagami to the top of the first ridge of trees: all slash to be cleared and burned; all logs to be removed from the water by summer; and no summer log booming.

Protection of the Skyline Reserve was later enshrined in the *Tenets for Temagami*, which became official lake policy in 1994 and is now the foundation for all municipal planning. The tenets also ban the construction of new public roads and access points, and allow cottaging on islands only.

In 1936 the Association tried to have the 1935 restrictions enforced but many were violated, despite provincial pledges. Some slash was piled and burned, and some logs were confined in a bay by means of a boom. However, cutting timber within the Skyline Reserve continued. After several meetings with government representatives, President Frank Todd concluded that it was the intention of the government to allow all the timber in the Temagami forest to be harvested.

"We are not at all sure that the cutting of timber should be stopped, but we are very sure that it should be done in a manner not detrimental to the beauty of the lake," Treasurer Mal Scovil wrote during a 1936 membership drive. "We believe this can be accomplished by having the restricting portions of the leases enforced." At the 1936 Annual General Meeting (AGM), the executive urged all members to write letters to the minister of lands and forests (who, unfortunately, was no longer William Finlayson) imploring him to adhere to the 1935 restrictions.

Several forest fires burned near the lake during summer 1936. One was blamed on slash left by a lumber company. The incident sparked the Association into lobbying the province for a plane to be stationed on the lake during the summer and for updates to the department's firefighting equipment. The first fire-spotting plane arrived at the Bear Island forestry base in 1938.

Responsible logging was at the top of the priority list. In a 1938 membership renewal letter, Mal wrote, "This is a job that there must be no let up on, and it is the Association's intention to see that the lumbering companies are forced to live up to their contracts in the matter of clearing slash, cutting only ripe timber and having the lakes clear of logs before the summer season starts."

New President George "Cecil" Ames and Secretary Gib Cochrane met with Lands and Forests Minister Peter Heenan during winter 1939. They presented a memorandum requesting tougher regulations and a meeting with lumbermen in the minister's office. They left feeling that the minister and senior staff were fully aware of the desirability of preserving the shoreline beauty. By summer 1939 the department cooperated fully. Forest rangers were clearing portages of overgrowth, installing shelters and keeping a close eye on log boom towing to eliminate stray dead heads.

Gib Cochrane returned as secretary in 1937, replacing Frank Cassie. Frank Todd exited as president but returned in the early 1950s to the executive committee. Frank died in 1977. His son H. Arnold Todd had taken over the Todd Insurance Agency and was one of the founders of the Cobalt Mining Museum in 1953. He shared Island 159 with his sister Frances Seymour. Arnold passed away in 1992. His son Frank Todd of Cobalt owns the northern half of the island, while his cousin Lenore, née Seymour, and her husband Peter McGuire of Toronto, own the southern half. Frank's grandchildren are the fifth generation of Todds at Island 159.

A Mining Man for President

Cecil Ames had discovered Temagami's wonders via Cobalt. In 1927 he leased Island 1075 on the North Arm. Cecil worked for a company whose interests included part of what is now Noranda Mines. It was hoped that his Toronto residency would help him tap into Queen's Park when taking up causes with the province. He resigned as president about 1940. He died in 1951 and Island 1075 was sold a few years later.

Cecil's sons Jack and Bill went on canoe trips with Camp Cayuga counsellors. Daughter Mary Kane recalled that when the family visited Cayuga, they had to approach slowly and noisily to give fair warning as the boys sometimes lounged in their birthday suits, a common but potentially embarrassing practice at some of the boys' camps.

Bill's summer job was driving for the boat line. His navigation skills helped him become a member of the first group of Royal Canadian Air Force (RCAF) sergeant-pilots flying patrols over the Atlantic during the Second World War. Later, he flew land surveys for the Ontario Provincial Air Service. One of the areas he surveyed was the Temagami forest. Engineer Jack built military training planes such as Tiger Moths, Ansons and Mosquitoes.

Incentives and Initiatives

In the mid-1930s the first membership incentive was introduced – a free boat pennant to every new member. It was made of blue felt with the Association's pine tree logo stitched in black. The same incentive would be used in the 1980s. This time the pennant was blue nylon printed with the modern-day loon logo.

James Ross Sproat's Temagami Boat Company had taken on the job of restocking, with fish supplied by the lands and forests department. The Sproat boat line would ply

Temagami waters until 1944 when the TNOR acquired it. Again with the cooperation of the boat company, additional buoys and lights were placed in the main channels by the federal transportation department in 1941. The Association started providing painted buoys, complete with chains and anchors, to mark shoals and rocks in secondary channels. These could be had for the asking.

SOUTH ARM

— READ DOWN —				— READ UP —	
Daily June 15 to Sept. 15	Daily June 28 to Sept. 5			Daily June 15 to Sept. 15	Daily June 28 to Sept. 5
10.30 a.m.	3.00 p.m.	Lv. ...... TEMAGAMI ...... Ar.		6.00 p.m.	9.50 a.m.
11.40 a.m.	3.50 p.m.	...... AGAMIK		4.50 p.m.	8.50 a.m.
12.05 p.m.	4.05 p.m.	...... WABI-KON		4.35 p.m.	8.40 a.m.
12.30 p.m.	4.25 p.m.	...... CHIMO		4.10 p.m.	8.20 a.m.
1.00 p.m.	4.40 p.m.	...... COCHRANE		3.40 p.m.	7.50 a.m.
1.50 p.m.	5.25 p.m.	Ar. ... ACOUCHICHING ... Lv.		2.50 p.m.	7.10 a.m.

SOUTH WEST ARM

Daily June 15 to Sept. 15	Daily June 28 to Sept. 5			Daily June 15 to Sept. 15	Daily June 28 to Sept. 5
10.30 a.m.	3.00 p.m.	Lv. ...... TEMAGAMI ...... Ar.		5.50 p.m.	9.45 a.m.
11.20 a.m.	3.50 p.m.	...... FRIDAYS		5.00 p.m.	9.00 a.m.
11.30 a.m.	4.00 p.m.	...... TEM. LODGE		4.45 p.m.	8.50 a.m.
f11.40 a.m.	f4.10 p.m.	...... OGAMA		f4.35 p.m.	f8.40 a.m.
12.00 noon	4.30 p.m.	...... WIGWASATI		4.05 p.m.	8.10 a.m.
12.40 p.m.	5.00 p.m.	...... WHITE BEAR		3.35 p.m.	7.40 a.m.
1.10 p.m.	5.30 p.m.	Ar. ...... NORTHWOODS ...... Lv.		3.00 p.m.	7.10 a.m.

NORTH WEST ARM

Daily June 15 to Sept. 15	Daily June 28 to Sept. 5			Daily June 15 to Sept. 15	Daily June 28 to Sept. 5
10.30 a.m.	3.00 p.m.	Lv. ...... TEMAGAMI ...... Ar.		6.10 p.m.	9.50 a.m.
11.45 a.m.	4.00 p.m.	...... BEAR ISLAND		5.00 p.m.	8.55 a.m.
f12.01 p.m.	f4.15 p.m.	...... CAYUGA		f4.45 p.m.	f8.45 a.m.
12.30 p.m.	4.30 p.m.	...... KAKEENA		4.20 p.m.	8.30 a.m.
12.45 p.m.	4.45 p.m.	...... WABUN		4.05 p.m.	8.15 a.m.
1.15 p.m.	5.10 p.m.	...... KEEWAYDIN		3.35 p.m.	7.50 a.m.
1.25 p.m.	5.20 p.m.	...... OJIBWAY		3.20 p.m.	7.40 a.m.
1.55 p.m.	5.45 p.m.	Ar. ...... WANAPETEI ...... Lv.		2.45 p.m.	7.00 a.m.

f—Flag Stop. Will only stop on signal when there are passengers in or outbound

TNOR Temagami Navigation Ltd. route timetable.
The daily cruise fare was $2 plus a 30-cent war tax.
Courtesy: Jack Glenn

War Times

As of September 10, 1939, Canada was at war with Germany. The executive reassured American members in 1940 that the federal and provincial governments were making every effort to minimize the evidence of war, so tourists spending their holidays (and money) in the "Canadian Woods" would not be inconvenienced. Village merchants informed the executive that the hostilities abroad would make no difference to daily life, despite controlled prices and rationing. Milne played its own unique role in the war effort by providing red pine veneer logs used in the assembly of Mosquito bombers.

The Japanese attack on Pearl Harbor in December 1941 forced the U.S. into the conflict – and everything changed. It ended the façade of normalcy in Temagami. A slight majority of Association members were American. Therefore, the annual meeting was cancelled in 1942, the first and only known time in the Association's 80-year history. The executive also decided no dues would be collected for 1942 and the Association would carry on with the same officers who would normally be elected at the AGM.

The war took a toll on the youth camps. Keewaydin reached a low point in 1942, luring only 43 campers. Wanapitei's boys' section didn't even open, and the focus switched to fishing and hunting. There would be no youth camp at Wanapitei again until 1956, when Stan and Laura Belle Hodgins of Kitchener, Ontario, bought it and established a boys' and girls' camp. The resorts saw guests dwindle. Acouchiching temporarily closed about 1942.

Gas rationing shuttered many cottages and some resorts. Federal restrictions were imposed in 1941 on the sale of gas to non-essential users. It couldn't be sold from 7 p.m. Saturdays until 7 a.m. Mondays, prime car trip times. Restrictions further tightened the following summer. American visitors could purchase only 20 gallons of gas during their stay. It meant some couldn't get to and from Temagami, let alone fuel their boats. Rationing eventually encompassed everything from tea and coffee to booze, all considered essential to the Temagami experience. Another hindrance to travel was a federal ban on buying new tires.

The war-time president was Harry Schumacher, a real estate developer from Buffalo, New York. He leased half of Southwest Arm Island 496 in 1939, after vacationing at Camp White Bear. He patented the 4.5-acre island in 1942. An Association goal during Harry's presidency was to have a "much needed" public dock built in Temagami harbour. However, government funds for anything but the war effort were difficult to come by.

The offer of a $50 reward for information leading to the apprehension of offenders was so effective in curtailing break-ins that by 1941 they were almost non-existent. More police protection was needed to solve a bootleg liquor problem. Though not 100 per cent enforced, the skyline and shoreline reserves, and other restrictions on logging licences were still helping to preserve the area's scenic splendour.

New Ventures

The Association was instrumental in the 1942 passage of legislation allowing lease holders to obtain freehold patents. The province removed islands from the Temagami Provincial Forest, formerly the Temagami Forest Reserve. Buyers could patent islands or parcels up to 10 acres in size. The cost per acre for an island was $45, while parcels were available for $22.50 per acre plus a 15-cent per foot frontage charge. A building worth $2,000 was to be erected within 18 months, and for each additional acre over five, $500 had to be invested. A postwar boom in cottaging can be partially attributed to this provincial bill, giving seasonal residents a sense of security.

Peter Nordby, better known locally as Pete Norby.
Photo: Temagami Historical Society

The Association was again collecting $5 annual dues in 1943. Members were asked to contribute to a charitable fund to help area residents struck by misfortune. Some of the money collected in the 1940s was earmarked for Bear Island health care.

Not expecting a full house for the 1943 AGM due to the war, the executive mailed out ballots so members not in attendance could still vote on several proposals. There was a vice president again in 1940. Ed Higbee had leased 10 acres of Rabbitnose Island 1119 in 1933 and patented his holdings in 1943. His connection to the lake traces back to 1909 when his first cousin Russell Cleminshaw was a Keewaydin camper. Ed's family and a partner founded the Higbee Department Store in Cleveland in 1860. The Higbees sold it in 1929. The flagship Cleveland store, part of a chain, figured prominently in the 1983 movie *A Christmas Story* before closing in 2002.

Ed ventured into mink ranching in 1937. He hired George Linklater, a mail clerk and fur bearer at the post, to manage his ranch. George purchased blue mink from eastern Quebec. In a single year 150 females could give birth to 500 offspring. He paid a paltry $2.65 per animal and the peltry could fetch as much as $30 apiece. The operation supplied smaller ranches at Temagami Inn, Cochrane's Camp, Frank Goddard's Papa John's Place at Herridge Lake, and to Peter Norby, then residing on Island 1081.

Ed joined the armed forces in 1942 and the Rabbitnose mink ranch went out of business. He was in Europe and cash flow problems

Temagami harbour. The *Belle* is loaded with picnickers. *MacLean photo on a Temagami Outfitting Company postcard. Postcard photo: Reg Sinclair*

developed. The property was sold two years later, and a fish and hunt camp opened its doors.

Larkspur

Peter Norby had his finger in many pies during his 56 years of living in the Temagami area. Departing the family farm in Norway, he boarded a passenger ship in 1928. After landing in Quebec, he trekked out to Alberta to harvest wheat but returned to Ontario. He worked as a carpenter at the Golden Rose gold mine south of Obabika Lake and as a blacksmith at various lumber camps, before settling down on Lake Temagami. His surname was actually Nordby, but the federal government erred in processing his naturalization papers, so he was legally required to adopt the shortened version.

Pete worked at Camp Northwoods and built cottages, including one for Kenneth Wismer on Island 1086 and another for Stuart and Barbara Paltrow. The couple was awed by his skills at building with only the simplest of hand tools. Stuart's family acquired a portion of Island 378 on the Southwest Arm in 1949. He was sent to Temagami to meet the craftsman with whom he was to spend the summer building the cottage.

Barbara recalled Stuart's first impressions of Pete in the *Temagami Times*. "A sturdy, sinewy outdoorsman dressed in rough work clothes and a worn cap into which he had poked a sprig of fresh larkspur, a first hint that this was no ordinary man." He grew the plant in a window box to attract hummingbirds and the larkspur in his hat invited the birds to travel with him. Pete cherished all creatures great and small. He once tried to raise an orphaned black bear cub. Barbara, a New York state resident, still owns the cottage.

Pete also worked as a gas and boathouse attendant at the post where his great strength was noticed. When the *Belle* pulled in, he stacked his wheelbarrow high and pushed it upgrade with ease. After purchasing three acres on a southwest corner of Garden Island in 1949, he became a Wabun caretaker and also took care of Eagle, the camp horse.

Tom and Shirley Drake of St. Catharines, Ontario, had a cottage on Island 1091. They purchased Pete's other property, the one-acre Island 1081, in 1955. Pete subsequently moved his 10 by 15-foot log cabin across the ice to Garden Island, pulled by Eagle. He grew fruits, vegetables and flowers, sharing the abundance with friends. He lived alone in his cabin until his death in 1984 at 87. The O'Hallaran family purchased the Norby property from a speculator who had bought it from the estate. It was for sale in 2011.

A Working Vacation

Fred Dinsmore of Temagami Inn became the Association's secretary around 1940. Joe Spitzig had sold the inn in 1933 to Charlie and Audrey Spittle, and Fred and Phyllis Dinsmore, all from Toronto. While Fred catered to the tourists, Charlie was responsible for upkeep and, later, the mink ranch. Many Bear Islanders worked there over the years. A waitress named Kay married guide Phillip Potts and they had six children. Their first son Gary became the dynamic leader of the Teme-Augama Anishnabai.

Mal Scovil remained treasurer well into the 1940s. He died in 1950 at 57. His son Sam served as chair of the membership committee in the late 1950s. Sam was an executive at Cleveland-Cliffs Iron Company and was

Minawassi Hotel in the 1950s. *MacLean postcard photo: Reg Sinclair*

active in the business dealings which led to the opening of the Sherman Mine. The open pit iron ore mine operated from 1967 until 1990 with close to 500 employees. It was a joint venture between Dofasco steel of Hamilton, Ontario, and Cleveland-Cliffs.

Neither the president nor vice president was available to conduct business in summer 1943. Vice President Ed Higbee was in the armed forces and President Harry Schumacher was ill. He died at his island about one year later. Torontonian Harold Shannon became acting president and, by the end of 1943, had replaced Ed as vice president. He would soon assume the presidency.

Harold had leased part of Turner Island 342 in 1938. He bought 10 acres of the isle in 1950. The president of Shatco Steel, a car body builder, he was not content to simply lounge in his dock chair while on holiday. He formed a company called Shannon Enterprises. The Temagami Air Service (soon to be renamed Lakeland Airways) became airborne in 1948 with Harold's financial backing as a silent partner. The manager-pilot was Glendon Simms. Veteran RCAF flying ace Lou Riopel became the principal pilot. He bought out Glendon's share of the business in 1955 and became the manager.

A Lakeland flight from Temagami to Bear Island cost $12 in 1955, while a trip to the South Arm was $4 more. Bringing his own float plane with him, Dave McConnell, son of Camp Acouchiching owner Reg McConnell, worked as a Lakeland pilot in the 1950s. Dave had bought a Piper Cub in the '40s to fly guests and supplies to and from Couch. Bob Gareh bought Lou's one-third stake in 1973 and, a year later, purchased Harold Shannon's two-thirds share.

Shannon Enterprises purchased the Ronnoco Hotel in 1950 from the Ontario Northland Railway (formerly the TNOR). It had closed four years earlier. Harold and his wife Fran reopened it as the Hotel Minawassi, meaning "happy hunting grounds." It was

refurbished with 40 rooms for up to 75 guests, a dining room and a cocktail lounge. Minawassi advertisements stated Association members were "particularly welcome at any time to use all of the facilities of our hotel, upon entering or leaving these beautiful lakes at Temagami."

A Student's Lot

John C. Allan, a student about to start graduate school in Illinois, was hired in summer 1950 as a Minawassi desk clerk. He earned extra cash by working in the cocktail lounge. Under Ontario liquor laws, food had to be served alongside alcohol. "Most of the time nobody ate the cheese and crackers. The little plates went from table to table during the evening until the cheese looked somewhat less than edible," he recollected in a 1990 *Temagami Times* piece.

The enticing views of the lake led John to buy a battered cedar canoe from Minawassi carpenter Elly Zimmerman for $35, splitting the cost with a starving novelist/hotel bartender. He spent days off exploring the top of the Northeast Arm and Snake Lake, or hunched over a lands and forests map showing lake properties. His interest turned to the unpopulated Island Bay.

Lakeland Airways pilot Glendon Simms offered John a free flight to Island Bay as he was going to be flying in that vicinity. The canoe was lashed to the pontoons. As he paddled around on a shopping spree, he espied a little island with four rock toes, making it easier to explore than the thickly-wooded remainder. He was feeling quite smug when he went to pay for Island 649, as its size was exactly an acre and he wouldn't have to pay a penny more than the $45 charged per acre. He was taken aback by a hidden $25 cost for the 1904 survey.

John returned to his island a week later, accompanied by a University of Toronto commerce student/hotel bookkeeper. With the patched-up canoe atop the *Vedette*, the boys were dropped off at Wigwasati and then paddled over to discern the best cabin locale, a good view being the top priority. "It was a very still day with no wind and I chose a site with the best view of the bay. Had it been blowing half a gale, as it often seems to do, I might have chosen a site away from the prevailing wind on what I now call the "Florida side" of the island," he wryly observed.

When it came time to return, the boys learned the *Vedette* had hit a log and was out of service. Having work first thing the next morning, the pair had no choice but to paddle back. By the time they reached Bear Island it was pitch black, so they overnighted at Lakeview House. The bill came to $1.20, leaving no room in the budget for breakfast. They canoed back to be greeted by an apoplectic manager who "saw no humor in two of his staff arriving late for work with some cock-and-bull story about a boat that didn't show up. It was too near the end of the season to fire us, but he urged us not to push our luck in the future."

Following John's rough start as an island owner, things didn't get much better. He

Pop Culture

Temagami Dry ginger ale originated at North Bay's MacDonald's Beverages Limited, established in 1907. It was sold in thick green bottles with the brand embossed on the glass. A white paper label with a row of green trees came later. The bottler linked the area's pristine setting with the pure taste. Temagami Dry's unique ingredient was spicy natural ginger rather than the extract most producers used. Large quantities of Temagami Dry were delivered by truck to the Dionne quintuplets' home in the late 1930s.

The "Experience Temagami Dry" can, introduced in the 1960s, featured green trees on the upper half and blue waves on the lower. The name and logo also appeared on orange and scotch sodas. New Liskeard's Bastien's Beverages Limited produced the pop through the 1970s until the company became a Pepsi distributor.

Fortier Beverages Limited purchased the formula rights in 1979 but stopped production in the mid-2000s. It was so locally popular that students away from home arranged for parental deliveries to dorms.

Temagami Dry was unique to the north because it was only available there. A vintage Temagami Dry bottle can fetch up to $25 U.S. from collectors. Canada Dry started claiming to use "real" ginger in 2009.

planned to build a small cottage with John Turner's help. He bought glass for 18 windows and stored them in his bachelor apartment until 1956. The main problem was a shortage of vacation time. Thirty years later he was finally able to enjoy an annual vacation at his beloved Four Toes Island. Illness prevented John from coming north after 1996 and he passed away in 2002. John's wife Nancy and their children Christopher, Doug and Saliha all live in the U.S., including Hawaii, and are able to come to the lake infrequently. The island, however, is never far away in their minds.

The Shannons sold the Minawassi in 1959 to Temagami resident Lockie Goddard. Back at Island 342 they indulged an unusual hobby – raising imported ornamental pheasants with the help of their caretaker George Turner. One thing led to another and they had a novel though flighty business on their hands. Shannon pheasants were featured on the menus of Toronto's Royal York and King Edward hotels.

The Shannons originated the Temagami winter carnival in 1958 in partnership with the Temagami and District Chamber of Commerce. It was the first of its kind in Ontario. Featuring tea boiling, snowshoe baseball, curling, log chopping and dog sled races, it became a major event. As larger communities hopped on the bandwagon, the village couldn't compete. The last winter carnival was held in 1976 until it was successfully revived in 1996. Cochrane's Fortier Beverages Limited donated cases of Temagami Dry ginger ale.

In retirement Harold Shannon promoted land sales for residential development in the Sunshine State. Fran did not stay in her husband's shadow. She stood in hotel lobbies and restaurant entrances in downtown Toronto in 1957 handing out yellow flowers to call attention to the symbol adopted by the Canadian Cancer Society. An anonymous donor had 5,000 daffodils flown in from Victoria, B.C. Fran tried giving them away, but everybody wanted to pay for them. The idea for an annual, international Daffodil Day began then and there.

Harold died in 1982. Fran kept the cottage for a few more years before selling to Alexander and Patricia Donald of Burlington, Ontario. Alexander was no stranger to the lake, having earlier attended Camp Temagami. Fran lived to a great old age, spending her twilight years at a Toronto nursing home.

Association Concerns

Some Association concerns in the 1940s were the need for adequate garbage disposal and regulated water levels. It was also hoped that the province's fish stocking program could be supplemented by a government-run fish hatchery in Temagami. Dues for a property-owning member rose to $15 by 1947, triple the 1943 rate.

Although relations between cottagers and Bear Islanders had been generally positive, there were a few bumps along the way. Harold Shannon wrote to the director of Indian Affairs complaining of alcohol consumption by native guides employed by camps. For the safety of summer visitors, he urged police supervision. He also asked for more attention to health conditions amongst Bear Island residents, suggesting a periodic medical clinic. For many years, he added, doctors belonging to the Association had volunteered treatment, aided in recent years by the Association's charitable fund. Although they had been able to treat specific cases, they could not improve general conditions.

An Indian agent replied, suggesting members request a health certificate from their guides. Dr. W.C. Arnold of Haileybury was visiting Bear Island every two weeks, he added. Dr. Arnold was a member with a lot on Island 79. His widow Christina continued to own the cottage for many years after his death. It is now owned by Tom and Sarah Keating. The Indian agent blamed non-native and Métis guides and servants – arriving every summer from "all over" – as the source of all contagious disease and liquor.

A short-lived OPP summer detachment opened on Bear Island in 1949. It was replaced in 1951 with a radio-equipped patrol launch named the *Temagami*. It was the first police boat in the province. It was replaced in 1966 by a 22-foot cabin cruiser named the *George Caldbick* in honour of the first provincial officer to be stationed in northern Ontario. George was sent to the Cobalt camp in the 1900s to tame boisterous brawlers.

A Wabun hubbub during the 1940s. *Photo: Russell Tuckerman*

Let's All Go to the Ball Game

The summer ritual of hitting a fast one out of the park gripped Bear Island in the 1940s, especially when Hilliard "Sonny" Moore was pitching. He could better the best at home, Bass Lake, Camp Pinto, Cochrane's Camp and Wabun. He started league pitching in 1947 at the age of 18. For five consecutive years Bear Island won the Tri-Town and Temagami championships.

Major league scouts scoped Sonny and, in the late 1940s, he was offered a position playing professional ball in the U.S. But he resisted the draft because he didn't want to leave home. His ball-playing days spanned 55 years and he passed his skills to successive generations as a coach and mentor. He competed against four generations of Lewises at Wabun. Since the camp's 1930s inception, a friendly rivalry has played out annually when the Bear Island sluggers meet the Wabun staff. The former have a slight edge in the wins column. Sonny's final game was at Wabun in 2002 and he died in 2004.

CHAPTER 9

POSTWAR GLORY DAYS

James Cleminshaw described the postwar period as "a simpler time. People were happy as long as the boats ran on time and the mail arrived on schedule. The attitude of the times was 'the resources will go on forever.' There was no super stack in Sudbury. Property protection and fish were big on the agenda. The meetings were short, maybe one hour, and more of a social occasion. There wasn't much worry about logging or pollution. People were there on holiday."

James' father Russell served as Association secretary in the 1950s and '60s. The immediate postwar period was a quiet time, a chance to recharge batteries. People were content to return to cottages, ponder the good fortune that brought them back to their beloved lake and remember those who would return no more.

Youth camps and resorts generally thrived and new cottagers flocked to the lake. There were 407 property owners by 1957, double the number at the Association's 1931 founding. The fact that islanders could now own their properties was a measure of security for early arrivals and a drawing card for new ones.

One hundred Temagami residents served during the Second World War, while 33 had enlisted during the First World War. A total of eight residents made the ultimate sacrifice. The Royal Canadian Legion Branch 408 Temagami counts four Second World War veterans as members. Temagami Indian Band members also fought in both conflicts. The band didn't lose anyone in combat although several soldiers were wounded. During World War One only one of Bear Island's enlisted men, a sniper, returned home unscathed.

Aboriginal World War One soldiers: front (l-r) Joe Friday, unidentified commander and John Turner. Back (l-r) John Katt, Charlie Potts, Raney Wabi and Charlie Moore.
Photo: Moose to Moccasins by Madeline Katt Theriault

The province didn't always treat aboriginal war veterans with respect. Walter Becker learned that his trapline had been given to a non-native. Bill Twain was fined and jailed after picking up the hind quarter of a deer killed by a wolf. The band's sole surviving veteran is Tommy Saville, living in a North Bay seniors' residence at the age of 90 in 2010. He was honoured during the Grand Entry at the 2008 Temagami First Nation powwow.

Anishnabai Warriors

Temagamis battled Nadoway (Iroquois) raiders at Temagami Island, Rabbit Lake, the Stinking Islands and the Temagami River in the 1600s. Their clever strategies included floating a lynx skin as a decoy, digging hidden lookout and ambush pits, and setting adrift or slitting the bottoms of enemy canoes while they slept. Lookout pits can still be found on Garden Island.

In 1763 a confederacy of native tribes, including area aboriginals, launched the Pontiac War to drive British soldiers and settlers out of the Great Lakes region. During the War of 1812 three Temagami warriors helped the British capture Fort Mackinac, an American military outpost in the straits between lakes Michigan and Huron.

The Logging Scene

The number of forestry companies operating in the area reached a peak in 1947-48 with 18 pine and veneer operations. Most of the province's best pine originated in the Temagami forest through the 1950s and went to mills in Temagami, Goward, Latchford, Field, Sturgeon Falls and Timmins. Most seasonal residents were not aware of all the cutting, thanks to the skyline and shoreline reserves championed by the Association in 1935, and the fact that most activity took place in the off-season.

Logging still had a picturesque aura. Frank Panabaker, one of Canada's Group of Seven contemporaries, visited Temagami several times. He oil-painted a winter logging scene depicting two horse teams hauling logs along a tree-lined trail. The reproduction has since adorned millions of Christmas cards. Temagami was a hot spot for Canadian artists during the late 1920s and '30s. David Milne, a renowned landscape painter, and Group of Seven member Franklin Carmichael also recognized the unique beauty of Temagami.

Timber companies mainly practised selective logging, taking the more robust pine and leaving the scrappier ones behind so the forest was able to regenerate more quickly. Logging occurred on the mainland near a number of cottages but several cottagers said the only impact – and it did not adversely affect their enjoyment of the lake – was short, narrow, temporary trails down which Milne skidded great rafts of pine logs to the water's edge. They were then towed away with either the *Tom Tom* or *Andy Milne* tugboat up the Northeast Arm. Logs from all points of the lake were jackladdered (an engineered staircase

Frank Panabaker's famous Temagami logging painting.
Photo: The Temagami Experience by Bruce W. Hodgins and Jamie Benidickson

used to lift logs) into Turtle Lake on their way to Milne's sawmill at Link Lake northwest of Temagami.

Many older cottagers fondly remember the *Andy Milne*. It was a 37-foot high-bowed wooden tug, built in Owen Sound, Ontario, in 1945. Since Milne's demise in 1990 *Andy*

Back to the Wild

Wondrous Temagami, Wasacsinagama,
Low waves that wash up the
shadowy shore,
North of the Nipissing, up the Timiskaming,
We will come back and sing
to you encore.
Back to the wild again show me the way,
Make me a child again just for a day.

Crystal Temagami, Wasacsinagama,
Swift running rivers and skies
that are blue,
Out on the deep again, rock me
to sleep again,
Rock me to sleep in my little canoe.
Back to the wild again show me the way,
Make me a child again, I want to play.

Cy Warman, *Weiga of Temagami and Other Indian Tales*, 1908

has been a retired hobby tug privately owned in West Island, Michigan. Log booming was suspended during the summer, but occasionally, a family would arrive to find its dock dismantled by a log boom or nowhere to dock due to Milne caching a boom. Propeller sales bounced when wayward logs caused damage after a boom break. Compensation was usually offered.

It wasn't until the mid-1950s that all-weather bush roads began permanently scarring the landscape, as wood sources were located further from sawmills. Mechanical skidders replaced horses. River runs and log booms were replaced by truck transport though Milne continued to tow logs to the Temagami mill. Milne was one of the few forestry companies in Ontario that did not switch exclusively to road hauling.

Candy Culture

Cy Warman who wrote Weiga of Temagami and Other Indian Tales, published in 1908, once wrote a love poem to his girlfriend Marie, which, in time, was put to music by a songwriter. A chocolate company capitalized on the tune's popularity and the ubiquitous "Sweet Marie" bar was born. Cy was an American living in London, Ontario, with a railway background. He came to Temagami in 1905 while chronicling Ontario railway construction. Weiga is a fictional Ojibway maiden who falls for an ill Algonquin brave with a pet moose.

How Not to Build a Cottage

During the postwar cottage boom, most newcomers hired local contractors to construct their cabins – but not the Wilsons from Toronto. Marion Wilson's father George M. Kelley had explored Temagami's canoe routes in the 1890s. She decided it was high time for the family to put down some rustic roots by building a log cabin. The Wilsons were the proud new owners of tiny Island 958 in the South Arm. Marion read a brochure on log cabin construction and was convinced that with a few carpenters' tools the family, Donald and Marion and their two sons Kerry, 16, and Robert, 8, would have no problem building a cabin.

The family set off for Union Station in June 1951, boarded the red-eye CNR train, and arrived well-fed and rested in Temagami. "We didn't realize it at that moment, but that was the last comfortable, dry night's sleep and the last decent meal we would enjoy for the next two months," Kerry wrote in a short memoir.

Having stowed endless supplies aboard the *Modello*, the Wilsons awaited the arrival of a captain: "After an unexplained delay of about 40 minutes, a quite round, quite red-faced, nonetheless distinguished, man exited the Steamboat Authority building and slowly began to amble down the long wharf toward our ship. After several conferences with a diverse variety of local citizens, Captain [Ted] Guppy finally reached the *Modello*'s gangway and swung himself aboard. In a minute, bells rang in the engine room and a powerful diesel

The *Modello* arrives at Cochrane's Camp amid mid-season madness.
Photo: Carol Cochrane

rumbled to life; were we off? Well, not quite. Our good captain disappeared into the engine room for another half hour or so. Dad was just about to reach the boiling point when our good captain appeared on the bridge and shouted to the deck hands below to "cast off all lines." At last, we were truly on our way," Kerry wrote.

The Wilsons were deposited at Camp Acouchiching from where they were transported by motorboat to Island 958 to set up their tents and wooden army cots. Waking up the next morning to a steady drizzle, they learned that their waterproof tents weren't. Marion sent Donald and Kerry off to get logs for cottage construction. They donned Eaton's latest rainwear to row the kilometre stretch to the mainland. "Wrapped in air-tight cocoons of plastic, we were soon rendered soaking wet, inside and out," Kerry recalled.

Erroneously believing logs could only be harvested at least 90 metres from the water's edge, they scrambled over large boulders and tangled vegetation. After much disagreement, Donald and Kerry settled on a candidate tree. They had read a booklet about felling a tree and somehow managed to saw it down without crushing themselves. "Neither Dad nor I, even for a moment, thought our skill had anything to do with our success. We didn't really know our trees, so its classification remained something of a mystery to us."

After attempting to sever the top growth and trim the branches without the right tools, the duo lugged their seven-metre log back down a rugged non-path. At long last they were able to push the log down an embankment to the water where it landed like a torpedo and disappeared. It finally surfaced 15 metres away with just a small bit of it visible. Having forgotten to bring along a rope or chain to tow their harvest back to the island, they improvised with an old clothesline being used as a boat rope. Repairs were made to the towline as they inched their way back. The first thing Marion asked was why it had taken hours to get a single log and when they were going back for more.

The family quickly realized they had to rethink their grand plans and conferred with Couch owner Reg McConnell. While he listened to their tale of woe he barely managed to stifle a smirk. Plan B soon evolved, involving skilled builder Alex Aird. Alex and his wife Peggy had a large log house and carpentry shop on the mainland.

For a man in his 60s, Alex was remarkably strong and agile, easily carrying 20 to 30-pound foundation boulders in each arm from his workboat to the shore and on to the building site. Putting the Wilsons to shame, he was able to fell and tow six perfect logs in a couple of hours. Alex set the family to barking the logs. Blisters and sore muscles notwithstanding, the pile of soggy, sappy bark debris soon threatened to sink the small isle. A fire seemed the answer. The dense smoke drew a lands and forests ranger in a float plane. He circled twice, dropped his side window and gave a thumbs-up sign. He likely concluded these fools were going to burn down the island but posed no threat to the rest of the lake or the mainland pine.

Alex proceeded to lay and notch his logs expertly without measuring. Donald and Kerry's hardscrabble struggle in the bush was not for naught; Alex used their sole log in the cabin's east wall. It can still be identified. Then the Wilsons went achinking and acaulking with surprisingly good results.

"Finally our cabin was finished. I will always remember the day, shortly after the shingles were put on, that it started to rain. The new beds were soft and no drips of water came

Alex Aird (l) and Kerry and Donald Wilson work on a log during cottage construction.
Photo: Robert Wilson

in anywhere. It was a great feeling of protection and well-being," wrote Kerry. When it came time to settle up, payment of about $600 passed hands, although the lamb shearling winter coat Marion bought at Eaton's for Alex and the blueberry pies Peggy baked for the Wilsons rendered that dollar figure meaningless.

Drinking and Driving

The majestic *Belle of Temagami* had been a welcome sight to two generations of summer visitors. The war years weren't kind as passengers vanished and she started showing her age. Ontario's last steamer, she was dismantled in the mid-1940s. She was replaced in 1946 by the faster diesel-powered *Aubrey Cosens VC*, named for a Latchford World War Two hero posthumously bestowed the Victoria Cross.

The *Aubrey* was built as a motor yacht in 1910 in South Boston, Massachusetts, according to Angus Scully of Island 1087 in an article he wrote for the *Times*. She was employed as a rum-runner during Prohibition

Captain Ted Guppy commanded lake vessels for nearly four decades. Here he is aboard the *Aubrey Cosens VC*.
Photo: Temagami Experience

and ended up being impounded by the American government. On Lake Temagami she stayed on the right side of the law and was beloved by the lake's youth for her ice cream bar and the joyful thrill of riding her waves in a rowboat or canoe.

The late Darryl Lalonde worked as a purser on the *Aubrey* in the late 1950s and '60s. He reminisced about his experiences in the *Times*. An unnamed captain got into a heap of trouble during a run down the Northeast Arm to Bear Island. A couple of passengers approached Darryl and asked him if he knew what the captain was up to. "With some trepidation, I walked up the deck towards the wheelhouse and looked in the side window. The captain of the *Aubrey Cosens*, a one-time captain on the Great Lakes, was holding a mickey of rye up to his mouth and having at it."

Darryl's first thought was, "How do we travel up to the end of the north arm and back to Temagami with a captain under the influence?" Captain Ted Guppy, the tipsy captain's supervisor, told the purser to keep a close eye on the situation. Ted couldn't take over the controls due to a stroke he had suffered.

"The people at the Bear Island dock that day were surprised at how the *Cosens* landed... Instead of pulling along the long side of the dock, we somehow ended up docked on the narrow end out front." Muriel Swann, the wife of boat lines' superintendent Jack Swann, ran the *Aubrey*'s snack bar. The force of the landing chipped some of her dishes. As the vessel left the dock, the captain pushed the throttle control

Gordie Howe with his children Mark and Marty at Chimo in the 1960s.
Photo: TLA Archives

arm into reverse by mistake and the boat nearly crashed into the dock. Darryl shouted at the captain who threw the lever into forward. A near disaster was thinly averted.

Darryl decided to stay in the wheelhouse and sat on a seat cushion. By the captain's demeanour, he realized the mickey was hidden under the cushion, so he spent most of the rest of the day plopped on the pad. "Upon our return to Temagami, the *Aubrey Cosens* made the longest slowest approach to the dock that anyone had ever observed. Jack Swann released this captain from his job that same day."

Another change in transport was the TNOR's takeover of the James Ross Sproat boat service in 1944. It became part of the

Ontario Northland Boat Lines (ONBL). The TNOR was renamed the Ontario Northland Railway (ONR) in 1946 to end its confusion with the Texas and New Orleans Railway. Because both lines used the same initials, the Ontario railway lost boxcars to the U.S. while it received invoices and rental charges meant for the Texan line.

More VIPs Discover Temagami

Mel Hundert of Toronto bought Camp White Bear in 1947. It had once been a secluded retreat for Hollywood celebrities. He brought in a grand piano expressly for Percy Faith, a celebrated Canadian band leader and composer. Percy was a regular guest who practised and entertained other patrons.

After the Second World War, the Gooderhams of Camp Chimo hosted Prince Alexander of Teck, the Earl of Athlone, a younger brother of Queen Mary. The earl was Canada's governor general from 1940 to '46. Accompanying the earl was his wife Princess Alice, a granddaughter of Queen Victoria. A number of Canadian cabinet ministers were part of the entourage. Detroit Red Wings legend Gordie Howe was a guest in the early 1960s. He stayed about two weeks and stick-handled a mess of bass with the help of his Bear Island guide Phillip Potts.

Temagami Inn became a private retreat for some of Toronto's prominent Jewish families in 1943 and became known as Temagami Lodge. The lodge reinvented itself as a co-operative. Guests were also the owners, including flamboyant, cigar-chomping Nat Taylor. Nat bought an Ottawa movie theatre in 1938 and subdivided it so he could show two films simultaneously, thus inventing the world's first multiplex theatre. Nat coined the name "cineplex" as a short form for cinema complex. He and partner-protégé Garth Drabinsky opened an 18-screen cineplex at the Eaton Centre in Toronto. Nat also produced a handful of thriller flicks, including 1961's *The Mask* – the first Canadian film to be distributed in the U.S.

Alex Solway was another Temagami Lodge visitor-proprietor. His wife was Frannie Rodenburg, whose family owned Toronto's Park Plaza Hotel at Bloor Street and Avenue

Road. It is now the Park Hyatt Hotel. The hotel chef spent his summers at Temagami Lodge, concocting gourmet dining experiences for guests, recalled sisters Elaine Lowery and Patricia Delarosbel.

After dinner Nat Taylor provided first-run movies, Elaine said. She waitressed there, beginning in the mid-1950s, joined by Patricia in the early '60s. "They treated us like family; they had watched us grow up across the bay," Elaine added. The Lowery cottage on Temagami Island is just a stone's throw from the resort. They worked with managers John and Nellie Longhi who had a two-storey house beside the lodge.

The Posluns were also Temagami Lodge regulars. They had been immersed in the downtown Toronto garment industry since the turn of the 20th century. Designer Irving Posluns' *I Love Lucy*-style women's coats and jackets are in high demand at vintage-wear boutiques. Wilfred Posluns founded Dylex Limited in 1966 and acquired the faltering Tip Top Tailors men's clothing chain, charting the company on a steep growth curve. At its height Dylex owned 17 chains, including Fairweathers and Thriftys. Rough times forced Dylex to sell its holdings in 2000.

Tip Top Tailors was established in 1910 by Polish immigrant David Dunkelman and quickly rose to an apparel giant. The Dunkelman children grew up in luxury on Sunnybrook Farm, an estate northeast of Toronto, now the site of Sunnybrook Medical Centre. David's son Benjamin succeeded his father as company head while Joe, another

IT WALKS— IT SWIMS— IT FLIES!

The Goodyear amphibious travel ad included this artist's conception of
a futuristic Temagami camping scene. *Courtesy: Reg Sinclair*

son, was considered less conscientious and was consigned to a backroom role.

Living Large

Joe Dunkelman patented 10 acres of Ogama Island 843 in 1957. He and his wife Claire were bon vivants who knew how to throw a party. They became fast friends with Harold and Fran Shannon and replicated their pheasant farm on a smaller scale. The Dunkelmans sold to a developer in the early 1970s.

Local legend has it that the Dunkelmans were the first on the lake to own personal watercraft. Bombardier offered Seadoos for sale in 1968 and '69. Engine problems led the Canadian company to abandon Seadoo manufacturing after just two seasons. Kawasaki successfully revived the product in the late 1980s. On Lake Temagami jet skis are either reviled or rejoiced without compromise.

The Dunkelmans also brought in a personal aircraft. "It Walks – It Swims – It Flies!" declared a 1945 Goodyear Aircraft Corporation advertisement for amphibian travel in an American magazine. Amphibians or flying boats, equipped with both floats and retractable wheels, were used widely by the U.S. military during the Second World War in air-sea rescue and anti-submarine patrol. Postwar they linked remote Far North communities with the outside world and fought forest fires.

The large centrefold ad was aimed at Temagami tourists. "It will take you places in a hurry – set you down on water as well as on land – it will carry four passengers in limousine comfort – and its cost will be just a fraction of the price of pre-war amphibians." An "artist's conception of a future camping scene at Lake Timagami, Ontario, Canada" depicted a pilot unloading camping gear onto a beach while a smiling couple prepares to go fishing.

At the time of the ad's production Paul Litchfield was Goodyear's CEO. He also owned Camp Pinto on islands 709 and 710 where Goodyear management training programs were conducted. There is little doubt he had a hand in the ad's creation and the company's promotion of amphibious travel to and from the lake.

Island 1067's Brad Hall conned Paul into giving him a ride in an amphibian. He had stopped at Pinto to check out a Goodyear Duck, a light amphibian that Goodyear was testing. In exchange Brad promised Paul a ride in his 14-foot runabout. Not accustomed to such sporty transportation but being too nice a man to say no, Paul reluctantly climbed aboard and held on to the gunnels for dear life for the next 10 minutes. More importantly, Brad got his amphibian thrills.

Island 488's John Eberhard was one of two people aboard an amphibian that went down off town in modern times. No serious injuries were sustained. Designed with the Florida Everglades and the odd alligator in mind, airboats, also classed as amphibians, are now a useful mode of transport, especially during freeze-up and break-up. George Mathias, Rick Lockhart and the Temagami First Nation each own one. They are manufactured in Ontario by 1000 Island Airboats and designed for northern conditions.

First Co-ed Camp

Irwin Haladner established the first co-ed youth camp on the Wabi-Kon site in 1945. He called it Wabikon. After purchasing the adult fish camp, one of his most pressing tasks was collecting the empty whiskey bottles littering the beach front.

Renovations undertaken by maintenance foreman Mel McDonald and his assistant Charlie Reeder included the addition of tennis and volleyball courts. Mel hauled two railway cars loaded with gravel over the ice road in 1946 for the courts' base. A riding ring with six kilometres of trails was cut through the bush. Thirteen horses, procured from a Toronto riding school, were barged in from Temagami every summer. Wabikon was sold in 1970. Irwin died in 2000 and the Haladner family still owns a cottage on Temagami Island.

Accommodation rates had more than doubled by 1957 since the birth of the Association, with White Bear at the top of the scale at $75 to $90 per week. One could stay in a two-bedroom cabin at Chimo for $63 per week, in line with Acouchiching's rates. All Chimo cabins had flush toilets and hot water, but a shower stall cost an extra $3.50 a week. A "chore boy" and "cabin girl" stocked firewood and clean linens.

CHAPTER 10

EARL RODGERS: THE WATCHDOG

Records do not show how long Harold Shannon remained president. It is believed that Charles "Earl" Rodgers of Toronto was helmsman by 1950. Earl was destined to carve a deep notch in the Association's history. As its presumed longest-serving president, he also served as treasurer. He gave selflessly of his time.

Earl was a mining engineer who discovered the lake through professional contacts. The family rented a cottage on Wingfoot Island 864 in 1938 when it was leased to Burt Knapp. Earl and Burt had met in the Kirkland Lake mining camp. The Rodgers took a shine to Island 990 west of Bear Island. There was only one problem – somebody already had it. Florence Mack had visited Temagami about 1900, canoeing with her father, an HBC employee. She occupied Island 990 by 1914.

Florence maintained an exotic lifestyle while roughing it in the bush. A wealthy New Yorker-Californian, she travelled by private rail car with an entourage of servants, including a Chinese chef. Promptly at 4 p.m. every day, Bear Island guides arrived to accompany her fishing parties. She had three cabins built by local contractors. The main cabin was luxurious with Oriental carpets on polished hardwood floors, a quartz fireplace and an ivory baby grand piano. She, meaning the servants, raised chickens on nearby Island 984 to supplement the dinner fare. That isle is now owned by David and Gerry Reid of North Bay.

Florence organized a garden party on Bear Island in the mid-1920s with the aid of post manager Sherman Thorpe and his family. The combined social, bake sale and flea market raised over $500, which she gave to the people of Bear Island to build a path from the post to Lakeview House and the forest rangers' base.

Tragedy struck when a guest's infant accidentally plunged to death off the high cliffs at the south end of the island. Her own son drowned near Bear Island in a canoeing mishap when he was a young man. By the mid-1940s her health was failing. Lloyd Matchett, a friend who owned neighbouring Island 989, negotiated the island's sale to the Rodgers.

A Toronto dentistry student, Lloyd first came to the area as a fire ranger on Smoothwater Lake from 1910 to '14. He was one of 130 rangers who cruised the Temagami forest. On his days off, he and a fellow ranger would venture down to Bear Island for some socializing. Rising at 4 a.m., they would paddle as many as 92 kilometres over 27 portages. Then they would stay put for three days before commencing the return trip.

Lloyd took over the lease on Island 989 in 1914 but was away from the lake until 1919 due to military service. He became a real estate

Roots of Origin

In 1889 Albert Alexander "A.A." Hyde founded the Mentholatum Company in Wichita, Kansas. Mentholatum Ointment was a salve that became a medicine cabinet staple.

A.A.'s son George was wounded during the First World War, leaving him with a weakened heart. He had enjoyed stream fishing at the family cottage in Colorado, but his doctors advised him to find a vacation spot where he could expend less energy by trolling. He and some brothers bought out the lease on a Cattle Island property. He came north occasionally but it was a long trip from Kansas where he was married and raising a family.

Shortly after the death of his father in 1935, George moved to Wilmington, Delaware, where the Mentholatum Company consolidated its holdings. Temagami was more accessible and the family went up during the late 1930s.

The main cabin was razed by a lightning fire in 1940. George's old college pal Norm Duffield had been renting the cottage. The two decided to divide the lease. George would rebuild the cottage while Norm furnished it. After they passed away, George's widow Patsy purchased the lot. She transferred the title to her sons John, Art and Steve Hyde.

The Mentholatum Company was privately held for 89 years, until it was acquired by a Japanese pharmaceutical consortium in 1988. Mentholatum is still on store shelves today.

developer and had three children. Son Boyd went to Cochrane's Camp as a camper and counsellor from 1933 to '41. He and his family now own the island. Boyd's sister Elizabeth was married to the late Canadian publishing mogul Jack McClelland. Octogenarian Boyd was elected a TLA director in 2009.

John Hyde of Cattle Island 849 informally acted as recording secretary at a few AGMs in the early 1950s. He was a young American serviceman whom Earl had taken under his wing. John's father George Hyde had arrived on the lake in 1924.

John recalled that Earl's Lakeview House meetings lasted about three hours, following a catered lunch. About 50 members attended. Hot button issues were logging and fishing, and the district forester from North Bay was often raked over the coals. Earl was a vigilant watch dog over members' concerns. In order to keep tabs on the doings and undoings of logging companies, he booked flights with Lakeland Airways.

Logging Looms Large

The peak volume of wood harvested from the Temagami District was reached in 1955-56, though there were actually fewer logging companies in the area than in the late 1940s. The operators often left high waste stumps and marketable tops. Clearcutting was more profitable so few left seed trees or practised selective cutting.

A Lifelong Friendship

George Hyde's next door neighbour in the College Hill section of Wichita was none other than the Standish Hall family. George had gone to the same school as Standish's future wife Helen Brooks. Standish's son Bradford and George's sons George Jr. and John were about the same age and played together. A.A. Hyde lived nearby in a three-storey Victorian mansion, which was sold by the family in 1937 after A.A.'s death. Island 1067's Brad, a San Franciscan, and George Hyde Jr. of nearby Oakland, remain close friends.

Earl Rodgers is believed to be the Association's longest-serving president.
Photo: Larry Rodgers

Earl sent "strong protests" in 1953 to the district forester regarding logging operators "rapidly destroying our virgin forest heritage." Most were ignoring the 1935 licence restrictions. Transgressions included trees being felled beyond the Skyline Reserve on hill crests so that scarred areas were visible from the lake. He also complained about abandoned logging camps left to deteriorate into an unsightly mess, and companies leaving behind piled brush, adding to the fire risk.

He viewed logging in a resort area as "a wholly unjustified destruction of natural timber beauty," causing "irreparable damage and disfigurement." He concluded that the signs of "deterioration in this still beautiful land are unmistakably clear and ominous. Only prompt, fully effective government control will stop this Lake border area devastation."

In 1955 Earl was prepared to take legal action on behalf of the Association to stop illegal cutting. He believed the forest industry was exerting too much clout with the province. He drew media attention to the Association's cause in southern Ontario.

Rebranding the Association

The first constitution was approved in 1953. The aims and objectives were: protection and promotion of the common interest; maintaining and improving health, sanitation, safety and general welfare conditions; and preservation of the natural scenic beauty of the lake and its surroundings. These are some of the keystone objectives listed today under the preamble to the TLA Bylaws, though the wording has changed.

Earl was concerned with protecting not only Lake Temagami but its interconnecting waterways. The Temagami Association's name was changed to the Temagami Lakes Association about this time, to reflect the geographical extent of its interests. Members set in their ways continued to refer to "The Association."

There were four classes of membership by 1953, consisting of Class A (cottage owners); Class B (commercial camp owners with a year-round caretaker); Class C (commercial camp owners without a year-round caretaker); and Class D (non-property owners called associate members). All but Class D members were entitled to vote. Fees were: Class A and B - $15; Class C - $30 (higher than Class B because they required property patrol); and Class D - $5.

The officers consisted of a president who was also treasurer, a vice president and a secretary. They were elected each year at the Annual General Meeting (AGM). There was an executive committee headed by the president. All members were eligible for appointment to the executive committee at the AGM for a one-year term.

Committees Draw an Interesting Mix

Aside from the executive committee there was also a logging committee, chaired briefly by Howard Baker. He attended Cochrane's Camp in the 1920s. His son-in-law Dick Grout would become president in 1989. The Baker Island 857 was sold in 1971 to Sid and Elva Starkman of Toronto, who purchased it from Howard's widow Sheila.

Also on the logging committee was Howard Chivers, a Keewaydin trip leader who was appointed camp director in 1948. He owned the camp from 1960 until '75. The vice president was Ralph Marshall and Russell Cleminshaw took on secretarial duties. Ralph acquired Island 1102 in Gibson's Bay in 1932. His long association with the lake ended abruptly in 1977 when all but his boathouse was destroyed by a massive forest fire. The elderly Ralph didn't rebuild and the island was sold.

Russell arrived in 1909 as a Keewaydin camper. All three of his brothers learned the ways of the wilderness there. He returned in 1936 to take a second look, staying at Brooks Shepard's Island 1175. The Cleminshaws leased Island 1113 and began building in 1937. Russell was an engineer but switched to teaching during the Depression. Although the economic climate was the reason for his career change, longer summer holidays spent in the north were a fringe benefit – for him and for the Association.

Members of the executive committee in the early 1950s included Gib Cochrane, Frank Todd, Marty Taylor, Jack Swann and Wally Denny. Wally had purchased Gibson's Bay islands 1097 and 1098 after staying at Goodyear Canada's Camp Wingfoot. His wife was Edith Litchfield, a daughter of Goodyear Tire CEO Paul Litchfield who owned Goodyear's American Camp Pinto.

Striking Out

Jack Swann remained with the boat line from 1945 until '66. He began as a timekeeper and shipper, jobs that kept him from seeing the lake. During time off, he learned his way around in the decommissioned Kokomis. One morning after he was promoted to manager, the boat drivers went on a wildcat strike. Since the Ramona was already loaded for Keewaydin, Jack took the helm. The police were awaiting his return, alerted by the striking drivers.

Although Jack wasn't charged with operating a vessel without a commercial licence, he immediately hopped the train to Toronto where he wrote a temporary master's ticket exam the next day and returned to Temagami the same day. He arrived at work the following morning with all legalities resolved, just in time to watch the drivers return to work.

Committee member George Pleasance of Lakewood, Ohio, was a son-in-law of Charles Anderson who had settled on Island 974 south of Bear Island in 1911. The island was later bought by Jack and Nora Walker of St. Catharines, Ontario, and is now lovingly owned by Jack and Nora's grandchildren Wendy Mitchell, and Ian and Geordie Walker.

Sam Seaman was another committee member. Also from Lakewood, he was a son-in-law of Frank Anderson (Charles' brother) who had occupied Whispering Pines Island 976 and Happy Isle 977 in 1910. Sam purchased Island 976 in the early 1940s and built his own cabin. He was vice president in charge of sales and, later, chair of the board of Imperial Type Metal Company. It supplied more than half the type metal used in the U.S. The firm was founded by Karl Nibecker, a son-in-law of Frank Anderson and father of Marilyn Corl Brinkman who now owns Island 977. Frank's great-great-grandchildren are fifth generation islanders.

The First TLA Directory

One of the most notable accomplishments in the early 1950s was the production of the first *Directory of Camp Owners and Services.* It has been published every year since then. It was the brain child of Earl Rodgers and Sam Seaman. Until then, members only heard directly from the executive at the AGM and via a newsletter sent with membership renewal notices.

The directory was edited by Sam Seaman who had it printed by one of his contacts. It was about one-third the dimensions it is today. The front cover logo was a circular sketch of two men paddling between pine-blanketed shores. There was a single alphabetical list of members and advertisements from merchants spanning New Liskeard and Toronto. The centrefold was reserved for a postcard photograph, often an aerial view of the post or village.

The directory dispensed motherly advice until 1971. Here are a few samples of the words of wisdom:

"If you can't swim, stay away from deep water."

"Never go in the water directly after a meal."

"Avoid canoeing after dark, if possible."

"Poison ivy can cause great discomfort."

Another 1950s venture was the production of a four-piece set of navigation charts indicating shoals in large-scale detail. Much of the information was gathered during Earl's logging reconnaissance missions. The charts were available to members on paper for $15 or linen-backed for $25.

The Keevil Legacy

A potential menace appeared on the horizon in 1955. The Temagami Mining Company, established by Torontonian Dr. Norman B. Keevil Sr., was incorporated the previous year to consolidate holdings on and around Temagami Island. Among the claim stakers he bought out were Dewey Derosier and the Friday family. Copperfields Mine was born, employing about 100 people on the richest copper discovery in Canada at the time. Copperfields was the taproot of Teck Corporation, later founded by Norman Sr. His son, also Norman, is chair.

Armed with a PhD in geophysics from Harvard, Norman Sr. discovered the high-grade deposit by inventive means. Recalling the use by the RCAF coastal command of an aeromagnetic device to detect enemy submarines during the Second World War, he concluded the gadget was simply a high-powered metal detector. He installed one on his Grumman Goose and flew over Lake Temagami where he detected a strong magnetic anomaly. His airborne surveys changed the face of mining exploration.

While Norman was scoping the Temagami area for its mining potential, he discovered another gem – Island 1114 near Gibson's Bay. He bought it from the Crown in the late 1940s. Son Harold built his dream cottage after purchasing Island 1255 in Sharp Rock Inlet in 1995 from Peter and Helen Bates of Belleville, Ontario. Helen's mother Florence Thompson served as an Association director in the late 1970s.

Norman Sr. was inducted into the Canadian Mining Hall of Fame before his death in 1989. Daughter June bought the family island from his estate. The Keevils also had a cottage in Island Bay now belonging to Norman Jr.'s son Scott, an Association director in the early 1980s. Scott's sister Laura and her husband Danny McDonald have a cottage west of Bear Island. Rosemary Keevil-Fairburn, the widow of Norman Sr.'s son Brian, owns islands 1097 and 1098 near Gibson's Bay. They formerly belonged to Wally and Edith (Litchfield) Denny.

In the early 1990s June was the artistic director of Roots and Wings, a youth theatre program on Bear Island. The group's play *n'Daki Menan* was presented locally before the amateur thespians embarked on a tour of northern Ontario and the western provinces.

Noting considerable diamond drilling on Temagami Island, Earl contacted Queen's Park regarding cottagers' concerns, and soon had copies of Temagami Mining Company-government agreements for reference and potential legal action. "It is unfortunate that mining should have been added to our troubles," he wrote in the 1956 directory. Despite the unease, fishing seemed better than it had been for years. The Ontario government's restocking program was ongoing. Association volunteers assisted with aerial planting, and fish netting and tagging for population surveys.

The Good Times Roll for the ONBL

The boat line was thriving, having made numerous postwar acquisitions. Gasoline and diesel-powered ships, barges and World War Two crash boats ferrying passengers and freight threatened gridlock. They included: the *Modello, Aubrey Cosens VC, Vedette* (built in Ohio in 1906 with an 11 ½ knot-Cummins engine), *Ramona* (a 46-foot 1923 Gravenhurst Ditchburn with a 13-mph Chrysler engine), *Gull Lake, Sesikinika, Wakimika* (three World War Two air-sea rescue launches now carrying freight), *Metagami, Grey Owl* (a 1933 Bracebridge Minett-Shields with a 15-mph Kermath engine), *Ojibway* (a 1926 Ditchburn with a 15-mph Kermath engine), *Marco, Naiad* (built in Toronto in 1890 and sumptuously modelled after the royal yacht *Britannia* with a closed cabin panelled in bird's eye maple and black cherry), *Sharp Rock, Cross Lake I* and *II* (three barges), *Kokoko, Wendigo* (the fastest boat on the lake for a time), *Kaniki, Gracie* and *Chico.*

The *Modello* was dismantled and burned in 1955 due to a rotten hull, according to Carol Cochrane, while the *Naiad* was taken out of service in 1966. Collisions, dry rot and obsolescence due to the Copperfields Mine Road would be the fate of many. Displaced by diesel fuel, the last steam-powered locomotive rumbled through T-Station in 1957. The boat line converted gradually to diesel and the village's towering coal shute became redundant.

The ONBL administrative building and upper restaurant overlook the docks.
Postcard photo: Reg Sinclair

110

The *Aubrey Cosens VC* makes her daily stop at Bear Island.
A launch on the other side of the dock is the *Illawarra*.
MacLean postcard photo: Reg Sinclair

The ONR and ONBL delivered from 30 to 40 bags of mail a day during high season in the 1950s to the lake's five post offices and other commercial camps. The large volumes are no surprise; people couldn't simply pick up the phone for a yak with Aunt Mabel. Some vestiges of civilization began to appear on the lake: one could call Temagami from a phone at the post for 25 cents and the Temagami Mining Company installed a radio phone for long distance calls.

CHAPTER 11

A CAST OF CHARACTERS THROUGH THE 1950S

Dr. Joseph Sullivan began a long relationship with the Association in 1955 as a logging committee member. He had discovered the lake as a Cochrane's Camp boy. Joe bought Island 496 about 1946 from Gladys Schumacher, the widow of former president Harry Schumacher. He later purchased nearby Island 498 and built a boathouse.

Joe's Toronto housekeeper in the 1940s and '50s was Rita O'Sullivan, née Moore. They developed a lifelong friendship. Rita later became second chief of the Teme-Augama Anishnabai. Rita's sister Laura McKenzie also worked for Joe. She too served her people, as a band councillor until her death in 1979. The Laura McKenzie Learning Centre on Bear Island, opening in 1983 with 38 pupils up to Grade 8, is named in her honour. It replaced a wood-frame school built in 1958.

Joe attended the University of Toronto where he excelled academically and athletically. He was a member of the gold medal winning 1928 Canadian Olympic hockey team. As goalie, Joe recorded shutouts in all three of the games he played. The team was coached by Conn Smythe. He was the Toronto Maple Leafs principal owner during their Stanley Cup glory years from the 1930s through the '60s. Joe was invited to Boston to play with the NHL but his mother convinced him that post-graduate studies would offer better security. He was inducted into the U of T Sports Hall of Fame in 1988.

After studying in Europe, Joe became a leading ear, nose and throat surgeon. He regularly boarded the train to treat patients in Haileybury and Kirkland Lake, returning immediately afterwards to resume duties at St. Michael's Hospital in Toronto. Joe did much philanthropic work. Another claim to fame came in 1957 when he was summoned to the Canadian Senate by Prime Minister John Diefenbaker.

"He Shoots, He Scores!"

Joe chaired the logging committee in 1956. New to that committee was Foster Hewitt. He went to Cochrane's Camp in 1917, returned as a staff member and later as an adult guest. He and his wife Kay had a cabin on "adult point." By then Foster was famous as the voice of the Maple Leafs and the name on the front of his cabin was SEE KAY FH – see Kay and Foster Hewitt and also CKFH, the radio station he started in 1951 which carried his Leafs broadcasts.

Foster pioneered hockey play-by-play announcing. He logged 3,000 broadcasts over a career spanning more than 50 years. It all started in 1923 when he sat in a cramped

A young Foster Hewitt.
Photo: Canada's Sports Hall of Fame

for CBC's *Hockey Night in Canada*. He gave the play-by-play for the historic 1972 Summit Series between Canada and the Soviet Union. He retired in 1978. Son Bill Hewitt became the TV voice of the Leafs for 30 years. Bill died on Christmas Day 1996.

Foster bought Island 850 on the South Arm in 1949. When he died in 1985, the island went to Bill's son Bruce Hewitt. He started building a large log home but, as rumour has it, he ran low on funds. Syd and Cathy McDougall from Kirkland Lake purchased the island from Bruce in 1995 and completed the project. Temagami's Cathy Dwyer-Smith and her landscaping company hauled in loads of top soil to plant several stunning gardens.

Sandy and Debbie Nixon of Toronto bought the isle in 2005. A lawyer, Sandy was a White Bear camper and counsellor in the 1960s. The Nixons had honeymooned on the lake by canoe in 1971. Few artifacts from Foster's glory days remain. His small cabin is now used for storage and houses some of his old fishing gear.

Foster Hewitt's honours include the Order of Canada and induction into both the Hockey Hall of Fame and Canada's Sports Hall of Fame. Locally, the Foster Hewitt Foundation has donated generously to the Temagami Area Fish Involvement Program (TAFIP). Bill Hewitt was a TAFIP volunteer. Foster was vice president by 1957, replacing Ralph Marshall who continued to serve on the executive committee.

glass box far above the ice for the world's first live radio hockey broadcast. It was relayed by telephone to a radio station. Before the puck dropped, Toronto stores ran out of radio batteries. It was during this game, between Kitchener and Toronto, that Foster first uttered his famous phrase, "He shoots, he scores!" When Foster grabbed a megaphone, stood at the end of the Cochrane dock and did play-by-plays of the annual regatta action, people more or less took it in stride.

Foster's talents found a new medium in 1952 when he moved to televised broadcasts

Camps and Resorts Influence Cottage Locales

In 1957, 68 per cent of cottage owners on the South Arm were Canadian, due to their connections with Cochrane's Camp, Chimo and Acouchiching. About 70 per cent of cottage owners on the Southwest Arm were American, as a result of affiliations with Camp White Bear, Wigwasati and Northwoods. On the North Arm, 85 per cent were American, due to ties with Keewaydin and Wabun.

Canadians made up 83 per cent of cottagers on the Northeast Arm. That arm had 113 cottages, more than any other arm, yet only nine belonged to the Association. Many Northeast Arm dwellers lived in Temagami and the Tri-Towns, and likely believed they didn't share the same concerns as their southerly neighbours. Nowadays there is a more eclectic mix.

Men of Distinction

Dr. Maurice Eisendrath and his wife Rosa discovered Temagami via Camp White Bear. Born in Chicago, Rabbi Eisendrath was the spiritual leader of Toronto's Holy Blossom Temple. He leased Island 565 on the Southwest Arm and became a member of the fish committee.

White Bear owner Arthur Judson brought his New York City chauffeur Frank Preston up north one year to work at White Bear. Frank

and Maurice met and connected. The rabbi asked him to design and build a log cabin. Maurice was so impressed that he asked Frank to craft some knotty pine furniture too. This marked the beginning of what would become Pioneer Handcraft, the classic furniture maker of Muskoka. Frank used red and white pine he harvested right on the island.

Frank went off to war in the early 1940s as an airframe mechanic, then moved to Severn Bridge in 1948. He died in the late 1950s but his widow Kay Preston continued Pioneer Handcraft. The business was sold to John Bell in 1971. He has advertised in the TLA directory every year, a nod to the business's roots. He set up furniture displays at the flea market and craft sale during the 1990s. Frank was a skilled multi-tasker: not only a chauffeur but also proficient at architecture, tree cutting, construction, design, carpentry, furniture making and airframe mechanics.

The Eisendraths were friends of Canadian actor Lorne Greene and his wife Rita. Maurice had officiated at the Greene wedding in 1938. Born Lyon Chaim, Lorne visited the lake several times where he enjoyed fishing. He called Temagami "a gorgeous part of the world" in the mid-1980s when contacted by *Temagami Times* editor Pam Glenn. After Rosa Eisendrath's death and the Greenes' divorce in the 1960s, Maurice married Rita Greene. Lorne went on to play Ben Cartwright, the family patriarch on the long-running TV series *Bonanza*.

By the time of his Association involvement, Maurice was living in New York City where he was the president of the Union for Reform

LAKE
TEMAGAMI
COMMUNITIES

the early years. Don was a U of T professor, destined to become the post-1971 coup d'état board member with the most years of service.

The lumber market slumped from 1956 to '59, so there was less cutting than usual in the Temagami forest. The Association became much less vocal against the industry. According to Earl Rodgers, the government and lumber companies were complying with its appeals for shoreline border protection.

A perceived breach of trust by the Department of Lands and Forests was raising Earl's hackles in the late 1950s. The Association had been promised that if a Copperfields concentrator or processing plant was to be built, it would be on the mainland. But Ontario issued the mine a permit to construct the plant on Temagami Island. It was feared that an island plant would pollute the water, and become a noise and odour nuisance. "The discharge of tailings and effluent constitutes a hazard wholly without justification in a well-established vacation area," Earl wrote. He appealed to the province in 1961 to demand strictly enforced safeguards and to have summer operations curtailed.

"If surface blasting, diamond drilling and other work is carried out in the midst of the summer season, it will destroy what pleasure is left to Temagami residents in this area," he

Judaism from 1943 until his death in 1973. Some of the causes he championed were the civil rights movement, opposition to the Vietnam War and inter-religious cooperation. He presented President John F. Kennedy a Torah scroll in 1961. Island 565 is now owned by Larry and Sharon Enkin of Toronto.

Trouble in Paradise

New to the logging committee was Don Fraser who became chair in 1958. Don's family had leased part of Alexander Island 992 near Bear Island in 1935. His mother was a Michie. Michie and Company was a main supplier of cottagers' grocery orders in said in a letter to the deputy minister of mines. Dr. Senator Joe Sullivan, by now the executive vice president, added his weight. He strongly denounced the "indiscriminate, unseasonable and obnoxious exploration and mining activity," adding "if necessary, I propose to take it up with the Premier."

Build It and They Will Come

The 19-kilometre Mine Road was being built by 1958. Until then Copperfields Mine shipped ore by barge to Temagami, headed for a smelter in Noranda, Quebec. The Association had been informed that no access to the lake would be permitted for any other activity than forestry. Little did the executive know that within the next decade there would be multiple lake access points, a large public parking lot, boat slips, a privately-run boat line, and the Association itself would be erecting a headquarters building off the road.

After the Mine Road opened, islanders began bypassing Temagami and the ONBL by driving their cars to the south end of the Northeast Arm, where they jumped into their own boats. The mine had installed a gate and charged $1 per day for private parking plus a $2 road toll. The convenience of not having to synchronize plans with the boat line's schedule and ticket purchase savings made the Mine Road attractive.

Ice Fishing: The Lake's Ruination?

A perceived threat to the Temagami experience reared its head in 1958. Noting that summer fishing had recently been poor, the Association laid blame at the door of ice fishing huts. Adding to the allegation, "reports appear to confirm that garbage and other unsanitary refuse is left on the ice by fishermen," Earl Rodgers wrote. By 1960 he was hoping to convince Ontario to ban ice fishing until the summer catch improved.

There was a fish committee by summer 1959. It was chaired by Dewey Derosier, soon-to-be president, whose number one priority was to stamp out ice fishing. Born in Huntspur, Michigan, in 1898, Dewey's family moved to Temagami in 1912. His father became the keeper of the Diamond, Temagami and Sharp Rock dams. One of Dewey's summer jobs as a teenager was working as a bellhop at Temagami Inn.

From 1922 until '30 Dewey used his 40-foot Ditchburn launch the *Ogania* to transport Wabi-Kon guests on fishing expeditions. The vessel held 30 to 35 passengers, including eight guides with a flotilla of canoes towed behind. One passenger was Archie Belaney who guided at Wabi-Kon during the 1925 season.

Dewey built a camp on the east side of Temagami Island in 1923 from logs cut and milled on site. It was originally called Eucoroma, an amalgam of the owner's three daughters' first names. New owners in 1943 renamed it Stone Turtle and ran it as a Girl Guide camp. The White family purchased the lodge in

1947 and renamed it Adanac (Canada spelled backwards). It is still owned by the Whites. Lance White also runs a bait and tackle shop.

Rumours have swirled for years that Frederick Banting and Charles Best stayed at Adanac and used a back kitchen as a makeshift lab in their pursuit of a medical breakthrough for diabetics. However, the doctors discovered insulin in 1921, two years before any footings were laid at Eucorama. It is possible that the pair stayed at Adanac at some point but their goal was likely relaxation. The men had two local townships named for them.

Camp Ogama

Dewey married nurse Kathryn Bishop in New York in 1930. He and a partner leased 10 acres of Island 843 near Temagami Island in 1933 and built Camp Ogama, run by Dewey as a summer resort until 1943. In the mid-1940s, Dewey built White Gables Lodge (now Deepwater Lodge) on Island 203, which expanded into housekeeping units, a store, bakery and tearoom.

Ogama was comprised of a log main lodge and dining room featuring a large stone fireplace, and

rustic cabins and floored tents. According to a brochure, the resort was famous for fish breakfasts, Sunday chicken dinners and silver service on white linen tablecloths. Some cabins had running water, electric lights and fireplaces. Guests could tuck in for the night under Hudson's Bay blankets. There was a bathhouse with hot running water. Amusements included ping pong, deck quoits and horseshoe tournaments.

Camp Ogama was owned by a Newark, New Jersey, resident by the early 1960s. The main lodge met a fate similar to other cottages and resorts. It was razed by fire, leaving only the stone fireplace. A developer bought most of Ogama Island in the mid-1970s and subdivided it into five lots. Five acres are still Crown land. Patricia and Ray Delarosbel of North Bay bought a 2.5-acre lot in 1978.

The bishop of the Anglican Diocese attended St. George's 50th anniversary celebration in 1961. Attendees included Olive Lanoie and Mrs. Lloyd Matchett. *Photo: John Hyde*

They nearly doubled the size of their property by buying the 66-foot wide shoreline reserve from the MNR. On some patents, the Crown reserved these shoreline strips adjacent to private land to preserve aesthetics and spawning locations. The MNR made them available for sale to land owners in the late 1980s. Early maps used a chain scale with one chain equal to 66 feet. That is how the reserves came to be 66 feet wide.

God's Country

Sam Seaman resigned as directory editor in the early 1960s. As an avid angler he had other fish to fry. He was also involved with St. George's Anglican Church on Bear Island. The small chapel was built in 1911 to serve cottagers, Scottish post employees and a few native families who hadn't converted to Catholicism.

During St. George's 50th anniversary celebrations in 1961, Sam presented a plaque "in appreciation of the dedicated leadership of Olive Lanoie." Olive and her witty French Canadian husband Joe Lanoie had arrived on Bear Island from Winnipeg in winter 1930. They stayed with Olive's sister and her husband George Hutchings. A former Ka-Kena Inn carpenter, George ran a Bear Island store until the Hutchings established White Top Cabins in Temagami in the late 1930s.

Joe's first impression was that there were three non-native families, 90 natives and 150 dogs living on Bear Island. One of his earliest jobs was helping John Turner with the construction of six buildings and docks at

Homer and Eva Graftons' Camp Wigwasati. In 1930, the Graftons' first summer in operation, the Lanoies' only child drowned off Wigwasati. After losing six-year-old Eddy, Olive didn't return to the camp for 25 years.

Joe worked at the Bear Island post from 1932 until '65. He maintained its fleet of 52 canoes and rented them out to tourists. He was also a caretaker, guide and friend to three generations of cottagers. He unofficially adopted about half the children on the lake, fretting over their school grades and their being on the lake in a kicker during windy weather. He was often stationed on the post dock, asking, "Where's the pretty one?" former Island 1067 cottager Ted Hyde recalled. A bevy of little girls would call back, "Here I am, Joe!"

Joe Lanoie in the 1950s with
a nice lake trout caught off Cattle Island.
Photo: John Hyde

118

Olive Lanoie was St. George's guardian angel in her roles of elder, caretaker, recruiter, usher and refreshment provider. She was active on the Association's membership committee in the early 1960s and ran a proper English tearoom in the summertime. She died in 1967. The last service at St. George's was held in 1971. Sam's plaque was quietly removed by Joe and adorned a wall of St. Simon's Anglican Church in Temagami. Joe died in 1979 in North Bay, where he had retired a few years earlier.

Sam Seaman died in 1977. Today Island 976 belongs to his daughter Allyne "Rusty" Portmann. Gloria Seaman Allen, another daughter and former Cayuga camper, purchased Joseph and Barbara Shaw's Island 1024 lot close to Slide Rock in 1998. Their log cottage was lost to fire in 1980 and rebuilt three years later. They operated Granada Investments, a real estate investment firm in Aurora, Ontario, and acquired land on Chimo Island in the 1970s for subdividing, as well as some Temagami waterfront property, including the Shell Station, now PetroCanada.

Following Sam's resignation, the directory editor was Henry "Hank" Dow, secretary-treasurer of a Toronto printing company. He became acquainted with the lake in his teens, when he attended Cayuga. After camp closed, he would spend time at his friend Jack Ames' island. His father Cecil was president in the late 1930s. Hank and his wife Edith "Deed" spent three months on the lake in 1947 searching for an available island. They patented a lot on Island 1005 in 1955.

New Blood

A membership committee made its debut in the late 1950s under Chair Sam Scovil, son of former treasurer Mal Scovil. Committee members included Joe Barnett from Pennsylvania who had bought Dr. Fred Clarkson's point on Island 985 west of Bear Island. A discriminating seller, Fred required the Barnetts to stay with him to ascertain their suitability as prospective owners. Apparently they passed muster. Fred's strict standards were a result of his long association with the lake. He arrived in 1918, bringing 10 or more relatives and friends with him every year thereafter. As a medical doctor, he delivered a few Bear Island babies and extracted innumerable fish hooks from campers' limbs.

Others on the membership committee were Jack Swann and John Rykert, a Toronto

Smooth Operator

Dr. Harold Rykert was a leading heart surgeon whose most famous patient was silent film star Charlie Chaplin, upon whom he operated in France. Dr. Sen. Joseph Sullivan of Island 496, an ear, nose and throat surgeon, treated commoners and royalty alike. King George VI came to Canada expressly to have Joe perform an operation. After King George's daughter Elizabeth II ascended the throne, Joe was appointed her official surgeon during a Canadian tour but his services were not called upon.

investment analyst. Dr. Harold Edmund Rykert of Toronto, John's father, leased Island 308 near Cross Bay in 1934, having been introduced to the lake as a Cochrane boy. John arrived on the lake as a babe in arms, staying at Chimo with his grandparents. He later went to Cochrane's Camp.

John Rykert replaced Foster Hewitt as vice president in 1960. He also chaired a new Mine Road parking committee whose mandate was to plan for the expansion of lots and docks. Dr. Philip Greey of Toronto and Island 775 was a member. His son Phil Greey would become TLA president in 1973.

A new face at the executive committee table was Herbert "Stoky" Stokinger. A staff member at Keewaydin from 1929 until '31, he switched over to Wabun in 1941 and became managing director in the late 1950s, a post he would hold until 1976. Stoky died in 2006 shortly after his 100th birthday. Another recruit to the executive committee was Doug Gardner. A year later he was head of the membership committee.

The trip shed in the 1960s when
the Gardners owned Camp Temagami.
Photo: Robert Gardner

Historic Cochrane's Camp Changes Hands

Doug Gardner ran a youth camp on the shores of Georgian Bay and another in Algonquin Park. When his park lease expired and provincial land policies changed, he learned that Cochrane's Camp was for sale through connections at Toronto's Upper Canada College where he taught science and chemistry. For years the camp was virtually Upper Canada College's summer program but, by the late 1950s, it was beset with financial difficulties. Just two weeks before his death in 1959, A.L. Cochrane sold his camp to Doug who also bought Acouchiching and established Camp Metagami for girls. Doug's wife Barbara became Metagami's director.

One island at Cochrane's Camp was inadvertently omitted from the sale. The water level was low at the time and it appeared that Island 768, under an acre in size, was part of Island 762. Carol Cochrane eventually gave Island 768 to her daughter Linda Bangay. It is used for family picnics and bonfires.

Some positive signals were evident by the early 1960s that Dewey's campaign to improve the fishery was working. The province reduced the daily lake trout limit and established four alternate-year fish sanctuaries. These were abolished in 1985 and later replaced with others. The Department of Lands and Forests was expected to stock double the average number of fish.

The Association's tough stance against ice fishing rubbed Temagami's chamber of commerce the wrong way and the chamber president aired his beefs in a *North Bay Nugget* story. Wilfred "Butch" Spooner accused cottagers, whom he erroneously identified as mainly American, of giving the area a black eye by sullying its reputation for good fishing. By 1960 approximately 55 per cent of property owners were Canadian as were some 48 per cent of Association members.

The Nanette

Fresh recruits included Bill Russell on the Mine Road committee. One of

Wabun's founders, he had recently assumed responsibility for Doug Gardner's Camp Temagami canoeing program. Bill captained the *Nanette* for Doug from 1959 to '72. She was a 32-foot Hamilton Boatworks mahogany launch, built to order for A.L. Cochrane in the 1930s, according to Bill's grandson Russell Tuckerman.

The *Nanette* was powered by a 12-cylinder Kermath engine. For a time she was the fastest boat on the lake, Russell noted. He recalled riding in the *Nanette* with his grandfather, often stopping at the post for ice cream. She had a displacement hull which pushed the water to the sides, rather than planing over the surface. "You could drink a proper cup of English tea without spilling a drop," he claimed.

The vessel was sold in 1972 to a North Bay Liquor Control Board of Ontario (LCBO) inspector for $500. After Bill Russell died of a heart attack at his Garden Island cottage

Gib Cochrane driving the *Nanette* in 1942 with Cochrane's Camp foreman Alec Steadman in the cockpit plus 15 passengers.
Photo: Carol Cochrane

in 1974, the family borrowed the *Chimo III*, another classic craft, to spread his ashes. Russell has spent many years attempting to trace the fate of the *Nanette* and bring her home.

Earlier, the *Nanette* had been under Gib Cochrane's care. She typically carried a canoe party of nine or ten. Gib was the only one allowed to drive her, accompanied by camp foreman Alec Steadman. "Between them, they rescued many trips from different camps on the lake after a canoe had been swamped or upset," Gib's daughter Carol Cochrane recalled.

When Carol and her husband Jim Hasler visited Dorset, Ontario, a few years ago, she was astonished to see a photo of the *Nanette* on a buy-sell notice board. The asking price was $100,000. It took her by such surprise that she didn't think to go back and jot down the information. She supports Russell's search and rescue efforts. "If it is found, no one would be happier than myself to see this wonderful

launch back on Lake Temagami where it really belongs," said Carol.

A Winter Adventure

The Association hooked up with Alfred "Alf" Cook, a veteran Camp Acouchiching fishing guide. He guided at Couch for 15 years, starting in 1927. His first winter trip was in the late 1920s, to help owner Reg McConnell arrange for ice for the icehouse and wood for the stove and fireplaces. They started their journey at the only village hotel open in the winter, belonging to Alex Guppy. The next day they managed to walk to Friday's Camp on a partially frozen lake, where they stayed the night.

Reg and Alf walked over to Temagami Island the next day, broke into a boathouse and borrowed a Peterborough skiff. Then they rowed to Chimo where they faced more open

---

Paranoia

W.G. Gook was on the membership committee. A Hiram Walker & Sons employee from southern Ontario, he bought Sharp Rock Inlet Island 1255 in 1950 from a woman suffering from cabin fever. Staying alone in her isolated cottage, she imagined faces staring at her through the windows. Terrified, she paddled away in the middle of the night to an occupied island and never returned. The Gook family is remembered for the fish fries it hosted for Sharp Rock area neighbours.

W.G. Gook died in the mid-1960s and his widow sold the island to Peter and Helen Bates of Belleville, Ontario. The island is now owned by Harold Keevil of Bracebridge. Flat rocks on Island 1255 bear carved names dating back to the early 1900s. The island originally served as a campsite for adventurers heading into Diamond Lake through the Sharp Rock portage.

water down the South Arm. They met up with Chimo caretaker Dennis Laronde who lived in a nearby log cabin. He is remembered for the many fine stone fireplaces he built. His daughter Jeanette married Archie and Angele Belaney's grandson Albert LaLonde. The LaLondes and Larondes still have summer homes on Chimo Island.

Dennis tried to start an outboard motor for Alf and Reg but it kept freezing up. They finally paddled a canoe to Cochrane's Camp. They arrived at Donald McKenzie's ancestral home in the bays at the end of the South Arm where four aboriginal families were hunting and trapping. Reg and Alf stayed with them for about five days. While they were there, Eva

McKenzie was born. They ate rabbit stew and dumplings, and shot a moose.

The pair lived at Couch all winter with a weekly trip to Bear Island to shop and a monthly sojourn in Temagami to take an overdue bath. Normal standards of cleanliness were suspended; the men would occasionally nail their tin plates to the kitchen table to avoid dish washing and the dogs would sometimes rinse them.

Tragedy struck the McConnell family in fall 1952. Reg, 49, drowned while closing up at Couch. He was a strong swimmer, according to his daughter Pat Bonnell, and his only known health issue was a smoker's cough. It was never known exactly how he met his fate. Reg's wife

A Life of Conviction

Connie Cook would have been a huge asset had she the time to serve the Association. At home in Ithaca, she balanced motherhood with a career in New York state law and politics. She earned her law degree at Cornell University in 1943.

From 1962 until '74 Connie was a Republican assemblywoman. She co-wrote an abortion rights law, legalizing the procedure. The State Senate passed the Cook-Leicher bill in March 1970 calling for no restrictions. A month later the contentious bill was narrowly passed in amended form by the State Assembly. The bill's passage paved the way for the Supreme Court's landmark Roe v. Wade decision three years later.

Connie was the first woman vice president of Cornell from 1976 through '80. She took up the cause of an ordained Episcopal woman priest who was refused a licence in 1976. Connie put the case before the U.S. Equal Employment Opportunity Commission, which ruled in the priest's favour. As a result, the Episcopal Church passed a resolution declaring that "no one shall be denied access to ordination on the basis of sex."

Connie died in 2009 at the age of 89. Cornell's Advisory Committee on the Status of Women annually confers an award co-honouring her on students making positive contributions to women's issues.

Winnifred and their son Dave continued to run the resort, selling it in the late 1950s to Doug Gardner. Pat returned to the lake one time only in 1961. She walked the main Couch Island 938, now Camp Metagami, and was disappointed to encounter no one.

Alf Cook became president of Honey Butter Products in Ithaca, N.Y. His wife Connie was vice president of Cornell University. The Cooks settled on Island 884 near Couch in 1945 and later purchased Island 854. Alf entertained friends and family with French Canadian ballads and by playing his harmonica.

Logging Roads Encircle the Lake

All-season logging roads made their permanent appearance around the perimeter of Lake Temagami by the early 1960s as wood was cut further from the sawmills. Rumours were flying that certain roads were to be improved for residential development in areas such as Fasken's Point, Obabika Inlet and across from Camp Cayuga.

The Johns-Manville company built a road, now known as the Red Squirrel Road, to get at jack pine on the sand flats just north of Ferguson Bay. Running west from Highway 11 and passing north of Sandy Inlet, it was a dusty, noisy and ecological irritant for the Hodgins family who had bought Camp

Wanapitei from Ed Archibald in 1956. The road was lengthened in 1970 to gain access to jack pine through the Sharp Rock portage near Diamond Lake. It was opened to the public as far as a gate west of Wanapitei in 1972.

Cottagers in Shiningwood Bay were upset over an access road constructed into the bay in the early 1960s to facilitate log removal by Milne. They believed that this entry point was contributing to break-ins and creating a fire hazard.

"If the government permits main shoreline settlement, your past and present island isolation will be quickly destroyed; the scenic beauty of Lake Temagami ruined," Earl Rodgers declared. His presidency would soon come to an end, and the issues of access roads and mainland development would not again attain a high profile until the time of a 1971 coup d'état.

The lake's watchdog and defender of the Lake Temagami experience succumbed to cancer. A lands and forests Beaver arrived at Island 990 in summer 1961 to take him aboard for his final flight over his beloved lake. Island 990 ultimately ended up in the Smellie family. Mary Smellie, one of Earl's daughters, served as a director in the 1980s.

The Smellies and the Maurice "Mac" McKenzie Jr. family of Bear Island dealt with wrenching tragedy in summer 1988. Two young men from Toronto were killed when a Smellie boat came into collision with a McKenzie boat on a main channel at the northern point of Temagami Island. The Smellies' only son Brian died in his mid-30s in the early 1990s. He had been aboard the Smellie vessel when the accident occurred.

Earl's son Dr. Larry Rodgers, a Toronto pediatrician, purchased Island 318 near High Rock Island in 1971. He owned it until 1999 when Malcolm and Louise Wilson bought it. Louise is a daughter of the late Art Avard who became president in 1997. Malcolm was elected a director in 2007. Mary Smellie, her husband Gary and her brother Larry all died within weeks of each other in 2003. Island 990 was inherited by Lynn Hinds, a Smellie daughter.

CHAPTER 12

DEWEY DEROSIER: THE SHOWMAN

The 1961 AGM proceeded without a president or acting head for the only time in history. Members asked Dr. Sen. Joe Sullivan to accept the presidency. He declined, citing too many pans in the fire. Members then voted unanimously to entrust him with complete authority. Joe decided to ask Vice President John Rykert but he too refused, citing time constraints. Joe's next choice was Fish Committee Chair Dewey Derosier who accepted the offer.

Some members distrusted Dewey because of his involvement with the mining industry as a part-time prospector. However, he was enthusiastic and had some ambitious plans. He wrote to John Rykert, "I do hope to put a little more life into the Association from all angles. And I see no reason why we can't at least increase our membership by 50 per cent within the next year." While Earl Rodgers had done "an excellent job," he "carried about 90 per cent of the responsibility without the co-operation and assistance of some of the executive and committee members."

Dewey Takes Charge

Every year of Dewey's 10-year tenure yielded an increase in membership. With his boisterous personality, he was able to raise the Association's public profile to previously unheard of levels. The directory listed 150 members in 1961. By 1967 membership had more than doubled to 338. Dewey was also successful at boosting attendance at meetings, from about 50 during Earl's era to as many as 125. His bid to spread out executive responsibilities would not prove as successful.

Dewey's main focus was improving angling opportunities. One of the first things he did was buy a new 10-hp motor and a 16-foot steel boat for the new patrolman he hired. The patrolman's job was vastly expanded to include installing trap fences for catching suckers, thought by Dewey to consume walleye and lake trout spawn. He was to check all navigational aids and inspect all portage docks, so the Association could request government repairs. He was also expected to assist the collection of creel census information.

Seventy-five barrels marking shoals on secondary channels, which were retrieved by the patroller come autumn, were put out in 1963. The barrel program continued until the early 1980s when too many runaways and potential liability problems sank it.

Dewey made few executive changes by 1963, despite his earlier vow. Officers were the same ones who had served under Earl Rodgers, with Joe Sullivan as executive vice president, John Rykert as vice president and Russell

The Gooderhams aboard the *Annabell Lee* in the 1960s.
Clockwise from left: Tim, Sam the dog, Steve, Meg, Jane, Mary, Bill,
Sue, Nancey, Gerry, Pat and Cathie. *Photo: Gerry Gooderham*

Cleminshaw as secretary. One of the few new boys on the block was Bill Gooderham, joining the executive committee.

An Oakville, Ontario, accountant with a degree in forestry, Bill embarked on a relationship with the Association that would span a generation. He was a son of Gordon S. Gooderham who opened Camp Chimo in 1926. After his mother died in 1951, Bill ran Chimo with his father until 1958. Bill and his wife Nancey assumed the operation in 1958 following Gordon's death.

Dewey saw no redeeming qualities in ice fishing. "This is one of our greatest problems and will get worse if not checked in the near future," he wrote. "The increased use of auto

An Untimely Death

Stories abound about the colourful Chimo regattas. But how many know about the drowning of a Bear Island post manager off the Chimo dock?

Looking forward to a two-week canoe trip with his parents, Bill Gooderham bounded down to the dock one fall morning, only to discover the body of Bill Gourley, a Scotsman who had been the manager since 1941. He had apparently fallen out of a boat during the previous windy night. The incident fed grist to the rumour mills regarding the goings-on at Chimo, an outwardly dry lodge...but given the family's distillery past...Bill's father was not amused. Bill's nephew, young non-swimmer Tim Gooderham, caught his first look at a dead body. After glimpsing his possible future, a traumatized Tim decided learning to swim was a better alternative.

toboggans [snowmobiles] has enabled winter fishermen to go farther afield on the lake and catch more trout and leave more garbage and possible pollution. Your Association will keep pressing for a complete closing of winter fishing on Temagami Lake while we still have a few fish left and can still drink the water." He called ice fishermen "unwelcome winter visitors."

Negotiations were underway with the Temagami Mining Company to have more docks built at the end of the Mine Road. Dewey imposed the condition that a recently-granted liquor licence to Stan and Marion Liddiard be rescinded. The Liddiards built Camp Manito Hotel on Island 336 about 1956. Lou St. Germaine bought it and called it Ket-Chun-Eny Lodge. The Liddiards built again on Island 205 in 1963, transferring the Manito name. Their Mine Road landing docks were just a stone's throw away from the hotel. Dewey hoped that if the Manito couldn't serve alcohol, the ice fishers would go somewhere else.

The agenda at the 1963 AGM included a lengthy discussion about the feasibility of dredging a canal across McLean Peninsula between the South and Southwest arms. The pros included a short cut between the two arms and lower ONBL rates. The cons included the creation of a huge island, which might become a massive cottage subdivision. Tom Romans of Island 1250, attending his first AGM, concluded that this was not a serious organization if it could entertain such a notion. He didn't return to another meeting for 15 years. "Clearly, I now have a different view," he said, after serving as president from 1987 to '89.

The 1963 AGM marked the first time it was not held at Lakeview House. The historic Bear Island lodge would soon close. The new venue was Camp Wabun, the start of a tradition of rotating the meeting to different places.

Comings and Goings

A side view of Lakeview House in 1945.
The *Iona* passes by. *MacLean postcard photo: Reg Sinclair*

Dewey injected some new blood by 1964 while dropping the logging and Mine Road committees. After 13 years as secretary, Russell Cleminshaw passed his steno pad to Dr. Percy Ross of Island 213 and Detroit. Island 213 now belongs to Steven and Terese Wrightson of California. Russell died in 1968, followed by son James in 1997. Island 1113 and 1107, a second Cleminshaw holding, are now owned by the families of James, his brother Bill and sister Elizabeth Felix.

John Rykert stepped down as vice president in 1963. He rated a listing in the 1975-76 edition of *Who's Who in Canada*. At the time he was a director and treasurer of a Toronto investment trust and was involved with many volunteer boards. Five years later he took his life at the age of 51. He left behind his wife Carol and children Serena, Liz, Pam and John. Liz became a website consultant and is

---

2010 Members Who Couldn't Hitch a Trailer from Home

Daniel Carpenter Sr. of Island 1171 and Pembroke, Bermuda; Thea Cleminshaw of 1113 and London, U.K.; James Gray of 1200 and Paget, Bermuda; Tom Haladner of 234 and Ciudad, Panama; Herbert Schrade of 804 and Schwenningen, Germany; Lore Ulrich-Rommel of 150 and Weinstadt, Germany; Nancy Wiles of 25 and Victoria, Australia; William Willitts of 1219 and 1221, and Earlwood, Australia; and Jack Goodman Jr. of 352 and Mosman, Australia.

1963 Members Who Couldn't Hitch a Trailer from Home

Mel and Lela Saunders of 749 and 750, and Lima, Peru.

---

a published author. She is married to former Toronto mayor John Sewell. Pam was a gifted photographer who died suddenly in 2009 of a heart attack in her 48th year. Islands 307 and 308 belong to Serena, Liz and John.

Mel Saunders of islands 749 and 750 southwest of Temagami Island stepped into the vice president's shoes for a year, the same brief term as his successor Bill Gooderham. Mel was an International Petroleum executive living in Peru. He and his wife Lela retired to the lake and furnished their rustic cabin with exotic South American treasures.

The Saunders befriended many of their neighbours, including Dr. William Pace and his family of Ohio and Island 677. Bill first visited Temagami as a Wigwasati camper. His father William G. Pace Jr. bought the Newcomb Island 680 in 1952. Mel was largely responsible for the Paces' purchase of two snowmobiles and many winter trips to the lake in the 1960s and '70s.

Bill was a director from 1968 to '71. Mel was tragically killed when his snowmobile went through the ice on a Friday the 13th in 1973 while on his way to open a neighbour's cottage. Islands 749 and 750 are now owned by the Davis family of North Carolina.

Built Ford Tough

The Paces once resurrected a 1932 Model A Ford truck which had lain on its side in six metres of water behind the McMillens' Island 684. Local cottagers found the rusting carcass a great trolling spot until Bill Pace's son Tom decided to raise the truck from its watery grave. He dove and tied four large inner tubes to the corners and inflated them with an air tank aboard the Pace boat *I'm Tired II*.

Once towed to shore, Tom discovered three of four tires were still full of air. The fourth Goodyear tire was a bit low, so Ralph McMillen Jr. proceeded to fill it until it blew. "We guessed he was trying to see just how good the tires were from the company his father worked for," Tom jested. Surprisingly, the Paces were able to turn the engine over, though their plans to rebuild the body never materialized. The only part left in 2010 was the engine. "If anyone wants it, please take it!" Tom added.

A second 1932 Model A Ford truck remains in its aqueous resting place. Owned by Gordon S. Gooderham, it was used to haul supplies around Chimo Island and to bring blocks of ice for the icehouse. It was lost through the ice in about 20 metres of water at Skull Narrows behind Boatline Bay in 1943. While scuba diving in the early 1980s, Gordon's grandson Gerry Gooderham removed the ignition key. He still has it.

Sparks Fly

Hydro lines were strung down the Mine Road in 1963 and nearby residents were slated for service. Chessman Kittredge Jr., one of Chess Sr.'s five children, sent letters to all members that winter, apprising them of Ontario Hydro's plan to string wires from island to island. He enclosed a photo showing wires running from the mainland to Manito Island 205. Chess's action stirred up a brouhaha. Dewey felt Chess had circumvented proper channels and accused him of "harassment." Joe Sullivan echoed his words, labelling his campaign "intimidation."

Due to maintenance costs, Ontario Hydro decided water crossings would be via underwater cable, much to everyone's relief. However, the Association wasn't ready to move on. At the 1964 AGM Dewey demanded disciplinary action. Joe moved that the constitution be amended to include a bylaw giving the executive the power to oust any member discrediting or interfering with the executive.

The resolution was passed but not before it was amended to say that a decision to expel a member would be subject to appeal at the following AGM. Members were unsettled by the harshness of the original motion because it vested the executive excessive authority, and because the Kittredges were well-respected.

Once the main underwater cables were placed in the lake, many cottagers balked at having to pay for cables running to their islands. In addition, potential hydro customers had to reside within 30 cottages per mile at standard rates or 15 cottages per mile at double rates. Most eligible cottagers opted to stay off the grid. In some high density areas neighbours eventually shared cable costs.

Chess Kittredge Jr. was given Kokomis Island 1155 on the North Arm in 1918 by his grandfather Albert Gifford as a 'getting born present.' In the late 1920s the family leased Granny Island 1158. Chess attended Keewaydin from 1926 to '31. After retiring in the late 1960s as an auto products executive, he became the president of an Ohio tree nursery. He went on to work for the Association after the 1971 coup and revamped its constitution.

Kokomis

An Anishnabek oral legend tells the story of a cranky manitou, or spirit, who turned his elderly wife Kokomis to stone, according to The Keewaydin Way (2004) by Brian Back. The rock formation perched on the shore of Granny Island bears a resemblance to a small woman and was a local shrine where tobacco offerings were left for good fortune.

The Association was "like a corporation being run by a single man. If I stood to ask a question at the annual meeting, Dewey would say "Sit down! You're out of order!" Chess recalled. He died in 1998. Chess Sr.'s descendants share the two family isles. His grandson Chip Kittredge, who tripped at Keewaydin as a camper and staffer in the 1970s, was elected a director in 2007.

Today's TLA Bylaws were kick-started by the Kittredge controversy. They state that the decision to expel a member must be made at a board meeting called for that purpose, by a resolution passed by a two-thirds majority vote of directors. There is no provision to appeal the decision or to reapply for membership. No member has ever been ousted.

Trees Take Centre Stage

Vandalism of trees on private property, for which the OPP couldn't investigate or lay charges, was vexing the Association in 1965. Under the Ontario Public Lands Act, timber on many private rural lands was reserved to the Crown. Thereby, the Department of Lands and Forests could license a lumber company to harvest the trees without having to pay compensation to the landowner. Should a landowner cut down his trees, he was expected to get permission in writing first and then compensate the department. These restrictions applied even if the trees were diseased or damaged, or about to crush the boathouse. Dead trees were the exception.

The reserves were applied unevenly on the lake. Some leases and deeds reserved timber rights, others did not, and some specified pine trees only. It all depended on what year the Crown land was leased or patented. They were often ignored by islanders who sawed dock cribs and cabin footings from their own cedar assets. Frank Preston, Harry Smith, Dewey and others built cabins from standing pine.

Joe Sullivan made a motion at the 1965 AGM for the Crown reserves to be overturned. Rarely if ever enforced, they were lifted in the early 1970s. Mineral rights are still reserved to the Crown though most islands are withdrawn from staking. Ontario phased out leases on cottage lots in 1988 and now grants patents only.

Smokey Goes Undercover

The OPP and the Association maintained close ties during Dewey's presidency. Earl Cooke and Jack Burke became cottagers and members. Both were transferred to the Temagami Detachment in 1963. Its manpower doubled, going to eight officers plus a new commander, to deal with an increase in crime.

Herb Stokinger thanked the OPP on behalf of the Association at the 1965 AGM. "They seem to be constantly apprehending the same criminals who are responsible for the break-ins and vandalism on Temagami Lake," Dewey noted. "The discouraging part of it is the leniency of the court in dealing out sentences to those habitual criminals."

Due to his previous experience in northwestern Ontario, Jack Burke was assigned to Lake Temagami policing issues. His first assignment, to conduct a clandestine investigation of a rash of cottage and post break-ins, occurred shortly after he arrived in June of 1963 – as a newlywed of one week.

"I was an unknown face to the community and I, accompanied by my new bride [Cecile], spent a week undercover on Lake Temagami, posing as tourists. My wife and I were given a 16' steel skiff somewhere along the Mine Road and off we went. We had no idea how long we were to play this game and few resources. A portable Coleman stove, a few cans of wieners and beans, a few clothes and toiletries, and we were on our way," Jack recalled.

"We arrived at Red Pines Island and were met by Newk and Pearl Newcomb. We settled into a small log cabin on the south end of the island with a pretty good view of Bear Island. It had no electricity and a kerosene lamp was the only light. We had dinner with the Newcombs and at dusk I left my lovely bride and locked myself into the Hudson's Bay warehouse to spend the first of many lonely nights waiting for the inevitable break-in to occur."

The Post Abuzz

The post continued to be a gathering place for cottagers, tourists and youth camp canoeists. "In its heyday, the post was so big it had branches and it ran like a department store," said Patricia Delarosbel, née Lowery, then a Temagami Island cottager working in the tuck shop in the mid-1960s. There was Joe Lanoie in the boathouse, Louise Friday in dry goods, Doug Drake in souvenirs, Bernadette Gibson in the post office, and John McKenzie, a shelf stacker and "floater," she recalled. Patricia was the first female tuck shop employee, and it wasn't unusual to sell $200 worth of candy, snacks and drinks in a day. That's the equivalent of $1,360 today.

A Bear Island chef concocted "good solid Canadian food" and there were usually dinner guests. "The Newcombs were great hosts and Newk was an amazing storyteller. One evening he sang us his version of the "Temagami Song." He also invited us to use the 'bath house' which was his pride and joy. It was situated on the east side of the island, not far from our little cabin. As the years went by, we would boat by the island on occasion and fondly point out our little cabin and the bath house to our growing family and tell the story of how we came to be there."

On his last night staking out the post warehouse, Jack heard several boisterous youths approaching the door. He knew he was outnumbered and wouldn't be able to arrest them all. Suddenly, he heard a loud explosion. It was the post manager who had heard the commotion and fired a warning shot with his 12-gauge shotgun. The young people quickly dispersed and the undercover assignment was terminated the following day. "In today's policing environment, this type of operation would never be undertaken," Jack remarked. "As a police and TLA venture, it was a joint public relations success which very few people are aware of."

In Jack's day, Bear Island elders were very supportive of marine patrols. "I so clearly remember docking the police boat at the MNR [forestry base] dock and walking the boardwalk on a Monday morning. Somewhere along the way, I would be asked in for a cup of tea. In the following gossip, over a cup of tea, I would have a pretty good idea of where the parties had taken place over the weekend."

Officers like Jack often worked solo, a practice unheard of today. When making arrests in town, he could always count on some civic-minded civilian jumping into the cruiser and driving it to the OPP station, while he struggled with an uncooperative passenger in the back seat.

Jack and Cecile bought one and a half acres on Chimo Island 665 in 1969. They put up a Pan Abode cottage and some outbuildings. Jack was transferred out of Temagami in 1972 and retired from the OPP in 1993. He and Cecile live in Barrie, Ontario, and stay at the cottage from mid-May through October. Their three daughters are frequent visitors.

Temagami Detachment's Earl Cooke and his wife Terry bought Island 582 near the top of the Southwest Arm about 1965. They built cabins with the help of friends and fellow officers. After Earl was transferred to North Bay, he kept the cottage and used it extensively. His health later deteriorated and he sold the island in 2003 to Doug Davis of Columbus, Ohio. Earl died in 2005.

Nowadays Bear Island is policed by its own First Nation Constable Tom Saville. A program was introduced by the OPP in 1975 allowing Indian reserves to be policed by trained aboriginal residents. John McKenzie was the first Bear Island constable, from 1978 until his retirement in 2008. He was serving his second term as TAA chief in 2010.

Eying the Huts

The patrolman's duties expanded to take in the enforcement of game and fish regulations, following his appointment as a deputy game warden. The Association bought him "the best autoboggan on the market" so he could check ice huts in any weather. Dewey had a winter home in North Bay and arranged for the patrolman to live at his cabin near the Mine Landing "where he can keep a close eye on the fishermen who use the mine road and where he is handy to the mine telephone when needed for help," Dewey wrote.

The Toronto *Globe and Mail* ran a story about a petition submitted to the Ontario legislature by the Association in 1965 requesting a complete halt to ice fishing, after the chamber of commerce started holding a

Sail Away
TO A LAKELAND PARADISE

D. S. AUBRY COUSENS, V.C.
Snack Bar on Board

LAKE
TEMAGAMI
Special Daily Cruise Fare

Prices on Application at the Dock Office
CHILDREN: Under 5 Years FREE
Under 10 Years HALF FARE
12

SIX HOURS
CRUISING A LAKELAND PARADISE

Cover of the 1966 Shell boat line schedule – the final T-Station schedule, marking the passenger boat era's demise. Note the spelling of the *Aubrey Cosens VC* and the handwritten correction. *Courtesy: Jack Glenn*

winter fishing derby. Chamber representative Butch Spooner branded Association members "selfish and hypocritical" in the *Globe* article, saying that they wanted the lake closed except in summer. He again wrongly asserted, thus perpetuating the myth, that the majority of cottagers were American.

The Ontario Northland Transportation Commission sold its ONBL holdings, including the docks, boats and restaurant, to Shell Canada in 1965. Shell's focus was the ONBL Highway 11 property rather than the traditional boat service. The gas station and restaurant were profitable while the boat line bled $26,000 in the single 1966 season that Shell ran it.

Boatline Bay is Born

Partners Bill Swift and Ron Johnstone formed the Temagami Development Corporation and acquired the boat line, a shell of its former self, thanks to the Mine Road. Bill's agreement to the partnership hinged on finding a boat terminal site with road access near the centre of the lake. Relocating there would reduce passenger and freight rates by eliminating 19 kilometres of the Northeast Arm. They reached a deal with the Department of Lands and Forests. The ONBL's Fasken's Point was traded for the road accessible Twelve Mile Point, soon to be known as Boatline Bay. The department turned Fasken's Point into a campsite.

At the 1966 AGM the membership approved relocating the boat service in principle, thereby acquiescing to the creation of a new access point. A caveat attached to the motion stated "that the Association maintain its frequently resolved position against further development of the mainland shoreline."

Bill and Ron began to develop the 10-acre property in 1967. Ron took out a mining lease on the Briggs landfill site and had 150,000 yards of gravel fill brought to the bay. A row of red pine provided dock cribs and held the fill. The office was a four-unit motel the men purchased from organizers of Expo '67. They hauled it from Montreal and put it back together. They began offering passenger and freight service in summer 1967.

The Temagami Development Corporation acquired some of the ONBL vessels from Shell. They included the *Vedette*, *Ramona*, *Ojibway* and *Grey Owl*. The *Ramona* was discarded after the 1972 season. Others broke down or wore out and were replaced by more practical, but less charming taxi boats. The ONBL sold

Sail Away
TO THE LAKELAND PARADISE
LAKE
TEMAGAMI
SPECIAL DAILY CRUISE

Featuring New Modern Boat
"TEMAGAMI BELLE"

All Service From Our New Location
at BOAT LINE BAY
On the Temagami Mine Road
Turn Four Miles South of the Town of Temagami

CRUISE FARE $3.00
CHILDREN (under 12 years) HALF FARE

Two and One-half Hours Cruising a Lakeland Paradise

Leaves Boat Line Bay 10.15 a.m.
July 3rd to September 3rd

1967 boat line schedule, the first season Ron Johnstone and Bill Swift ran the service out of Boatline Bay. *Courtesy: Jack Glenn*

Roger Robbins and Bill Johnson rebuild White Bear's front dock
in June 1961 in preparation for its reopening as a youth camp. *Photo: John Eberhard*

two barges. The *Temagami Copper* went to Copperfields Mine and later the TFN and the other, the *Cross Lake II*, eventually went to Berubé Repairs Limited. Ron and Bill operated Boatline Bay for 15 years, keeping parking rates at $1 per day.

From 1965 to '71 Ron was the Association's vice president. In 1961 he and his wife Mickey, from London, Ontario, had purchased Camp White Bear, once a secluded playground for Hollywood stars. They opened a camp for boys in July and girls in August.

The First Board of Directors

The Association amended its constitution in 1967 to incorporate an eight-member board of directors, elected by a show of hands at the AGM. The executive positions, previously elected annually by a show of hands, would now be elected by the board. Inaugural directors were Dewey Derosier, Joe Sullivan, Jack Moulton, Percy Ross, C.F. Nichols, Doug Gardner, Herb Stokinger and Ron Johnstone. Considerable discussion ensued as to whether Joe's role as executive vice president was superfluous, and how to define his duties. The Association decided to retain this position and defined it as "in charge of good will."

During the AGM Chief Ranger John Rumney reported that Northeast Arm Island 150, and Alexander Island 992 and Island 993, both west of Bear Island, were being surveyed for squared subdivisions. Association officers responded by asking about winter brown foliage on pine trees. John replied that it's a

natural occurrence. The issue of small plots, laid out row upon row, spoiling the unique landscape, wouldn't gain traction as a serious threat until the Association reinvented itself four years later.

A plan was afoot in 1968 to open up the shoreline west from Temagami for a distance of more than 6.5 kilometres and build private mainland dwellings. "Our Association will protest vigorously any extensive opening for development along the south shore of the northeast arm and down to Shiningwood Bay," Dewey vowed.

An Improvement District

Temagami became an improvement district in 1968. The boundaries stretched down the Northeast Arm to include Temagami Island, the mine there being a good source of tax revenue. The Association objected to the boundaries, saying services to lake dwellers would be non-existent and they should not have to subsidize village commercial development.

Many Temagami residents weren't happy either, taking exception to the district's appointed, rather than elected, representatives being thrust on them. The Department of Lands and Forests unveiled a proposed Lake Temagami land use plan at public sessions in summer 1971; Northeast Arm mainland development formed a cornerstone.

By 1970 the growing village of 500 was desperate for a sewerage system so raw sewage would no longer flow into the Northeast Arm. An urban renewal study pegged sewerage costs

What's in a Name?

Temagami is derived from the Anishnabek words for deep 'Teme' and water 'Augaming.' In 1906 Canada's Board on Geographical Names decided the proper spelling was Timagami. Local residents and provincial agencies continued to use the traditional 'Tem' spelling, while federal agencies adopted the 'Tim' spelling. For more than 60 years, the sign at the train station read 'Tem' while the post office shingle read 'Tim.' When the province established the Improvement District of Temagami, the spelling of the lake, island and river was officially declared Temagami. The Association used the 'Tim' rendition in its early years.

from $400,000 to $1 million. The Ministry of the Environment (MOE) set the cost at $2.5 million, seen by Phil Hoffman, chair of the improvement district, as a "politically inspired" way to nix sewerage system plans.

He authored a 1970 flyer titled "Why Should this Village die?" after Ontario froze Temagami development. Phil wrote about the intention of the province to move residents to a new townsite, away from the lake-based tourism on which many depended. "Is Ontario to become a totalitarian society, in which people are forced to move without consultation, without debate, and as a result of bureaucratic decisions?"

The development of Sherman Mine had begun in the mid-1960s. Many believed that the development ban was tied to a concern

that once the mine was operational, flying rocks from blasting could result in injuries and property damage. The Temagami North townsite became an essential community as Temagami proper lacked land for outward expansion to house mine workers, being bounded by rocky hills and lakes.

Temagami got its sewerage works in 1978 when a low-pressure system, the first of its kind in Ontario, was installed. It uses grinder pumps to keep the pressure in the pipes low. This allowed pipes to be run under just two to three feet of ground cover. It's ideally suited to Temagami's rocky terrain where traditional sewers, dependent on gravity, would have entailed blasting down to three or four times that depth.

The Temagami Mining Company began trying to unload the Mine Road in the mid-1960s. The Department of Highways was subsidizing maintenance costs and the gate levies helped. The company reached a maintenance agreement with the improvement district by 1970, a move opposed by the Association. It had asked the Department of Highways to take over the road.

Dewey's Grand Plan

Dewey criticized the methods and locations of the Department of Lands and Forests fingerling aerial plantings. Young lake trout were dropped in water that was too deep and at the wrong temperature, he said. The department agreed to allow observers on the scene to "verify our complaints." He noted that allocations to Lake Temagami would not be increased, even though a new fish hatchery had opened in North Bay.

Taking matters into his own hands, he informed the membership in winter 1968 that a planned headquarters building would include a basement trout and walleye hatchery. "The main obstacle to the hatchery plan is the Department of Lands and Forests and the Fish and Wildlife Division. They feel we are infringing on their rights," Dewey wrote. However, "we intend to stick with it."

The province managed all stocking programs until the 1980s, when it began encouraging public participation under government guidelines – hence the birth of the successful Temagami Area Fish Involvement Program (TAFIP). Dewey convinced the department in 1969 to stock 30,000 yearling trout, three times the usual number. He regarded this as one of the Association's greatest achievements but it did not deter him from his hatchery scheme.

He was busy in 1968 seeking land near the end of the Mine Road. A mainland site close to the parking lots was leased due to the availability of pure spring well water, hydro, telephone, and road and water access. The building would serve as another case of mainland development by the very organization which had come into existence with a strong mandate to preserve Lake Temagami's shoreline in its natural state.

The TLA building was still beckoning cottagers to stay a while and chat through 2010.
Photo: Pam Sinclair

The irony of the situation was not lost on a number of members.

Just a year earlier Dewey had vociferously disparaged a proposal to build private homes along the shoreline of the Northeast Arm. He had also opposed the relocation of the boat line to Twelve Mile Point in 1966. "In my opinion, that was the opening gun for public development of the shoreline of Lake Temagami," he later said. He was now ready to fire the next round.

Dewey was soon circulating pledge forms to cover the building costs, estimated at $30,000. Sherman Mine donated $8,000 while Copperfields Mine gave $2,500. A 1968 Department of Lands and Forests letter to the Association's lawyer spelled out the regulations: "No person shall take any fish or spawn from Ontario waters, or have such fish or spawn in possession for the purpose of stocking or artificial breeding except with written authority of the Minister."

"It is highly unlikely that such authority would be granted, since Temagami Lake is the property of the Crown and the fisheries management there is this Department's responsibility," the letter added. Joe Sullivan responded with his support of the hatchery, using Canadian Senate rather than Association letterhead, a move that would likely prompt a scandal today.

Dewey sold White Gables to Bob and Cathy Brown in 1968 and retired to North Bay. John Seguin, a neighbour of Dewey in both North Bay and Temagami, was the general contractor for the headquarters building. The two-bedroom raised bungalow, completed in 1971, cost $28,000.

By that time Lands and Forests Minister Rene Brunelle had confirmed that the Association could not stock fish in public waters. Not one to easily admit defeat, Dewey later said the hatchery plan was axed because government biologists in Toronto were afraid that he would be so successful he would put them to shame. Hope springs eternal: "The plans are still to use part of the building for research and hatchery under government supervision if the need should arise in the future, with the Minister's permission." The building has never raised a single fingerling.

Many members were already red-faced over the headquarters building fiasco when the *North Bay Nugget* ran a story describing how a 70-year-old ban on mainland development was broken. While noting some earlier lapses in the policy, the newspaper focused on the Association's bungalow and the mine's posh executive lodge on the Northeast Arm. Sherman Lodge's fate was sealed in 1995 when Township of Temagami Council voted unanimously to have it torn down – with the TLA's best wishes.

A Tornado Strikes

Instead of a political firestorm, the lake was struck by a vicious tornado around the dinner hour one day during summer 1969. Bob and Marie Richmond had just bought a cottage on Island 1058 and had to rebuild after the violent storm almost levelled their property. The twister also toppled the Bear Island fire tower and cut a still-visible swath across Bear Island.

Boyd and Rose Matchett of Island 989 were away when the twister struck. They lost 60 mature red and white pine which they replaced; the hand-planted trees have since thrived. "The tornado tipped over a bunky, more of a shack; we were very lucky other buildings on the island were spared," Boyd said in retrospect.

Pam Morgan was a teenager returning to the cottage following a trip to Bear Island that fateful day with her boyfriend and younger brother Jay Myers. They hadn't gotten far when the wind churned up treacherous waves which crashed over the transom. She turned back to Bear Island and made land just as the boat sank like a stone. Pam's parents Everett and Jean Myers owned Island 1128 on the Northwest Arm.

CHAPTER 13

THE PALACE REVOLUTION

At the 1970 AGM an avid nature lover from Troy, New York, spoke ardently about the need for the Association to broaden its activity base. He proposed a land use planning committee – a formal body that would respond to development plans by the Department of Lands and Forests. The department had already sold off 22 cottage strip lots on Narrows Island 660 and was planning subdivisions elsewhere, some on mainland. The Narrows Island project had gone through with nary a peep of protest from the Association.

Jim Flosdorf, an English professor, was appointed to chair the new Committee on Land Use and Environment (CLUE). Jim had witnessed first-hand the devastating effects of uncontrolled development. His family had a cottage on a man-made lake in the Pocono Mountains of Pennsylvania, which had been spoiled by reckless overdevelopment. "It was so bad that the water was coffee brown with displaced mud from bulldozing along the river, and a black oil slick from outboard motors left a line on all the boats moored in the lake," he said. "There was practically wall-to-wall cottages and houses all along the shore. It was the playground for swarms of people from New York City and Philadelphia."

Jim learned about Temagami from Bill Plumstead when they were graduate students.

One of the many islets dotting the lake. *Photo: Jack Goodman*

Also a professor, Bill has been a cottager on Island 658 since 1955. He invited Jim to help open up in 1958. Jim fell hard for the lake's charms and began looking for his own place. He bought Island 588 on the Southwest Arm in 1961 from a distant relative of Bill – sight unseen.

CLUE was the first step non-board members took to steer the Association in the direction of environmental issues. Jim brought in CLUE members Bill Plumstead and Doug Buck, Milne's woodlands manager since 1966 who, with his wife Marianne, bought a cottage on Island 300 in Shiningwood Bay. Others he recruited were Jack Goodman, a Chappaqua, N.Y. publisher and a cottager since 1953; and Don Fraser, the only Association veteran.

Dewey's last presidential actions were to increase annual dues and change the membership structure. Earl Rodgers' Class A, B and C memberships were merged into a Class A, covering all private and commercial property owners who would pay $25. Class D associate members remained intact though dues rose to $10 from $5.

Eager to get down to work, CLUE was not supported by some board members, including Dewey and Joe Sullivan. A groundswell of opposition rose against the old order. The reformers thought of the Association as a fishing club.

The first meeting was held at Jim Flosdorf's island. Some 30 disgruntled members sat on folding chairs and boat cushions in a blueberry patch in front of his cabin. The rebels' strategy included enlarging their pool of support. The

time and place to topple Dewey's regime in a coup d'état was set for the August 1971 AGM, to be held at Camp Temagami. It worked. The executive was swept out of office in what was called "the palace revolution." After the smoke cleared, a new slate and a new era were ushered in.

Vice President Ron Johnstone offered his recollections of the coup: "In the midst of the 1971 revolution, Dewey turned to me and indicated that he didn't know how to handle all the questions, and would I take over and chair the meeting. Both he and I had been challenged and accused of running a closed shop. I had tried to get Dewey to hear the concerned members at an executive meeting. I am sure that it would have answered the concerns and there would have been no need for a public challenge – but it was not to be."

Bill Pace was one of the ousted directors. He gave a speech of resignation with the understanding that the rest of what he called the "rubber stamp slate" would do likewise. Board members hated to depart under trying circumstances and never abandoned the conviction they had done a great deal of good for cottagers. Bill died in 1996. His youngest child Tom Pace and Tom's wife Linda from Columbus, Ohio, now enjoy Island 677.

Since the coup Dewey has been branded "a dictator" and "a man of great rigidity" running "a tight ship" with "a self-perpetuating executive." Others remember him as a "sincere man," "a hard worker," "a spark plug" and "Mr. Association." Ron, Dewey's vice president for six years, summed up his polarizing persona well: "He was a kind and gentle man who was quite rough around the edges, but had a heart as big as Temagami country."

While Earl had turned the Association into a virtual oligarchy, it differed from the regime Dewey created. Earl was so admired that one colleague called him "a saint." While he tried to get a handle on all diverse issues that came his way, Dewey chose the issues that inspired him and neglected others. The membership allowed Earl as much control as he wanted. Dewey seized control and was not willing to delegate.

Earl the watchdog was all about defending core members' interests. Growing the Association into a political tour de force took second stage. Dewey the showman dreamed big and drew many new members with his energy and passion, but his tunnel vision set the Association on a narrow course. These days, directors (and potential presidents) can only serve two three-year terms before they are required by bylaw to take a two-year breather to smell the balsams.

Dewey's legacy is the TLA building, much maligned over the years for its mainland location, but a boon for past and current uses as a communications centre, post office, library, rental home, administrative office, meeting quarters, shop, Internet access provider, and a gathering place for the annual flea market, welcome back barbecue and mid-summer corn roast.

Dewey was crestfallen at the loss of his Association, central to his life for the past 10 years. The new board tried to lessen the blow by making him an honourary life director. He attended one more AGM, circa 1980, to listen to a discussion about a proposed copper mine behind the North Arm's Ferguson Mountain which never went into production.

Four years after the coup, his wife Kathryn died. He was as feisty as ever at age 79 and got married again to a woman he met through the Golden Age Club. He stayed active and in the spotlight until the day he suddenly died in 1981, right after performing in a seniors' club skit.

Spurred by 1970s director John Everett "Ev" Choat, who transformed the building from a liability into an asset, the Association placed a Dewey Derosier commemorative plaque inside the building in 1982. It is inscribed: "It was through his endeavours and foresight that this building was conceived and erected in 1970."

Joe Sullivan continued to serve as a figurehead executive vice president. He was made an honourary life member in 1973. He remained in contact with several board members and attended some AGMs through the early 1980s. His long and fulfilling life came to an end in 1989. His cottage is now owned by Richard and Dawna Armstrong, Canadian expats living in Texas.

CHAPTER 14

THE WINDS OF CHANGE

By the time of the coup d'état, the clock was ticking down on several fronts. The Mine Road had sounded the death knell of large passenger boats. The *Aubrey Cosens VC* rammed a dock at Wanapitei in 1966. Her remains were trucked to Marten River in 1969 for rebirth as a restaurant but she was destroyed by fire.

Lakeland Airways owner Bob Gareh and marine rental shop owner "Trapper" Tom Warring tried to revive the passenger boat era in 1982 by bringing in a 44-foot cruise boat. The *Trapper Tom* made a daily cruise to Bear Island, a Wednesday evening dinner cruise and could be chartered. The vessel didn't lure enough tourists and the venture sank after three seasons.

Sellers and Buyers

Tourist resorts on islands near the end of the Mine Road included White Gables, Ket-Chun-Eny, Adanac and Can-Usa, and the newer Manito and Malabar. This central area became known as the Hub.

Some resorts were shuttered for good in the mid-1960s including Friday's and Lakeview House. Friday's was hurt by the disappearance of deer (and deer hunters) in Temagami by 1965 due to severe winter snowfalls and an intestinal infection carried by moose. Lakeview House became the Temagami Indian Band's recreation centre.

In 1971 Stanley and Laura Belle Hodgins' sons Bruce and Larry and their wives Carol and Nancy, along with some associates, formed a co-operative company. They bought and reorganized Camp Wanapitei. A Trent University history professor, Bruce soon became active in the Association.

Wanapitei head guide Dick Twain (1956-78) shows campers how to sharpen an axe.
Photo: John Clarke in Wanapitei on Temagami by Bruce W. Hodgins

Doug Gardner closed Camp Temagami in 1972 after 69 years in operation. His Metagami

143

In Simpatico

Bruce Hodgins and Camp Wanapitei have always enjoyed good relations with the Anishnabai, supporting their land claim and employing them. Bella White worked at Wanapitei for more than four decades. Her mother Charlotte (McLean) Morrison was one of Caroline Brown's sisters. Caroline spent decades as a cook at Keewaydin. Bella passed away in 1998.

Bella's daughter Bunny Miller is a respected Temagami resident. She, along with others, has raised more than $40,000 for the Canadian Cancer Society. A cancer survivor, she ran a non-profit used clothing shop called Bunny's Boutique in the 1990s and sent children with cancer to camp. Variety shows are another innovative fundraiser she has been involved with. Bunny and friends craft frustration-venting "Dammit Dolls," which they give to Temiskaming Hospital chemotherapy patients and soldiers serving in Afghanistan. In recent years the name has come to apply to the women themselves. They spread cheer and small gifts wherever needed.

its construction from Cross Lake using the camp launch the *Nanette*, according to Carol Cochrane. Gerald kept the building intact as a large living-dining room while adding bedrooms and a kitchen. The dining lodge is also a refitted cottage. Trout Island 759 is now owned by Donald and Cameron Crawford. The *Nanette* is long gone from the lake though her boathouse remains (see Chapter 11). Deacon's Island 762, where Bill Russell had a cabin, was sold to former Camp Temagami staff member Dick Grant.

Toronto-area residents Don and Donna Battersby purchased Metagami from the Pearson family of New York in 1973. The Battersbys had discovered the lake a few months earlier, staying at nearby Island 948. The Battersbys continued the on-going endeavour of fixing up the old place, even cement-basing some of the cabins because they were sinking. They later built a less labour-intensive cottage. Someone filched the original Metagami boathouse twig sign about 1999, which they replaced with arched plywood lettering.

Windshift, a small boys' camp on Island 1222 in Sharp Rock Inlet shut down in 1971 after 21 years in operation, according to Ottertooth.com. Owner Oliver Quickmire reopened from 1973 to '78 on the nearby smaller Island 1219. A new camp called Langskib opened at the former Windshift site, run by David and Karen Knudsen. It emphasized survivor-oriented boys' canoe tripping. Cayuga and Wabikon were closed by 1970 but both were soon back in business, with Gordon Wolfe at Wabikon and Don and Jeri Moore at Cayuga, now co-

girls' camp closed about a year earlier. Doug's cottage on Kabekwabika Island 765 was turned over to his children Ann, Susan and Robert after his death in 1999.

The core of the Camp Temagami property was transformed into cottage lots. Gerald Kluwak purchased the adult lodge on Island 758. Gib Cochrane had towed all the logs for

ed and called Lorien Wilderness. Gordon and Don were both briefly involved with the TLA.

The Graftons sold Camp Wigwasati, meaning "birch" in Anishnabek, to two Maryland teachers in 1967. They ran the boys' camp until 1978. Clarence Gallagher was a long-time Wigwasati

The *Naiad*'s bow as she departs Camp Temagami. The small brass cannon was fired to announce her arrivals and departures.
Photo: Robert Gardner

doctor until the camp closed in 1965. He then served as Wabun physician for many years. His son Michael was a Wigwasati camper and staffman from 1955 until '65. He also lent Wabun a medical hand as did sisters Marilee Gallagher and Molly Henn, owner of Island 757. In summer 1994 all four Gallaghers were Wabun doctors. Michael died in 2008. His wife Mary Beth maintains their cottage on Ogama Island 843.

Wigwasati staffman Gordon Deeks, a former senior Camp Temagami staff member, formed Pays d'en Haut in 1975. Jim Tatman, another staffman, partnered with Gordon in 1977 and the pair took over the Wigwasati site in 1979, offering adult and youth co-ed canoe trips.

After nearly 140 years on Lake Temagami, the Hudson's Bay Company sold the post to Bill and Joan Zufelt in 1970, financially backed by several cottagers. They had recently operated

Zufelt's Camp, comprised of a snack bar, store, water taxi and gas bar near the Manito Landing. Zufelt's was sold in 1971 becoming Malabar and overnight accommodation was added. Bill and Niki Plumstead bought and renamed it Loon Lodge in 1973. Their Wednesday smorgasbord dinners enticed hordes of cottagers. The Plumsteads also offered accommodations, a craft shop and taxi service.

The Zufelts ran their Bear Island Bay Post for four years while beset with business losses, break-ins and vandalism. Gary Potts' brother Henry Potts attempted to fill the void by running a small band-sponsored grocery store in the old Bear Island community hall, starting in 1976.

Stan and Marion Liddiard sold Camp Manito Hotel but had to repossess it a year later. Under the ownership of Glenn and Barbara Fehrman, from 1974 to '86, Manito became "the place to go on a Saturday night." Lounge entertainment included *Suckergut*, a musical duo composed of cousins Wayne Potts and Ted Leduc who wrote a ditty called "Manito." Wayne's oldest brother Gary raised the roof and brought it down with local hits such as "Bear Island Man." The late great blues-rock-jazz musician Jeff Healey performed there in 1984 and '85. Following the Fehrmans' departure to sell real estate, Manito was briefly in the hands of two other owners. It was converted to administrative purposes for the Teme-Augama Anishnabai (TAA) in 1991.

Chimo Bids Adieu

Chimo closed its doors in 1974 after 48 years of treating guests to a taste of the Temagami experience. Many property owners were introduced to the lake at Chimo. In one of its last brochures, the resort charged $94.50 weekly for a cabin for four. Guests paid extra for boats, motors and guides, but camp excursions to the post were complimentary.

A legion of locals, spanning three generations, worked as guides and staff members, including: Charles Paul, Donald McKenzie, David Faubert, Maurice McKenzie, George Peshabo, George Becker, Joe Laronde, Kush Paul, Shorty Belanger, Felix

Longhi, Willie Turner, Pete Commanda, Sonny Doucette, Alex Laronde, Walter Becker, Vincent Laronde, Dennis Laronde, Albert LaLonde, Raymond Becker and Gary Potts.

For young Bear Island women, it was almost a rite of passage to work at least a few summers at Chimo, in the kitchen, waiting tables or cleaning cabins. The Gooderhams carried their weight as well, starting with Gordon Stuart, then his son Bill and his wife Nancey, Bill's brother Gordon Alexander, Gordon A.'s son Tim and spouse Cathie, their kids Megan and Steve, and Bill and Nancey's children Gerry, Patricia, Susan, Jane and Mary.

Much of the property was purchased by real estate developer Joe Shaw of Aurora, Ontario, and divided into cottage lots. The Gooderhams' guest launch the *Chimo III* also came into Joe's hands and was eventually sold to Muskoka cottagers who restored her to exhibit at boat shows.

Chimo servers in the 1960s. From left, unidentified, Bonnie Price, Bonnie Hut, Linda (Potts) Mathias, unidentified.
Photo: Gerry Gooderham

Mine Road Goes to the Ducks

Copperfields Mine closed by summer 1972. Once the richest high-grade copper mine in Canada, it had made relatively few waves on the lake despite earlier concerns. Mining activity was mainly confined to the interior of Temagami Island. The road had been in terrible condition since 1970. Tim Gooderham recalled rounding a bend that summer and having to brake for a family of ducks swimming, not waddling, across. The Temagami Improvement District said it couldn't afford upkeep costs, prompting calls again from the Association to turn the road over to the Department of Highways. The toll gate was removed and the parking lots became public, supervised by the Department of Lands and Forests.

Tim followed up with a tale of unrelenting rain in spring 1998, which became front page *Temagami Times* news. He described a creek running smack down the middle of the road that washed it out for 90 metres. It had never happened before and the new Municipality of Temagami was forced to post "road closed" signs while it imported ton after ton of gravel.

There were more than 500 property owners on the lake by 1971, 60 per cent of them Canadian. More began enjoying the winter wonderland for cross country skiing, ice fishing, snowmobiling and snowshoeing. Many central cottages had or would soon get hydro, which had arrived on Bear Island in 1965. The advent of electricity ushered in a sea change. Some went for indoor plumbing and water heaters, two-channel TV reception, and stoves and refrigerators turning on with

Temagami circa 1970.
The ONBL administrative building and restaurant have been
replaced by a Shell station. *Photo: McIntosh family*

nary a match being struck. Coal oil lamps were electrified, the icehouse morphed into the tool house and stone irons were reworked as doorstops.

Despite the arrival of modern conveniences, the essence of the Temagami experience remained intact. When you wanted to get away from it all, you slid the old Peterborough canoe into the sun-dappled water and explored your favourite bay. The call of the loon in the still of dusk, the sound of those industrious dam builders startling you with a paddle-tail whack, the silent appearance of a mama sheltering her downy ducklings on her back, and the descending sun reflecting cathedral pines on tranquil waters – all still cast their spell.

Arrival Rituals

The Manito Landing became a place where many annual arrival rituals were performed. Jeff Carew wrote about these rites in a 1991 *Times* tribute to his late father Donald Carew of London, Ontario. "It's been more than a few years since I first stood on the dock at the end of the Temagami Access Road and watched my father back our boat into the water – window down, head stuck out, the steering wheel turning like it had a mind of its own. It wasn't a matter of driving technique, but an almost orchestrated manoeuvre of man and vehicle against the endless invasion of mosquitoes.

"Once the boat was in the water, Dad would drive back up the Mine Road in search of a parking spot. We always knew that within minutes he would be back yelling the immortal verse, "The plug! Is the plug in the boat?" With swarms of mosquitoes or blackflies hovering over our heads, it was in with the supplies, a turn of the starter, another turn of the starter, a trip to the back to plug in the fuel line, then a few squeezes of the ball and we were off.

"It was now time for the yearly renewal of the eversame landscape – Washing Machine Island, Camp Chimo and Chimo Bay, cold and usually the roughest part of the trip to Island 941 in the South Arm. The next morning we knew something was different. There was no telephone ringing, no alarm clock, no race to get to work or school. When we opened our eyes and took the first smell of the new day it was like someone had thrown sand in our eyes but it was just Father starting up the wood stove.

"Dad had woke an hour ahead of us and was doing his best to send smoke signals back to London. It was a jump in the lake with a five year old bar of Ivory (which seemed to get bigger each year), a run back to the cottage to sit in the old arm chair beside the woodstove which by now had cleared its throat and was roaring away famously. Life was at its best."

CHAPTER 15

THE TLA RETURNS TO ITS ROOTS

The post-coup executive consisted of old guard members Ron Johnstone, Joe Sullivan and Bill Gooderham as president, executive vice president and treasurer, respectively. Reformers included Secretary Annie Fenn and Director Jim Flosdorf. Several new committees were created, including archives chaired by Bill Plumstead, commercial and youth camps headed by Gordon Wolfe, pollution chaired by Don Crawford of Toronto and Island 759, and winter coverage and area co-operation with Doug Buck in charge.

As a cottager and Milne's woodlands manager, Doug played a dual role over the years. He was an effective liaison between the Association and Milne in regard to timber cutting and log towing timetables. He pioneered experimental strip cutting in the Skyline Reserve around Shiningwood Bay and Joan Peninsula, and helicopter logging on Temagami Island – all the while attempting to bring the Association on side of these methods' aesthetic and scientific value. Doug's wife Marianne served as a director in the mid-1980s.

Air and water pollution, island subdivisions and proposed mainland development gave the reinvented Association its impetus. The TLA, as the Association shall be called from now on to distinguish it from the old order, faced its first major challenge the same summer as the coup. The Department of Lands and Forests embarked on a long-range lake plan and public hearings were held in summer 1971.

Mainland Subdivisions

The department declared that the lake's "vacation user days" must increase by 50 per cent. Too many cottagers and campers were visiting Muskoka and Algonquin Park, squeezing recreational capacity to the limit. To disperse vacationers northward, the proposed plan called for the development of two mainland cottage clusters with road access off the Mine Road. One would be on the Northeast Arm, the other on Shiningwood Bay, carrying a maximum of 100 cottages.

It was an about-face from the government's nearly exclusive islands-only policy. Another 75 cottages were to be located on islands in the South and Southwest arms. There would be three additional youth camps in the North Arm, each with a population of 150.

CLUE authored an important document titled *Man and the Environment*, providing a framework for the TLA's response. It supported the principles of land use planning while opposing development that was to the detriment of existing youth camps and cottages.

Land Cautions Freeze Development

The final plan, little altered from the draft, was released to the public in 1973. It was stopped in its tracks not by TLA criticism, but by the actions of the Temagami Indian Band and its new chief Gary Potts. The band claimed that no Temagami native representative had signed the 1850 Robinson-Huron Treaty ceding its ancestral lands to the Crown. It filed three cautions in 1973 claiming title to Crown land in Temiskaming, Nipissing and Sudbury districts. A caution is a legal warning that the land title is in dispute.

The cautions covered 110 townships over 10,000 square kilometres. They excluded all private land but halted Crown land sales, mining exploration and any expansion plans in Latchford, Temagami and Elk Lake. It was business as usual, however, for the logging companies. They were still issued licences by the Department of Lands and Forests, which evolved into the Ministry of Natural Resources (MNR) in 1973. The band allowed cottagers to continue converting leases to patents, saying its struggle for justice was with the colonial government, not its neighbours.

The band had been assigned a 2.5-square kilometre Indian reserve on Bear Island in 1971, transferred from Ontario to the federal government for that purpose in the 1940s. It was a far cry from the 259-square kilometre reserve promised in 1885.

The cautions forced the MNR to delay more than 200 planned cottage lots, because Ontario could no longer issue Crown land grants. The spectre of mainland development, periodically raised throughout the 1970s, continued to haunt the TLA. And the TLA, in turn, commissioned professional studies showing shoreline cottaging was not desirable.

The Voice of the TLA

One of the TLA's first moves after the coup was to start its own quarterly newspaper, a novelty amongst Ontario cottage associations. The first issue of the *Temagami Times*, "the voice of the TLA," was hot off the press in winter 1971. Edited by Island 661's Don and Annie Fenn of Kettleby, Ontario, Vol. 1 No. 1 was four pages long and interspersed with advertisements. It featured a front page picture of the new board while banner headlines shouted, "IT'S YOUR NEWSPAPER." Ron Johnstone explained that "it was obvious at the last GM that we as an Association had not been doing a good job of keeping the membership informed."

As "staff photographer" for the *Times,* Jack Goodman offered portraits of mergansers, blue herons and hummingbirds in flight. Jack owned two New York state companies that published educational videos and films, widely sold throughout Canada and the U.S. His Canadian partner, Toronto's Tom Whyte, owns Island 388 in the Southwest Arm. Jack would go on to serve as a TLA director half a dozen times.

Jack's photographic pursuits have multiplied since his retirement and a move to Vermont. He'll get up at 4 a.m. to capture a nature scene and shoot 100 images for that one perfect frame. His photos have appeared in a wide range of publications and websites. A TLA placemat set is complemented by his waterfowl photos.

Two female common mergansers stick close to shore.
Photo: Jack Goodman

Jack and his brother Dennis first arrived on the Southwest Arm in 1953 to help their cousin Bob Goodman build a log cabin on his newly purchased Island 406. Bob had been head counsellor at Northwoods. Jack and his wife Barbara bought Northwoods founder Karl Kist's Island 352 in 1967. Dennis and his wife Laura Beth purchased Island 416.

The annual directory sported a new look. It was larger and a front cover Jack Goodman photo replaced the 1950s-era canoeing logo. Cheaper newsprint inside the directory replaced book-quality paper. The change was

economical as was the TLA's scrapping of the traditional AGM lunch.

The Super Stack

The mining and smelting industry in the Sudbury area annually discharged over two million tons of sulphur dioxide (SO_2) – more than half of all SO_2 discharged annually in the entire U.S. from smelting sulphur-containing ore. In 1972 a Sudbury super stack – then the world's highest chimney – started puffing malignant clouds of sulphur and nitrogen gases higher into the atmosphere. This cleaned the air in the Sudbury moonscape but sent pollutants Temagami way. Ron Johnstone wrote to INCO and Falconbridge nickel mines, and Queen's Park, requesting attention to the problem.

The TLA was one of the first organizations to sound the alarm over the noxious effects of SO_2 pollution on plant and aquatic life. It lobbied for change long before acid rain became an international buzz phrase. An SO_2 committee was struck, spearheaded by Carol Cochrane. She lives in North Bay and cottages on Island 817 in Cross Bay. It was not until the late 1980s that American and Canadian governments got tough on industry to reduce emissions and not until 1994 that scrubbers were installed in the super stack.

Saving Maple Mountain

By 1972 the Ministry of Industry and Tourism was planning a mega-resort atop one of Canada's most scenic peaks. The Maple Mountain resort would accommodate 3,500 tourists, amusing them with tennis, golf, swimming, horseback riding, skiing and fine dining. The first phase was to cost $82 million. Problems such as isolation, rough terrain, severe climate and pesky bugs were glossed over. From the TLA's perspective, the Maple Mountain project would destroy an enchanting wilderness area.

Local politicians and chambers of commerce lined up behind the proposal, believing it would be a boon to the economy. Temiskaming Tory MPP Ed Havrot defended the grandiose scheme at the 1973 AGM and tarred TLA members as southerners trying to tell northerners how to run their affairs. Gary Potts, who attended virtually every AGM after he became chief in 1972, shot back that he was as northern as northerners get and that he too was opposed to the project.

Bruce Hodgins, Wanapitei shareholder Jamie Benidickson and Hugh Stewart formed a Save Maple Mountain Committee (SMMC) in 1973. A permanent resident of the lake, Hugh was involved with Headwaters, a canoe-trip program initiated by some former

Camp Temagami staff members. The SMMC launched an aggressive publicity campaign.

Hugh suggested the proposal was not designed to benefit local communities and they would not see significant economic spin-off. Ontario New Democratic Party Leader Stephen Lewis raised the subject in the legislature and threw his support behind the SMMC. Opposition members belittled the Conservative government's project as a "million dollar hot dog stand."

At its peak in 1974 the SMMC had more than 1,000 members. As effective as their lobby was, it did not stop the resort plan; the band's land cautions scuttled it for the same reason aspects of the MNR's land use plan were shelved. The band viewed the scheme as an invasion of sacred ground, the mountain being known as Chee-bai-gin, "the place where the spirit goes after death."

The land claim and the Maple Mountain issue soon landed Ed Havrot in hot water at Queen's Park. Inflammatory comments were reported by the national media. His invective, "I could buy the Indian chiefs off with a case of goof," and "We should have given them a bunch of teepees and some cordwood," got him fired by Premier Bill Davis from his post as chair of the Ontario Northland Transportation Commission and as parliamentary assistant to the transportation minister.

Gary Potts feared Ed's sacking would cloud the real issue by offering him up as a scapegoat without the province moving closer to dealing fairly with native people. While condemning Ed's racist sentiments, the TLA was also concerned about misconceptions he had perpetuated in the media. The Toronto *Globe and Mail* reported, "Havrot looks at the Indians' caution as a ploy by U.S. cottagers to keep the area a private preserve." The *Times* was quick to point out that the majority of members of both the TLA and the SMMC were Canadian.

A President with a Long History

Philip Greey led the TLA through the Maple Mountain issue. He succeeded Ron Johnstone as president in 1973. Before his death in 1994, Ron served as president of both the Ontario and Canadian camping associations, and as founding president of both Canoe Ontario and Canoe Canada. With John Eberhard he co-founded the Canadian Recreational Canoeing Association.

Philip's father Dr. Philip Greey of Toronto was a camper and then counsellor at Cochrane's Camp from 1914 to '19. The Greeys possess three cups Philip Sr. won for proficiency at camp that were dug up at a South Arm garbage dump about 1980. Philip and his brother Steve leased Island 775 southwest of High Rock Island in 1921. They cut 150 red pine on the mainland. It would have been considered a huge breach because mainland trees were protected within the Temagami Forest Reserve. The brothers paddled the logs to their island, barked them and built a log cabin still standing today.

A boathouse was built in 1928 to house the Greeys' Minett launch, crafted from east African mahogany in Bracebridge. Bert Minett

opened his built-to-order boat yard in 1923. He was a perfectionist and didn't craft many. Philip Jr. had the classic watercraft refinished in 1990; she still had all the original boards but one and all the original hardware. The family referred to her as "the launch," never giving her a name.

Today wood is the lake's aristocrat and fibreglass less sophisticated. Aluminum is the errand runner and steel the workhorse. The canoe is the poet and the kayak the fitness buff. Jet skis are the party boys and houseboats the RV fans.

Philip Jr. first ventured to the lake in 1938 and attended Cochrane's Camp from 1943 until '47. He went into real estate development and restoration. In the early 1970s he renovated several old downtown Toronto buildings and helped to revitalize an historic district. Sometimes at Christmas he would visit his tenants dressed as Charles Dickens' miser Scrooge, who was Philip's polar opposite in character. Philip Sr. served the Association in the early 1960s as a Mine Road committee member.

Philip Jr. resigned as TLA president in 1974 to work for the SMMC. He was succeeded by Bill Allen, a Toronto lawyer and owner of the now private Wingfoot Island 864. He worked at Camp White Bear during the mid-1940s.

Gord Lak followed Bill Allen in 1975. The owner of an electrical installation business in southern Ontario, his company ran the overhead power lines into the Sherman Mine pits in the mid-1960s. He discovered the lake a few years later when he visited friend Cyril

Elston's Island 887 cottage. Gord and his wife Doreen were hooked and bought South Arm Island 771 in 1969 from Dr. Richard Weaver, a Cochrane's Camp alumnus who sat on Earl Rodgers' logging committee in the 1950s.

Not wishing to mix business with pleasure, Gord never electrified the isle, dubbed Crosswinds. The Laks bought a second, more remote island in Cross Lake where they are the sole cottagers. Gord served as membership committee chair from 1973 until the president's gavel was passed to him while Doreen became recording secretary. An acquaintance of the Laks designed the familiar TLA loon logo in 1971.

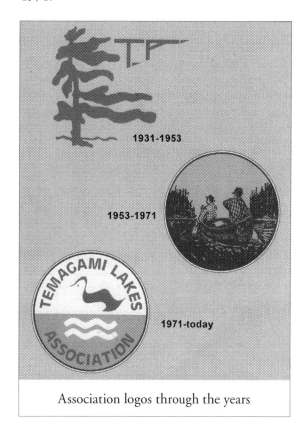

1931-1953

1953-1971

1971-today

TEMAGAMI LAKES ASSOCIATION

Association logos through the years

The TLA had dropped Dewey Derosier's membership schedule by 1973. Class A now consisted of property owners, Class B of associate or family members, Class C of sustaining members (organizations and businesses) and Class D of junior associates. Fees did not rise. The eight directors would be elected by paper ballot to serve two-year terms with four elected annually. Until then all eight directors were elected annually by a show of hands.

Women Given a Vote

For the first time in the TLA's history, associate members had the right to vote. Until then only commercial and private property owners had that privilege at the AGM. At least 90 per cent of the time it was the husband who joined as the property owner, regardless of who legally possessed the cottage. The wife might then join as an associate member but could not vote.

This male-dominated membership set-up and traditional gender roles are partly why women were sparsely represented on the Association executive prior to the coup. They now had equal voting rights as Class B members. It was another 22 years before the TLA elected its first woman president.

The Deep Water People Unite

The Temagami Indian Band could appoint two directors with full voting rights. Soon Chief Gary Potts and Mac McKenzie were attending board meetings. But Gary wasn't entirely happy with the arrangement. "There was some discomfort for the two representatives on the board, because we weren't paying the regular dues. It felt like we were token representatives," he said in 1991. Yet dealing with the TLA since the coup had been a time for "dialogue" rather than "friction," as was sometimes the case in earlier times.

"After the caution went on, the pressure on the relationship was relieved. There were no major developments to worry about," he added. "The caution has enabled the TLA and ourselves to have a chance to grow, without having day-to-day development plans to contend with. It's been a time of growth, a time to plan and assess what has happened."

The band passed a resolution in 1975 that non-status Indians and Métis (those not recognized by the federal government under the Indian Act and living on or off-reserve) who were descended from the original Temagami tribe would be included in the land claim. To prove occupation of ancestral territories prior to the 1850 Robinson-Huron Treaty, genealogical charts of band members (the federally-recognized status Indians under the Indian Act living on Bear Island) and non-status natives were put together.

Status and non-status natives met for a key tribal assembly in 1978 and adopted a constitution authorizing the Temagami people to define their own membership. Band Chief Gary Potts was also elected chief of the tribe (including both status and non-status Indians) while Métis Rita O'Sullivan became second chief. (Rita regained her status following Indian Act amendments.) This tribe, to be called the Teme-Augama Anishnabai (TAA) or "Deep

Water People," unanimously approved a unity resolution stating that all descendants of the Temagami Indians from time immemorial should share in land claim benefits.

The TAA council would be responsible for the land claim and the negotiating process. The new tribal council soon agreed on the boundaries of n'Daki Menan or "the homeland" after consulting with neighbouring bands. The Temagami Indian Band continued with its traditional composition.

Navigation Chart Revamped

The TLA's 1950s navigation chart was reworked in 1974 due to complaints about the difficulty of juggling four sheets in an open boat. It was reduced to one sheet and new information about garbage dumps, campsites and tourism services was added. Another chart was printed in 1984 following complaints that the print was too fine to read. This one solved that problem – it was eight feet long. Information was updated by Reg Sinclair, then MNR lands supervisor and a TLA director. The chart showed campsites, buoy locations, primary and secondary channels, and shoals.

Committee Commitments

The 1970s could be categorized as the decade of committees. They included SO2, youth, constitution and bylaws, real estate, archives, commercial and youth camps, and publicity. There were also the traditional trappings of property protection, fish and membership.

The TLA even grew an offshoot; the Temagami Region Studies Institute (TRSI) is a non-profit research agency, legally independent of the TLA but supported by it. Bill Allen prepared all the paper work for its incorporation so tax receipts could be issued for donations. The TRSI's mandate was and still is to conduct research into the "human and natural history" of the area.

Denis Benson of Stittsville, Ontario, was the founding chair. He and his wife Dorothy were canoe tripping when they became storm-bound at the top of the Southwest Arm during several days of rain, fog and wind. They sought an island in the storm, purchasing 820 in Cross Bay in 1963 from the Crown and building a Pan Abode prefabricated cottage. The couple spent their retirement summers on the lake. They gave Island 820 to their grandson Sean Murray of Marquette, Michigan, in 1998. Denis died in 2008 at the age of 87.

Early TRSI activities included water quality tests for acidification and E. coli from sewage systems, and monitoring SO2 effects on pine stands and soils. Denis's career as a field biologist lent professionalism to his work. Most of the studies were conducted in cooperation with three Ontario universities, the MOE and the MNR.

Results indicated that water quality in the Northeast Arm near Temagami was "grossly impaired" due to intensive cottage development and raw sewage from the village. Caution

was needed to ensure that sewage systems met approved standards because of the lake's sensitivity. No evidence of acidification was detected, though SO2 emissions were found to be harming white pine, manifested in stunted growth rates.

A Lake Capacity Study

The MNR passed an order under Section 17 of the Public Lands Act in 1975 whereby, for the first time, the ministry got involved in the management of private land in unorganized townships. Under the order, property improvement and building construction could not be undertaken without a permit from the Temagami District manager.

These regulations were meant to prevent owners from building too close to shore and disturbing the treescape and fish spawning areas, or adding a bathroom without an adequate sewage system. The order was intended to fulfill controls in the 1973 plan and ease islanders' fear of haphazard, unregulated private development. Due to the cautions' freeze on Crown land development, pressure was mounting to accelerate private development.

President Gord Lak arrived at the 1976 AGM "somewhat bitter, disillusioned and rather discouraged." He had recently attended a meeting of the district manager's advisory committee, comprised of local interest groups. It provided input into MNR plans. A proposal to subdivide former Camp White Bear into 24 cottage condominiums was on the table. It was approved by other committee members; Gord's was the lone dissenting voice.

The membership voted to oppose the proposed White Bear subdivision. A revised plan calling for 18 lots still engendered TLA criticism due to potential ecological damage and overcrowding. The project was blocked by the Ontario Municipal Board, though 17 lots were eventually developed. Adding to the TLA's dissatisfaction was an MNR decision to revive plans for the Shiningwood Bay mainland cottage clusters. The MNR thought the lifting of the land cautions was imminent.

The TRSI concluded it was high time for a detailed study of Shiningwood Bay and some large islands to calculate their development potential. A major fundraising drive ensued with a target of $16,500. While the TRSI spearheaded the fundraising, CLUE, now chaired by Dr. Norm Flett of Island 664, oversaw the study. Norm is a son of the late Dr. Ross Flett who first beheld the lake in 1928. Norm went to Cochrane's Camp from 1949 to '56.

The TRSI met its monetary target by summer 1979; 36 per cent of donors were non-TLA members. In his pitch TRSI Chair Ed Searle of Belfountain, Ontario, and Island 623, used a hook few could resist: "If you do not care what may happen to the lake, if you wish to see another Lake Muskoka on Lake Temagami where your neighbour is 100 feet away, where you can't drink the water and you can't catch a fish, then please don't send any money."

The TLA hired Hough Stansbury and Associates to conduct the study. "To date, no one including MNR or MOE has been able to tell us how much pressure our lake can withstand," Ed wrote in the *Times*. "The TLA's position is that no further development should be allowed to take place until such time as we know if the lake can withstand increased usage, in what form and in what areas."

The thorough study included field work, meetings with MNR, chemical water sampling, day use surveys and a bio-physical terrain analysis. First viewing of the document, more than two years in the making, occurred when Norm Flett, Ed Searle and Don Fenn presented a copy to Natural Resources Minister James Auld. The encounter was hailed by the *Times* as "one of the most important meetings ever held by representatives of our Association." The report concluded that the lake could ecologically support more development, but the traditional policy of islands-only development and limited road access should be maintained so its semi-wilderness character would not be compromised.

CHAPTER 16

CONFLAGRATION

In May 1977 an immense forest fire raged through the bush for 18 days, ravishing 27,000 acres, including much of the shoreline along the Northwest Arm. Sparked by lightning south of Obabika Inlet, the inferno burned between Gull and Obabika lakes before jumping into Gibson's Bay, and Granny and Devil's bays on the North Arm.

A total of 250 firefighters, assisted by five water bombers, worked the blaze in shifting winds, which caused constant change in its direction. Crews were called away to Cobalt to tackle another fire and the Temagami fire was left to spread out of control.

Carol Cochrane, a soot-covered eye witness to the devastation, wrote about what she saw, smelled and heard in the *Temagami Experience*:

"There were virtually hundreds of small fires cropping up all over as the main fire crowned and sent missiles of burning pine for thousands of yards. I heard the ominous booming in the distance and the sound of flames crackling in areas where just days earlier, there was only the sound of wind and water.

"I saw the scattered, charred remnants of buildings which appeared to have virtually exploded, glass which had melted into incredible twisted heaps on the ground, melted and unrecognizable masses of metal, two propane tanks within 10 feet of each other, one completely intact while the other had split and been completely flattened.

"I had watched the water bombing, an intriguing site to see at close hand. Two were huge amphibious machines (Canadair I believe). Of the two pontoon-type planes,

Much of Obabika Inlet was torched. New growth was thriving in 2006.
Photo: Harold Keevil

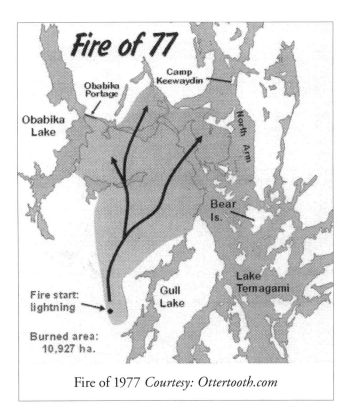

Fire of 1977 *Courtesy: Ottertooth.com*

was stopped and the cottages preserved," Steve Drake said in 2009.

The Carpenters have been affiliated with the lake since 1936 when Daniel Carpenter Sr. was a Keewaydin camper and staffman. His son Dan Jr. was a camper in the 1960s and a trip guide in the 1970s. He was a camp director from 1991 to '98, as was his late brother Bill until 1996. The family bought their patch of paradise a mere two years prior to the conflagration. They set about rebuilding almost immediately.

Rebuilding Benefits Economy

Dan Carpenter Sr., in his late 80s, is a retired high school math teacher living in Bermuda. In the early 1990s he described what it is like to lose everything, including your dock and trees, and the long process of starting from scratch to replace it all. The Carpenters are a ripe example of how cottage owners put money into the local economy and beyond.

Dan contacted North Bay's Kennedy Insurance. The company was "a great help as we rebuilt," he said. The family purchased a pre-cut Viceroy cabin and a Bear Island barge was hired to transport it to the island. Contractor Mac McKenzie began construction with a crew of four. Dan's wife Jane and the Carpenter sons pitched in too. When summer ran out, they had just enough time to insulate so they could return and work indoors over Christmas vacation.

The family purchased a woodstove in North Bay and began interior finishing, using

one was a Beaver and one an Otter. The Otter was able to touch down, refill and get airborne once again within one minute. I watched them discharge what appeared to be such pathetically small loads in comparison to the overall size of the fire."

Three cottages were razed. Island 1102's Ralph Marshall of Shaker Heights, Ohio, was 80 years old when he lost his cottage and chose not to rebuild. On Island 1144 in Eye Lake, the Valkenburg family lost its summer retreat, as did the Carpenters of Island 1171 in Devil's Bay.

The late Norm Keevil of Island 1114, who established Copperfields Mine on Temagami Island, is credited by the Drake family with saving several islands, including his own, the Drakes' Island 1091, and islands 1097 and 1098. Norm strategically placed water pumps on the mainland just a stone's throw north of his isle. "It is evident to this day where the fire

From left, Dan Carpenter Sr., his wife Jane and their children Dan Jr. and Bill in the 1980s. *Photo: Dan Carpenter Jr.*

wood from a Temagami lumber company. They bought tools as well; all they were able to salvage from the ashes was a crowbar. The interior was completed during summer 1978. The Carpenters purchased a propane stove and refrigerator from Bob Louks. He operated a marine supply and propane sales and service shop in Temagami from 1958 until the late '70s. Kitchen cabinets and counters were crafted at a North Bay shop. Furniture was bought locally. Boats were also lost in the fire. Three were replaced, two from local marinas.

The replacement process was gradual and went on for several years, Dan said. The Carpenters then tackled the boathouse. Supplies were acquired from local merchants, including lumber, roofing and windows. A portable generator and power tools came later.

The fire left the island devoid of greenery. North Arm friends offered trees from their properties and the Carpenters shopped area nurseries to accelerate regeneration. "Throw in the new insurance, taxes, propane for the summer, winter boat storage, car parking, food, and contributions to local needs such as the fish hatchery [TAFIP], and the upshot is, a cottage owner does help the local area," Dan concluded.

Dan Jr., who like his father became a teacher, said in 2009 that the family still hauls in pine needles and soil to deepen the thin organic base of the burned humus layer. Soon after the fire a few birch and poplar took hold. The Carpenters thinned the saplings so they could grow into sturdy trees. Any small patch of greenery, however spindly, was tended. "The growth has been incredibly lush in the last five or six years," Dan said. So lush, that they recently cleared a few trees in front of the cottage that were obstructing lake views.

In the immediate aftermath of the fire, Milne's timber crews went to work in a salvage race against the pine sawyer beetle. The insects could be heard chewing their way into the wood and left sawdust piles at the base of trees. Although some of the destroyed forest contained trees between 150 to 200 years of age, Milne's losses consisted mainly of plantations rather than future timber allocations.

CHAPTER 17

A LIABILITY BECOMES AN ASSET

The TLA building, completed in 1971, was used to hold board meetings and to house property patrolmen and the archives collection. The dock was handy for cottagers picking up guests or heading to town. At the 1977 AGM a motion was tabled to look into the possible sale and removal of the building from its mainland site.

"Many past directors of the Association have expressed dismay at having to speak to authorities on behalf of an organization which stood for no mainland development while owning property permanently established on the mainland," said Tim Gooderham. Tim succeeded Gord Lak as president in 1977. Members agreed and a motion to possibly scrap the building was passed.

Two committees were struck, one to propose potential building services and the other to present reasons for disposal. Based on their reports, the executive voted unanimously for disposal. By the time the 1978 AGM rolled around, the membership was at loggerheads. Both committees presented their case in the *Times*.

The group favouring retention was led by Director Ev Choat, a Toronto businessman. In 1924 Ev began working for Dr. Frank Wood who was setting up Camp Cayuga on Island 1088. The camp opened with some 30 boys from private schools in southern Ontario. Ev was put in charge of the sailing program, receiving room and board. He purchased a lot on Island 1088 in 1950. Other members on Ev's side were Doug Buck, and Director Don Moore and his wife Jeri.

They argued that the TLA would lose its original $28,000 investment, now valued at $45,000. They suggested a citizens band radio communications centre upstairs and an historical display downstairs. CB radio had become popular with cottagers, residents and the OPP boat. The TLA might someday require a salaried administrator needing a permanent office, they added. Besides, if the TLA truly wished to be consistent in its stand against mainland development, then members should stop using the Mine Road, and the hydro and telephone services originating there.

Members urging the building's sale were represented by Annie Fenn, Gord Lak and Ed Searle. They argued that its location made a sham of the islands-only development stand. "Our credibility in negotiations with various government agencies is absolutely zero when the Association itself blatantly violates its own policies."

Voting by mailed ballot, 99 members said dump the building while 98 said keep it. The building was, in all likelihood, saved by a Canadian postal strike. The 197 returned ballots represented less than 40 per cent of eligible voters. Many ballots never made it because of the mail disruption. "The question then arises: Can the Association dispose of its only capital asset on the say so of so few of its members?" asked Tim Gooderham in the *Times*. The board decided to review the matter "just one more time."

Ev convinced the executive to set aside $7,000 for a CB radio centre – almost 70 per cent of the annual operating budget. A rift soon divided the board. Ed, Gord and Annie accused the others of acting irresponsibly, by committing huge sums without seeking membership approval. They feared environmental issues and normal operations would be left under-funded.

Despite the discord, Ev barrelled ahead. He bore a resemblance to Dewey Derosier in his determination. While not opposed to the radio service but rather its location, Ed Searle nevertheless agreed to install and maintain the equipment. He could not have chosen a better set; his Radio Shack model transmitted its summer signals into the early 1990s. Ed left the lake in the late 1980s and moved to Owen Sound, Ontario.

Ev hired Tom Dymond, a blind ham radio operator from Toronto, and Temagami resident Norm Thompson as cook and housekeeper. The telephone was on a party line shared with a downstairs pay phone, plus phones at the Manito Hotel and the Mine Landing. Early radio operators often had to ask other parties to conclude their conversations when a dire situation arose. Dialling the operators was a frustrating waiting game to get past the busy signal.

Island 1003's Pam Glenn became a radio operator in August 1979 and was promoted to

---

Breaker! Breaker!

CB radios are affected by an 11-year sunspot cycle. During high sunspot activity, refracted signals called skip travel over long distances and can reduce or shut down local communications. Cottagers knew the frustration of waiting for a message from the TLA only to be blasted out of the room by a trucker: "Breaker Breaker 1-9!"

Conditions were sometimes ripe for "skip talking." Over the years TLA radio operators conversed with "good buddies" in Alabama, Mississippi and elsewhere. These chats would go something like this: "Hey Tea Lay, you're comin' through like an express train!" And the operator would reply, "Likewise Buckshot. You're really walking the dog!" These exchanges weren't entirely counterproductive; American truckers became familiar with the charms of "Lake Mahogany, Ontario, Canada."

Skip was at its lowest ebb by 1984. Its next phoenix-like rise to loquacious lunacy would occur in 1989 and '90. Not surprisingly, those would be the years when droves of cottagers rushed to Canadian Tire to buy reliable Very High Frequency (VHF) marine radios.

head operator until 1986. Acting on members' suggestions, Ev and Pam introduced additional services such as laundry, mail and a lending library. Ev planted pine trees on the front lawn and raised a flag pole with the familiar loon logo on the banner. Other staff members have included lake residents and cottagers, most of them students. "TLA out. XM4716505 clear" meant the operators were signing off for the night. A steady stream of "good night" salutations often kept staff on air for another 15 minutes. Ev left the lake in the mid-1980s when the annual trip from his Vancouver retirement home became too long. Honoured as Member of the Year in 1982, he died in 1991.

Predictions that the radio service would break the bank didn't materialize. Headquarters services became immensely popular, stilling earlier doubts. A CB fund was established with contributions from service users. The amount received consistently topped the amount budgeted. Staff wages have often been subsidized by government grants.

By the 1981 AGM the CB radio service was a fixture on the lake. Aside from typical "please order my propane" calls, doctors, ambulances and veterinarians were summoned. The *North Bay Nugget* ran a story that summer about the service helping to save a heart attack victim's life. And Temagami OPP Sgt. Bud Mitchell said at the AGM that "CB is the best thing the TLA ever got on this lake."

TLA Hires Executive Secretary

In summer 1979 the board hired Tim Gooderham as its first executive secretary. Prior to the coup, the Association had only seven known presidents over 40 years. Two expired while still in office and two served for 10 years. In the eight years since the coup, the TLA had gone through five presidents, none serving longer than two years. From past experience, the board strove to ensure members did not stay in office long enough to stagnate. The emphasis shifted from the president's persona to the issues, with the power base spread out amongst a larger, more diverse and ever-changing board.

The injection of new blood created a problem with continuity. Tim is a good example. Elected to the board in 1977, he was immediately installed as president with no previous TLA experience. It took him a year to get on top of its workings. His two-year term was up the following year. A more immediate reason the TLA needed this salaried position was that the incoming president – Bruce Hodgins of Wanapitei in summer and Trent University in winter – was hard-pressed for time to devote to presidential duties.

Tim was introduced to the lake as a toddler in 1936 and spent summers at Chimo, the family's resort. Chimo didn't serve alcohol, but guests were encouraged to bring their own supply. Tim was sometimes sent over to the ONBL's Fasken's Point to use a hand crank phone connected to the village's ONBL building, to relay liquor orders to the LCBO. When in use, the sound of wires banging against trees was audible. He recalled William Mulock, Canada's first postmaster general, ordering cases of scotch. No word on whether it was blended or single malt.

Tim entered the Royal Military College at Kingston, Ontario, in the mid-1950s. After

A Chimo shore lunch with all the fixings.
Photo: Ontario Ministry of Travel and Publicity in The Temagami Experience by Bruce W. Hodgins and Jamie Benidickson

training as an aircraft navigator, he worked at the North Bay Canadian Forces Base, flying CF-100s. He later did search and rescue work in the Far North aboard modified Lancaster bombers. He settled into family life as a North Bay high school history teacher in 1966, retiring in 1993.

Tim's executive secretarial duties included chairing the membership committee. This lifted

a heavy load off Jeanne Underwood who had replaced Doreen Lak as recording secretary. Until then the secretary's job was to record minutes, process membership applications, and address and stuff envelopes. All correspondence was now channelled through Tim's address. He excelled at keeping members informed via the *Times* and regular executive reports. When things were going as planned, his report masthead featured the loon logo. When things hit a wall, so did the loon, depicted by Tim as a bedraggled victim of choppy waters.

He was also expected to deal with lawyers, consultants and government agencies. Tim's role was later expanded to the property protection committee. His starting salary was $5,000 per year plus expenses. It stood at $11,000 by 1992, adjusted periodically as his duties expanded and membership rose. The membership voted in favour of a constitutional amendment in 1981, which addressed the continuity issue. Three directors would be elected per year for a three-year term. Previously, four were elected for a two-year term.

CHAPTER 18

THE PACE OF CHANGE ACCELERATES

The 1980s made their grand entrance with a hike in membership dues. Class A property owner fees went up to $40. The reasons given were inflation, the executive secretary's salary and legal costs stemming from two subdivisions. Few new cottages had been built due to the land cautions' freeze on Crown land sales.

The land claim was to be decided by the Supreme Court of Ontario. As the Teme-Augama Anishnabai's respect for their indigenous roots grew, so did pride in their heritage. Gary Potts described the 1970s and '80s as "a tremendous time of growth. Bear Island...has been through the growing pains and the people have evolved from being guides to contract businessmen in this one generation. Our concerns have turned from putting in ice at the camps to governance issues."

The Temagami Indian Band purchased the post property and opened the Bear Island Trading Post in 1981. It was subsidized by a federal grant through the Local Employment Assistance Program. The store operated at a loss, prompting the band to hire a consultant to identify and address concerns. Gladys Farr became assistant manager in 1983 under manager Kim Montroy. Gladys took over the store's management from 1984 until '89. Under

Doug McKenzie's coordination, it became a co-operative with Liz Potts among others managing the flow of commerce.

Indian Act Amendments

For almost 130 years the federal government has labelled Temagami aboriginals status or non-status, based on an arbitrary acceptance of treaty payments. Status Indians are band members with rights under the Indian Act to live on a reserve, vote for band council, and own and inherit reserve property. Ottawa's early policy was aimed at assimilation: a native woman who married a non-status man lost her status and band membership, as did her children. Men and their descendents kept their status when they married non-native women.

A second assimilation policy was called enfranchisement. Aboriginals were encouraged to give up their status for the right to vote in federal elections or to earn a university degree. If a male became enfranchised so did his wife and children.

These discriminatory provisions led women's organizations to take on the Indian Act in the 1960s and '70s all the way to the Supreme Court of Canada and the UN Human Rights Committee. The Department of Indian Affairs and Northern Development amended the act in 1985. The most significant change was that native women would retain or regain their status and band membership rights after marriage to non-natives, as would their children – but not their grandchildren. The so-called grandchildren clause would become a major concern in the 2000s.

On-reserve status Indians (First Nations people) benefit from federal tax exemptions on reserve-earned income. Goods purchased on or delivered to a reserve are federal Goods and Services Tax (GST) exempt. Ontario gives First Nations people sales tax exemptions anywhere in the province provided they show their registration cards.

The Taxman Cometh

Status Indians' favourable tax position almost ended when Ontario introduced a Harmonized Sales Tax (HST) in July 2010, bundling provincial and federal sales taxes on products and services. GST rules were to apply to the entire HST, meaning First Nations people would have had to pay provincial and federal sales taxes (13 per cent) on off-reserve purchases. The province's First Nations threatened protests at the June 2010 G8 and G20 summits hosted by the federal government in Huntsville and Toronto. An 11th hour deal exempted First Nations from the provincial portion of the new tax.

Many Anishnabai who have gained status since 1985 live off reserve. They receive some benefits, such as tax exemptions when purchases are made on a reserve and better positioning in the land claim settlement. Acceptance of status by the Indian affairs department is not always easy.

Island 1182's Peter McMillen described his 1993 pursuit of status with the aid of TAA researcher Jim Morrison. He first followed a paternal link. His grandfather Peter Brown was never registered, nor were his parents John Brown and Mani Ann Simon. Peter then pursued a maternal connection. His grandmother Caroline Brown received Robinson-Huron Treaty payments in error as a youngster. (Her father Malcolm McLean was non-native.) He had to delve further back but the trail went cold on the Golden Lake Reserve. He plans to pursue one "final clue" someday. The reason Peter, an American resident, strove to claim status was "a sense of heritage."

The Mayor of the Southwest Arm

Change was a constant within the lake community. Northwoods, the Cleveland YMCA boys' camp established in 1937 in the Southwest Arm, closed in the early 1970s. William "Bill" Crofut III and his wife Susie bought Northwoods islands 355 and 356, using them as a retreat for literary figures, musicians and artists. Bill's grandfather William Crofut originally bought the two islands in the late 1920s as a fish camp. As chair of the board of the Cleveland YMCA, he subsequently gave the camp to the Y. Northwoods expanded to islands 352 and 353. They are now owned by Jack Goodman.

Bill's first trip to the lake was in 1938 as a four-year-old. He was a camper and staff member at Northwoods. He became enamoured of folk music after attending a Pete Seeger concert. He helped Pete build his house in exchange for banjo lessons. Bill became an internationally-acclaimed classical banjo artist. On the lake he was known as "the mayor and chief gadfly" of his Southwest Arm neighbourhood. He enjoyed touring aboard *The Loon Boat*, one of two solar-powered vessels he built, a first for the lake. Bill died in 1999 at his home in Massachusetts.

Camps Buck Tradition

Canoeing was enjoying renewed popularity. The MNR estimated canoeists' use of Temagami District increased more than 60 per cent between 1975 and '85. Wabun added a girls' section in 1977. It was "a mark of the times," said Dick Lewis who became managing director in 1976. Off-season he was

the headmaster of a Vermont co-educational school. He watched girls keeping up with the boys on demanding hikes and realized they were capable of holding their own despite the "understated expectations" of Wabun administrators. Dick's wife Marg was instrumental in implementing the decision.

"The girls' program has exceeded my wildest expectations. It opened up whole new relationships and tempered the chest-thumping Neanderthal dynamics," Dick said. "The girls' presence introduced new channels of empathy, understanding and communication." Keewaydin Camp waited until 1999 to admit girls after decades of hand wringing, according to Brian Back.

Dick, Marg and their children Jason and Jessica spent several years on the lake as permanent residents. Parents taught at Bear Island and the family immersed itself in community life. Dick followed Mac McKenzie on his trapline and served on the Township of Temagami's planning board. The Lewises created lasting friendships with native and non-native residents.

One camp did not follow the path of the paddle and didn't really offer canoe trips. Skip Connett's Canadian Adventure Camp opened in 1975

Wabun began admitting girls in 1977. *Photo: Camp Wabun*

on 160-acre Island 1104 in the North Arm. It mainly offers water skiing and gymnastics. Toronto trampoline gymnasts Karen Cockburn and Mathieu Turgeon honed their skills there before heading to the 2000 Sydney Olympics where they won bronze medals. Karen went on to clinch silver at the Athens and Beijing games.

Another untraditional youth camp opened on Rabbitnose Island 1119. Appleby College, a private co-ed school in Oakville, Ontario, became the official owner of Rabbitnose Lodge in 1977. Stuart McLaughlin had donated property on the north half of the island, according to Appleby Archivist Tracey Krause. He purchased Rabbitnose from William Sinclair in 1973, intending to turn it over to the school. Earlier that year Stuart attempted to buy Wanapitei to establish a northern campus. The McLaughlins were Toronto land developers. The campus was named for a program called Northward Bound, based on sea cadet training that emphasized survival skills. Tenth graders were required to spend one supervised month there.

The program underwent changes in 1986 and $35,000 was spent on upgrading buildings and equipment. Telephone and hydro arrived in the early 1990s. A new radio system allowed off-site staff to communicate with base camp during overnight outings. The one-month session was split into two nine-day sessions to minimize missed classroom time.

Nine campers in the Northward Bound program suffered trauma in February 1990 when their canvas tent caught fire and burned

to the ground northeast of Keewaydin. Four students received burns and were hospitalized in Sudbury. One required plastic surgery. It is the only serious incident for the northern campus in its 35-year history.

The Rabbitnose facility was renamed the McLaughlin Northern Campus in 2006 in recognition of the McLaughlin gift. A 2008 Appleby gala raised $50,000 for renovations. Three dorms were expanded and a fourth added. Improvements were also made to the main lodge. Today students participating in week-long trips learn wilderness skills.

Businesses Change Hands

Bill and May Metcalfe purchased Temagami Lodge in the mid-1960s. Bill tried to have the leaky, unused lodge restored for its historic significance but government funding wasn't forthcoming. What had once been a grand pine log resort with two and a half stories and a gable was burned down, on purpose, in 1980. Bill and Niki Plumstead sold Loon Lodge in 1981. After several owners, it gained long-term stability under the ownership of John and Jenny Moskwa. They operate a winter and summer fishing lodge and snack bar serving their signature loon burgers. No loons are harmed in the process.

Niki Plumstead became the first deputy reeve of the Township of Temagami in 1976 under its inaugural reeve Butch Spooner. The Temagami Improvement District with an appointed council moved from village to township status with an elected council. One of Niki's most valued accomplishments was helping seniors obtain a 10-unit apartment building and support services. Built in 1988 the Ronnoco House sits on the site of the historic Ronnoco Hotel. The hotel's front steps were incorporated into the design. The original structure was destroyed by fire in 1973. In its twilight years the hotel made more profit from the bar than from its rooms.

Temagami Township's inaugural council consisted of front (l-r) Niki Plumstead, Reeve Wilfred "Butch" Spooner and clerk Len McAnulty. Standing (l-r) Bob Louks, Jim Kitts and Angus St. Jean.
Photo: *Temagami Experience*

Bill and Niki served as TLA directors after the 1971 coup. Bill was the first chair of the archives committee and returned in the late 1980s. Bob Rannie succeeded Bill as chair. He and his wife Frances "Frankie" purchased Cross Bay Island 813 in 1969. Bob's history on the lake went back almost as far as the archives. He was a kitchen boy at Keewaydin in the mid-1930s. He served two terms as a director and chaired the taxation committee. Bob died in

1993. His daughter Claire Rannie now owns Island 813. She became involved with the TLA in the 1990s.

Under Chair Peter Moes the archives collection was used for the first time by another organization. Material was borrowed by Niki for her accounts of bygone days in the *Temagami Experience*, a breezy summer tabloid published by the chamber of commerce in the late 1970s. Island 647's Peter had discovered the lake in 1963 and was a University of Toronto French professor. He passed away in 2007 and the isle remains in the family.

In partnership with Charlie and Georgette Reeder, the Plumsteads revived Boatline Bay in the early 1980s and expanded services. The Plumsteads opened a second marina in North Bay in the mid-1980s and sold their share in the lake operation in 1990. Boatline Bay Marine became a family affair. Charlie Reeder, who had opened Reeder's Marine in 1959 with an expansion in 1971 to become Reeder's Marine and Electric, died in 1995. Charlie's son Ken and his wife Carol took over the business. They were grief-stricken when their three-year-old daughter Avery was accidentally killed at Boatline Bay Marine in 2004.

New Faces

Narrows Island 660's Howard Hoegy of southern Ontario became acid rain scientific co-chair about 1980. With a master's degree in chemistry, he used his expertise to set up 24 water sampling stations for analysis by the MOE. The results revealed that most of the lake was at an acceptable acidity level, the main exception being Sharp Rock Inlet, which was extremely sensitive. He wrote *Times* articles, noting that acid rain came not just from Sudbury but also the industrialized northeastern U.S. Howard drowned in a boating mishap on the lake in 1989, leaving his wife Sandra and two young daughters.

Carol Cochrane and the acid rain committee liaised with other groups, including the Canadian Coalition on Acid Rain. The coalition took the view that Canadians and Americans must work together to reduce emissions. It would become a valuable environmental ally. Carol was elected to the board of governors in 1982.

Island 938's Albert Beust, an Ohio accountant, had been chair of the property protection committee since 1978. By 1980 he was also headquarters committee chair and soon added the budget committee to his work load. He retired in 1976 and, along with his wife Judy, lived on the lake from break-up to freeze-up.

Although Al only joined the TLA in 1976, his ties predate its birth. The Worman family started trekking to Camp Acouchiching in 1927 and then leased Island 942. They lived

It didn't take Carol Cochrane long to learn how to paddle her own canoe as a youngster at Cochrane's Camp.
Photo: Carol Cochrane

two doors down from the Beusts in Dayton and their kids were good friends with the Beust kids. The Beust parents heard so much about Temagami that they decided to give it a whirl. Al's father Carl was so impressed that he talked Couch owners into sub-leasing the southwestern portion of Island 938 to him. Reg McConnell and a co-owner built the Beust cottage in 1931.

In 1998 Norman and Denise Gofton of Guelph, Ontario, bought the Worman island. "It incorporated more of what we wanted, not the brash and noisy Muskoka lakes," said Denise. "Besides, we are more interested in the natural environment, the tranquility and beauty, and had canoed up in the area. Another major consideration was the lower prices up in Temagami." Judy Beust died in 1994. Al was seen as "the grand old man of the South Arm." He was 93 when he headed up in summer 2009. He sold his place in 2010.

Jack Glenn succeeded Bruce Hodgins as president in 1981. An executive with a Toronto life insurance company, he had served on the membership committee just after the coup. He was elected a director in 1980 and appointed TRSI chair. The Glenns' history of TLA service extends back to the 1940s when Jack's mother Gladys Glenn, née Trethewey, did committee work. In those days Jack worked as a Cochrane's Camp counsellor.

The family's history in the north stretches back to 1904 when William Trethewey, a mine

was soon squaring identification posts for his discoveries and marking witness trees to delineate plots. He called his abutting mines the Trethewey and the Coniagas – an amalgam of metal symbols Co (cobalt), Ni (nickel), Ag (silver) and As (arsenic).

William was shortly joined by Jack Glenn's grandfather John Trethewey, William's cousin. But the real treasure for John was not to be found down a mine shaft. Lake Temagami beckoned in 1905. He chose a small one-acre island and called it Silver Birches. He liked Island 1003 because it was an easy paddle to the post and obscured from view by an adjacent island. John built the lake's first water boathouse in 1907.

John reinvested his mining profits in dubious mining ventures further north. All he was left with were dozens of worthless stock certificates. Sadly for his living descendants, the family mines eventually reverted to the Crown and the MNR sold the tailings to Agnico-Eagle Mines Limited in the 1970s for $1.5 million.

Jack Glenn's wife Evelyn, née Lillie, was the granddaughter of

Jack Glenn at Island 1003 in the late 1920s with a great mess of fish for a little guy. *Photo: Jack Glenn*

and real estate developer, arrived at the rough and tumble Cobalt camp, fast becoming the stage for Canada's richest silver boom. He

the first mayor of Sturgeon Falls. The same year Jack became president, his daughter Pam took over the publications committee. Her Cobalt connection came alive when she later worked as northern bureau chief for the *North Bay Nugget*. Her Silver Street office was mere steps from a safety fence enclosing the underground workings of the family's old mines. A house next door was torn down about 1990 when the stopes crumbled and the ground subsided.

In the 1980s and early '90s Carol Lowery, another daughter, served on the advisory board as the Lake Temagami Permanent Residents Association (LaTemPRA) liaison. LaTemPRA was founded in 1980. Carol's husband Biff began operating Temagami Barge in 1982.

Development Concerns

As a follow-up to the Hough Stansbury environment study, the TLA engaged Hanna Associates and Hough Stansbury Michalski to proceed with a Lake Temagami planning assessment. While the study had shown the lake could sustain some development, the follow-up would determine how much development lake dwellers felt the lake should support. The MNR relaxed its Section 17 order regulating private land development. The explanation was that only Crown land was within its mandate. The TLA believed the easing of building controls would exert pressure on the 15 per cent of the lake's island shoreline that was privately held but undeveloped.

The TRSI embarked on a $30,000 fundraiser. The assessment would initiate the planning process with a firm set of guidelines to direct future development. The first step was sending questionnaires to all lake users to formulate a profile of the quality of experience desired.

Results demonstrated overwhelming support for planning controls on both private and Crown lands with islands-only development and new cottages spread out evenly. Most wanted cottages to be built on lots no smaller than two acres and desired no additional resorts. Half was in favour of three or four more youth camps.

TLA and Township See Eye to Eye

The board discussed the survey results with the Township of Temagami and started investigating a joint planning board to control private development. It planned to input survey results into a new Temagami District land use plan being developed by the MNR to update its 1973 plan.

A steering committee for the proposed Temagami planning area was formed in fall 1981 with lake and township representatives. The TLA chose Tim Gooderham. Dick Grant – a lawyer, Camp Temagami alumnus, town resident and Island 762 cottager – was appointed chair. The steering committee had become the nine-member Temagami Planning Board by summer 1982. The planning area covered the lake (excluding Bear Island) and the township.

The planning board hired Robert Lehman Planning Consultants in 1984 to draft an official plan. Completed two years later, following public consultation, the Official Plan (OP) specified islands-only development. Proposed cottage lot sizes varied by location, from a minimum of one acre on the Northeast Arm, Shiningwood Bay and Temagami Island. Elsewhere, lots would be a minimum of two acres.

The OP also called for a maximum of 20 new private lots per year for a total of no more than 226 over a 20-year period. The 20 lots per year provision and the special lot-size treatment of some parts of the lake would come back to bite the TLA following 1998 municipal amalgamation and the need for an expanded OP.

Wilderness versus Logging

One component of the new MNR plan was a proposed provincial wilderness park in the Lady Evelyn River region. It would cover 468 square kilometres and encompass traditional canoe routes and landmarks such as the Trout Streams, Maple Mountain and Ishpatina Ridge. There would be no logging and no new road access permitted inside the Lady Evelyn-Smoothwater Wilderness Park.

Battle lines were drawn with many of the same players taking the same sides as they did during the Maple Mountain resort controversy. Temiskaming MPP Ed Havrot opposed the park, as did local chambers of commerce and municipalities.

The Alliance for the Lady Evelyn Wilderness was basically the Save Maple Mountain Committee with a new name. Arguing the alliance's case in the *Times*, Hugh Stewart

The Golden Staircase on the Lady Evelyn River in the wilderness park in 2009. *Photo: Harold Keevil*

eloquently asked, "Do people want wilderness areas which involve canoe routes winding around clear-cut areas? ...Wilderness uplifts the human spirit. It is the music, the fine art, the literature, the theatre of the natural world." Hugh and his wife Carin ran Headwaters, an adult canoeing program from 1974 to '83, first on Lake Temagami, then out of Anima-Nipissing Lake west of Haileybury. The alliance pointed out that the park would cover just two per cent of Ontario's productive forest.

Three logging companies had timber agreements inside the proposed park and their representatives were the most vocal opponents. Arguing Milne's case in the *Times*, Doug Buck cited the threat of single versus multiple use of resources to the company's future existence and to increased unemployment. Milne was in the process of modernizing its sawmill to the tune of $4 million, basing its refit partly on the 20 per cent of its wood allocations that was to flow from the proposed park.

The board reached an impasse and put the issue before the membership at the 1981 AGM in the form of two motions. The first endorsed the Lady Evelyn-Smoothwater Wilderness Park, conditional on forestry companies receiving allocations elsewhere. Bruce Hodgins reminded members that the TLA is the Temagami Lakes Association, not a more narrowly defined Lake Temagami Association. The second motion stated that the TLA did not want to take a formal stand. The first motion narrowly passed after a lengthy debate. A year later the MNR greenlit the park, though it was slightly smaller than proposed.

Liskeard Lumber Road, running through the park, would remain open.

A New Land Use Plan

The MNR released a proposed Temagami District plan in the early 1980s. It included 200 cottage lots from Crown and private land on islands and possibly the mainland of Joan and McLean peninsulas. In addition, a gate preventing public access to the lake on the Red Squirrel Forest Access Road west of Camp Wanapitei would be removed. The road connects with Highway 11 north of Temagami, giving direct access for logging companies at Whitefish Bay and Sharp Rock Inlet.

The TLA soundly rejected the MNR's proposal to remove the Red Squirrel gate, citing policing problems, environmental degradation, fishing pressure and forest fire danger. It agreed to the MNR's 200 cottage target, provided they were dispersed on islands only.

The lake was also being reached through roads at the south end. The Field Lumber Company and others had established bush roads northwest from River Valley to Baie Jeanne at the bottom of the Southwest Arm. Islanders were becoming the victims of break-ins and theft. The TLA requested that the Baie Jeanne access point be controlled by a locked gate.

The MNR's final product, the Temagami District Land Use Guidelines, was released in 1983. The TLA scored on many points. The guidelines called for 200 dispersed islands-only cottage lots and for the Red Squirrel gate to remain in place. The Baie Jeanne access point was not mentioned because the MNR recognizes it as a legal access point.

Memberships Tumble

1980 memberships tumbled by 66 from 1979's 495, partly the result of some disapproval of the executive decision in 1979 to retain the TLA building. To add insult to injury, Class A property owner fees rose by $15. Most members don't hold a grudge for long; memberships rebounded in 1981, soaring to a then high of 509 – despite another hike in dues. This time, the TLA went after Class B associate or family members, upping their levy to $25 from a $10 fee set 10 years earlier by Dewey Derosier. A compulsory $10 Legal and Professional Fees Fund charge for Class A and B members was also introduced. Held in its own account, it would help position the board to react to continuing development pressures.

From Trash to Treasure

The TLA held a trial flea market on the front lawn of the TLA building in 1982. It has been staged every year since except for 2010. It was the brain child of cottagers Ernie and Helen Taylor, David and Mettajean Gerstner and David's secretary Jean Wilson. They were trying to devise a way of getting members together for a social occasion while raising funds for the radio service. From 1985 to '96 Helen Taylor organized a bake table which continues today under other floured hands, selling like hotcakes. Anticipated delights have included Sally Pride's lemon loaves, Catherine Morrison's cinnamon buns, Nancey Gooderham's blueberry muffins and Tuuli Lowery's rum cakes.

The inaugural flea market netted $300. Today it has been known to bring in more than $8,000. Proceeds are no longer restricted to funding the radio service and have supported such diverse projects as a Temagami skateboard park and CPR training.

Among flea market founders, only David Gerstner remains, at the highly-suspect self-proclaimed age of 50. He has enjoyed the Temagami experience since 1934 when he took a camping trip with a Dayton high school friend. Neither lad had a driver's licence but such matters were of no concern to the constabulary, because they weren't required. David had been driving since he was 11, conveying his mother to market on Saturdays. The pair witnessed several accidents on the gravel Ferguson Highway involving much more senior motorcar operators driving too fast.

The boys explored the South Arm, trolling as they paddled. Everything was right with the world until David's buddy felt a tug on his line and pulled up a nice bass. It suddenly flipped the lure, piercing his swimming trunks and jabbed his nether regions. David had the unenviable task of cutting off his pal's trunks with a filleting knife and carefully extricating two hooks while keeping his manhood intact. He poured whiskey on the wounds to sterilize them, but most of it went into the poor sod's mouth to mute the screams carrying across the water.

Whether David's friend had the bollocks to return is unknown; David did, accompanied by his wife Mettajean. World War II was raging and David was about to join the army. They rented a canoe from Marty Taylor's marina and headed up the North Arm and straight into four days of relentless rain. Sodden and sullen, they packed it in and beelined for town. Somewhere along the way, David lost his billfold containing his money and gasoline ration stamps. Adding to the couple's woes, a storm whipping up five-foot swells almost swamped them. They made land at Friday's Camp, overturning the canoe on the dock to protect their gear.

While enjoying coffee and cake offered by the Fridays, the Gerstners glanced out a window to see their canoe flying through the air. Two Friday boys made a rescue mission and the couple was invited to share dinner and breakfast after a restful night, compliments of the family.

As they paddled up the Northeast Arm the next day, they met a couple who lent them $20 and enough gas stamps to get back to Dayton. Then the skies opened up and someone came to their rescue once again. This time a cottager provided a warm shelter, a hot meal and a tow to town. After recounting their tangled tale to Marty Taylor, he also lent the pair a 20-spot.

It took David several years to talk Metta into giving the lake a second chance. The weather was perfect and she was enchanted. They built a 20 by 20-foot cottage in 1950 on Island 830 and David named his dog Friday. Friday once chased a 250-pound bear up a tree as the unsuspecting Gerstners approached. They paid favours forward by rescuing stranded canoeists and boaters in groups of up to 24 people who drained their hot chocolate stores.

Sue Gooderham, a daughter of Bill and Nancey Gooderham, chaired the bazaar committee for about a dozen years starting in 1986. She was honoured in 1992 as Member of the Year. "Oops!! Inevitable! Bound to happen! Surprised it didn't happen before!" read a 1991 *Times* headline. In the midst of flea market set-up madness, unsuspecting cottager Jane Macdonald dropped off a box of

Mettajean and David Gerstner, at far right, announce raffle prize winners at a 1980s flea market. *Photo: Pam Sinclair*

linens to be picked up by New Liskeard launderers. They got priced and sold. The TLA pleaded for their return and offered a refund to no avail. The story provided grist for the *Cottage Life* magazine mill.

From its humble beginnings, the flea market expanded to include a 50-50 draw and children's activities. Area merchants generously donate items for an auction and, for many years, Ty Morrison, "the backwoods barber," trimmed and teased. Temagami Barge sells pop and hot dogs, and donates all proceeds to the TLA. The sale of handicrafts and not-so-new stuff remains the bricks and mortar.

Literally hundreds of unsung heroes have helped make the flea market the hullabaloo it is today, by performing mundane grunt work such as sorting and pricing major and minor fleas, soliciting donations, manning stations, juggling boats, and disposing of the unlovable. Some of these volunteers have been Member of the Year honourees, including Ernie and Helen Taylor, their son David Taylor, David and Metta Gerstner, Jean Wilson, Duff Shaw (for handling flea market finances and running TLA elections), Robin Campbell, Lorie Jocius, Barbara Olmsted, Heather Windrem and Bobby Morrison.

Flea market volunteer David Taylor poses with his dachshund Weasel and TLA Executive Secretary Peter Healy at the 2009 flea market. *Photo: Pam Sinclair*

Most Devious Sleight-of-Hand on the Steering Wheel

In the 1940s Bob Morrison told his wife Catherine that they owed a visit to his cousin in Toronto, quite a stretch from their Ohio home. As Bob drove through the night, he suggested Catherine crawl into the back seat for some shut-eye. When she awoke, Bob was still driving — through towering pines, not the office towers she expected. Bob had another surprise in store; when he opened the trunk, inside were a boat motor and gas can, likely squashing the city attire Catherine had packed. They purchased Island 731 in 1949. Today, Catherine and her children Ty and Sue Morrison Jennings enjoy the cottage every summer. Son Bobby owns Island 718.

CHAPTER 19

PINTO, WINGFOOT, STINKING ISLANDS AND MORE...

As the struggle to save wilderness was heating up, most members were aware of the issues, including the Red Squirrel Road conflict. Yet appreciation of the simpler and finer things in life commanded their attention. Late North Arm cottager Daniel Felix, a Cleminshaw in-law, wrote a witty compendium of daily impressions in what he called *Dan's Delirious Digest*.

His (a)musings included a crash landing straight into the OPP launch due to a sticking gear shift. Dan described 12 characteristics making the lake "a very special place." They strike a familiar chord and include "blueberries at arm's reach, a mirror lake to reflect sunsets, sunrises and full moons, cooling north winds for sleeping, the haunting call of the loon, the sleep-lulling sound of the water lapping on the rocks and comfortable quarters, each with its own super view."

Pinto

Ted Underwood, a recently retired engineer with Goodyear Tire and Rubber Company in Akron, Ohio, was elected president in 1984. He wore two other hats – chair of the property protection and headquarters building committees. Ted was initially a director in the late 1970s. He and his wife Jeanne, the TLA's recording secretary and a director from 1987 until '90, became permanent residents of Island 988 in 1983.

Ted was introduced to the lake at Goodyear's Camp Pinto in 1961. Pinto's roots ran deep. Paul Litchfield ventured to Muskoka with a business associate from Goodyear where he had started work in 1898. "He had the vision to foresee that the Muskoka Lakes would become overdeveloped," said Paul's grandson Alan Hyde.

Paul arrived at T-Station in summer 1905 – a trip he repeated every year until his death in 1959. He stayed at Friday's Camp until about 1911 and then camped on Island 709. He later leased it while his wife Florence leased Island 710. In 1942 their daughter Katharine Litchfield Hyde bought Island 1248 in Whitefish Bay. Katharine died in 2001 at the grand age of 96. Her son Alan, his wife Polly, their children and grandchildren trek to Island 1248 every summer. Alan's brother Paul died in 2005. Paul and his wife Sherry had three sons who still enjoy cottage life. Paul Litchfield's great-great-grandchildren are the fifth generation on the lake.

As CEO of Goodyear, Paul's time on the lake was limited and Pinto received little family use. Islands 709 and 710 were handed down to Goodyear by Paul and Florence. Pinto closed in the early 1980s as a cost-cutting measure.

The company donated it to the Cleveland Y, which operated the camp for three years as Litchfield Islands YMCA. It was put up for sale in 1986 and purchased by Graham and Carol Hall of Bay Village, Ohio, about 1990.

Graham was an executive at a printing press company. He had attended Northwoods and was later a Cleveland Y trustee. The Halls rebuilt all the cabins except the triple-slip boathouse. They worked with a Cleveland architect and George Mathias Construction to create a luxurious but low key summer retreat. A distinctive feature is an arched log bridge connecting the two islands. The Hiner-Robbins family of Ashland, Ohio, bought the property from the Halls in 2006.

Moving North

Ted and Jeanne Underwood searched for their own piece of Pre-Cambrian rock in the mid-1970s. Due in part to the land cautions, undeveloped lots were in short supply. "The first realtor we approached knew of nothing for sale, but the next one had one lot available – and we bought it," Ted said. "We often kid now about how smart we were to pick this site, as if we had a great choice to make."

Before moving north in 1983, "We had spent a total of, maybe, six hours on the lake in the winter; we had attended a TLA meeting at the headquarters building one January," Ted recalled. "We got lots of advice from oldtimers – and we took it all! Most of the first summer and fall were spent getting ready for a completely new experience. Bought our

first snowmobile, got in enough groceries to last forever, and hoped that we hadn't burned our bridges too soon." Initial fears were soon forgotten and they made plans to stay put as long as health permitted.

Another "landed" immigrant couple is Hilton and Dora Young. She was recording secretary in the late 1980s and he was elected a director in 1990. The Youngs began enjoying four seasons on the lake in the 1990s and have spent part of every winter there. They have chalked up a combined 30 years of TLA service. Dora chaired the AGM committee for about 10 years, taking over for Nancy Davis who helmed it from 1986 to '92.

Elizabeth Currier of Dundas, Ontario, took over as recording secretary, a position she held from the mid-1990s until the early 2000s. Her daughter Ann Rice and husband Don own the South Arm's Tamar Vacations. Liz and her family bought property on Northeast Arm Island 90 in 1974. Liz's husband died of natural causes at the island. She had the grim task of driving the boat to town in the middle of the night to summon police. Liz passed away at the cottage in 2003 following a courageous battle with ALS.

Camping Out

William Stanley "Stan" Funnell, a University of Toronto chemistry professor, camped with friends on Island 1087 back in 1918. He took out a 21-year lease at $20 per year in 1922, the first year his wife Ethel and children Joan and Hugh visited the island.

Joan later recalled a family-essential loaf of bread floating in the bilge water of a rowboat they took from Bear Island to Island 1087, according to Angus Scully. The family spent two summers in a tent before Stan, Ethel, Stan's brother A.R. "Bert" Funnell and Stan's father Albert Funnell built a cabin.

Stan bought his first motorboat in 1923. It was a Dispro, produced in Port Carling, Ontario. Disappearing propeller boats, fondly known as dippies, feature a device that allows the prop to be lifted into an interior housing. They could go almost anywhere a canoe could with as little as an inch of prop blade protruding.

The Funnells' trip from T-Station to Island 1087 took more than five hours putting along at five kph. Kenneth and Ellen Wismer heard so many good things about Temagami from Stan back in Toronto that they camped on nearby Island 1086 in 1925 and subsequently leased it. Ken died in 1994 at 96. William John Taylor of Port Colborne, Ontario, now owns the island.

A Nobel Cause

When Island 1086's Ken Wismer wrote a student thesis in 1924 investigating the superheating of liquids, he never dreamed his research would be used in the development of a bubble chamber, one of nuclear physics' basic tools. His research led Donald Glaser to use the correct chemical fluid in scientific trials. Donald went on to win the 1960 Nobel Prize for inventing the bubble chamber.

Stan purchased Island 1087 in 1943 when his lease expired. When Stan died in 1948 ownership passed to Ethel. She died in 1990 at the ripe old age of 102. Her daughter Joan Iddon became the owner and, in turn, Joan's daughter Jill Scully. Jill and her husband Angus renovated the original 1924 cabin from 2002 to '09.

Most Infamous Islands

Wingeganahkweshin translates as "Stinking islands." The name refers to islands 1086 and 1087 in the North Arm, purported to be the site of a bloody battle between the Iroquois and Temagami natives back in the 1600s. The bodies left to decompose gave the islands their ghoulish name. Another less sensational version relates to the islands' sloping rocks where fish were supposedly cleaned and dried.

The Funnells of Island 1087 have unearthed a treasure trove of ancient artifacts, including spear heads, shot and clay bowls. They even discovered a French trade axe under a fallen 300-year-old cedar tree. One of the roots had grown through a hole in the handle. Some of these archaeological wonders were lent to the Temagami Historical Society by the late Hugh Funnell for an early 1980s exhibit at the TLA building. The island is owned by Funnell descendent Jill Scully. The Scullys' marine radio call sign is WinGee, a more manageable version of the aboriginal name.

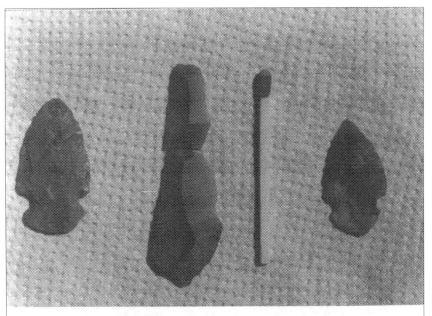

Arrowheads and a flake knife unearthed at Witch Point
by archaeologist Thor Conway in 1982. *Photo: Pam Sinclair*

Funnell descendents are fifth generation islanders.

Fish Heads

London, Ontario's Don Cooke finished Hugh's term. He ran a soft water business, which he sold to Culligan upon retirement. Don and his wife Florence purchased Island 185 in the early 1970s where they spent every season but winter. They died in 1996. Since then Island 185 has been enjoyed by the Cooke children Donald, Richard and Elizabeth, and their families. Don had been chair of the fish committee, replacing Alf Cook who had served in various capacities for about 25 years.

Alf passed away in 1998, partly due to the stress of being physically unable to make the trip to his beloved lake, his daughter Catherine Cook speculated. His wife Connie died in 2009. Islands 884 and 854 are now co-owned by Catherine and her brother John Cook.

Subsequent fish committee heads were Island 985's Wib Walker and Island 970's Gaye Smith. From Paisley, Ontario, Gaye hooked that position in 1990 and held it, with the patience of a lake trout angler, until 2004. "Fishing was the reason for my coming to Lake Temagami initially and the improvement of the sad state of fishing in Lake Temagami is

Albert Funnell, his wife Emily and their son Bert built a clapboard cottage on a Garden Island lot in 1933. They had only one mode of transport – a 10-foot lapstrake rowboat built by Toronto's Ned Hanlon. He was a 19th-century world champion oarsman. Having just a rowboat was not an impediment; the boat line made a daily stop at Wabun. Bert purchased the 1.1-acre lot in 1954 when the 21-year lease expired. The property was handed down to Bert's son Owen.

Hugh, a retired toxicologist born in 1918, joined the directors' team in 1984. He was known for his poetry, published periodically in the *Times*. Hugh and his wife Nora built a second cabin, named Easthaven, on Island 1087 in 1966. Hugh died before his three-year term as director was over. Nora died in 1994 and Easthaven went to Rheanon Funnell, one of their four daughters. The youngest of the my first concern," he once wrote. For a few years Gaye had a co-chair – Island 732's Dick Crum of Perry, Ohio. Dick was a college football coach prior to his retirement in 1992. He became a director in 1995.

No Dial Tone

First Vice President and TRSI Chair Ralph McMillen became the determined leader of a new telephone committee in 1984. Permanent residents had obtained phone service but there were not enough lines for seasonal residents. Ralph's aim was to have the service extended at reasonable rates. The only service then available to cottagers was radio telephone, costing $1,000 for installation, plus $500 in annual service charges.

Ralph's initial tactic was to urge members to write government officials and apply pressure. A turning point came when the committee convinced the Ontario Ombudsman's office that the Ontario Northland Telecommunications Commission was discriminating against seasonal residents. His battle was to last seven years but it ended on a happy note – the ringing of phones. Sixty-eight cottagers were on a waiting list. The initial wave didn't put much of a dent in the number of calls to TLA radio operators.

Ralph was beguiled by the lake's charms in 1954 as a guest at Wingfoot Island near Bear Island. Goodyear Canada acquired the island in 1945. It was named for their logo – the winged foot of Mercury, the Roman god of commerce. Karl "Charlie" Zwygart managed

Wingfoot and the lodge was equipped with a light plant. Charlie would ask guests when they wanted lights out and then carefully measure the fuel; when it ran out so did the lights. All activity ceased and guests retired to bed in pitch blackness.

Weekend guests were Goodyear customers while mid-week guests were employees. The employees were selected from all segments and individuals usually didn't know each other. The outcome was often lasting friendships. Charlie met the night train from Toronto with the camp boat *Pathfinder* and visitors were overwhelmed by the bountiful supply of skiffs, canoes and sailboats by the light of day. "And we didn't have to lift a hand to fill a gas tank, bail out a boat, or prepare for fishing trips – the boys looked after everything. It was living in a dream world," Ralph recalled.

New Owners

Charlie and Edith Zwygart became Cattle Island cottagers. Ralph and his wife Dorothy rented the Zwygart cottage from 1956 to '58 and then bought half of Island 681. Ten years later they moved to electrified Island 684, previously belonging to John and Mary Pheiffler. Ralph died in 1997. The Zwygart cottage became the year-round home of Bob and Gladys Farr until they moved to Bear Island in the early 2000s. Wingfoot guests Don Murray, Wally Denny and Fred Wilmott also went on to purchase property. Fred was a member of the logging committee in the late 1950s.

Grant McMillen, one of Ralph's two sons, was a director in the mid-2000s. An accountant, Grant chaired the finance committee. Peter and Susan Sleegers of London, Ontario, purchased the 7.5-acre Wingfoot Island from Bill and Doris Allen in 1992 and restored it to modern rusticity. Bill had served a second term as president in 1983.

By the mid-1980s some camps and resorts were in the hands of new owners. Island 808 cottager Jack Janssen of Muskoka bought White Gables from the Browns and reopened it in 1986 as Janssen House. Brian and Margaret Youngs bought the resort about 1989 and renamed it Silverwater Lodge. The Metcalfes sold Temagami Lodge to Paul Forsythe in the late 1980s and moved to town after nearly 30 years on the lake, including five summers at Broom Lodge.

Camp Wabikon was sold to Frank Saul by Gordon Wolfe in 1980. He teamed up with Marcello and Margaret Bernardo of Toronto. The Bernardos assumed sole ownership in 1983. Langskib owners David and Karen Knudsen purchased Camp Lorien in 1985 from the Moores to operate a co-ed canoeing camp called Northwaters.

A Father of a Different Ilk

Since 1984 non-denominational summer services have been held at the gracefully aging St. Ursula's Roman Catholic Church on Bear Island, built in 1924. Cattle Islander John Hyde, an American history professor at Massachusetts' Williams College, was the unpretentious preacher. Although he had no theological

training, years of keeping the attention of a lecture hall full of students honed his skills. His services consisted of prayers, hymns, and his own Temagami-leaning biblical adaptations.

Now a professor emeritus, "Father" John marked his 25th and final summer as a cottage minister in 2009. He was bestowed a photo of himself as the "Bishop of Bear Island" and some shots of the congregation. All told, the offering plate raised roughly $20,000 earmarked for preserving and restoring the church building. Island 1088's Ray and Martha Banghart stepped up to the pulpit in 2010 to take the tradition forged by John in new directions.

"Father" John Hyde at the church entrance carrying a pastoral staff crafted by a Bear Islander upon the occasion of his retirement. *Photo: Temagami Times.*

> **Wings**
>
> *Riding on wings of moonlight*
> *I suddenly see so far*
> *Darkness has less power now*
> *Over night, less beauty marred.*
> *Starlight stipples inky black*
> *Pin drop holes of light*
> *Lasting so long, piercing so deep*
> *The lake's secrets theirs by rite.*
> *A call far-off heard, so soft*
> *Erie voices of loons unite*
> *To form a banner of raucous sound*
> *So shocking in the velvet night.*
> *Riding on the wings of the moon*
> *Stealing calm from silence*
> *Quiet as the sleeping loon*
> *Starlight reflections conquer distance.*
> *Winded chariot waves*
> *Shatter the silent stillness*
> *Rushing through the satin shades*
> *Of night's eternal flame.*
> Tracy Banghart, 1996

TAFIP is Hatched

The MNR began promoting a Community Fisheries Involvement Program in 1984. It was a reversal of past government policy that discouraged private clubs and associations from participating in egg hatching, habitat improvement and restocking. The MNR now welcomed a hands-on approach by non-professionals. While the government provided technical guidance and partial funding, local groups contributed labour and raised private funds. The Temagami Area Fish Involvement Program (TAFIP) was spawned in 1985. It brought together many diverse organizations, including the Township of Temagami, the Temagami and District Chamber of Commerce, the Royal Canadian Legion, the Temagami Tourist Operators' Association (TemTOA), LaTemPRA and the TLA.

With an eye to raising $50,000, TAFIP launched the largest pledge fundraiser ever undertaken in the area at the time. It was spearheaded by Island 1058's Bob Richmond. He had recently retired as senior vice president of the world's largest fundraising firm. He and his wife Marie were guests at Chimo, starting in 1957, and bought their cottage in 1968.

TAFIP elected Bill Metcalfe as its first president. Pledges more than doubled the goal by summer 1986. The largest donor was Sherman Mine. A fish hatchery was built in Temagami and 259,000 walleye eggs were milked, fertilized and transported to hatchery tanks. Some 172,000 jar-hatched fry were released into local lakes. To improve survival rates, TAFIP soon built several fingerling rearing ponds. Bob died in 2002 but his legacy lives on.

Countless volunteers have contributed to the program's success in many ways, from raising funds and babysitting the egg jars to readying the rearing ponds and cleaning spawning shoals. The program was bearing fruit by 1989 as local fishers began reeling in

Ivan Beauchamp (l) and Wayne Adair carry pens to separate male and female walleye during TAFIP's first egg capture in 1986 at Red Squirrel Lake. *Photo: Pam Sinclair*

lots of small walleye in spots where there once were few.

An annual winter Ling Fling, organized by Jerry Burrows and others, lures some 200 permanent and seasonal town and lake residents to Wabikon Bay for a fundraising fish fry. The inaugural bash took place in 1992 and attracted roughly 50 feasters. The TLA includes a TAFIP donation form with its membership renewal notices and makes an annual $1,000 donation to TAFIP at the AGM.

Like other businesses, Jerry Burrows' charter fishing venture was a beneficiary of TAFIP's good deeds over the years. In the early 1990s he crafted two Cape Islanders, similar to the vessels used by maritime fishers. They are 39 feet long with 12-foot beams and the wood hulls are sheathed in fibreglass. He kept one of the five-ton boats and named it the *Ketch III*. The other went to his son's James Bay charter

fishing outfit. Jerry's custom-furnished craft features a bathroom, a holding tank for grey and blackwater, galley kitchen and a boom to launch two electric fishing boats. He had previously built a large wooden launch to transport Wabikon campers and their gear to and from the landing. Jerry and his wife Louise were caretakers there for 25 years until their retirement in 2007. They now reside in New Liskeard.

Pitching in

Another area where local residents and groups stepped in to assist the MNR is campsite and canoe route maintenance. Until the 1970s canoeists tripping Temagami's routes practised no-trace camping. The Department of Lands and Forests' ranger crews kept trails and portages in good shape in case they were needed as fire routes. Youth camp guides and counsellors were designated backcountry fire wardens by the department and given badges to wear during canoeing season. Island 1005's Russell Tuckerman has a collection of his grandfather Bill Russell's badges, spanning several decades when he worked for Keewaydin,

Jerry Burrows' *Ketch III. Photo: Andy Stevens*

undertook with Doug Adams of Northland Paradise: "Beautiful weather, but a demoralizing situation. We managed to keep each other laughing though. Doug's biggest disappointment of the day was the realization, at lunch time, that his lunch (a sandwich, slice of chocolate cake and a banana) was in a plastic bag under about 1 ton of garbage. We shared what we had and Doug topped off the meal by producing some after-dinner mints. Who says you can't be refined even when you're picking up other people's litter."

Project CANOE (Creative and Natural Outdoor Experience) was born in 1976 when some Toronto Children's Aid Society youths were taken on a canoe trip in Algonquin Park. The focus shifted to Temagami and Project CANOE opened a base in 1999 at the former Briggs Junior Ranger Camp off the access road.

Charting a New Course

New to the board of directors in 1985 was Island 1005's Jim Dow. He was a commercial pilot from Toronto. His father Hank Dow had

Wabun and Camp Temagami. The MNR initiated a dedicated canoe route maintenance program in the 1970s but cancelled it in the late 1980s.

Youth camps from southern Ontario began sending groups to Temagami in the early 1990s. No reservations or permits were required, access road parking was free, routes were well-mapped (by MNR park ranger Hap Wilson in his *Temagami Canoe Routes*), and the area was remote and scenic. Overuse and neglect resulted. The TLA, youth camps, LaTemPRA, TemTOA, Friends of Temagami (FOT), Project CANOE and others stepped in to keep Temagami pristine.

In a *Temagami Wild* newsletter published by FOT, Mike Pepall described a snafu occurring during a garbage clean-up he

Jim Dow displays his second Member of the Year award in 2010. *Photo: Pam Sinclair*

Temagami Dawn

Only the soft
Gurgling of his paddle
Broke the silence until
A fish jumped
Spreading
A galaxy of ripples
Across the flat surface.
A grunting cough.
Slowly he turned and
Could just discern
A moose,
Come from the swamp for
Its morning drink and
To escape the flies.
Dawn was near;
There came the distant
Sweet song of
A Thrush
Near by, the Piccolo piping of
A white throat.
He turned to the East.
The sky was goldening behind
The inky black silhouettes
Of trees
Ringing the shore of
Lake Temagami.
Hugh Funnell, circa 1975

earlier edited the TLA directory. Jim chaired the navigation committee and acted on gripes about the unwieldy and easily ripped 1984 navigation chart by reducing its size to two by three feet. He had it printed on both sides and reproduced on plasticized waterproof and untearable paper. More than 400 of Jim's maps had flown off the shelves by 1987. After 30 years of trial and error, it seemed the TLA had finally got it right.

The chart was enhanced in 1993 when four colours were added, including red and green for the buoys. The cost to members was $10 while non-members were charged $25. The shoal map was updated again in 2008 and is now GPS-compatible. It sets members back $20 and is available on CD.

CHAPTER 20

WILDERMESS

Preserving Temagami wilderness is a compelling issue. The Red Squirrel Road conflict was back in the news in 1985. The MNR wanted to extend the east-west running forestry road to connect with the north-south running Liskeard Lumber Road. That road ran smack through the Lady Evelyn-Smoothwater Wilderness Park. The objective was access to jack pine and spruce so Liskeard Lumber could haul it north to the Elk Lake Planing Mill. Red and white pine would be harvested and moved east to the Milne sawmill. No timber was to be harvested within the park.

The 15-kilometre Red Squirrel extension would create direct access from Highway 11 north of Temagami to the wilderness park

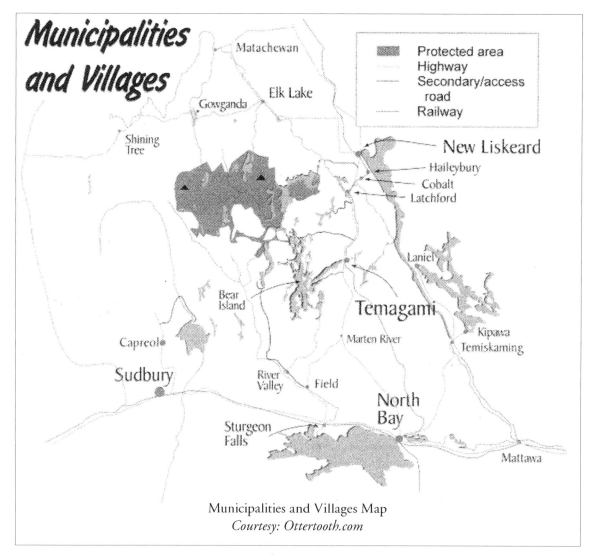

Municipalities and Villages Map
Courtesy: Ottertooth.com

188

and from Highway 560 near Elk Lake to Lake Temagami. The TLA believed it would put enormous pressure on the MNR to remove gates and provide unrestricted access from all directions to the lake and the park, thus undermining the area's unique wilderness character.

The Association of Youth Camps on the Temagami Lakes (AYCTL) vigorously opposed the extension, fearing that wilderness canoe routes were threatened by the invasion of motorized recreationists. Lake organizations and the TAA called for an environmental assessment prior to any road work, supported by New Democratic Party (NDP) Temiskaming

Historical researcher, author and Temagami Wilderness Society-Earthroots founder Brian Back in 2009. *Photo: Brian Back*

MPP David Ramsay. The province acquiesced and DeLCan Limited was hired to oversee the study, the first ever conducted on an Ontario forest access road.

At one public session, a delegation of Sturgeon Falls area fish and hunt clubs pressed for the link-up, plus an additional link with Highway 805 north from River Valley. They hoped it would open up the area to sportsmen along the Highway 17 corridor. If roads are to be built with public funds then the public should have unrestricted access, they reasoned. As expected, a 1987 draft assessment report recommended the link-up proceed, with access-controlling gates and other mitigating measures to lessen the impact.

Temagami Wilderness Society

The Temagami Wilderness Society (TWS) emerged in 1986, dedicated to Temagami conservation. It was conceived at Keewaydin by Brian Back and Claire Muller, a naturalist and summer resident of Temagami Island. New Liskeard environmentalist Terry Graves was another founding member. Brian became the executive director. Born and raised in North Bay he spent summers at the family's Northeast Arm cottage. From 1970 until '75 Brian was a counsellor at Wabikon. He joined Keewaydin's trip staff from 1976 until '80. Brian authored *The Keewaydin Way*, a sweeping history of the camp published in 1983 and sequelled in 2004.

The TWS's first donation came from Fred Reimers, owner and director of Keewaydin from 1975 to '90. He kept track of campers, guides and supplies via the TLA's radio service. When his authoritative voice came booming through the mic, the radio operator on duty jumped hoops to answer ASAP. Due to his U.S. Air Force background, Fred became known in-camp as "the Major." His contribution was used to send out a mailing to solicit members.

T-shirts were also sold sporting a provocative message: "Temagami Chainsaw Massacre." The society grew into the largest single-issue environmental group in Canada with almost 14,000 members by 1988. The TLA joined the TWS in 1986, along with the AYCTL, TemTOA and the Lady Evelyn Tourist Operators' Association.

The TWS proposed a 2,750-square kilometre Temagami Wildlands Reserve to preserve one of the country's last tracts of unspoiled wilderness and old-growth forest. The protected land would encircle the wilderness park and extend from the Elk Lake area to Lake Temagami. Most access roads would be closed, except for the Lake Temagami Access Road. Mining and timber extraction would be banned. The wildlands concept was embraced by environmental groups across Ontario and caused a kerfuffle the likes of which northeastern Ontario had never before seen.

Bitter opposition sprang from the forestry and business sectors, the Timiskaming Board of Education, politicians from Timmins to North Bay, and hunt and fish clubs from Sudbury through Mattawa. In Elk Lake, a highway sign was erected stating, "Closed – Population 0 – Gone Canoeing."

A Cause Célèbre

Support for the reserve concept was wide-ranging and went well beyond northeastern Ontario. The International Union for the Conservation of Nature, based in Switzerland, added the wilderness park to its global register of threatened areas.

Former TLA president Bruce Hodgins led a canoe trip through the road-threatened area in summer 1987. His entourage included author Margaret Atwood, former federal cabinet minister Judy Erola and novelist M.T. Kelly. The VIPs specified a leisurely trek but Bruce was anxious for them to see everything, M.T. Kelly quipped in a *Toronto Star* piece. "We expected to see the Lady Evelyn and not to travel through it on a forced march." Bruce had squeezed a seven-day trip listed in the Wanapitei adult schedule into five days.

Soon the Canadian literati and cultural elite threw its collective weight behind the wildlands reserve proposal. Many joined the Save Temagami Committee based in Toronto, including writer-broadcaster Pierre Berton, author Farley Mowat, publisher Jack McClelland, Jack's brother-in-law Boyd Matchett, lawyer and Cochrane's Camp alumnus Julian Porter, and wildlife artist Robert Bateman. Temagami had become a cause célèbre. The interference of outsiders infuriated many residents who interpreted the situation as a local jobs issue. The struggle was once again spun by the media as pitting northern livelihoods against southern tourism.

Entrance to Dirty Heart Bay. *Photo: Harold Keevil*

Dozens of national and international environmental groups sided with the TWS. The wilderness issue loomed so large it was featured on the current affairs program *W5* and David Suzuki's *The Nature of Things*. It also warranted a big spread in *Canadian Geographic* magazine.

Few northern residents publically endorsed the reserve. They were likely so intimidated they kept their green leanings to themselves. Advocates belonging to the Temiskaming Action Committee would later join road blockades and protests. Their long-term goal, versus a perceived short-term gain of forestry jobs, was to preserve a rich natural environment for future generations.

Temagami Area Working Group

The Liberal government called an election in 1987. To diffuse the tension, it announced the formation of the Temagami Area Working Group, a citizens' committee whose mandate was to reach a compromise and make recommendations. Though its cutting permits had been put on hold, Milne was allowed to cut pine in the Gull Lake area via water access only.

The TLA initially spurned the working group. President Tom Romans, an economics professor with the University of New York at Buffalo, said a conclusion of multiple use was expected, preventing the wildlands reserve option. Even so, Tim Gooderham was appointed as its representative. Tom was elected president in 1987. He had canoed the area in 1958 as a university student.

Tom and his wife Joanne bought isolated Island 1250 because they believed most of the lake was over-populated. It is the only island inside Hammerhandle Bay or Dirty Heart Bay, the traditional name preferred by the Romans. Arriving on the lake in 1966 with an infant, they were likely the first cottagers to install CB radio, to keep in touch with the post manager. The narrow, shallow entrance to their bay limits the size of boat they can drive. Depending on the water level, there is a short paddle with the motor up. If the water is low, the boat is moored outside the bay's entrance and access is gained via canoe.

Temagami Front and Centre

For the first time in history, Temagami was one of the main issues in a provincial election campaign. MPP David Ramsay proposed a wilderness buffer zone between the lake and the wilderness park in 1986. There would be no logging and no access road construction in the buffer zone. He was publicly opposed to the Red Squirrel Road extension and suggested the creation of a forest management authority to resolve conflicts.

David was then an NDP member and the Liberal government didn't pay him much heed. In the meantime, he defected to the Liberals and no longer promoted his buffer zone or the wildlands reserve, which he now branded "absurd." Then, at the 1989 TLA AGM, he called himself "a conservationist." He touted his new party's line by supporting the working group initiative, similar to his earlier proposed forest authority.

Former Conservative MPP Ed Havrot, who had disgraced himself during the Maple Mountain resort fiasco, was once again on the hustings. He never let an opportunity to slam David Ramsay for "flip-flopping" slip by. He accused the government of "practically selling

us down the river to an elitist environmental gang down south."

The NDP was in favour of protecting the environmental integrity of wilderness areas. Leader Bob Rae hung the local candidate out to dry on the eve of the election by stating that no logging should be permitted in the Temagami forest until the land claim was settled.

The local campaign culminated in a heated candidates' debate in Temagami. Outside, some 100 log-filled transport trucks clogged the town while protesters demonstrated against the wildlands reserve. Resource industry workers moved their peaceful protest to the Red Squirrel Road during a wilderness celebration weekend at Camp Wanapitei.

David Ramsay was re-elected although Ed Havrot was the clear victor in resource-based towns like Temagami and Elk Lake. David was an unsuccessful 1992 Liberal leadership candidate. During his lengthy political career, he served as minister of natural resources, aboriginal affairs, correctional services, and agriculture and food. He retired in 2011.

Hearings Draw Extreme Views

The Temagami Area Working Group was composed of representatives of area municipalities, forest and mining industries, tourism, permanent and seasonal residents, youth camps, and fish and game clubs. It held three gruelling days of public hearings in winter 1988 in Elk Lake, Temagami and North Bay. They were well-attended and the vast majority of speakers were pro-development. The North

Bay forum caused the biggest rout.

An overflow crowd, some bused in from Sturgeon Falls, Mattawa and Sudbury, toted placards and sported buttons proclaiming "Access Is Our Right" while chanting the same theme. The North Bay police patrolled the auditorium. To a chorus of boos, TLA President Tom Romans recommended compensation for forest industry workers who would lose their jobs, via user fees and taxes from those who would benefit from the proposed reserve.

Environmentalists were incensed that no public hearing was held in southern Ontario where they believed the majority of speakers would have been in favour of the reserve.

The working group folded prematurely when pro-development members rejected a draft report by Chair Dr. John Daniel, president of Sudbury's Laurentian University, because it failed to provide unrestricted road access for sportsmen. John submitted it to the minister of natural resources anyway,

Men with an ATV and boat trailer emerge from beyond the Whitefish Bay gate on the Red Squirrel Road. The ineffective gate was moved in 1987 to the Eagle River Bridge.
Photo: Temagami Wilderness Society

although it bore only his signature and none of the 15-member working group. His report recommended the MNR establish a council to advise it on Temagami matters and to act as a Red Squirrel Road extension monitoring panel. While rejecting the wildlands reserve, he said the section of Liskeard Lumber Road running through the wilderness park should be closed by 1996 so it would only form a temporary link.

Three minority reports were submitted to the MNR with the TLA subscribing to the one bearing the most member signatures. They were committed to the wildlands reserve and believed the Red Squirrel Road should not be linked to any roads, including Goulard Lumber Road off Highway 805, potentially giving additional access from the River Valley area.

Road Extension Approved Amid Controversy

The final environmental assessment report echoed the draft recommending the Red Squirrel extension proceed with gates to restrict access. The name of the consulting firm was conspicuously absent. DeLCan would later accuse the MNR of watering the report down to downplay possible ecological damage. Despite calls for public hearings, the minister of the environment approved the report without holding any on the grounds of "undue delay."

Mirroring a suggestion in John Daniel's report, the Temagami Advisory Council (TAC) was set up. One of its tasks was monitoring the road extension's construction and impact. To

mollify conservation groups, the MNR created three new waterway parks – Obabika River, Solace Lake and Sturgeon River. The TLA was not granted representation on TAC, but two lake appointees held similar views.

At a TAC meeting in River Valley, a recommendation that the illegal Cross Lake access point be closed permanently caused a hubbub. About 125 protesters nearly forced the meeting's cancelation while threatening violence down the road. Agitators carried picket signs declaring "We will never surrender Cross Lake" and chanted "Cross Lake! Cross Lake!" TAC Chair John Daniel's tires were slashed. The MNR dynamited the Cross Lake access in summer 1989 but two weeks later "persons unknown" re-established it. The problem was temporarily solved with bulldozer trenches.

There were threats of burning down camps and resorts. The only gas station in Elk Lake had started refusing fill-ups to canoeists including Bruce Hodgins. The dispute got dirtier when the forest industry reported equipment damage due to spiked trees – a serious threat to the safety of bush and mill workers.

A New Lease on Life

Doug Buck was recovering from a heart transplant in 1985. He was the second oldest heart recipient in Canada and the only one in northern Ontario. Doug had contracted a rare and fatal weakening of the heart muscle, induced by a viral infection.

Doug's new lease on life prompted him to refocus his priorities. He became an independent forestry consultant and developed a more holistic and sustainable approach. He also aspired to new heights. Sponsored by Transplant International, Doug and two other organ recipients climbed Mount Kilimanjaro as a gesture of gratitude to organ donors. He had to abandon the ascent part way up on his doctor's advice due to a low heart beat rate. The expedition doctor was Peter Nichol who would succeed Carol Cochrane as acid rain committee chair. Doug's remarkable life came to an end in 1992.

Chief Gary Potts and Second Chief Rita O'Sullivan meet Attorney General Ian Scott at Bear Island in 1986 to consider a land claim settlement offer. *Photo: Pam Sinclair*

Ontario Offers Cash and Real Estate

The Temagami Planning Board sent its Official Plan (OP) to Ontario's minister of housing for final approval in winter 1986. However, approval was withheld due to renewed provincial negotiations with the TAA. The Ontario Supreme Court had overturned the TAA's claim to aboriginal title in 1984. The proceedings were covered extensively by *Times* editor Pam Glenn. It was one of the longest civil cases in Ontario judicial history, involving 3,000 exhibits, lasting more than two years and filling 68 volumes of transcripts. Pam went on to read every page at the Bear Island library as a research assistant to Bruce Hodgins.

In his 300-page decision, Justice Don Steele found that TAA interest in its ancestral lands was extinguished by the 1850 Robinson-Huron Treaty. No one from the Temagami Indian Band had signed it because, at the time, the band was so small it was represented by a prominent chief from Lake Wanapitei. After treaty annuities began being paid in 1883, the band was held to have adhered to the treaty. The band, therefore, had a claim to unfulfilled treaty obligations, which the Crown was bound to honour. The TAA intended to take its case before the Ontario Court of Appeal.

One courtroom exhibit was a birchbark canoe from the Matchett family. Lloyd acquired it in 1912 for $16 from a native artisan he met on the Montreal River. The canoe strengthened the argument that the band was a distinct tribe with entrenched traditions at the time of the treaty signing. With its uniquely curved bow and stern, the canoe is a fine example of the local building style. Today it hangs in Boyd and Rose Matchett's Island 989 cabin.

In fall 1986 Ontario presented the TAA with a $30-million land and cash settlement package. After studying the offer, the TAA rejected it. Government funding was available to proceed with either the appeal or to resume conciliatory talks but not both. "To accept a negotiated position of the provincial government while that [the impending appeal] was a reality, it seemed it would compromise our integrity," Chief Gary Potts reasoned. Had the offer been accepted, lands chosen by the TAA within the planning area would have been subject to compliance with the OP, which had just been greenlit.

A Village of Poker Players Raises a Cottage

Toronto-area physics teacher Graeme Thompson served as TLA president from 1986 to '87. His father Ken Thompson had canoed the area in the mid-1930s and bought Island 198 about 1949. The original 8 by 12-foot cabin housed a family of four. On rainy days they had only a deck of cards to keep boredom at bay. The island later went to cabin fever survivors Graeme and his brother Ian.

By the 1970s Island 198 could no longer be seen as "a beautifully isolated island, about a half-mile off the main channel, and adjacent to its own private bay," Graeme reflected. Boatline Bay Marine and a Milne landing directly across from the Thompsons' had arrived.

Graeme's uncle and aunt Gordon and Florence Thompson bought Island 179 in 1942 and took an active interest in TLA affairs for more than 40 years. Their idyllic log cabin inspired Graeme to build his own. Starting in 1974 poker-playing buddies were lured north with promises of cards and beer, only to be handed stripping tools to bark logs. It took six years of heavy labour, which is how the cottage got its name – Stagger Inn.

Ken disagreed with Graeme's decision to put in hydro, preferring fish camp rusticity. Several invitations to come over for a hot shower met resistance. One day while Ken was alone on the island, Graeme came back and noticed the shower stall was wet. No words were exchanged between father and son.

After construction dust settled, Graeme had some time to devote to the TLA. One of his pet projects was Cottage Watch, modelled after its urban counterpart Neighbourhood Watch. Members taking part left their VHF radios on at night in order to summon emergency help in case of a fire or medical crisis. The program assisted several emergencies during summer 1994. One was a fire engulfing Joe and Sarah Seivold's main cabin on Island 1088. An "All Stations" bulletin was answered by Graeme and by Carol Lowery. Calls were made and islanders with fire pumps responded. Brisk action prevented the fire's spread to other cottages on the island.

CB Signal Fades to Black

Graeme authored a radio operators' handbook. When the TLA installed a VHF radio in 1987, there were only 20 marine stations on the lake. The service was controlled by the federal Department of Communications and operators required two documents – an operator's certificate good for life and a station licence requiring annual renewal. This licence has not been required since 1999.

For several years Graeme was known as "Mr. Radio Communications" for the certification courses he taught on behalf of the Georgetown Power and Sail Squadron. Cottagers leapt onto the bandwagon and the biggest jump in VHF-rigged vessels was in 1990. TLA radio operators had their hands full keeping track of all the new call signs. Graeme retired as chair of the marine radio committee in 2002 and Tim Gooderham took over. Only 13 members were still using CB radios by 1992 and six of them had telephones. In light of those statistics and the aural trauma of listening to skip 11 hours a day, the TLA discontinued monitoring its "good buddy."

Saying Goodbye

In 1986 following 23 years of service, Bill Gooderham resigned as treasurer. Gerda Glenn, former president Jack Glenn's wife, took over his book-balancing act. Jack was again on the board, having been re-elected a director. He chaired the budget committee until 1992 when both Jack and Gerda stepped down. Jack's four grandchildren are fifth generation island dwellers.

His daughter Pam obtained full time work as a newspaper reporter and photographer in 1985 and, a year later, found the work load of toiling on two newspapers too consuming. For the first time since its birth in 1971, the *Times*

was not published. Jeanne Underwood stepped into the breach in 1987. After 10 years of note-taking, Jeanne was succeeded as recording secretary by Director Bryan Plumstead, son of Bill and Niki.

Carol Cochrane bid adieu in 1987 after 15 years of championing acid rain reductions. Her successor, Director Peter Nichol, was a cardiologist at the University of Western Ontario. He and his wife Judith purchased Island 459 in 1982. They moved to Alberta in 1994 but kept the cottage.

Peter soon found himself in the thick of things on the acid rain front. In 1989 he reported that INCO would reduce its SO2 emissions by 50 per cent by 1994. In 1991 he reported that the U.S. would reduce SO2 emissions by half by 2000. According to Peter, it wasn't time for the TLA to rest on its laurels. Another water quality threat emerged when members sent samples to the Temiskaming Health Unit for analysis. Many had unacceptable levels of fecal coliform, spurring Peter to try to document the extent of the problem.

The committee, now called environment, conducted a three-year sanitary survey starting in 1992. Funding for two students was secured through the MOE's Environmental Youth Corps. They inspected marinas, cottages and pleasure boats for compliance with MOE sewage disposal regulations. Only three per cent had infractions and they were reported to the MOE.

The parameters were widened in 1993 to include greywater disposal, privies, cesspools and lagoons. A total of 109 inspections were carried out on the Northeast Arm. Some minor problems were uncovered. Most involved greywater disposal and non-vermin-proof privies, and were resolved by the owners. A 1994 re-inspection showed some non-compliance. The MOE planned to fine owners if problems were not resolved.

Temagami Comes Courting

Reeve Ron Prefasi made an annexation pitch at the 1987 AGM held in Temagami. He said annexation of the rest of the islands (excluding Bear Island) by the township would give property owners a say in how the area is managed, instead of being at the mercy of the MNR. Pressure was mounting from the Sturgeon Falls region for the MNR to improve access points to the lake, he added. Council shared the TLA's concern about upgraded access points but for a different reason – they bypassed Temagami's commercial core. A union of the lake and township could block those clamouring for better access, he argued.

Members responded with misgivings, the major ones being: tax increases of 40 to 50 per cent above provincial land and school board levies with few services rendered; U.S. citizens, comprising more than one-third of the membership, being disenfranchised; subsequent councils insensitive to the TLA's desire to preserve the lake; and with the closure of Sherman Mine looming, Temagami's real concern was boosting its tax base.

An elementary school teacher, Ron proposed the formation of a fact-finding committee to study the pros and cons. He assured members

that the township would not move forward if a significant number of lake dwellers were opposed following a year-long review. The TLA cautiously agreed to representation.

A Resignation

Leaps and bounds in membership can be attributed in part to a need for cottagers to present a unified front against annexation and the perceived erosion of wilderness values. In 1991 membership topped the 700 mark. While the TLA's voice grew stronger, Bryan Plumstead resigned from the board in 1987. As a Township of Temagami employee, he said his credibility was stretched to the limit trying to represent both ends of the preservation versus development spectrum.

Following the closure of Sherman Mine and Milne, the Temagami and Latchford Economic Development Corporation was created, funded by the province. Bryan was appointed tourism coordinator and assigned the task of promoting economic diversification.

The TLA appointed Island 708's Shelley Timms, a southern Ontario lawyer, to serve the remaining two years of Bryan's term. Her late grandparents Stewart and Nina MacInnes first experienced Temagami in the 1940s, staying at Camp Adanac. They later purchased Island 708 from Doris Wurth. Shelley became an elected director and first vice president. Her mother Nancy Davis also served as a director and coordinated preparations for six AGMs.

CHAPTER 21

A BACKCOUNTRY BATTLEFIELD

The TAA reacted strongly to government approval of the Red Squirrel Road extension. They established a blockade and encampment on the road where it passes Sharp Rock Inlet beyond the MNR gate near Whitefish Bay. The TWS reacted by suing Ontario for ignoring calls for public hearings.

Nearly 100 Temagami-area sawmill workers and supporters met with five cabinet ministers to prod them into action but were told the extension was being held up by the blockade and the lawsuit. Tensions exploded on Friday of the 1988 Labour Day weekend when 200 protesters blocked the Lake Temagami Access Road near Highway 11. They were hoping to prevent cottagers from reaching their destinations.

The stand-off was brief but tense as about 300 OPP officers arrived and a helicopter circled. The crowd was ordered to disperse. The riot squad later broke up a "sit-down." Arrestees included Reeve Ron Prefasi. Wilful obstruction charges against those arrested, labelled the "Temagami 51" in the media, were dismissed a few months later.

The TAA was ordered by the Ontario Court of Appeal to dismantle its seven-month-old blockade in December 1988. The court also ordered the government not to proceed with the road extension until the TAA's appeal of the ruling against its land claim was dealt with. The TAA lost its appeal in February 1989. The court found that any TAA land rights had been extinguished either by the Robinson-Huron Treaty or the Temagami band's adherence to it.

The TWS also lost its lawsuit. The road extension was approved. A Sudbury construction company was awarded the $3.5-million contract – the most expensive primary forest access road ever built over such a short distance. In a TWS bid to amp up public support, a benefit concert was held in Toronto in April 1989, in cooperation with Beaver Canoe Limited, featuring Gordon Lightfoot and Murray McLaughlan.

Temagami's Economic Future Dims

The Milne sawmill, employing about 140 people, went into receivership. Roger Fryer, former Milne co-owner and owner of Field Lumber, attempted to buy the company, offering 50 cents on the dollar to Milne's creditors. The deal was contingent on an assured wood supply via the Red Squirrel Road.

In winter 1989 Dofasco announced the closure of the Sherman Mine and Kirkland Lake's Adams Mine. Faced with a catastrophic loss of tax revenue, the Township of Temagami intensified efforts to annex the lake. The study group's Dick Grout conveyed the TLA's opposition, citing tax benefits for the township and few services for the lake.

There was a bid to revive the Maple Mountain resort proposal. Former MPP Ed Havrot suggested a Las Vegas-style casino. It fell flat for the same reasons the scheme was dropped 15 years earlier. Another suggestion came from Benoit Serre, an unsuccessful Liberal candidate for the Timiskaming MP's job in the 1988 federal election. He recommended the land claim be resolved by giving the TAA the Lady Evelyn-Smoothwater Wilderness Park containing Maple Mountain.

Dick Grout was elected president by the board in 1989, having joined the directors' team in 1988. His initial encounter with the lake came in 1936 when he vacationed at Camp Acouchiching with his parents Harold and Esther Grout. Harold bought Island 943 near Couch in 1946. The family pitched in with local builder Alex Aird to construct a cabin. From 1942 to '45 Dick was a counsellor at Cochrane's Camp and later a fishing guide at Couch where he met his wife Sally. She is a daughter of Howard Baker who served briefly as chair of the logging committee in the 1950s. Dick was with Imperial Oil for 35 years after graduating

from the University of Toronto with a bachelor of commerce degree.

Holiday Houseboaters

Dick served as chair of the new boating committee, set up to investigate the alarming growth of the houseboat holiday industry since the early 1980s. By 1988 there were two principal commercial operations, renting out a total of 16 vessels – Peter and Annemarie Drenth of Leisure Island near town, and the late Bob Gareh who had a Three Buoys franchise from leased town docks. There were also a number of privately-owned houseboats, some rented out.

A Leisure Island houseboat finds a sandy tuck-away.
Photo: Mike Drenth

The board viewed houseboats as floating cottages whose occupants were free of the restraining knots of taxation and the OP anchor on development. By 1989 nearly 70 of the 226 cottage lots set out in the OP had been accounted for through severances and subdivisions. The consensus of the board was that the impact of houseboats should be considered in development plans.

Under Chair Charles King, the boating committee produced a map in 1991 in conjunction with the MNR. It designated overnight mooring sites and the maximum number of houseboats permitted at each. The committee pressed the province for greywater containment regulations and houseboat population control.

Ontario proposed in 1991 that all houseboats be equipped with greywater holding tanks within two years. A year later legislation was postponed. The MOE instead recommended the use of phosphate-free and non-toxic soaps, discouraged discharge of greywater overboard and suggested holding tanks be installed. While blackwater (sewage) requires containment by law, greywater was, well, a grey area.

It is difficult to enact rules that bind a single recreational activity and exclude others. Campers, for example, could wash dishes and bathe in the lake, and their discharge was not regulated. Youth camps have for years used biodegradable soaps and disposed of greywater back from the shore. "These practices differ dramatically from the practices of in-the-lake bathing and rinsing dishes in bygone days," said Dick Lewis.

The waters shared by houseboaters and others are not always calm. Canoeists once pelted a houseboat with stones. A cabin cruiser nearly swamped another. One evening a family with children and guests ran shrieking down to the lake for a skinny dip, hoping to deter a houseboat moored 10 metres off their dock. The tactic worked. A houseboater was prosecuted for shooting a loon. Others chattered on the TLA VHF monitoring channel in oblivious disregard of federal penalties, although some have used VHF radio to report forest fires. Fleets often crowded popular spots such as Sandy Inlet, Witch Point and Ferguson Bay.

Sam Scovil once sent houseboaters running for cover. They moored off the end of his island. When informed they were on private property, they refused to leave. Sam went to the cottage to get his 22-calibre rifle. On his way back, he picked up a piece of two-by-four lumber. He threw it into the water between the island and the vessel. When the occupants saw the firearm, they concluded that he had fired a warning shot and beat a hasty retreat. Sam died in May 2010. He first summered at Island 1161 in 1925 and only missed four due to World War Two and health problems in 2008. He has 13 grandchildren and his many great-grandchildren are fifth generation islanders.

The late Don Willits was a mild-mannered cottager until houseboats arrived on the lake. According to his daughter Bonnie Willits Lendrum in a *Times* story, Don muttered, "They should never come into Sharp Rock Inlet or else." The family learned what "or else" meant one afternoon when Don saw a houseboat creeping toward his Island 1221. He set off five shotgun blasts. "We were shocked. But that was not the end. He got out the chain saw and ripped into a pile of logs for the next 30 minutes. The houseboat left."

Canadiana

Charles King, known on the South Arm as the night owl "Uncle Charlie," was elected to the board in 1988. His great-great-uncle Alex Mackenzie was a stonemason from Sarnia, Ontario. All of Canada came to know him as Prime Minister Alexander Mackenzie from 1873 to '78. The prime minister's niece married Ralph King and their son C. Mckenzie King was Charlie's father. C. Mckenzie went to Cochrane's Camp from about 1919 to '23 then leased part of Island 770 in 1926. The family switched allegiance to the Tories and he became chief fundraiser for the Ontario

Conservative Party, working for Premiers John Robarts and Bill Davis. Charlie died in 1998 and the island is family owned.

TWS Mounts Blockade

In September 1989 the TWS blockaded the Red Squirrel Road construction site from a base camp on Wakimika Lake. About 200 environmentalists arrived on the opening weekend. They were a determined lot. Participants had to drive 37 kilometres from Highway 11 then switch to a canoe, or embark on a 25-kilometre portage and boat shuttle from Whitefish Bay, via Diamond, Larn and Pencil lakes.

The base camp used radios to coordinate the shuttle service from Smoothwater Outfitters, owned by Hap and Trudy Wilson. A few even chartered bush planes. In a notice circulated to members, the TWS warned that the site was a remote wilderness area: "Please be prepared for hiking up to a mile with your camping gear and for wet weather. September can vary from hot summer days to cold fall weather."

Blockaders used tried and true tactics. Some chained themselves to bridges and bulldozers with Kryptonite bicycle locks while others were

Accoutrements surround a Cochrane's Camp fireplace.
Photo: Carol Cochrane

buried up to their necks in sand and dirt. One spent 13 days up a white pine in the road right-of-way.

Then Tri-Town resident and TWS Director Jean Trickey was one of the first to be arrested and charged with mischief, according to Brian Back. She remained unruffled; after all, she had braved racial hostility back in 1957 as one of the "Little Rock Nine," the first nine black students admitted to an all-white Little Rock, Arkansas, high school. Every day a human blockade was lifted off the road and carried away in a paddy wagon, allowing construction to resume until the next blockade. The OPP drove about 85 kilometres down the Liskeard Lumber Road from Elk Lake to make arrests.

One high-profile arrestee was provincial NDP Leader Bob Rae, soon to be Ontario's premier. Following his brush with the law, he

No Mischief-Making

Beatrice Dora Campbell was born in June 2009 to Hugh Campbell and Sarah Layton. Hugh is Robin Campbell's second son and Beatrice is her first grandchild. The Layton and Campbell families get together in July at the Campbell Island 972. Family members include federal NDP Leader Jack Layton, Bea's maternal grandfather, and his spouse Olivia Chow, a federal MP. Unlike his former provincial counterpart Bob Rae, Grandpa Jack manages not to get arrested and charged with mischief.

said, "This government is spending millions of dollars on a road that will supply wood for a short time and solve no long term problems." The Temiskaming NDP Riding Association slammed his opinion as typical of Toronto people who never leave the city except for summer vacations.

Tim Gooderham spent two weekends ferrying TWS supporters from all walks of life to Sharp Rock Inlet from Wanapitei. He profiled some of his passengers in the *Times*: "One man was born in Syria and had just completed his medical training in Moscow. He met somebody in a bus station in Toronto heading for the blockade and decided to tag along. He had a whole pocketful of low denomination rubles which he could not change and was handing them out to anyone as a souvenir. He helped gas up Annabelle from jerry cans, wearing his trendy city clothes. We last saw him heading cheerily down the portage to Diamond Lake with virtually no overnight gear. We wonder how he got along."

TAA Resumes Blockade

The Supreme Court of Canada agreed in 1989 to rule on the land claim, while the Ontario Supreme Court rejected a TAA injunction to halt Red Squirrel Road construction. An angry Chief Gary Potts said of the province, "They're going to rewrite history and there's going to be a new version of Little Big Horn. They're out to avenge Custer." The TAA resumed its blockade, moving it to a site just two kilometres west of the Sandy Inlet-Camp Wanapitei turnoff.

Wanapitei was turned over to the TAA as an advance operations base. The TAA unfurled its tribal flag, depicting six ancestral clans, on the Wanapitei pole. "We had truly but peacefully been taken over," said Bruce Hodgins. The flag was later bestowed on the Hodgins at a Bear Island appreciation ceremony and now hangs in the dining hall. Gary was granted an honourary doctor of law degree by Trent University in 1991. On the front lines the TWS shared Thanksgiving turkey dinner with a road crew. Remembrance Day ceremonies were conducted by the TAA, joined by OPP officers.

Gary was arrested and charged with mischief along with a somewhat motley crew from across Canada. Supporters from Wanapitei and Trent were also arrested, including Bruce and Carol Hodgins. When the TWS halted its blockade, it showed respect for aboriginal rights issues by donating equipment and moral support to the TAA blockade, following some criticism that the TWS had obscured TAA efforts to highlight their struggle for justice.

Despite building the extension from both ends to foil protesters, it was completed in December 1989. MNR personnel drove a truck across soon after and discovered a 90-metre section had collapsed into a swamp. The link-up cost more than $6 million, including roughly $1 million in policing costs. The OPP charged 348 protesters with mischief. A total of 35 TWS supporters were fined $500 each. Charges against TAA members were later dropped while non-native supporters were prosecuted. Some chose short jail terms in lieu of fines to focus media attention on aboriginal issues. The blockades were then the largest act of peaceful civil disobedience in Canadian history.

During this tumultuous period protests were also staged on the Goulard Lumber Road, running north from Highway 805. The Goulard Lumber Company extended the road in 1989 to reach pine in the Wakimika Triangle. During the TWS blockade Goulard's licence to the stand was revoked, according to Ottertooth.com.

Environmental activists in Toronto used such pre-election antics as camping in Queen's Park trees and stalking Premier David Peterson with a 12-foot replica of a rasping chainsaw. They depicted him as the

Chief Gary Potts and other blockaders await arrest.
Photo: Peter McMillen

Many were arrested at the Temagami Wilderness Society's blockade, including future Ontario premier Bob Rae who can be seen in the photo. *Photo: Earthroots*

Peter Quinby and his Tall Pines Project. The TWS hired him in 1988 and he determined that Wakimika Triangle red and white pine were old growth using criteria he developed. It was the earliest recognition that old growth existed anywhere in eastern North America. Peter identified the world's largest stand of old-growth white and red pine near Obabika Lake. It is inside the protected Obabika Waterway Park.

Old growth was the focus of 45 artists camping as TWS guests in the Wakimika Triangle in summer 1990. Amongst the skyscraping pines were Robert Bateman, Glen Loates and Toni Onley. Their goal was to create wilderness paintings to be donated to the Temagami Wilderness Fund to raise money for the TWS.

The Township of Temagami spruced up its waterfront in the late 1980s. The façade of the old red brick ONBL building was refurbished as the Waterfront Pavilion, to be used for community events and retail operations. Bush pilot Ted Krofchak and his wife Leona bought the building in 1996 and opened Lady Evelyn Outfitting, changing the name to Temagami Outfitting in 2001. Dean Pearson of Pennsylvania bought the business in 2005 and has since relocated across the road. The

ultimate environmental villain – a heartless tree killer. The premier referred to "the Temagami problem" as the most complicated mess he had ever dealt with.

Aftermath

In spring 1990 the Liberal government tried to bring voters on-side by pronouncing the Red Squirrel Road extension dead. The MNR assured the TLA board that there would be no more clearcutting of red and white pine stands. Harvesting would involve shelterwood techniques, leaving about half the trees standing to aid regeneration. The extension has never been used due to a prolonged downturn in the forest industry.

Ontario acknowledged old-growth forests as an entity for the first time in spring 1990 due to the work of forest ecologist Dr.

former Langskib guide also owns property on Island 79 near Axe Narrows.

The Welcome Centre was built in 1990; construction faults would come back to haunt the municipality. It housed a 93-seat theatre and other facilities. Exhibits at the Welcome Centre gallery would showcase Grey Owl's wilderness, the TAA's history and struggle for justice, local and international artists, and more. The first of several Grey Owl festivals was staged in 1990. Temagami's continuing summer festivities centre around Canada Day.

TAA and Ontario Enter Treaty Talks

The TAA and Ontario signed a memorandum of understanding in 1990, committing them to negotiate a treaty of co-existence based on shared land stewardship and to establish a joint land stewardship council. The council was to manage four logging-suspended townships as a model for how diverse interests could work together to satisfy everyone's economic, recreational and cultural needs. The townships were under the land cautions and took in parts of the Goulard, Red Squirrel and Liskeard Lumber roads.

Much of the area was within the Wakimika Triangle, having enormous spiritual and cultural significance to the TAA. It contains an old village site, two spirit rocks, thousand-year-old nastawgan, ancient pictographs (rock paintings), a traditional winter fishery and a

Temagami's waterfront in the mid-1990s. *Photo: Andy Stevens*

vision quest site. The province provided three years of funding to the TAA.

Perceptions Shift

The battle to keep the Milne sawmill afloat hit the skids the same day the stewardship agreement was announced. The province made a backroom deal with owner Roger Fryer to protect the rest of his northeastern Ontario operations. Milne assets were acquired by the province, allowing Roger's company to pay off loans and free up money.

Milne's demise came hard on the heels of Sherman Mine's closure, throwing about 340 mine employees out of work, including roughly 100 Temagami residents. It left some area residents feeling that the government was sacrificing jobs to pacify Toronto environmentalists. A sawmill union representative warned that angry northerners might "just take a whack" at "an Indian or a tree hugger, or just the first person who is closest." Loggers blew off steam by roaring their engines and blasting their air horns when skidders, chip trucks and other logging vehicles converged in front of the Temagami MNR office. The protest was repeated in Sturgeon Falls.

In reality, a financial tsunami had swept over the company. Milne management held massive debt on a modernized mill at a time when interest rates were around 10 per cent. The Bank of Nova Scotia indicated in 1988 it would foreclose against the company.

The Sherman Mine shutdown was not linked to the conservation movement. World iron prices were depressed and the mine was no longer profitable. Management cited "costs and disadvantages which cannot be overcome." Dofasco contracted EcoLogic to clean up about 175 tons of hazardous PCBs left behind at a cost of $15 million. All PCBs had been removed by 1995 under MOE approval and transported to Swan Hills, Alberta.

Some Temagami residents gradually adjusted their attitudes toward preservation, believing their future might lie not in the boom and bust cycles of resource-based industry but in the value of their natural heritage. They banded together in the early 1990s to keep Goulard Lumber Company chainsaws out of the 3,000-acre old-growth White Bear Forest to preserve it as a trail system. It was part of the Whitebear family's traditional lands. Peter Quinby wrote an interpretive guide. Global TV aired a show about the project and the *Globe and Mail* featured a full-page spread in its travel section in 1993.

On the Municipality of Temagami's website, old growth was mentioned in the first sentence of the opening screen in 2011: "Temagami is the reality that fuels the popular perception of Canada's great Northland: Old growth pine forests." The introductory remarks were accompanied by a sweeping aerial photo of dense forest.

A Rough Road to Hoe

Early in 1990 the land claim was before the courts again, prompting the Ministry of Municipal Affairs and Housing (MMAH) to cease annexation discussions. That summer the township put the brakes on its regular maintenance of the Lake Temagami Access Road. Teeth-clattering washboards became the norm while exhaust pipes littered the road. The township was refused an increase to its 50 per cent road maintenance subsidy from the Ministry of Transportation (MTO). An avenue explored by the township was having the MNR hand over supervision of the parking lots so the township could charge fees and defray road costs.

The TLA, LaTemPRA, TemTOA and AYCTL proposed that the township turn the access road over to the province. This would pave the way for the unorganized area to form a local roads board and remove its financial burden from the township. The road would then be financed by user groups and Ontario.

The TLA was asked by the MTO in 1991 to contribute toward maintenance costs. The board recommended to members a one-time contribution, provided the township launch an application to revise its boundaries to exclude the road, the Northeast Arm, and Temagami Island and its adjacent islands. The contribution would also hinge on the results of a TAA bid to have the road designated a federally-subsidized Indian Reserve Access Road.

In a 1991 letter to the MTO, president and municipal committee chair Dick Grout debunked the perception by many mainland residents that the road's maintenance was an unfair burden for the township to bear. He noted that the total tax bill for lake residents within the township's boundaries was about $23,000 in 1990. Since the only benefit to the majority of taxed islanders was road upkeep and since the township's net costs after deducting the provincial subsidy averaged $24,000 per year, the heavy burden argument was without merit.

A TLA proposal for a Township of The Islands slowly evolved. It would be modelled after the Township of The Archipelago in Georgian Bay incorporated in 1980. The goal was to help preserve and protect the lake in perpetuity, including the shoreline and the Skyline Reserve.

Grand Plans Grounded

Proposals to bolster Temagami's sagging economy included a Northern Hemisphere Environmental Research Centre, promoted by rancher/politician Eugene Whelan who had a cottage on nearby Red Cedar Lake. The centre never came to fruition because Temagami was deemed too isolated. Plans by Pyrok North America for a particle board plant at the Sherman Mine site also turned to dust. Pyrok cited renovation and shipping costs.

In the wake of the late 1980s strife, Temagami's profile again loomed large in the early 1990s. This time no one faced OPP charges or a paddy wagon ride. Suzy Lake, a professor of fine arts at the University of Guelph,

A photo-collage triptych from "Cautioned Homes and Gardens" by Suzy Lake of Barbara Twain (l) and Janie Becker. National Gallery of Canada collection. *Photo: Suzy Lake*

participated in land claim symposiums through Trent University's heritage department. While staying at Wanapitei, she took photographs, which would become one of the central subjects of a major art installation originally exhibited at Guelph's Macdonald Stewart Art Centre before touring the country.

With its double-entendre title "Cautioned Homes and Gardens," the Temagami component is comprised of several nearly life-size photographic triptychs of TAA members. One called "The Three Peters" features a central panel merging generations of the Brown family. In another the late Barbara Twain and Janie Becker emerge from a dense forest.

"I wanted to give names and faces to the "angry band" that was so often seen in the newspapers. I wanted the photos to indicate to urban centres that these people are like us – that there are things we have in common." Suzy's

landscape backgrounds were shot throughout the land under caution. "My method of collage was left to be seen as if the figures were being re-placed into the landscape they should never have been challenged to be displaced from."

A 1990 township bid to build a single runway airport at the Sherman Mine tailings site never took flight despite a federal grant. The tailings' contents, unresolved ownership issues and the township's deficit position grounded that one. Temcor Limited, a consortium of businesses and the aboriginal community, announced grand plans in 1989 to bring a $60-million destination resort to town. Dubbed Evergreen, it would have featured a 350-room hotel, convention centre, golf course, ski hill and a native cultural centre, all tied together by eastern Canada's first sky tram. Echoes of Maple Mountain?

Temagami was dealt another blow in 1991 – by *Cottage Life* magazine. It unleashed a reporter to sniff through cottage country for butter tart excellence. Each taste-tested treat was assigned a rating, five tarts being perfection. Of 22 samplings, Temagami's Busy Bee fared the worst. Although some outlets were assigned 0 tarts out of 5, the Bee rankly ranked "2 Maalox tablets." Here's what the critic had to say: "This is a tasteless tart with very little filling and a shell you can pour coffee into. A few dozen could have blocked the Red Squirrel logging road for a week." It made us laugh and the Bee was busier than ever.

Two Fires Two Causes

The Bear Island shoreline was forever altered in May 1990 when the old post burned to the ground. A wiring short had ignited an upstairs apartment. The Bear Island community was running a co-op store at the time under manager Joe Katt. The post was originally established by the Hudson's Bay Company of Adventurers on Temagami Island in 1834. A new one was built on Bear Island in 1876 due to fur trade competition.

Following a 1937 fire the store was rebuilt on the same foundation. A nearby restaurant building, once a Northwoods dining hall, was spared in the latest fire and put to use as a store and post office. An historical plaque, erected on the lawn in 1958 by the Archaeological and Historic Sites Board of Ontario, survived

Dignitaries, Bear Islanders and cottagers at the dedication of the HBC historical plaque at the Bear Island post in 1958. *Photo: John Hyde*

the blaze – as did a 1934 plaque dedicated to founding president Robert Newcomb.

A fast-moving line of thunderstorms swept across the lake in July 1990. A lightning strike started a fire destroying the Corls' Island 977 boathouse. A rapid response by the Bear Island community kept the flames from spreading.

It was pointed out at the 1990 AGM that the MNR's mandate is to suppress forest fires, not cottage fires. A suggestion was made that neighbours band together to buy and maintain fire pumps. By the end of the year, there were four new pumps in the Hub alone. By 2010 there were 70 pumps scattered throughout the lake on docks and in boathouses, available to anyone in an emergency. Over the years this equipment has stopped many blazes from consuming cottages and forests.

Security Issues

Winter 1990 proved a bad year for break-ins. The OPP reported some 15 incidents. The lake had become a busy place in winter. Temagami Trails, a four-season club, was keeping local snowmobile routes groomed for the thousands of snowmobilers traversing trails linking Temagami to Sudbury, and Cochrane to Algonquin Park. While most sledders were responsible, improper cottage close-up was asking for trouble. The Temagami OPP Detachment had been slashed from 13 to six personnel and was no longer able to mount regular winter patrols.

Following a series of break-ins in March 1994, resulting in the conviction of local

youths, the TLA decided to revive winter patrols, discontinued in the 1970s. Members were given the option of two winter patrols to supplement the traditional spring and fall checks. Patrolman Jerry Burrows was joined by Don Twain and Peter McMillen. Other recent property patrolmen have been builder Gerry Gooderham and Keewaydin caretaker Matt Ambler.

Typical problems included cash, alcohol and valuables left in plain sight, and doors and windows left unlocked. Someone must have had to cancel his credit card after Jerry found a non-expired Visa card on a path. Even when cottage owners closed up by the book, they were still vulnerable to malicious vandals and non-malicious four-legged invaders, especially bears.

Promoting Dialogue

One of the best things to emerge from the turmoil of a divided community premiered in 1991 with the goal of "promoting dialogue." The monthly *Temagami Talker* blossomed into a newsy tabloid with subscribers from Yellowknife to Yosemite under managing editor Marion Russell and a group of dedicated volunteers. Topics ranged from the White Bear Challenge to the Whitebear clan and soaring taxes to the Seniors Friendly Group. It became so popular that anyone caught filching a copy from a donation box was run out of town.

Brian Back founded Earthroots in 1991, a conservation organization based in Toronto, which replaced the TWS. Earthroots returned to Temagami in 1996 to stage another logging road blockade. It has 12,000 supporters across Canada. Brian later moved from Ontario to Wisconsin and developed Ottertooth.com, a website initially devoted to Temagami canoeing and backcountry issues. He moved back to Ontario in 2011.

By the late 1980s it wasn't all work and no play for TLA radio operators. Hali Denis' nightly sign-offs featured a joke of the day. Steve Scheleny and Brent Carbno introduced a trivia quiz. The two students converted a bedroom into a ping pong room and installed a basketball net on Ev Choat's old flag pole.

Blue Box Blues

The City of North Bay started a blue box program in spring 1991 and cottagers were encouraged to drop off their recyclables at its depot. The TLA launched a recycling program that summer, overseen by Steve and Brent. It started as three cardboard boxes in a hallway corner, which proved sorely inadequate to handle the deluge. The operation was moved outside and mounds of recyclables mounted. Cottagers volunteered to transport the mess to North Bay. Since some islanders neglected to rinse out cans and bottles, the first trip on a hot day was often the last.

Tim Gooderham was soon pleading with Northern Pinewoods to stock can crushers, to reduce the volume and the number of haulage trips. "Did you know you can get 84 crushed beer cans into an A & P shopping bag? We

have experts," he quipped in the *Times*. The TLA was selling crushers a year later.

The recycling program was relocated to the Mine Landing in 1992. Despite MNR and MOE grants, the TLA lost thousands in the four years it was the lone local recycler. It was the only non-municipality in Ontario taking part in an MOE Municipal Recycling Support Program. A problem developed when lazy, uncaring people tossed garbage in the recycling bins and vice versa, a problem that continues today. On the whole, recycling was so well-received that townies started running their detritus down the access road instead of disposing of it as trash. The township initiated a recycling program in 1995.

The MNR introduced fishing licences for Ontario residents in the late 1980s. Non-residents had been paying to drop a line since the late 1900s. The seasonal fee was $11.50 for Ontarians and $34.50 for non-residents. The federal government issued new rules by reducing the speed limit to 10 kph within 30 metres of any shore. In 1993 the TLA installed a "go slow" buoy near the TLA dock and another near the Manito Landing, where boats were creating dangerous wakes.

CHAPTER 22

MAKING PLANS

The 1990s was the decade for making plans. The province was doing it. So was the Township of Temagami. The TLA had plans of its own. The biggest plan of all – the aboriginal land claim settlement – would take a progressive stride forward before taking two steps back.

The Liberal government was swept out of power by Bob Rae and the NDP in fall 1990. They followed up on the Liberals' commitment to a joint stewardship council. It was named the Wendaban Stewardship Authority (WSA), meaning "whence the dawn comes" after the main aboriginal family that traditionally occupied the stewardship area.

Manito was purchased to house WSA offices and the TAA's negotiating unit. The TAA and the province appointed six representatives each. Director Bruce Hodgins was the TLA and youth camp representative. He co-authored *The Temagami Experience* with Jamie Benidickson in 1989, a definitive account of the history of the Anishnabai, resource extraction and recreational development.

In spring 1991 the Temagami Advisory Council was replaced by the larger Comprehensive Planning Council (CPC) with Nipissing University College's Roman Brozowski as chair. Its mandate was to manage the public consultation process in the development of an MNR Crown land and resource use plan. It would cover an area spanning the south end of the lake, Dymond Township north of

A map showing the extent of the comprehensive planning area.
Credit: Ontario government

New Liskeard, Lake Obabika to the west and the Quebec border to the east. The plan was to be completed in 1994 but its breadth and complexity delayed it until 1996.

Until the plan's completion, the CPC was to advise the MNR on land-use decisions and facilitate third party negotiations between the TAA and Ontario. Among the 12 appointees was Niki Plumstead, then co-owner of a North Bay marina. She was a TLA member at the time but soon let her membership lapse. Temagami Reeve Ron Prefasi claimed in the *North Bay Nugget* that three TLA representatives had been appointed. The other CPC lake representatives were Suzanne Gooderham, the wife of Bill Gooderham's son Gerry and Ivor Horncastle, who owned Ibi's Haven, now Becca's Haven. Neither Suzanne nor Ivor were TLA members.

To compensate for its lack of CPC representation, the TLA formed a forestry committee. Jim Hasler was appointed chair and its mandate was to monitor cutting plans, regeneration and illegal cutting in the Skyline Reserve. A recent arrival, Jim participated in a Sierra Club Temagami Wilderness Celebration weekend at Wanapitei in 1987 where he met Carol Cochrane. He was bitten by both the love and the Temagami bug. He moved to North Bay from the Niagara Peninsula where he had worked as an environment consultant.

As a licensed pilot, Jim used his own plane to get a bird's eye view of the Skyline Reserve, harking back to the aerial surveys of Earl Rodgers' presidency. He discovered no evidence of illegal cutting but was shocked by the scarcity of pine behind the reserve "curtain."

Jim Flosdorf once made a similar observation: "When one flies over the area it is looking more and more like a Hollywood movie set, with a false front of trees and desert behind."

In 1992 volunteers with the forestry committee's Project Pine planted 300 seedlings on the west shore of the North Arm where the 1977 fire had wreaked havoc. The amateur foresters discovered many pine naturally regenerating but covered by deciduous scrub. They returned the following summer and saw most of the seedlings had survived their first winter.

In November 1991 Temagami Transport owner Ivan Beauchamp was elected reeve with more than twice as many votes as incumbent Ron Prefasi. Ivan set a conciliatory tone toward the TAA and TLA by advocating an "approachable" council in the *Times*.

Good and Bad News

The TAA was dealt a blow in August by the Supreme Court of Canada. It dismissed their appeal of the two earlier court decisions, finding that the TAA's land rights were surrendered regardless of whether or not the Temagami Indian Band had signed a treaty. They adhered to it in exchange for treaty annuities and a 2.5-square kilometre reserve in 1971. Annuities amounted to $4 per band member per year until they were suspended in 1979. The land claim was the subject of a Global Television documentary in 1992 called *Temagami: A Living Title to the Land*. One segment captured reactions to the disappointing decision.

On a more positive note, the court found that the Crown had not lived up to its treaty obligations, the subject of ongoing negotiations for a Treaty of Co-Existence. Soon after the court decision, TLA representatives met with Barton Feilders, Ontario's chief negotiator, and with Gary Potts and council members, to stress that members' main interest was input into development plans and their environmental impact.

Celebration Time

The TLA hosted a barbecue for its 60th anniversary, taking place after the 1991 AGM at Wabun. A New Liskeard chef and his chuckwagon were transported to Garden Island by Temagami Barge. He grilled meat and potatoes to perfection. Members brought side dishes and Director Charlie King baked a cake. The 175 celebrators took home commemorative coffee mugs.

Carol and Bruce Hodgins in 1957. *Photo: Bruce Hodgins*

Up at Wanapitei Bruce and Carol Hodgins were celebrating the official provincial heritage designation of the Chateau, the camp's adult lodge and conference centre. A year later they secured a rehabilitation grant from the Ministry of Culture. However, restoration work undertaken by George Mathias Construction and a heritage architectural supervisor took two years and the grant money dried up. Much of the labour involved log work. The Chateau was constructed by Finnish immigrants between 1932 and '34. The Maki family used the Finnish chinkless style, scribing and copying each poplar log so it fit precisely over the one beneath. The logs had been attacked by wood beetles and wet rot, and the Chateau's condition deteriorated severely during the 1970s and '80s.

The TAA's Vision

After the court decision, the province was under intense political pressure to have the land cautions lifted. A draft framework agreement stalled for months in 1991 when the TAA was not willing to lift the cautions without the ability to protect its interests during negotiations. Head TAA negotiator Doug McKenzie rejected Ontario's position of sole jurisdiction over Crown land because it was contrary to the concept of co-existence.

The two sides agreed to hire a facilitator to break the impasse and meet an Agreement In Principle (AIP) deadline of March 1993. The facilitator recommended a joint review panel to consider individual requests for release from the cautions and "substantive" negotiations commenced in August 1992.

The TAA unveiled a *Vision of Co-Existence* in 1992, based on the concept of land stewardship for n'Daki Menan, which was divided into three categories. On sole stewardship lands, including Lake Temagami (excluding private land), the TAA would exercise authority. On shared stewardship lands, a joint native-non-native governing body would hold sway, similar to the WSA. The remainder would be administered by municipalities and the province.

The vision proposed TAA jurisdiction over about two-thirds of n'Daki Menan, stirring municipal councils, hunt and fish clubs, tourist operators and cottagers into a tizzy. Deep concern was expressed that the TAA and the province were conducting negotiations without input from the grass roots that would be the most affected by the results. Ontario's negotiating team rejected the TAA's vision.

Cracks were beginning to appear in the relationship between the band and the TAA. While the TAA represented the community in land claim talks, some band members believed the chief and council should have veto power over the TAA as a safety net to ensure decisions were in the band's best interest. One potential solution was granting ex officio seats on the TAA executive council to Band Chief Joe Katt and Second Chief Holly Mathias.

The Teme-Augama Anishnabai's *Vision of Co-Existence* map showing sole stewardship lands. *Credit: A TAA circular*

Author! Author!

"Many times, as he drove along the highway, Bill Plumstead heard characters carrying on conversations in his mind – so, in the interests of driving safely, he decided to get those imaginary speeches out of his head and on to paper," is how the *Times* introduced Bill's novel *Loon*, published in 1992. He composed nearly 80 per cent of his prose in his Island 658 cottage office. *Loon* tells the story

The bio-diverse Witch Point bog has been studied extensively by Claire Muller.
Photo: Elizabeth Sinclair

Mouse Tales

Claire Muller authored a *Times* story in 1999 titled "The Year of the Mouse." It all started when her husband Bernard heard "the patter of little feet. A flashlight beam revealed long whiskers, bulging eyes, enormous ears and delicate white paws holding the edge of the cookie bag while a tiny pink mouth sampled the goodies within. Suddenly, presto! The thief was gone."

The next evening there were three more. The Mullers patched a hole in a window screen but the rodents chewed another hole. They closed the glass and then tried some lethal Mousetreat, but the mice stuffed their faces and dashed off to a storeroom. The Mullers switched to fail-safe traps set under the window. Over 15 nights, the tally rose to 66 mice. They may have set a record for dispatching the most undearly departed.

A former Narrows Island resident holds the record for the most disturbing encounter betwixt mice and men. He bought sticky tape and placed it against the bottom of a wall where he knew there was a rodent run. Voila! The next morning he found a super-glued victim. He detached the tape and went outside to shake the varmint off. While waving it about, his generous beard got stuck to the tape. He was about to go back inside for scissors when a raven spotted its next meal and began trying to pick off the mouse. He had little choice but to let it rip. It took days for the redness and rawness to subside.

of a young New Englander who comes north to research the history and mythology of the Wendaban Indian Band. She meets a rough-around-the-edges bush pilot. Their adventures and love story form the main plot.

Jeanne Underwood retired as *Times* editor after putting the summer 1992 edition to bed. As a stopgap measure, Tim Gooderham penned several "What's Happening?" newsletters. The Underwoods moved back to the U.S. in 1998, having decided that northern winters were getting harder and longer. Ted Underwood died in 2010. Carol Cochrane took up the slack in 1994, becoming the *Times'* fourth editor. Claire Muller's "Nature Notes" were a must-read staple through the 1990s. A Temagami Island cottager, Claire imparted her extensive local knowledge about fluctuating bird populations, winter wildlife survival tactics and other nature lore.

Money Matters

The TLA's proposed Township of The Islands would take in all the islands, some withdrawn from the Township of Temagami. A lawyer advised the board to pursue its objective as part of the TAA-provincial negotiations. During Hilton Young's first term as president, the TLA launched a $100,000 fundraising campaign to retain professional negotiating and public relations assistance. Legal and consulting fees were projected to consume 75 per cent of the targeted amount. Thanks to director and chief fundraiser Sandy Navaro, the TLA surpassed its goal.

The TLA building was operating a veritable shopping kiosk, selling logoed t-shirts, maps, books and everything but the kitchen sink… Oh wait, they were sold too – at the flea market. Marketing committee members Dora Young and Phyllis Avard, wife of Director Art Avard, prepared a wish list for Christmas shoppers looking for stocking stuffers. Sales topped $3,500 in 1994. Between 1987 and '93 the TLA sold about 1,300 of its popular navigation charts.

Best Ever Stocking Stuffer

John Oliver II returned home from military service for Christmas in 1952. On Christmas morning he discovered a small box in his sock. Inside was a photo of Island 1178, a gift from his father John Oliver.

The rough ride over lack of access road maintenance came to a halt when the township received a special grant from the Ministry of Northern Development and Mines for upgrades. The township was required to match the grant and a total of $92,000 was spent to replace culverts and lay gravel. At the 1993 AGM Reeve Ivan Beauchamp proposed that lake and mainland residents unite in shared concerns.

Members' reactions were more favourable than when Ron Prefasi made an annexation bid at the 1987 AGM. Ivan's amalgamation proposition prompted queries about the access road, planning and development, assessment of properties and the role American cottagers would play. For the purposes of this book, amalgamation is defined as a consensual coming-together while annexation is defined as a hostile takeover.

Land Claim Settlement Gains Ground

Seven public consultations were held in fall 1992. At the Temagami assembly, attended by 120 people, fears about plummeting real estate values and the loss of property were raised. TAA representative Mary Laronde stated that patented lands would be unaffected by the settlement and declining values were a reflection of a Canada-wide recession. Attendees questioned the fate of leases, land use permits and other forms of tenure, as well as access to property, hunt camps and traplines. Queries could not be answered satisfactorily because the province's position on sole and shared stewardship lands was still in the early stages, Ontario negotiator Barton Feilders replied.

The TLA took the stand that TLA-TAA joint stewardship of the lake would bring joint consultation on planning and environmental matters. It hoped but failed to redirect the negotiating process before the Agreement In Principle (AIP) deadline. An application for the Township of The Islands, to include roughly 500 private properties, was filed with the Ontario Municipal Board in March 1993. The township would function as a recognized entity under the Municipal Act with an elected council, and be treated as an enclave within TAA lands. The application contained an entrenchment clause recognizing a mutually-

beneficial "treaty-trust relationship" between the new township and the TAA, which would enshrine shared stewardship values.

By spring 1993 the AIP was expected to be reached by the end of July. The original March deadline had been scratched. Frustrated by the extension, the Municipal Advisory Group (MAG) called on the province to take the land cautions to court for removal if a settlement

Who's Afraid of the Berries?

Before the HBC moved its post from Temagami Island to Bear Island in 1876, Bear Island was known by Temagami natives as Ma-Komin-ising, meaning "Berry Island," in reference to the abundance of wild strawberries, raspberries and choke cherries. The name was corrupted to Ma-Quamin-ising or "Bear Island," likely due to the similar pronunciation of the two Anishnabek and English-translated words.

was not reached by July 31. The MAG was set up to address the concerns of local mayors and reeves.

The MKA Enters the Picture

Another cog was thrown into the negotiating wheel when a splinter group emerged in winter 1993. The Ma-Kominising Anishnawbeg (MKA), translated as "Bear Island people," was composed of members of three traditional families claiming their ancestors did not

Part of Craig Macdonald's Historical Map of Temagami. It shows (l-r) Michelle Katt, Mishay-nis Katt and John Paul processing game from an autumn hunt.
Courtesy: Craig Macdonald

participate in the Robinson-Huron Treaty. They asserted sovereign rights over their traditional territories within n'Daki Menan, which they believed were being bargained away by the TAA. The MKA wanted to negotiate with the federal government for a new reserve.

To gain media attention the MKA felled old-growth pine in Delphi Township, one of four townships under temporary WSA jurisdiction. Haileybury resident and WSA Chair Jim Morrison, a former land claim researcher, obtained a court injunction against his one-time allies. Additional cutting on WSA lands, despite the injunction, resulted in arrests and charges. Main MKA spokesman Sherwood "Woody" Becker was later arrested for blocking a forest access road off Highway 805 to protest logging on lands claimed by the MKA.

Band Chief Joe Katt and a councillor were ousted by a community vote for improper conduct after aligning themselves with this breakaway group. Woody got into more legal hot water by allegedly raiding TAA offices on Manito Island for documents purportedly supporting the MKA's position. He was charged with break and enter, and theft, and detained at the North Bay jail. A fall 1995 fire razed the Manito offices. Valuable information was destroyed or went missing. Arson was suspected but Blaze, an OPP Labrador Retriever trained to sniff out fire accelerants and bodies didn't earn his kibble and no one was held culpable.

Chief negotiator Grant Wedge released Ontario's offer in mid-1993. The draft settlement offered the TAA 220 square kilometres of Crown land as development lands and $10 million in compensation over 10 years for

Te-mee-ay-gaming

The rich heritage of the aboriginal community was beautifully captured in a map published in 1993 by the Ontario Geographic Names Board. MNR employee Craig Macdonald spent 27 years exploring the Temagami region and studying the history, language and culture of the indigenous people.

Craig created the Historical Map of Temagami (Te-mee-ay-gaming). It embodies an invaluable contribution to the understanding of the aboriginal world that existed prior to European contact. The map features the Anishnabek names of 660 landmarks and nastawgan. Traditional land and resource use are depicted in artwork, and in Anishnabek names for bear-snaring place, for example.

grievances arising from the 1850 treaty. The land encompassed much of the eastern and northern shorelines of Lake Temagami, as well as the western shoreline of Cross Lake. It was conditional on the TAA informing Ontario if it wished to hold any land as a reserve and the involvement of the federal government to accomplish this.

Ontario would also transfer eight square kilometres as traditional family lands. The land cautions would be lifted as part of the deal. The MAG took the stand that Ontario should return to the negotiating table if the settlement offer was rejected only after the land cautions were removed.

A Stronger Voice?

A 1,295-square kilometre shared stewardship body would be centred on Lake Temagami. The TAA would appoint one-third of its members and Ontario would appoint the remainder. The board's initial response to the AIP was lukewarm. It wanted cottagers to represent at least 50 per cent of the remaining two-thirds of the governance body. The province indicated that the TLA, as just one of many "interest" groups, would not receive significant representation. This development prompted the board to open preliminary amalgamation discussions with the township.

Ontario said an enlarged township would receive significant representation. The board reasoned that amalgamation might accord the TLA a political voice rather than being classed as an interest group. The Township of The Islands concept had not won the support of LaTemPRA or the TAA and was no longer a viable option. The TLA was soon working with the township and LaTemPRA toward a local government study to investigate the terms under which the lake and township might amalgamate.

TFN Rejects Land Claim Accord

The draft agreement was subjected to tinkering before being sent to the TAA membership for ratification. The land base was enlarged to 290 square kilometres and compensation was raised to $15 million. The TAA narrowly approved the AIP in November by a vote of 83 to 75. The band, now known as the Temagami First Nation (TFN), turned it down by a close vote of 60 to 58.

The TFN held a second vote in March 1994 and rejected the deal by 59 to 29. The TFN formally severed ties to the TAA and the offer. It is possible that the agreement would have been ratified had the MKA not lobbied TFN members to oppose it. The MKA believed the agreement threatened TFN rights as federally-recognized status Indians. The province planned to proceed with a court appearance in April to petition for the land cautions' lifting.

The cautions' removal faced numerous judicial delays. Their eventual lifting would not directly open the land claim area to staking, the most highly-anticipated land use. Prospectors would have to await 1996 CPC recommendations and the MNR's approval. Frustration spilled over when 400 people crowded a New Liskeard hall to attend a MAG-hosted gathering in fall 1994. They were protesting the delays and the millions spent on a failed settlement bid they believed could have been more wisely invested in northern stimulus.

On several occasions TAA Chief Gary Potts reminded the citizenry that pointing a finger at the land cautions as the sole cause of Temiskaming's economic malaise wasn't realistic. Disheartened by the non-ratification of the AIP and the squabbling amongst his people, this long-serving and nationally-recognized chief chose not to run in 1995 elections. TAA negotiator Doug McKenzie succeeded Gary as chief.

Land Cautions Lifted

The case for removing the land cautions was heard in June 1994 by the Ontario Court's general division. The judge reserved his decision until November 1994 when he ruled the cautions could be lifted. However, the TAA, TFN and MKA filed appeals. They were extinguished in November 1995, spelling the near end of a 22-year Crown land freeze.

The Wendaban Stewardship Authority was winding down in spring 1994 and later released a 20-year Forest Stewardship Plan. Bruce Hodgins reported to the board that most of the Wakimika Triangle was designated a protected area. WSA member Rita O'Sullivan added an interesting perspective. Speaking at an environment conference, she remarked on the interplay between representatives, all bringing divergent opinions to the table: "By about the fourth or fifth meeting, when the people began to learn more and more about the land and what we needed to do, they didn't think of themselves as a non-native person or a native person, or a reeve or somebody else; they thought of the land first."

By combining traditional ecological knowledge and western scientific knowledge – a forestry technician learning about moose calving areas, bear dens or fish spawning locales from aboriginal observation and experience, for example – the group was able to lay out a thorough forest plan, Rita said. The four townships were rolled into the comprehensive planning area.

CHAPTER 23

THE TENETS FOR TEMAGAMI

March 8, 1994 marked a milestone. The Tenets for Temagami were adopted by the Township of Temagami and LaTemPRA, and became official TLA policy. The tenets are the foundation of all Lake Temagami planning and have guided Ontario government decision-making. They evolved out of a growing need for a set of guidelines when responding to development pressure from any direction, be it the land claim or the comprehensive plan. The township's acceptance of the tenets was a prerequisite for amalgamation discussions.

The tenets have their roots in a position paper former president Jack Glenn was asked to write in 1991. The TLA sought a clear definition of MNR planning policy on shoreline development, the Skyline Reserve and access roads. Jack combed MNR planning documents, the 1986 OP and borrowed some background material compiled by his daughter Pam (Glenn) Sinclair, who was writing *Temagami Lakes Association: An Historical Perspective.*

Jack described the TLA's definition of the Skyline Reserve as protecting the appearance of the natural skyline. "It must provide the viewer on any part of Lake Temagami with no visual evidence to the naked eye that timber cutting had taken place." He wrote that this definition had been verbally agreed to by MNR officials,

as had the meaning of the Shoreline Reserve – to consist of the area from the water's edge to the highest point of land.

He noted that the MNR had also interpreted the term less specifically to mean "the last strip of trees visible from any point on the lake," and very loosely in 1973 as a "reserve on the mainland shoreline." The OP stated the Skyline Reserve should be maintained to protect its pine component and that cutting should be prohibited in areas visible from the lake.

The MNR's 1973 land use plan stipulated no new access points were to be constructed, he wrote. Five access points had been accepted by lake user groups in 1982, consisting of three at the top of the Northeast Arm and two at the end of the Lake Temagami Access Road. The MNR's 1983 land use plan stipulated that "temporary roads will not be maintained and where necessary scarified to ensure that they do not become access points." The OP stated no additional access points should be provided. Jack wrote that almost all respondents to a 1981 Ed Hanna survey placed access point limitations and maintenance of the Skyline Reserve as top priorities.

An embryo of what would become the tenets emerged from Jack's document, known simply as "the white paper." After the TLA, LaTemPRA and the township began amalgamation talks, common ground was found in the tenet trilogy. Each of the participants fleshed out the three points into official document status. TLA Director Art Avard, Temagami Reeve Ivan Beauchamp and LaTemPRA's Biff Lowery wrote the Skyline Reserve, Road Access and Mainland Development elements, respectively.

Tenets for Temagami

Skyline Reserve: The mainland surrounding Lake Temagami and Cross Lake is to be zoned as a landscape ecology zone to preserve the beauty, restore the integrity and preserve the wilderness aspect of the Temagami Forest. This ecology zone would consist of 2 reserves which would be protected from natural disturbance e.g. fire and insect infestation, but would have separate management goals and prescriptions.

The two reserves would be the following:

1. Skyline: The Lake Temagami and Cross Lake reserves must protect the appearance of the natural skyline vista. It must provide the viewer on any part of Lake Temagami or Cross Lake with no visual evidence to the naked eye that any activities such as timber cutting or mining have taken place. The minimum dimension would be 200 metres. It would be preserved in its natural state and its permissible uses would be very limited.

2. Ecological Buffer Reserve: This would surround the skyline reserve to protect the natural forest and wildlife habitat ecosystems of the Temagami region. It would have a broader range of controlled activities but no

new public roads would pass through it except in the village of Temagami.

Road Access: The current ban on construction of new public road access points to Lake Temagami and Cross Lake is supported by our three groups. We define the existing public road access points to consist of the village waterfront, Finlayson Park, Strathcona Landing and the Lake Temagami Access Road landings. We agree that, where possible, parking areas must be screened from the main body of the Lake. Shiningwood Bay, Cross Lake, Austin Bay, Bleu Bay and any other illegal access points are to be closed using scarification methods. Existing gates are to be maintained and new ones are to be installed to prevent new public access roads to Lake Temagami and Cross Lake.

New skidoo trails accessing Lake Temagami/Cross Lake are to be no wider than ten feet and for winter skidoo use only. Proposals for these access points to Lake Temagami and Cross Lake are to be reviewed and sites inspected by the new governing body prior to construction.

Mainland Development: There should be no mainland development on Lake Temagami and Cross Lake with the exception of those potential lots immediately adjacent to the Township of Temagami that are able to be serviced by the Township's central sewage treatment facility. All other future development will occur on islands, the number and location to be determined by the revised Official Plan which will be sensitive to current ecological standards.

The tenets didn't happen overnight. "They are the result of countless hours of meetings and discussions with government officials, interested stakeholders, community leaders and ordinary citizens," Hilton Young said in 2010. Requests for TRSI funding from any organization, including the TLA, must be in line with the intent of the tenets. The tenets were later endorsed by the Cassels and Adjoining Lakes Association (CALA) and the AYCTL.

How We Stack Up

The TLA is not the largest property owners' association in Ontario, nor is it the oldest. Yet it is unique in two ways. The TLA appears to be the only association that publishes a newspaper; others have newsletters. Only one has a leg up on the TLA. The massive Lake of the Woods District Property Owners Association publishes five issues of a magazine per year.

The TLA is also unique in one of its mandates—protecting the mainland shoreline from commercial and private development. Lake Temagami is the only Ontario lake historically managed in a manner that has preserved the mainland shoreline in a virtually unaltered state.

A Powwow Revival

In 1994 the Bear Island community sought the power of a traditional powwow to help heal soured land claim negotiations. Such a celebration hadn't occurred since the 1920s when Catholic priests discouraged "heathen" behaviour. Rhythmic drummers, colourful dancers and sage elders from across Ontario and beyond gathered for four days of summer festivities. They were joined by Bear Island's own 20-member youth drum group *The Deep Water Singers* and two young hoop dancers. So successful was the gathering that it became a regular event.

Traditional practices were relearned, such as the Shaking Tent Ceremony, used by elders in vision quests to locate missing hunters. "This ceremony, like most of our ceremonies, were lost or practised in secrecy as the encroachment of the non-natives and the church people into our territory put such ceremonies in jeopardy. Our ancestors were told that our ceremonies were witchcraft!" Millie Becker explained in the *Times*. A traditional approach to healing was also adopted, by health services' use of a medicine wheel. "For health, it encompasses spiritual, mental, physical and emotional feelings and if one component is missing, a person is not in balance," Millie wrote in 1996.

A mid-1990s traditional powwow.
Photo: Andy Stevens

introducing wildlife corridors, 30-metre bands of trees to be left around lakes, rivers and wetlands. Harvesting on steep slopes was banned. Citizen advisory committees were also established. Jim would become the TLA's representative on Temagami's committee.

Local Government Study Underway

The inaugural meeting of the local government steering committee took place in fall 1994, attended by township, TLA (Art Avard, Hilton Young, Jim Hasler, Ray Delarosbel and Tim Gooderham) and LaTemPRA representatives, and consultant Bob Lehman. Bob's firm had prepared the OP. The Ministry of Municipal Affairs and Housing (MMAH) would fund 85 per cent of study costs. The tenets would guide it and be incorporated into a new OP. Amalgamation issues such as access road upkeep, taxation, council representation, services and costs were discussed.

Prior to the board agreeing to the study, it had surveyed the membership which acquiesced, based on these criteria: an August 1 voting date; equal council representation of lake and mainland residents; majority representation on the planning committee; a

Old Growth Protection

The decision of a Class Environmental Assessment on Forestry Practices in Ontario was released in 1994. It found that less than one per cent of Ontario's original white pine forests remained standing, and ordered conditions to protect them and their wildlife habitat, Forestry Committee Chair Jim Hasler reported in the *Times*. The MNR's timber planners addressed wildlife and erosion for the first time, by

Temagami

O Great Spirit, who filled
this ancient basin
With sparkling water, and strewed it o'er
With myriad island gems,
and rimmed it round
With pine-clad hills and shores and cliffs
Of ageless rock – we behold
The grandeur of your work and are lifted
By its beauty; and in its fastness
And solitude we find strength.
Blessed be this land; and blessed
All questing souls who hear a voice
In wind and wave, who quicken to
The freshness of the morning,
And know the peace of wilderness.

Ken Wismer, circa 1982

accordance with the earlier membership survey. The mayor would be elected at large in both scenarios.

Ivan Beauchamp's conciliatory reeveship came to an end in November 1994 when he chose not to stand for re-election. Wayne Adair, a retired OPP officer who spent all three decades of his career in Temagami, won handily over his sole rival Ron Prefasi. Ron, council and administrators had left Temagami's finances in a deficit position by the time he stood for re-election versus Ivan in 1991. Through prudent fiscal management, the township had moved to a modest reserve position.

CPC Survives a Withering Attack

The CPC was facing a firing squad by 1995. "The credibility of this Council is now under attack as no longer reflecting the requirements of local resident groups – those who live in, work in and pay taxes in the Temagami area," Hilton wrote in the *Times*. The board asked Ontario to turn the planning council's powers in the Temagami area over to the local government steering committee.

In a letter to the CPC, Tim Gooderham pointed out that the socio-economic costs and benefits of mining and logging were being covered in great detail while cottaging, youth camps, and backcountry recreation were taking a back seat. The TAA was also disillusioned and quit the council in 1995, after the MNR transferred a portion of the planning area to the Elk Lake Community Forest, territory that was part of its land claim.

reduced mill rate; and prompt revision of the OP. "In the final analysis, the most important question for lake residents may be how much control we will be able to secure over planning and development issues versus the additional tax cost of amalgamation," President Hilton Young said.

The local government committee held a series of information sessions. The final consultant's report addressed all issues except council's composition. An amalgamation vote by the TLA would not be undertaken until the issue was resolved. The township favoured a ward system that would elect a majority of mainland councillors. The TLA espoused a ward system with an equal number of lake and town councillors, in

Temagami Reeve Wayne Adair tried to address these concerns. He called on the council to protect Lake Temagami's shoreline by making it a conservation reserve, a new category of protected area introduced in 1994 under the Ontario Public Lands Act. It would allow hunting and fishing, but no logging or mining. Environmentalists thought the Temagami area needed more protection, while Temiskaming MPP David Ramsay and the MAG called for the province to disband the council because they believed it was too restrictive regarding resource use.

One new local organization was concerned that the CPC was favouring a pro-resource development stand. Friends of Temagami (FOT) believed the task force would propose that 75 per cent of Temagami's roadless wilderness be opened to development. Combined with the land cautions' imminent lifting, severe degradation of wild spaces could result. Some founding members were Tim Gooderham, John Kilbridge and Smoothwater Outfitters co-owner Francis Boyes. FOT held a Queen's Park news conference to denounce Ontario Premier Bob Rae as an environmental traitor. They accused him of changing his stripes from an environmentalist arrested with like-minded anti-logging activists in1989 to a logging industry crony.

1994 was proving a costly year. Class A membership fees were raised to $100 from $60 and the other classes were hiked proportionally to defray expenses related to the local government study, the AIP and the CPC.

The TLA had an internet connection and an email address by the end of 1994, as did about a dozen members. The world was on the cusp of a technological revolution that would see personal computers, digital cameras and cellphones become ubiquitous by the turn

Vintage-behatted Smoothwater Outfitters' Caryn Colman sells preserves and artwork at the 2009 TLA flea market.
Photo: Pam Sinclair

228

of the century, at which time the TLA had its own website.

The TLA had undertaken a survey in 1993 to determine how much was spent annually by cottagers and their guests. The results indicated expenditures between $5 and $7 million. The TLA wanted to show how vital cottaging was to the local economy and to raise the larger issue of how much development was sustainable before degradation ensued. A separate study for the MNR showed canoeists and camps spending $2 million per annum.

Something Fishy

While politicians and conservationists went fishing for CPC attention, anglers were putting words into action. A mistrust of MNR creel statistics led to the formation of the Temagami Fisheries Advisory Board in 1995 and its successor, the Lake Temagami and Cross Lake Focus Group. Its goal was to restore and protect the Temagami area fishery, and to advise the MNR on fishing issues. Gaye Smith and Dick Crum, fish and wildlife committee co-chairs, were the TLA's representatives.

A lake trout population survey, conducted by a retired MNR fisheries biologist in summer 1995, yielded alarming results. Jointly funded by the TRSI and TemTOA, it concluded that Temagami and Cross lakes were being overfished. Gaye and others conferred with the MNR for a year on the best ways to ensure rehabilitation.

A five-year strategy was endorsed by all local stakeholders, including the TAA. The plan called for a daily limit reduction from three to two lake trout and six to three walleye, slot-size limits so prime spawners would live to swim another day, and a scientific creel census as a fishery benchmark.

The district biologist was winding up a round of public sessions in North Bay, Sturgeon Falls and the Tri-Towns when the North Bay office stepped in. Progress sputtered while the MNR held more consultations and prepared questionnaires. A frustrated Gaye wondered if any regulatory changes would ever be made. They did happen, but not until 2002.

Dreaded slush rises on the winter road on the Northeast Arm.
Photo: Harold Keevil

It's No Wonder Bears Hibernate

So many members were enjoying the lake in all its winter-white splendour by the mid-1990s that Tim Gooderham put a daily ice report on the TLA's voice mail. The perils of winter vacations were driven home in a *Times* story by Island 985's Nadine Boles of Fergus, Ontario. She and her husband Gary spent three uneventful winter occasions at their cottage, despite hearing horror stories about slush.

"January 1994 was different," Nadine observed. "Having our own business makes it difficult to get away at all, so we sneak away at night hoping no one will realize we're gone." Just north of North Bay, "Gary mentioned that the truck behind us was flashing his lights and wondered if he might have a wiring problem. Upon peering out my side mirror I could see sparks flying from the trailer we were hauling and decided it was us that had the problem. Sure enough one of the tires was flat. Well actually it was gone. There was no rubber left. The other tire on that same side of the trailer was so hot it was like mush…One hour-and-a-half later we were on the road again. Oh well, a little time lost. It is now 1:30 a.m. Did I mention that it was -36 degrees?"

They finally arrived at 2:30 a.m. "What I really wanted now was a hot drink, no, a stiff drink and a warm bed but the night is still young. There is work to be done." Donning snowmobile gear after skiing to the cottage from Bear Island where they left their van and supplies, Nadine discovered dog kibble in her boot, stashed there by a family of shrews.

At 4 a.m. they set out on a quick sleigh-equipped snowmobile ride. "We loaded up the sled and started back only to realize that the sled was still sitting on the ice back at the van. Voila! A broken trailer hitch…Good old Gary to the rescue again. A quick patch job while I jump up and down trying to keep the circulation going in my feet."

"As we crawled into bed at 5:45 a.m. I remember mumbling "are we having fun yet?" Ahhh!! Winter at the cottage." The Boles left the lake several years ago but return regularly to islands 937 and 672 to visit old friends and neighbours.

Temagami in December

Revealed against the dreary waste
Of drifted snow and icy sheen
The stately pines that crown each isle
Retain their sombre green.
The sleeping cedars bound with snow
Demote and grace the rock-girt shore;
They dream of summer's bygone days
While storms around them roar.
Yet pulsing life will come again
With singing birds and sparkling wave;
Forgotten will be winter's gale
When spring returns once more.
A.L. Cochrane, circa 1920

First Woman President

The board shattered a glass ceiling in fall 1995 by electing its first woman president. Sandy Navaro, a trained botanist, was first elected to the board in 1991. But Sandy's story goes back to 1924 when buddies Charles Ault and William Mitchell canoed the Temagami area. They returned in 1925 and leased Island 1125. Cincinnati's Robert Muhlhauser visited in 1931 and was like one of those guests who refuse to leave. He became a co-owner and his wife Ann joined him in 1936. Sandy's great-grandfather, the son of a German immigrant, co-founded the Windisch Muhlhauser Brewing Company in 1866.

Strangest Reason for Coming to the Lake

Charles Ault, William Mitchell and Benjamin Lippincott grew up together in Cincinnati, then attended Yale University. The trio decided to take a canoe trip in summer 1924. Lake of the Woods on the Minnesota-Ontario border appealed to them but they changed their minds because the train connections from Cincinnati to Temagami were better.

Bob Muhlhauser was affectionately known as "Mr. Moose" for his stirring call, echoing throughout the Northwest Arm on still nights. The family ministered to and ran an amateur ambulance service for injured canoe trippers because, for many years, theirs was the first inhabited island travelling south from Obabika Inlet. Muhlhauser daughter Sandy and her husband Ralph Navaro owned Brown's Island 1186. Charles Ault's daughter Peggy Shardelow shares Island 1125 with the Muhlhausers' son Rick and owns Island 1127. Bob died in 1992 followed by Ann in 1994.

Sandy's two-year presidency would take her through a rough stretch as the TLA faced unprecedented media scrutiny over its struggle to modify claim staking in the Skyline Reserve and stop illegal Cross Lake access. She would also help guide the TLA through the complex union of lake and mainland.

CHAPTER 24

ONTARIO TIGHTENS ITS BELT

The 1995 election of Progressive Conservative North Bay MPP Mike Harris as Ontario premier changed everything for the local community. The land cautions were no longer in effect and the government yanked the Agreement In Principle off the table. It appeared that 23 years of court proceedings, negotiations, and time and money spent had come to naught.

In penny-pinching mode, the province introduced municipal restructuring, downloading of services and shrinking transfer payments. The goal was fewer and larger municipalities, and reduced service duplication. Driven by provincial politics, amalgamation of the Township of Temagami and the unorganized townships would become a fait accompli.

It was crunch time for the TLA as the CPC's mandate ticked down. The planning council proposed treating the Skyline Reserve as a special management area in which there would be no commercial logging although prospecting would be permitted. An all-day session attended by Hilton Young and Jim Hasler arrived at no conclusions.

The TLA was in favour of the Skyline Reserve becoming a conservation reserve, as it was an ideal tool to enshrine the tenets. "The mining fraternity remained adamant that they should be allowed to roam where they wanted…and put up claim posts, even if they are right on a cottager's front lawn," Jim reported in the *Times*.

Tim Gooderham and Director Ray Delarosbel spent a day in another CPC session on the topic of access to Temagami and Cross lakes. The TLA representatives and others suggested there should be no motorized access except at tenet-approved locations, while the West Nipissing groups asked for legal access to Cross Lake.

A final CPC open house was held at the Temagami arena in January 1996 with 200 attendees. Four OPP officers were present to maintain the peace should rumours of an environmental protest be substantiated. No protest ensued but an Earthroots member registered dismay that some areas previously allocated for protection would now be open to mineral exploration. Earthroots believed old-growth pine merited blanket protection as an endangered ecosystem.

MNR Abandons Temagami

A week before the CPC's draft plan was released the MNR announced the closure of the Temagami District office. It left villagers reeling. The MNR was its largest remaining employer. Wayne Adair called it "a catastrophe." At a council meeting, residents questioned how the CPC plan could be implemented with no MNR presence. Of the 50 jobs in the Temagami office as of May 1996, only 18 would remain in November and they would relocate to the North Bay District office. This was part of a massive provincial downsizing involving the layoffs of 10,600 civil servants and $2.3 billion in cuts to programs and services.

The MNR's roots were deep, beginning with the forestry building on Bear Island in 1901. A second office was opened on Forestry Island just off town docks in 1905 and relocated to the mainland in 1934. Forest fire fighting was a major TLA and TFN concern. There would no longer be fire crews in Temagami on a regular basis. During high risk situations, the MNR planned to dispatch a water bomber or helicopter. The area was also left vulnerable to illegal access, hunting, fishing and tree poaching.

The MNR moved to sustainable forest licences province-wide. Companies were expected to plan, harvest and regenerate. Many questioned the wisdom of having loggers monitoring themselves. However, non-compliant companies would be subject to penalties and fines. The controversial Temagami forest was the sole management area

not designated a licence by 2010. Englehart's Grant Forest Products was once considered a candidate, followed by the aboriginal community in partnership with the local government. The latter garnered widespread support but neither passed MNR muster.

Forest management plans would fall under the umbrella of the Crown Forest Sustainability Act. "The new act requires a far more detailed assessment of the flora and fauna of the woodland and what effect lumbering operations will have," Jim Hasler explained in the *Times*. Plans would have to be sensitive to all users, and protect canoe routes, traplines and native heritage sites.

The MNR began looking for alternative arrangements for the Briggs Township landfill, and the Mine and Manito landings, due to the local office closure and shrinking government funding. Ontario's belt tightening led the township to ponder the introduction of tolls on the Lake Temagami Access Road to fund maintenance.

Comprehensive Plan Unveiled

Despite the timing of the MNR closure announcement, the CPC report was released on schedule and contained several recommendations affecting the lake. Access at the middle of three unauthorized access points on the west shore of Cross Lake would remain open, and parking for up to five vehicles would be for day-use and out of sight of the lake. At Baie Jeanne historic access would continue. The MNR would facilitate the establishment of partnerships to address issues at Cross Lake and Baie Jeanne.

The Red Squirrel Road would be used for logging but not during summer months. Lumber roads into special management areas such as the Skyline Reserve would be gated while forest operations were in progress and closed when they ceased.

The majority of the land base would be opened to exploration and mine development, including Temagami and Cross lakes' skyline reserves under a special prescription yet to be written. The plan called for the withdrawal of all islands from staking except parts of Temagami Island. Mining would occur under but not on the surface of the Skyline Reserve. Mine infrastructure would be outside the reserve. No additional road access for mine-related purposes would be permitted in the reserve. There would be no Lake Temagami mainland development. Conservation reserves would be designated at Narrows Island and Temagami Island.

Though generally satisfied with CPC-MNR concessions, the TLA urged the MNR to incorporate these measures: creation of a conservation reserve surrounding Temagami and Cross lakes where no logging, mining or roads would be permitted; allowing motorized access to Lake Temagami and Cross Lake only through the five tenet-recognized access points; and establishing local governance with TLA representation to oversee the plan's implementation.

The CPC proposed buffer zones to protect the headwaters of the Lady Evelyn-Smoothwater Wilderness Park, engendering criticism from municipalities and the forest industry. Wayne Adair believed the added park protection was unnecessary and amounted to expanding the park. The Northern Prospectors Association agreed.

Plan Greenlit

The province accepted the comprehensive plan in June, making few changes to CPC recommendations, and paving the way for mineral exploration after a 23-year drought. Areas identified for resource development would be opened to staking in September 1996. Called the Temagami Land Use Plan (TLUP), it formally adopted the Skyline Reserve as policy.

Ontario also set aside 385 square kilometres to facilitate settlement of the land claim. The land encompassed the historic Austin Bay Tract, about half of the Skyline Reserve and abutted the west side of Cross Lake. The land would be closed to staking and forestry. It was set aside for two years and if no agreement was reached, the government would review its status. Camp Wanapitei was surrounded on three sides by the set-aside lands. Bruce Hodgins believed the area would be better managed under native jurisdiction than MNR's, as garbage piled higher each year from the occupation of Sandy Inlet by campers and houseboaters.

A Lane Change

A small but significant change was made to the entrance of the Lake Temagami Access Road off Highway 11 in 1996. A left turn lane for northbound traffic turning onto the gravel road was installed. A year earlier, with the backing of the Township of Temagami, LaTemPRA and TemTOA, the TLA had made a formal request for the lane to the MTO. Drivers attempting to leave the highway were unsettled by transport trucks fast approaching from behind. A traffic count by the MTO showed the numbers warranted it.

Life Memberships

To build a nest egg, the TLA began offering life memberships in 1996 for $1,500. It was hoped fewer requests for emergency contributions to the Tenets Legal Defence Fund would result. The tenets fund replaced the Legal and Professional Fees Fund set up in 1981. Amalgamation negotiations, fighting illegal access points and defending the Skyline Reserve from staking would prove a drain on the defence fund coffer. The TLA was forced to raid the life membership account in 1997, later refunding it. Tenets bulldog Hilton Young headed up a tenets defence committee during this period.

Cheryl Ruddock of Guelph, Ontario, became a life member. "The intent was to have funds readily available so the board could move quickly when any aspect of the tenets

was threatened," she said. Cheryl's physician husband Nick Ruddock, a director in the mid-1990s, would publish a novel titled *The Parabolist* in 2010, written mainly at his White Bear Island cottage. Primarily a love story, it met with favourable reviews.

Toronto's Liz Rykert and her late sister Pam Rykert of islands 307 and 308 also became life members. Being computer proficient, Liz assisted the TLA in electronically enhancing communications and creating work space online for directors. The life membership option had 20 takers in the first two years. It was dropped in 1999 when the funds were earning low interest rates and members stopped buying in.

Bear Island Construction

With the land claim stuck in the mud, the Bear Island community broke new ground in 1996, constructing the TFN Family and Wellness Centre and the Doreen Potts Health Centre. A new store replaced the one that burned down in 1990. A provincial grant covered 75 per cent of construction costs. A tendering process was used for its operation.

The business was purchased by Mac McKenzie and his daughter Melanie who rented the premises from the TFN. Named Mel's Market, they ran the grocery store until the business was purchased in 2006 by Fabian Grant, son of Dick and Vicki Grant. Fabian called his store the Temagami Post and Outfitters at Bear Island. Gladys Farr, manager of the retail outlet for many years in the 1980s,

The Bear Island store was operated by TFN Chief Roxane Ayotte in 2010.
Photo: Pam Sinclair

returned to work with both Melanie and Fabian. Roxane Ayotte, née Potts, acquired the store in 2008, renaming it The Pier Market.

The TFN elected a new chief in May 1996. Jim Twain, son of former band chief the late Bill Twain, acknowledged a difficult task ahead: bringing the community together with one common goal. He also desired more positive relationships with lake groups.

CHAPTER 25

SKYLINE RESERVE THREATENED

In July 1996 the TLA board was informed by the Ministry of Northern Development and Mines (MNDM) that the special prescriptions for staking in the Skyline Reserve would not be written into regulations in time for the opening of exploration. The MNDM tried to reassure the TLA that unenforceable good-faith guidelines would be attached to claim maps and work permits.

Unable to get its concerns about trailblazing, claim post tree-cutting and drilling across to the MNDM, the board initiated legal action against Ontario. The intent was not to interfere with economic development but to protect the mostly unspoiled Skyline Reserve.

TLA President Sandy Navaro faced the harsh scrutiny of the local media as an American requesting an environmental assessment of a Canadian land use plan. An 11th hour communiqué came from Northern Development and Mines Minister Chris Hodgson. He withdrew the reserve from staking, drawing a collective sigh of relief from the board.

It drew a collective sigh of disgust in the north. MPP David Ramsay said he had heard "just about enough from the TLA" in the *North Bay Nugget*. He suggested throwing the lake open to mainland cottage development would even the playing field, flying in the face of its historic management by the province.

Dr. Roman Brozowski, former CPC chair, accused the TLA of "self-protectionism to the extreme," and fielding "a very exclusionary policy." In a *Nugget* editorial dripping with sarcasm, members were labelled "an eclectic collection of rich Canadian and American cottage owners." This "privileged set apparently believes their shoreline is somehow more sacred than, say, Lake Nipissing's, or Lake Nosbonsing's, or Lake Temiskaming's or, for that matter, Lake Ontario's...Heaven forbid if a fern should get trampled or a twig snapped along the shoreline during prospecting and claim staking."

None of the vociferous critics cited the Tenets for Temagami. One credible oldtimer – Temagami's late Butch Spooner – weighed in to defend the Skyline Reserve, saying, "One of the last few forests of red and white pine in Northern Ontario, surrounding Lake Temagami, must be preserved for the future generations."

The first meeting of the 13-member Public Advisory Committee (PAC) on forestry was held in August. It was comprised of spokespersons from the economic development corporation, Friends of Temagami (FOT), and recreational and resource interests. Jim Hasler represented the TLA. The immediate task was to advise the MNR as it developed a two-year forest management plan. Jim noted in the *Times* that PAC found work on the plan difficult due to drastically reduced MNR staff. The stress would lessen when the next plan was created, he added, because much of the data gathered to build the first plan would be used again.

Staking Drought Ends

On September 17, 1996, 6,000 square kilometres of Crown land stretching through 103 townships was thrown open. A frantic one-day rush saw more than 600 prospectors beating the bushes. Aiming to be first, an American mining company hired high school track teams to sprint and stake claims. Helicopters carrying staking teams buzzed above.

Among the stakers were some amateurs. The Canadian Parks and Wilderness Society, the Wildlands League and Northwatch staked claims in environmentally-sensitive areas they believed should have been protected under the Temagami Land Use Plan (TLUP). Their goal was to highlight vulnerable old-growth white and red pine, yellow birch and eastern white cedar.

Prospectors had 31 days to record their claims. A month later, 3,440 claim units had been registered over 550 square kilometres. Some were made by local independents who would attempt to sell their earnings to bigger players like Falconbridge Ltd.

Owain Lake Siege

Another divisive aspect of the TLUP was the approval of logging in the Owain Lake forest while the White Bear Forest was protected. The CPC had recommended the Owain Lake block, a mixed stand of white and red pine, jack pine and spruce, should not qualify as a representative old-growth site. Earthroots mounted a blockade of Rabbit Lake Road on Labour Day weekend, just days before prospectors would descend en masse. The road was used by cottagers, canoeists, hunters, fishers and minnow trappers.

The Owain Lake cut was to be managed using a shelterwood technique, leaving about 40 per cent of the stand to protect habitat and aid regeneration. Earthroots claimed the 563 acres to be harvested by Goulard Lumber were old growth. The MNR, the Township of Temagami and Cassels and Adjoining Lakes Association (CALA) counterclaimed that parcels were logged prior to the 20th century, and again in the mid-1940s and 1963. Reeve Wayne Adair was eager to inform demonstrators they had established their tent camp on a former logging camp site.

Earthroots' three-month campaign of civil disobedience delayed logging by a month. Unlike the earlier Red Squirrel Road extension blockades, Owain Lake was neither a road-building nor an aboriginal justice issue. It didn't turn into a political hot potato at Queen's Park as the earlier conflict had. Owain Lake is about 45 kilometres southeast of Temagami, close to the Ottawa River, and isn't considered part of

Milne's horse logging in days of yore. Logs were sledded to a lake or river to be boomed to the sawmill after break-up.
MacLean postcard photo: Vintage Postcards

the traditional Temagami canoe routes. It is also outside the land claim area. Many of the protesters were southern Ontario students. It was a dirtier forest defence campaign, marred by a bomb threat and the discovery of more than 50 spiked trees, the work of radicals not associated with Earthroots.

A comedy of errors unfolded during fall 1996. Three prospectors were stopped from proceeding. Two minnow trappers complained to the OPP that they were denied access, resulting in a blockade leader being charged with mischief and intimidation. The same leader was rearrested the same day she showed *The Nature of Things* host David Suzuki around. The leader of the Green Party of Ontario was also charged with mischief and intimidation after two forest management workers collecting pine cones were halted.

With prospectors, protesters and OPP officers trampling the bush in all directions,

the UN World Commission on Forests and Sustainable Development decided it was a good time to visit. The commissioners camped at Wanapitei and heard from TAA, Northwatch, Wildlands League, MNR and CPC representatives. They also met with township representatives – who refused to talk with the 'forest protectors' at Wanapitei – on their own turf, and spent a night among Lake Obabika old-growth stands. Then it was off to Costa Rica and Cameroon.

Anger escalated when it was learned legal action had been launched by the Wildlands League and FOT. Represented by the Sierra Legal Defence Fund, they challenged MNR logging plans in Elk Lake, Temagami and the upper Spanish forest. The plans contravened regulations for old-growth forest conservation and wildlife habitat protection. The regulations had been set out in the 1994 class environmental assessment and reinforced by the 1995 Forest Sustainability Act. The league and FOT were seeking a court order forcing compliance from Ontario. They had to dodge flack from municipalities and the forest industry.

These organizations won a major legal battle in 1997 in Ontario Divisional Court, compelling the MNR to rewrite its forest management plans. The decision was unanimously upheld on appeal in 1998 and is considered precedent-setting by Ontario's environmental law community.

Earthroots' well-oiled public relations machine threw the Temagami area back in the national spotlight with widespread media coverage. In the U.S., the *Detroit Free Press*, *Cincinnati Enquirer* and *USA Today* all made forays into the Temagami issue. Earthroots held a Toronto media conference and invited some heavyweights to show their support. Late social justice activist June Callwood, prominent defense lawyer Clayton Ruby, NDP MP Svend Robinson, novelist Jane Urquhart and others resonated with rhetoric. They lambasted Temagami logging as everything from "an act of terrorism" and "both evil and mad" to "an environmental disaster of global proportions."

Three days later Ben Serre, Liberal MP for Timiskaming-French River, held a rally at the Temagami arena, drawing 1,500 people who sent a strong message to the protesters: "Go home." The MP inaccurately painted the Owain Lake blockade as a conflict between local residents desiring sustainable development and "urban yuppies" wishing to turn the area into a playground for the rich. He suggested northern Ontario should secede and become a separate province.

During the Owain Lake siege, an Oracle Research survey revealed that 75 per cent of Ontarians believed Temagami's remaining old-growth pine should be preserved. The highest level of support was in southwestern Ontario at 85 per cent and the lowest was in northern Ontario at 63 per cent. The results seemed to affirm a future for eco-tourism.

CHAPTER 26

ACCESS AT ANY COST

When the cat's away, the mice will play. A siege of a different stripe was taking place on lake trout-sensitive Cross Lake. In July 1996 Jim Hasler, chair of the environmental affairs committee, noticed that a previously-closed illegal access point had been reactivated. It was north of the middle one the MNR had approved in the Temagami Land Use Plan (TLUP) as a walk-in. The discovery was made during one of Jim's observatory flights.

"Calls to the MNR only produced the response that they were so short-staffed that they did not know when they could go and check it out," Jim related in the *Times*. He got the same response in August. In September, he noticed a 20 by 20-foot building. The MNR again pleaded inability to do anything promptly.

In the meantime members of the West Nipissing Access Group (WNAG) approached an MNR supervisor for permission to build a road access to Cross Lake, south of the MNR-approved access point. They were given verbal sanction by the employee who later declared he'd never heard of the TLUP. The WNAG built a three-metre wide road and a gravel boat-launching ramp.

Conservation officers finally inspected in November. The MNR notified the TLA and the MOE that the construction was illegal because no mandatory environmental assessment for small projects had been done. The MNR considered laying charges. It was the MNR itself that would soon be in the hot seat. Aggravated by the sluggish response and illegal authorization of the road and access point, the TLA and the Wildlands League teamed up with the Sierra Legal Defence Fund. They filed a request under the Environmental Bill of Rights for an investigation. The TFN was also concerned because the west side of Cross Lake was part of the set-aside lands.

The MNR began conducting a belated assessment in January 1997 to determine what if any access should be permitted. Some 70 organizations and individuals submitted suggestions. The majority requested closure of all three access points. They originated from a tertiary road off a main road, terminating about 130 metres from the shore of Cross Lake. It was built by the forest industry to haul gravel for road construction. "Parties unknown" to the MNR built another road to the shore in the late 1980s. The MNR discovered it in 1989 and attempted to destroy it with bulldozers and explosives.

Baie Jeanne Tampering

A 90 by 38-metre parking lot with graded gravel was added to the authorized Baie Jeanne access point by the WNAG in 1996. The

MOE decided not to prosecute the MNR due to the unlikelihood of a conviction based on evidence.

President Sandy Navaro was busy firing off letters to the MNR during summer 1997. The Cross Lake access point was being used despite the TLA's understanding it was to be closed until the environmental assessment was completed. In another letter she inquired about a trailer near Clem Lake at the Baie Jeanne access point parked beyond the 21-day limit. "Because this particular violation is at a site that is currently receiving a lot of attention, it leads TLA members to speculate on the future enforcement of any negotiated solution we might agree to for that site."

In a letter to members in the midst of these clashes, Sandy warned: "This is not just a South and Southwest Arm problem. As you know, roads encircle the entire Lake. If increased motorized access is allowed at Cross Lake and Baie Jeanne, there will soon be demands for drive-in access and motor boat launching at Sandy Inlet and Whitefish Bay or new road access from the west. The TLA needs to set a precedent for access planning with the Cross Lake and Baie Jeanne developments.

"All of this is happening because the MNR is treating Lake Temagami unfairly. More consideration is being given to people who will never pay taxes in the area and only care about how many fish they can take out of the Lake. These people don't care about the environmental damage their roads, parking areas and launching ramps cause."

Finding Common Ground

The North Bay MNR made desultory efforts to get the principal parties together to work on a Baie Jeanne site plan, despite a TLUP pledge to facilitate meetings regarding access issues. The TLA took the bull by the horns and arranged a 1997 discussion between board members, WNAG, the Sturgeon Falls Rod and Gun Club, Ontario Federation of Anglers and Hunters (OFAH) and the Southwest Arm Neighbourhood Association (SWANA). SWANA is an informal group of cottagers south of White Bear Island, focusing on environmental threats to its neck of the woods.

The meeting was mediated by Ed Hanna, a consultant who had worked with the TLA and OFAH in the past. Participants emerged with a draft agreement committing the TLA, SWANA and WNAG to work together on proposed regulations, including: a maximum of 10 parking spaces for vehicles and boat trailers; no upgrading of a recently constructed shallow boat launch; three overnight campsites and adjacent parking spaces would remain; and a boat cache for up to five boats to be located out of sight from the lake.

To maintain the integrity of the Skyline Reserve, no docks would be permitted. Signage outlining the rules would be prominently displayed. The township and LaTemPRA commented, and the MNR approved the accord, going into effect in 1999. "The agreement has worked rather well since it was signed and SWANA members are satisfied

Access or personal concerns seem to slip away
when you slip the canoe into the water. *Photo: Patricia Healy*

rudimentary and low quality access route from an existing forest access road over a 1 kilometre distance," the MNR stated.

The site would include a parking lot for 10 vehicles and boat trailers out of sight of the lake. There would be a shallow launching ramp for small boats. All other access points would be removed and no overnight parking or camping would be permitted. The MNR later signed a short-term Cross Lake management agreement with the Municipality of Temagami.

So, who won? The WNAG of course. Its members weren't charged and obtained their preferred access point – the original one illegally constructed in the late 1980s – with double the amount of parking approved in the TLUP.

Temagami Hits Another Bump

By the end of 1996 the owner of the Temagami Foodland grocery store wanted to sell. Due to the town's shaky economy, little interest was expressed. Knowing a community's grocery store is its life blood, residents formed a co-operative committee and went on a share-selling tear. In the spring Temagami Co-operative Incorporated took over ownership of

with it. MNR's signage has also helped," Jack Goodman said.

Government versus Government

In an odd twist, one arm of government took another to court in April 1997. The MOE charged the MNR with four counts of breaching the Environmental Assessment Act for approving access to Cross Lake. The MNR pled guilty to one charge and was fined $1,200. Although the penalty merely moved cash from one pocket to another, it was interpreted by the TLA as a symbolic gesture acknowledging that government agencies cannot be held above the laws they impose on their constituents.

Despite a majority opinion favouring closure of all Cross Lake access points, the MNR approved the WNAG-improved southern entry in May 1998. It was deemed the least offensive by the TLA. It would be "a

Foodland. The co-op had 506 lake and town members who had purchased $370,000-worth of equity shares by late summer.

Tim Gooderham was elected the inaugural president. Construction of a $1-million store, using loans, grants and share equity, started in fall 1997. One of the charms of the old premises, which shoppers fervently hoped would not be repeated, was the sloping floor and self-propelled carts. The co-op's mantra was "Shop locally" and, as desperation later set in, "Use it or lose it."

While a grocery store may be a town's life blood, the bank is its financial pulse. Scotiabank served notice it would shutter its Temagami branch and leave behind a faceless ATM. Too many town residents were banking in North Bay or the Tri-Towns, a problem exacerbated when the bank announced its decision. Council viewed the bank as an essential service. Months of discussions with bank officials secured Scotiabank's future. Curtailed winter hours were a temporary concession while the installation of an ATM was a new convenience. The decision to keep the branch open was, in part, influenced by an expected influx of business from a proposed birch mill and TFN income to be generated from Casino Rama revenue sharing. The TLA transferred its accounts to the local bank.

TAFIP was experiencing its own problems luring enough volunteers to aid with field and administrative tasks. In 1997 it appealed to council to have the township take it over. Instead, a membership drive spearheaded by Gene and Carol Diener and Tim Gooderham

saw TAFIP memberships rise by 110 per cent in 1998. They successfully approached the TLA membership for its support but, just two years later, TAFIP was again struggling.

A Temagami Times Controversy

Carol Cochrane resigned as *Times* editor in March 1997 citing a lack of community input. The newspaper had become a "Carol/Jim" production with very few regular contributors, she said. The last straw was alleged "unwarranted censorship" by the board of her "Carol's Corner" column. In a resignation letter, she said the intent of an unpublished column was to "bring about awareness of the need for more Canadian input and directors. In order to be credible and to be seen (by others) as a Canadian organization, this is a desperate need!" She cited recent *North Bay Nugget* articles denigrating the TLA as a rich American cottage association. While apologizing to five American directors of nine, she wrote of what she perceived as their misunderstanding of Canadian politics.

In summer 1997 the *Times* ushered in its fifth editor. A daughter of Island 813's Bob and Frankie Rannie, Claire Rannie was elected a director in 1996. She had worked for several years at lake camps, particularly Wanapitei where she met her husband Tim Roach. They were living in Pickering, Ontario, but moved to North Bay in 1999 to be closer to the lake. The *Times* would run its first colour photo in fall 1998. It was snapped by Chimo Island's Sue Gooderham and captured a fire smouldering on Cattle Island and a hovering MNR helicopter.

A Non-Confrontational President

Sandy Navaro's successor for one year was Island 711's Art Avard from London, and later, Huntsville, Ontario. He was acclaimed rather than elected a director in 1997, along with Bruce Hodgins and Hilton Young. The Avards had vacationed on the lake since 1969 and purchased their cottage in 1980. A Bell Canada retiree, Art was serving his second three-year stretch, having been first elected in 1992. He often worked behind the scenes, amending the TLA's bylaws and balancing the books as budget committee chair. He also kept the doors of communication wide open as LaTemPRA liaison during amalgamation discussions, a priority being the establishment of good relationships.

The Avards belonged to the Lake Temagami Bridge Club. Members played weekly in the TLA board room in the early 1980s but the surroundings lacked the right ambiance. They reconvened at the more convivial Manito Hotel and when it closed, the club moved to Ket-Chun-Eny Lodge. As the number of players dwindled, they gathered at their cottages. High-stake bidders boated home with an extra $5 on a good day.

Original card sharks included Gordon and Florence Thompson, John and Doris Schulte, Bob and Frankie Rannie, Murray and Eleanor Dickson, Jack and Gerda Glenn, Tuuli Lowery, Ed and Marie Hayes, David and

A Life of Conviction

Against the advice of female confidants and the disapproval of some of the men in her life, Island 1009's Daphne Schiff earned a master's degree in chemistry at the University of Toronto in 1947. She was a member of York University's faculty for 38 years.

In need of a "hobby," Daphne earned her pilot's licence in 1970 at the age of 46. She has flown in many Round the World and Transatlantic Air races. Her life was occasionally in danger. Both engines once sputtered near the coast of Chile; she coolly went through a procedural checklist and averted disaster. She was once escorted out of Iranian air space by two military jets. She's a member of the Ninety-Nines, the international women's flying club founded by Amelia Earhart.

Daphne's proudest aviation accomplishment is her aid work for Air Solidarité, a Paris-based humanitarian organization. Flying a single-engine plane to places like Cameroon and Senegal, she delivers medical and other essential supplies. She also checks on the progress of Air Solidarité projects including schools and hospitals. Daphne and a pilot friend are the sole North American partners. She flew her latest overseas mission in 2008 and has been temporarily grounded by a knee injury. Daphne, 86 in 2011, fully intended to fly future missions.

Metta Gerstner, Harold and Daphne Schiff and David Alexander. The bridge club nearly folded like a house of cards in 2009 when there were just enough players game enough to gather around a single table.

Amalgamation Moves Forward

Amalgamation talks bogged down for a few months but progress resumed in 1996 with changes to the steering committee. The TLA, the township and LaTemPRA appointed Tim Eby, former reeve Ivan Beauchamp and Gerry Gooderham, respectively.

The TLA asked for the voting day to be changed from November to August. This issue resolved itself when the province amended the Municipal Elections Act and made absentee voting legal. The amendment also smoothed the council representation hump. Only a small number of seasonal residents could vote in person in November and that's why the TLA had favoured a ward system. In elections-at-large the majority of votes would have been cast by permanent residents, even though voter distribution was roughly equal between the mainland and the lake (excluding disenfranchised Americans).

This imbalance was eliminated with absentee voting. A council elected at-large lessened the potential for polarization that a ward system could have generated. Council would consist of six councillors and a mayor. The council elected in November 1997 would take office on January 1, 1998.

The proposed union required council to uphold the tenets and they would be the foundation for planning policies. The restructured planning board would be renamed the Temagami Area Planning Advisory Committee (PAC) and would make recommendations to council on private land planning matters. The local government would have no legal authority over Crown land inside its boundaries. Once patented it would fall under the purview of the OP. PAC would be comprised of eight members. Island electors would represent 50 per cent of PAC membership with the chair selected by members.

The municipality would take in the Township of Temagami, all of Lake Temagami, as well as Cross, Cassels, Snake Island, Lowell, Wilson, Jumping Caribou, Hangstone, Red Squirrel, Gull and Snake lakes, and portions of Rabbit, Red Cedar, Diamond, Anima-Nipissing and Obabika lakes.

A big question remained. What is a fair percentage of property taxes the unorganized area should shoulder? The township gave some estimates but was hampered by an ongoing shift to actual value property assessments and continuing provincial service downloading. The taxation issue was deferred to the amalgamation council. If voters rejected amalgamation, Ontario would likely step in and undertake restructuring unilaterally in accordance with a bill committing the province to municipal streamlining.

Directors' views ran the gamut. Though she was ineligible to vote as a U.S. citizen, Sandy Navaro believed amalgamation would lead to the municipality becoming responsive to the concerns of permanent and seasonal residents.

Trail to Gull Lake. *Photo: Harold Keevil*

away if amalgamation was rejected. His answer: "Probably not."

The board was set to mail ballots to voting members in January 1997 when a new development appeared on the horizon. The Sturgeon Falls area was in the process of incorporating as West Nipissing and planned to annex the unorganized townships of Pardo, Hobbs and McCallum. Temagami's plan included these townships to ensure Cross Lake and Baie Jeanne access points were within municipal boundaries. They could potentially be regulated through MNR land use permits. Should they fall under West Nipissing control, pressure would mount to expand access with supporting infrastructure.

It was likely a tipping point for members sitting on the fence and a reason others planning to vote no had a change of heart. The Ministry of Municipal Affairs and Housing indicated that the assignment of unorganized townships would be on a first-come, first-served basis.

A majority of Township of Temagami residents and LaTemPRA members voted in favour of amalgamation, as did TLA members by an 81 per cent margin. By the closing date, 260 of 599 mailed ballots had been returned and 211 chose amalgamation.

Also without voting rights, Jack Goodman supported amalgamation mainly because he believed it was better than annexation.

Jim Hasler didn't support amalgamation, saying, "I do not believe that even with absentee voting we would have control of council and thus be able to stop any new development on the lake if the mainland people wanted it." His words would prove a portent of events in 2009. Claire Rannie asserted that the township was only interested in getting its hands on more tax revenue and likened the situation to "apartment dwellers who are paying their landlord's mortgage."

In a joint submission, Jim Flosdorf, Dick Crum and Jim Upson ran hot and cold, calling amalgamation a "watershed" moment and urging members to make up their own minds. Rather than influencing votes by revealing his position, Art Avard posed what he saw as the pros and cons. Past President Hilton Young weighed in, asking whether the issue would go

Uncharted Territory

The board met with Minister of Northern Development and Mines Chris Hodgson in fall 1996. It aired concerns about almost half of Lake Temagami's Skyline Reserve being held in limbo as part of the TAA set-aside lands. Both parties agreed that Temagami and Cross Lake's skyline reserves should be mapped for legal enforcement of restrictions before claim staking was permitted. These parameters would also be referenced should land claim negotiations resume.

A joint mapping project was initiated with Grant Forest Products. A producer of oriented strand board, the company was then a strong candidate for an MNR sustainable forest licence. Cottager Peter Bernie, eventual owner of New Liskeard's Wabi Iron and Steel Corporation, played a key role in the TLA-Grant partnership.

The map would make Lake Temagami and Cross Lake two parts of a single Skyline Reserve. Grant used satellite data, helicopter views and topographical maps to develop a unique and accurate map, completed in summer 1997. It was incorporated by the MNR and used in land claim settlement discussions.

CHAPTER 27

A MARRIAGE OF CONVENIENCE

The bride – the lake – would enter into a marriage of convenience in January 1998, hoping the groom – the township – would help protect her from corrupting influences. The groom wasn't in love but lusted after her assets. The honeymoon was over when the first tax bills arrived.

The Temagami and West Nipissing proposals were submitted to the MMAH, asking for the appointment of a restructuring commissioner to decide the fate of the three disputed townships: Pardo, Hobbs and McCallum. Following public meetings, the commissioner decided to hold the disputed townships in abeyance for three years, unless an agreement was reached between the two municipalities. By 2011 there was no agreement and the townships are still in limbo.

The commissioner removed Sisk Township, containing Marten River Provincial Park, from the West Nipissing plan and added it to Temagami's. It was a welcomed surprise for both the town and Sisk residents, whose affinity was closer to communities on the Highway 11 corridor.

The slate of candidates for mayor and council earned an eight-page pullout section in the fall 1997 *Times*. There were four hopefuls for mayor, including incumbent reeve Wayne Adair. The sole lake candidate was Barbara Fehrman. There were thirteen prospective councillors. Four were lake residents, including TLA members Jim Hasler and Bill Kitts.

Born and raised in Temagami, Bill was a former councillor and the owner of Temagami Marine. He and his wife Billie had owned a cottage on Island 86 since 1982. Jim had made presentations to the CPC, served on the local government steering committee, the earlier planning board and the MNR citizens' committee on forestry.

Candidates were asked a series of questions about the tenets, taxes, user fees and access points. Most pandered to the party line, knowing that the lake represented about 50 per cent of the electorate. An unsuccessful council contender did not supply a résumé or respond to the questionnaire. Former reeve Ron Prefasi who was running for mayor also disregarded the questions. One failed council hopeful simply replied "yes" in agreement with TLA positions and gave no explanation.

Wayne Adair was elected mayor for one of Ontario's largest municipalities, encompassing an area of 2,400 square kilometres. Bill Kitts won his council bid and was appointed to chair the general government and finance committee. The lake was also represented by Lorie Hunter, former president of LaTemPRA and a member of the local government steering committee. She would head up social services.

Biff Lowery, who had recently moved to town but kept his place on Temagami Island, was elected and put in charge of the planning and development committee. He represented LaTemPRA during land claim negotiations culminating in the failed Agreement In Principle (AIP). He was also a member of the steering committee and a new transition committee, charged with alleviating the growing pains of an enlarged municipality.

Ray Delarosbel and Tim Eby were TLA representatives on the transition committee. New Liskeard's Tim and his spouse Kelly were relative newcomers, having purchased property on Island 852 in 1989. The committee arrived at more than 100 recommendations, all published in the *Times*, giving members a good overview of the municipality's direction.

Who Pays for What?

Of key interest were services that would be core rated (everyone pays) and area rated (users pay). The transition committee recommended and council agreed that parks and recreation, library, school-crossing guard, bylaw enforcement, landfill maintenance, recycling, roads and social services would be core rated. Members would be paying for some services most would never use.

Council agreed that user-pay services would consist of water, sewerage, sewerage and water treatment plant maintenance, and garbage pick-up. Islanders would not be billed but there would be a charge for transferring trash from the Mine landing to the Briggs landfill. The lake would pay 50 per cent less for fire services. To keep taxpayers informed, the municipality began publishing a "Municipal Update" section in the *Times*. Consequently, the paper's distribution increased.

The Canadian Coast Guard announced it would no longer maintain the lake's 104 buoys and 16 shore lights. The transition committee recommended that the town assume responsibility for the navigational aids, to be core rated. Council agreed and the municipality began maintaining the markers in 2003 with hired local assistants. The long-range plan was to contract this work through a bidding process.

Death and Taxes

Islanders got their first interim tax bill in winter 1998. One commented succinctly, "Outrageous!" Another warned he would no longer be able to support the Tenets Legal Defence Fund. President Art Avard noted in the *Times* that council wouldn't have enough information about funding from Ontario to finalize its budget and issue final tax bills until summer. The province had recently introduced a property assessment system based on market value, which would have to be factored into the equation.

When lake dwellers received their final tax bills, they were a "shocker," according to one. The finance committee, headed by Councillor Bill Kitts and including Tim Eby, came up with a low mill rate. The gouge resulted from current value assessment – a double whammy for cottagers also owning principal property in Ontario.

After amalgamation became official, the TLA didn't rest on its laurels; Art Avard met with Wayne Adair. Then Hilton Young, Tim Gooderham and Art met with Wayne and LaTemPRA's Gerry Gooderham to review matters important to the lake. Hilton, Tim and Art were also attending committee of the whole and council meetings every month. Art drove all the way from Huntsville. "Initial meetings indicate that our objectives are similar for most issues and the thrust of the discussion was how we can work together rather than at cross purposes," he wrote.

The Planning Advisory Committee (PAC) was up and running by March 1998. Chaired by Biff Lowery, its TLA representatives were Ray Delarosbel and Jim Hasler while LaTemPRA's emissaries were Gerry Gooderham and Jerry Burrows. PAC would face the unenviable task of walking a tight rope between the preservation of the lake's semi-wilderness and the need for tax-paying development. The new OP would guide growth over a 20-year horizon.

User Fees?

The town was set to introduce parking and docking fees in July 1998. People could choose an annual/seasonal fee of $125 plus $50 for a trailer. Art Avard attended a council meeting to present the TLA's position that taxpayers should be exempt. Council decided to send an open letter to ratepayers asking for input. To Art's dismay, council instead approved fees

and circulated a letter after the fact. "To treat a ratepayer who spends two weeks vacation at his cottage the same as a camper or fisherman who spends two weeks on the lake and contributes very little to our community is not fair unless the main objective of Council is to tax and charge its new constituents to the maximum," he wrote in a letter fired off to council.

Council decided to postpone the collection of fees. It would instead determine whether traffic volume warranted a user-pay system. Major repairs were made to docks and breakwalls at the Mine and Manito landings over summer 1998. The municipality received $500,000 from the Northern Transition Assistance Fund in 1999 and earmarked $197,000 for the access road and Mine Landing. Work included a separate landing for commercial barges.

For Tim Gooderham and the radio operators, a liberating effect of amalgamation was the municipality taking over the recycling program in 1998. In the TLA's final summer Steve Wicary and Jen Wilson reported that monkeys had been set loose: "No matter how many spiteful announcements were made providing listeners with instructions on how to properly separate their recyclables, the mess kept getting bigger. Not only was there plastic in the glass bins and batteries in the can bins, there was household garbage (often rotting) everywhere. Someone even thought a chest freezer could be forced through an eighteen inch square hole and recycled." They added, "It is absolutely baffling that in a place as beautiful as Temagami people can be such pigs."

Access Denied

While the lake and mainland were divided over parking and docking fees, the municipality came together when the West Nipissing Access Group (WNAG) demanded a public access point and boat launch on the east side of Obabika Lake. It could lead to illegal access points on the western shore of Lake Temagami. Taking Highway 805, West Nipissing residents had access to Obabika Lake by way of a cottage until an altercation with the owner ended it. The proprietor of nearby Obabika Lodge, an upscale resort once offering paid parking access, became a target of blame. Several pounds of roofing nails were spread across his roadway, graffiti was spray-painted on signs and Obabika Lake buoys were removed.

At a public meeting, the MNR stressed that if a public access was designated, it would be accompanied by a management plan dealing with parking, length of stay and other issues. The TLUP stated an intention of "ensuring limited access to Obabika Lake." To the TLA's surprise, the MNR decided not to allow motorized access although several portages permitted access by foot.

In winter 1998-99 vandals struck the Baie Jeanne access point and cut two dozen trees in the Skyline Reserve. A sign was spray-painted with the words "Obabika Access Now!" This may have been retribution for the MNR's Obabika decision. The MOE and MNR investigated and Town Council offered a reward for information. There were no takers.

Train Station and Fire Tower Facelift

Restoration was a town buzzword in 1998. Ontario Northland Railway (ONR) closed the train station in 1996 as a cost-cutting measure and contracted out ticket sales. With its attractive exterior stone work, fashioned from boulders collected between North Bay and Cobalt, ONR didn't want to see the historic facility deteriorate. Constructed in 1907, the interior was rebuilt in 1909 following a fire. ONR leased the station to Richard and Claire Smerdon. Claire had been a Camp Metagami camper. She became a stage manager and met Richard, a technical director, through her work.

"I married him, taught him to paddle and brought him to Temagami to carry my canoe," Claire told *Times* readers. "Fortunately, he proved to be a competent bowman and, indeed, revealed an unsuspected talent for lighting fires in the rain."

Richard's specialty was theatre restoration while Claire's was building miniatures and scale models. The couple had revamped Cobalt's Classic Theatre and they melded their talents once again to refurbish the station to its former grandness. They set up a charitable restoration trust with a board of directors to receive donations. The trust was granted up to $200,000 from the Northern Ontario Heritage Fund, to be matched by donations. Individuals were invited to sponsor various items such as benches. The trust had brought $700,000 to Temagami by 2003 via federal, provincial and private funding.

The Smerdons discovered that the cathedral ceiling, supposedly destroyed by fire in 1976, was mostly intact behind a false ceiling. They put 19 Temagami youths to work

The train station in 2010. *Photo: Pam Sinclair*

restoring it. Other painstaking tasks included scraping eight layers of paint off interior oak trim. The couple established Temagami Station Enterprises Limited, a manufacturing business specializing in model kits, miniatures, engravings and custom products, sold in the station gift shop and at other outlets. ONR transferred ownership of the station to the municipality in 2000.

Richard and Claire set their sights even higher – the 30-metre fire rangers' tower standing on the summit of Caribou Mountain 120 metres above Temagami. It was a testament to days of yore when fire spotting was done from on high without benefit of an engine. The original 1910 square-timber tower was 13.5-metres high. The last in a series of steel towers was abandoned in the 1970s when aircraft became the standard for scanning distant

treetops for curls of smoke. The Smerdons and Temagami's Community Development Officer John Grass saw tourism value waiting to be tapped.

Richard was project manager and designer. The tower's outer skeleton was deemed sound but the inner workings, including an unsafe ringed ladder, had to go. The ladder was replaced with a 140-step staircase with several viewing platforms. A replica of the original cupola was placed atop the tower in two sections by helicopter. It commands breathtaking 360-degree views for 40 kilometres.

It's not often that one's worksite soars high in the sky. Richard had this to say about the challenges: "My work on this project has offered emotional swings between exhilaration, frustration and sheer terror. We are not trying to achieve the impossible but we are certainly trying to accomplish the difficult."

Although supportive of the project, the municipality said taxpayers would not be footing the bill. A $240,000 Northern Ontario Heritage Fund grant covered most costs. A Caribou Mountain Committee overseeing the project raised the remaining $60,000 through fundraisers like a revived winter carnival. The committee also sold tower steps and the

The refurbished Caribou Mountain
fire tower. *Photo: Mike Drenth*

cupola was available. A second $388,000 bounty from the heritage fund was spent on infrastructure such as bridges, washrooms, a parking lot accommodating tour buses and an interpretive centre. The fire tower complex was integrated into the nearby White Bear Forest through a network of trails and picnic areas. Forest supporters could purchase sections of trail and donations went toward maintenance and protection.

Land Claim Talks Resuscitated

Progress to resolve the land claim crawled along at a snail's pace through 1997-98. The TFN, TAA and MKA had all successfully argued grounds to appeal the 1995 court decision quashing the land cautions. Arguments were heard by the Ontario Court

of Appeal in summer 1998 but no decision was forthcoming. This was interpreted by the TAA as a sign that the court preferred negotiations over judicial proceedings. The court ruled in late 1999, upholding the 1995 decision. The TFN and TAA decided in 2000 not to appeal to the Supreme Court of Canada.

The TFN had cut ties with the TAA following the TFN's rejection of the 1993 settlement offer but they had since reconciled. The TFN voted in favour of a proposal closely mirroring the earlier AIP. It upped monetary compensation from $15 to $20 million. The province had withdrawn the AIP in 1995 and then set aside a parcel of potential Crown settlement lands in 1996. When the set-aside land offer expired after two years, Ontario extended it indefinitely. The Ontario Native Affairs Secretariat (ONAS) considered how to respond to the joint native proposition, which it had initially rejected.

At the 1999 AGM, TAA Chief Doug McKenzie said Ontario was willing to rekindle talks. The province wanted to renegotiate a new deal because Premier Mike Harris believed the 1993 offer was too generous. The federal government had announced it was prepared to join negotiations. The TLA continued to support a fair, just and equitable settlement endorsing the tenets. The board met with Ontario's chief negotiator Doug Carr of ONAS to underscore the importance of all lake stakeholders forming a primary advisory body.

For the Bear Island community, life in 1998 didn't revolve around the land claim. A

$5.3-million water and sewerage system was constructed to service about 65 households. The Laura McKenzie Learning Centre was transferred to TFN control. This step was part of a Canada-wide trend enabling First Nation schools to introduce native language and heritage courses.

Fire Season

Spring 1998 dawned hot and dry with a series of fires. Outbreaks in Sharp Rock Inlet, Whitefish Bay, the North Arm and Can-Usa Island were doused by islanders. A month later fishermen radioed TLA operators to report yet another fire, this one on Cattle Island. Doug Thompson, son of former president Graeme Thompson, rallied the troops and contacted the MNR. Firefighters' efforts were hindered by an inability of all but one pump, a powerful Wajax, to reach the top of the island with sufficient water pressure. Another problem was the incompatibility of different makes in attempting to connect equipment.

The MNR dropped an overnight crew to ensure the fire was truly out, stationed a stand-by crew in Temagami and readied a Twin Otter water bomber at its Link Lake base. Summer wasn't half over when houseboaters reported a fire raging high on a mainland ridge between Squirrel Point and Keewaydin. Deemed unsafe for amateur firefighters, the MNR was dispatched to drop water mixed with fire retardant foam.

All were caused by lightning strikes. The board used the 1998 flea market proceeds to purchase a Wajax pump with a set of adaptors for the TLA building dock. The fact all the fires were put out before they got out of control is a credit to the VHF radio system, the lake's network of water pumps and the swift response of islanders.

CHAPTER 28

PRESS FREEDOM FUELS DEBATE

A decision in spring 1998 triggered a heated dispute. The board received a piece co-written by directors Jim Flosdorf and Jack Goodman, taking issue with proposed municipal docking and parking fees. They suggested the board publish it in the *Times* as an editorial.

"If Art has some concerns about the editorial and believes it does not reflect the broad consensus of the Board, then Jim and I (and several others) would like to run it as a letter to the editor," Jack wrote to Tim Gooderham and Claire Rannie. Five directors (*Times* editor Claire, Art Avard, Hilton Young, Dick Crum and Jim Hasler) deemed it "unsuitable" as a letter. The copy was endorsed by four other directors (Jack, Jim, Bruce Hodgins and Jim Upson). The board voted, the majority prevailed and it was not published.

In their piece Jim and Jack labelled a plan to lump taxpayers together with day users, by charging everyone fees, "ill-considered" and "discrimination." "Rather than bringing town and lake residents together, it will create a wedge of annoyance and mistrust."

An uproar ensued over freedom of the press and minority opinion issues, culminating in a harsh statement read by Dennis Goodman at the AGM. He accused the board of "petty tyranny on the part of a self-appointed oligarchy," adding, "Every director has the right and the obligation to make his or her views known to the membership." President Art Avard defended the board's action, saying the tone and wording of the letter was "inappropriate" and counterproductive to its efforts to maintain good relations with the town.

Island 381's Jim Upson of Orchard Park, N.Y., surveyed the membership independently of the board on several topics shortly after the AGM. One of his queries was: "Should the *Temagami Times* publish both the majority and minority opinions of the TLA directors on all significant board votes?" 296 respondents said yes while just 43 said no.

To heal the rift, an ad hoc committee was struck, composed of three members with a journalistic background – Ray Dumont, Janet Kask and Pam (Glenn) Sinclair. They were to develop a set of policies for the Temagami News Association (TNA) and the *Times*.

The TNA was incorporated as a separate entity in 1986 to obtain a second class mailing permit from Canada Post and take advantage of lower rates. This permit was not available to the TLA because its primary activity was not publishing. The TNA was essentially a hollow shell with three inactive directors and no constitution or meetings. The ad hoc committee strove to turn the TNA into a living, breathing entity.

Lives of Conviction

Two South Arm cottagers distinguished themselves with exemplary military and public service. The late Dr. John Kask was a Canadian pioneer in fisheries conservation and oceanography. As a marine biologist, he advised governments and held high level positions with fisheries protection agencies in Canada, the U.S. and at the UN level.

In 1943 John joined the U.S. Army and was a senior fisheries official during the Pacific campaign and Japan's postwar reconstruction under General Douglas MacArthur. He often wrote the general's speeches. John bought two islands in 1950 but he never fished for sport. His daughter Janet, a Quebec broadcaster, writer and teacher, owns Island 922.

Admiral James D. Watkins of Island 953 since 1985 is a highly decorated retired U.S. Navy officer. During the Ronald Reagan administration (1982-86), James was chief of naval operations when work began on a strategic missile defence system. He was the secretary of energy during the first Gulf War. Time spent at his island refuge sometimes hinged on Washington DC averting a crisis. James was also appointed by two presidents to chair ocean policy commissions. He was presented the presidential citizens medal, one of the highest civilian honours, by President George W. Bush in 2008 for protecting the nation and its natural resources.

The committee put together a set of guidelines recommending the *Times* be operated as a newspaper, not as a newsletter, which the TLA had been accused of publishing. The editor should: strive to publish, rather than suppress, differing perspectives on controversial issues so that readers can make informed decisions; should not publish letters or other material considered slanderous, false or inaccurate; and if unsure whether a questionable item should be published, should request that the writer revise it. Failing that, the editor should request the TNA's intervention.

The ad hoc committee believed the TNA board should operate independently of the board, formulate long-term editorial policies and ensure the editor adhere to them. Directors should not serve on the TNA, nor should they interfere in the *Times'* operations or policies. To avoid conflict of interest, the editor should not be on the executive board, the report concluded.

The report was referred to the board. Recent policy changes at Canada Post meant it was no longer necessary to maintain a separate corporation to obtain a favourable mailing rate. The TNA was dissolved and the board transferred TNA duties to a publications committee. It adopted TNA recommendations but chose to contradict its own procedures by appointing a director as chair. It did not give the committee a mandate to develop editorial policies either.

Claire Rannie took the board-approved ad hoc panel's report as "the guiding principles" under which she operated, she said. The board began asking her in the mid-2000s to request approval for her editorial decisions. Had the middleman committee recommended by the ad hoc panel been in place, conflict resolution procedures would have kicked in. Citing a passage in the TLA Bylaws stating, "The President shall be, ex officio, a member of all Committees," the board passed a resolution in 2005 rescinding its previous endorsement of the ad hoc committee's report. Claire felt stripped of editorial independence and resigned.

Planning and Staking Pass Go

The municipality received $175,000 from the Ontario Municipal Restructuring Fund and allocated a portion to drafting the new OP. Planning firm Marshall Macklin Monaghan was hired. Public input was collected over summer 1998 and a list of planning topics was prepared. The Planning Advisory Committee (PAC) hoped to have a draft OP and zoning bylaw ready for public comment by summer 1999.

The recently mapped Skyline Reserve was opened to claim staking in October. Prospectors were to follow strict regulations approved under the Ontario Mining Act and the Public Lands Act. They were not permitted to cut trees to serve as claim posts but had to carry them in. Nothing was to be visible from the shore, including flagging tape and paint. The rules were developed with the input of the Lake Temagami Review Committee, including TLA representative Tim Eby. All proposed mining activity was subject to review by the committee. Just 10 staking crews tiptoed

around on opening day in steel-toed boots, while boaters patrolled for any sign of an axe blade protruding from the shoreline. None violated the regulations.

Tim Eby, a northerner and mining industry careerist, died in 2002. He packed in a mittful of community involvement during his time as a cottager. He worked for the betterment of Temagami's amalgamated future by serving on the transition committee and chairing its general government and finance subcommittee. He didn't abandon ship once amalgamation reached the dock; he joined council's general government and finance committee.

A Landmark in Ruins

In January 1999 Temagami was hailing its first hero of the year. The Temagami Inn restaurant and tavern, locally dubbed the White House, went up in flames. Pierre Leach, a son of owners Paul and Marcella Leach, was awakened by the smoke and thought immediately of a tenant who was hard of hearing. Prevented by smoke from reaching the tenant's room, Pierre crawled across the roof and climbed in a window to rouse him. Both escaped without injury. Jim Leach, another son, was a volunteer firefighter who helped try to save the business. Firefighters were assisted by the Haileybury fire department but the building was reduced to rubble.

Temagami had lost a landmark. Frank and Hazel Goddard opened Goddard's Hotel in the early 1930s. Agnes LaLonde, Archie and

Angele Belaney's daughter, was the first cook. The hotel was moved back for the widening and paving of the Ferguson Highway as Highway 11 in 1937. Guests included King

1970 where Vagn was caretaker. In quiet moments, the couple canoed bays and inlets. Vagn recreated their majesty in oil and pencil landscapes, treasured today by the owners.

The Red Indian gas station, from left, now Grant's Home Hardware,
Lloyd's General Store and Post Office, and Goddard's Hotel
and Tea Room, later the Temagami Inn, in 1936.
MacLean postcard photo: Reg Sinclair

Clancy who played hockey on two Stanley Cup championship teams and went on to plum managerial roles with the Toronto Maple Leafs. The Chicago Black Hawks and their coaches stayed at the Goddard resort while training in North Bay.

While Temagami lost the White House, it gained a fine dining establishment the same year. Vagn and Else Peterson opened the Copenhagen Dining Room, earning annual accolades in the *Where to Eat in Canada* guide. Vagn played host while Else devised divine Danish dishes. The Petersons immigrated to Canada in 1962, arriving at Wabun in

They went on to operate restaurants from the Tri-Towns to North Bay before returning to Temagami. Vagn succumbed to cancer in 2009.

User Fees and Y2K

A municipal parking and docking survey mailed to ratepayers in winter 1999 revealed that 95 per cent of respondents favoured fees, as long as those with no vested interest paid more. Director Jim Upson's independent membership survey reflected these findings. 290 of 342 respondents endorsed differential levies.

Despite overwhelming support, the municipality rejected fee implementation, because set-up costs would be prohibitive, especially for a two-tiered system. Instead, parking and docking would continue to be financed with core-rated taxes of an average of less than $25 per property owner per annum.

Almost every media outlet worldwide began sounding an alarm over the ascending apocalypse known as Y2K or the Millennium Bug. The *Times'* first warning came one year prior to January 1, 2000. The *Temagami Talker* planned to carry updates on the municipality's preparedness in every 1999 issue.

It was predicted by computer nerds that when the new century rolled over, computers would turn the clock back to 1900. And it wasn't just computers that would be afflicted; anything with a tiny but insidious electronic microchip, such as heating systems, could go wonky. The municipality struck a Y2K committee, chaired by CAO John Hodgson, to work with service providers to predict and address impacts. The school and arena were designated shelters.

The TLA asked cottagers to store their generators and VHF radios at the TLA building when they left the lake in 1999 so they could be used by the town in case of hydro and communications failure. More than the usual number considered spending New Year's Eve at the cottage where they believed they would be less affected. However, "EVERYONE WILL BE AFFECTED ONE WAY OR ANOTHER," the *Times* admonished in upper case.

We all know what happened. The year 2000 began with a trio of 0s – no planes fell from the

sky, the U.S. military didn't accidentally fire a missile at Toronto's CN Tower and the banks didn't delete their clients' accounts. However, for Temagami-area residents, the New Year started with a bang in the form of an earthquake with its epicentre near Temiscaming, Quebec. With the noise, shaking and things falling off shelves, some people thought a plane was falling out of the sky.

Tinder Dry

A measly 10 millimetres of rain fell between April and June 1999. Just a single log was pulled from the Cross Lake dam for a single week, so lakes and rivers downstream did not become completely dry. The Great Lakes were at their lowest level in more than 30 years. Lake Temagami in June was 45 centimetres below its normal level for that time of year.

Against this parched backdrop, a forest fire caused by human carelessness broke out early in May, just two kilometres south of town. Local firefighters were later lauded by the MNR for their quick response. Three water bombers and four MNR crews fought the flames, fanned by high winds. The fire jumped Highway 11. Several households were evacuated and the highway was closed. Bill and Billie Kitts came within metres of losing their home. The MNR spent five days suppressing the blaze and checking for flare-ups with an infrared heat scanner. 450 acres of mixed forest were destroyed.

Following an OPP investigation, arson was suspected in a fire that razed Jim Hasler and

Carol Cochrane's cottage in June. A shed was broken into and fuel oil taken. It was spilled on the cottage floor and a lit match was then tossed in. The couple posted an unclaimed $10,000 reward for information. They rebuilt a winterized main cabin.

The Privy Project

Although planners and consultants were consuming the board's time and energy, a few members decided to get physical. A committee responsible for backcountry, campsites, youth camps, and trails and outfitters issues took on a task worthy of Discovery Channel's *Dirty Jobs*. It built and installed box privies on 18 of the most heavily used campsites. Called the privy project, Ray Delarosbel described the first step – dealing with feculence and effluvium – in all its repugnant detail for *Times* readers. The volunteers buried the fetid evidence.

The bug-proof and ventilated privies were made of pressure-treated wood. Earlier efforts by canoeing groups failed because their privies were placed on the surface or over shallow, hand-dug holes, Ray said. The latest effort used a small excavator to dig deeper holes. Art Avard "was ultimately responsible for routing the seats and assures me there will be no slivers on his watch," Ray added. Financial aid to build the $200 privies came from businesses and organizations. Members got their hands dirty again the following summer, building and installing 45 more on Temagami and Cross lakes.

The TLA and TRSI financed a campsite and visitor survey in 2001. The results of 348 evaluations were posted on Ottertooth.com. Congestion, noise, illegal squatting and overflowing privy problems were identified. Recommendations included more privy construction and maintenance, regulating houseboats and the collection of user fees.

Wicked Weather

Mother Nature's disposition turned nasty in summer 1999. A microburst downed a large swath of trees on Chimo Island. Microbursts are like small-scale tornados caused by rapidly descending moist air. A similar anomaly in 2006 felled large-girth trees on Temagami Island. Some Northeast Arm cabins were split in half by the force of old-growth pine crashing down. Finlayson park lost at least 60 trees.

Island 150 cottager Ginty Jocius of Guelph, Ontario, was dying of brain cancer when the 2006 microburst struck and destroyed many of his trees. He chipped away, making cedar shakes from the toppled timber. After they purchased their property in 1998, Ginty and his wife Lorie jumped headfirst into the privy project, flea market and more. They had contracted Temagami-itis after canoeing the area while their children attended Wabikon.

Escalating incidents of extreme weather worldwide are a symptom of climate change. The summers of 2001 and '02 were hotter than normal. The mercury rose so high in 2003 that temperature records were shattered.

A Creel Census

The fisheries focus group was allocated enough MNR funds in 1999 for a bare-bones open-water walleye and lake trout creel census, according to Gaye Smith. Through Dick Crum's efforts, the group raised more than $20,000 in order to carry out a top-quality study. The municipality matched funds raised up to $10,000. The TFN obtained an $8,000 grant to pay some of the wages of two First Nation members hired to collect data.

Gaye was unhappy with the MNR's summary. The average trout catch rate of six

Trevor Sanders of Island 1091
was one of three lucky winners of the 2009
TLA children's fishing contest.
Photo: Temagami Times

hours was deemed "good fishing," an opinion he did not share. It took an average of 17 hours to land a walleye, which Gaye's guests called the "mythical fish of Lake Temagami," he wrote in the *Times*. He believed the MNR downplayed the significance of these figures.

Perhaps the younger set was having better luck. Fish and wildlife committee co-chairs Gaye and Dick began sponsoring a children's summer fishing contest in 2000. To enter, anglers sent photos of their catch to the TLA. Fishing gear prizes were donated by Gramp's Place on Highway 11 and later Camp Adanac.

Ottawa Tightens Its Hitch Knot

The federal government introduced new equipment regulations in 1999 for power and non-power boats. One key provision was mandatory life jackets within easy reach for everyone along for the ride. The rules were taken to a ludicrous extreme in 2003 when the OPP ticketed a senior summer resident enjoying a paddle around his island. His crime? He was without a compulsory whistle in the canoe.

Almost everyone powerboating in Canada would have to pass a written safety exam accredited by Transport Canada. Americans keeping their boats across the border for more than 45 days would also have to comply. Once a boater passed, he would be issued a lifetime pleasure craft operator's card. The TLA's Executive Secretary Peter Healy taught courses in anticipation of the September 15, 2009 date when all boaters had to have the card.

Despite the 10-year phase-in, more than half of Canada's boaters didn't have their cards in time. Private companies administering the test experienced a flood of skippers scrambling to take the test online just days ahead of the 2010 Victoria Day weekend, rather than risking fines of more than $250.

The goal is to reduce boating deaths. Critics branded it a cash grab because it doesn't require a driving test. The exam is riddled with online cheaters and the card cannot be revoked for infractions as can a driver's licence. Often inexperienced boat and houseboat renters are exempt in a nod to tourism industry concerns.

Draft OP under Scrutiny

A 76-page draft OP was released in May 1999. The board commended PAC for embedding concepts such as the tenets. There would be no new residential development in Kokoko, Pickerel and Couch bays or on Cross Lake. A lot's suitability would be assessed on a site-by-site basis. However, the board discovered a serious flaw. The draft carried a figure of 20 new lots per year, to be developed from patented and Crown land, and dispersed throughout the lake. It believed that number was far too high and recommended a reduction to five.

The draft was caught in the headlights at the 1999 AGM. Concerns were voiced about lot development and its impact on water quality, the fishery and the Temagami experience. A mouthful of a motion was carried by a vote of 58 to 10 "that the TLA and board are to explore every avenue to bring about the delay of the finalization of the Official Plan to enable further study and consideration ...and exercise due diligence to ensure the concerns of the membership are met within the plan policies and to further ensure that the studies necessary to address the Lake capacity issues are recommended with the plan."

The board didn't take its stand lightly. Four meetings were held with more than 140 members. Recommendations were submitted to PAC and Marshall Macklin Monaghan, including five dispersed lots per year, a lot creation and development study to determine where and how much cottaging should be allowed, a review with residents within line of sight of a proposed development, and enough time for PAC to review changes and for the TLA to communicate with its members.

A second draft addressed some of these issues. The annual lot target was reduced from 20 to eight with no carry-overs from previous years. Priority would be given to lots created from private rather than Crown land. The MNR did not intend to release any Crown land for five years or until the land claim was resolved. The draft proposed a lot creation and development study, which would also take into account future TFN development. Two-acre lots, with 90-metre frontages, two hundred-metre buffer zones and 10-metre setbacks were proposed. No lots could be within five hundred metres of access points or campsites.

CHAPTER 29

THE LAKE ADRIFT

The draft OP drew critical reviews. The Southwest Arm Neighbourhood Association (SWANA) and the Lake Temagami Group (LTG) were unhappy that the municipality was divided into five neighbourhoods with the lake treated as a single entity. SWANA didn't want the lake handled as one because it believed the Temagami experience is defined by individual neighbourhoods, each wanting a say in where development occurs and how much is permitted.

The LTG, representing about 30 property owners in the North and Northwest arms, believed little development should be permitted in its neck of the woods to protect its remote character. The group retained a lawyer and planner. It preferred the approach taken in the 1986 OP. That OP designated smaller lot sizes where development was already heavily concentrated, such as the Hub and the Northeast Arm, while the less developed North, Northwest and Southwest arms were treated to larger lots.

Another party, the Committee for the Preservation of the Temagami Wilderness Experience (CPTWE), had members from around the lake. They believed eight new lots per year were still too many and would lead to pollution, and "more of everything but the quiet and solitude we treasure." This group alleged that some Planning Advisory Committee (PAC) members doing business on the lake had a pro-development conflict of interest. The CPTWE was also concerned that the plan could be amended at the whim of council.

An OP amendment may be exempt from MMAH approval, provided the municipality gives notice of its decision and allows a 20-day appeal period. In the event of an appeal, a decision is made by the Ontario Municipal Board

The TLA refused to support what it labelled NIMBY protectionism, instead advocating that all residents should share "the pain" of development together on a fair and equitable basis. "Unbalanced application of special standards or exclusions could focus development activity disproportionately in other areas of the Lake," said Hilton Young, chair of the TLA planning committee. The board feared special interest groups could delay the plan's implementation by challenging it before the OMB. The old plan that did not encompass the tenets would remain in effect, allowing 20 cottage lots per year.

The board asked members to consider the fragmenting effect to the lake's collective voice of different groups providing input to the planning process. An expanded workload for Tim Gooderham led to the hiring of a part-time assistant. Matt Ambler was a Keewaydin caretaker for 16 years and a member of PAC. He lent a hand preparing an increasing number of communiqués such as "Member Updates" and "What's Happening?" They were an attempt to enhance communications and keep members aboard.

Second Woman President

Torontonian Albina "Al" Hake was elected the TLA's second woman president in November 1999. Harry Hake Sr. was first to lease a lot on Narrows Island 660, in 1929 when he obtained five acres. Bear Island craftsmen built a log cabin, which he named Arrowhead Lodge. Harry was a Cincinnati architect who designed the now demolished Crosley Field, former home of the Cincinnati Reds. A son Harry Hake Jr. and a grandson Harry "Jake" Hake III followed Harry Sr.'s career path.

The Department of Lands and Forests sold 22 Narrows Island strip lots in the late 1960s. "Harry [Jake] arrived one spring and looked around the corner to find all that development on his island. Needless to say, he was rather disturbed but could do nothing about it," Tim Gooderham recalled.

Al and Jake both had children from previous marriages. They resided in Toronto, Cincinnati and on the lake. Al was a retired chain store executive and would prove just as gutsy as Sandy Navaro in confronting rocky issues. Her challenges included controversial bylaw amendments, the touchy OP process and the splinter groups.

Negotiations Revived

Doug Carr, representing the Ontario Native Affairs Secretariat (ONAS), was meeting with TFN-TAA representatives to formulate a framework agreement modelled on the 1993 draft deal. A 30-month timeframe was established and an agreement was projected by the end of 2002. Like almost every Temagami political process, the deadline would be scrapped, scuttled and scratched again.

A 12-member public advisory committee was established. The TLA's representative was Hilton Young with Director Bruce Hodgins and Ray Delarosbel as alternates. The Municipal Advisory Group (MAG) was again part of the negotiations. The TLA asked ONAS to facilitate direct communication between the negotiating parties and the TLA, LaTemPRA, AYCTL and TemTOA, believing they would be most affected by the outcome. ONAS resisted because these groups were already represented on the advisory committee.

In addition to his MAG representation, Mayor Wayne Adair was made a member of the ONAS team. The municipality was not a party to negotiations but the mayor was expected to bring a local perspective. He signed a non-disclosure agreement and was not permitted to keep council or advisory group members informed. Workshops and open houses for public consultation were planned. The process had a more open-door policy than the earlier 1990s talks.

The set-aside lands would be the base from which 290 square kilometres of settlement lands would be negotiated. Up to eight square kilometres of family lands, based on the traditional territories of 14 families within n'Daki Menan, would be selected. One TFN member was living a traditional life on his ancestral lands at the mouth of the Obabika River. Elder Alex Mathias has been hosting a fall gathering since 2001 near Chee-skon-abikong or Spirit Rock, an ancient and sacred site. About 65 people attend, taking part in traditional ceremonies, Anishnabai stories and hiking old-growth forest.

Discussions would also cover methods whereby the aboriginal community could be consulted about new activity within n'Daki Menan. Financial compensation would be negotiated as would economic development incentives. These incentives would be woven into the local community to benefit everyone.

A Good News Story Goes Bad

A local wood opportunities study group was struck in 1997 with $25,000 in funding from FedNor, a federal business aid agency. The MNR later called for proposals for a small value-added sawmill processing birch, an under-used species. Former reeve Ivan Beauchamp, president of Temagami Forest Products (TFP), was the sole bidder.

The Milne site mill was approved and allocated birch from the Temagami District. TFP was granted $1 million by Human Resources Development Canada for its construction. It opened in 2004 with 50 employees and potentially more in related

manufacturing. However, workers were laid off just a year later as the mill was not profitable. TFP searched in vain for a buyer and went into receivership in 2006. Had the second stage – the value-added manufacturing – been reached, the outcome might have been a good news story.

In with the Old

The old OP versus the new draft was the object of a tug of war in 2000. Rick and Pauline Lockhart, then owners of Ket-Chun-Eny Lodge, applied for an OP amendment to build seven housekeeping cottages on Spawning Bay's Island 1022. The island is 7.5 acres in size and the Lockharts own three acres.

The TLA board opposed the proposed zoning change from residential to commercial because it believed it was a tactic to avoid the new plan's minimum commercial site size of five acres. The development also surpassed the maximum five cottages per year the TLA was advocating. "With a new plan a few months away, applying outdated 1986 standards to the current Lake situation is inappropriate and inconsistent with the intent of amalgamation and subverts the revision process underway," the board wrote council.

At a public meeting, the Lockharts explained their need to enlarge. "We are always full," Rick simply stated. Lance White, president of TemTOA, was on side as were many resort owners and contractors. The operator of Camp Adanac, Lance noted that several resorts had closed including Manito,

Fridays and Chimo, and there was a need for expansion. Tim Gooderham spoke against the development, backed by 10 letters from members.

The Lockharts' proposal was sent to PAC and council. Both approved it, a signal to the TLA that the new OP needed fast-tracking to avoid similar scenarios. The couple did not intend to generate animosity and eventually built three cabins. They are used to run a business whose sentimental name Wishin' You Were Fishin' sums up its nature.

Hornet Lake Disaster

The crew aboard an ONR freight train on a routine haul glanced back as it passed Hornet Lake to witness 25 cars containing sulphuric acid tumbling from the track. The derailment occurred in March 2000 about 15 kilometres south of town. A containment dam was immediately built at the end of a creek running under the track into Hornet Lake, to prevent the acid from spreading into Rabbit Lake, a popular fishing and cottaging lake.

The acid polluted about 20 per cent of Hornet Lake. Being heavier than water, the acid sank to the bottom. Treatment 24 hours a day seven days a week during April and May, with MNR and MOE consultation, consisted of pumping water from the bottom and adding a lime slurry. The ONR added 40 residents to its payroll to aid in the clean-up.

Although dead minnows and suckers were found near the creek in the immediate aftermath, it was estimated that 50 per cent of aquatic life survived. By summer, turtles, frogs and fish were observed along the creek and in Hornet Lake. Loons returned to their nesting areas. Sulphuric acid accounts for 25 per cent of ONR carloads. It is used in car batteries, pop, fertilizers and water treatment.

Third Draft Slows Lot Development

The latest OP draft was eventually deferred to Marshall Macklin Monaghan for fine tuning. Once it went public, a comments session would be held to determine whether more changes were required before council adopted it as the official plan. It would then be forwarded to the MMAH. Once approved, a 20-day OMB appeal period would be held.

The new draft acquiesced to the TLA's five non-cumulative lots per year request, down from 20 in the first draft and eight in the second. It recommended: a minimum separation of 200 metres between cottage lots when a lot is created from Crown land; no secondary cottages (for extended family) on lots smaller than two acres; and a limit on sleep cabins, based on the size of the lot, and not to exceed two. Boathouse upper quarters would count as sleep cabins.

Bylaw Blues

Revisions to the TLA Bylaws were causing a fuss within an already-divided membership by spring 2000. A lawyer had advised that the board was not complying with the Ontario

Corporations Act, which states that members of a not-for-profit organization are entitled to vote by proxy when not in attendance at an AGM. Proxy voting (the assigning of an absent member's vote to another person attending) is often the only way non-profit organizations can achieve a quorum to transact business. The act also requires directors be elected in a general meeting. Mail-in ballots are not acceptable because the election would not take place in the meeting.

Another concern was the low number of members, as few as 50, regularly attending the AGM. This meant a small minority of voting members could decide on an action affecting hundreds. The bylaw committee, headed by Director Art Avard, set out to rectify the situation.

In the proposed bylaws, the annual election of directors would be accomplished via proxy, instead of the traditional mail-in ballot. Electors would still vote for their choice of directors in a directed proxy. Other matters would be settled by resolution of the voting membership at the AGM by a show of hands. If a voting member requested a poll, voting members present or represented by proxy would vote on the resolution. Members could direct their proxy holders to vote on some matters but not others. The proxy system allowed the TLA to raise its quorum from eight to 15 per cent of voting members.

The board believed the system was more democratic and more accountable to members. A clause was inserted in the bylaws allowing in camera sessions at board meetings. It is a common tool used by boards and councils to discuss sensitive issues or negotiations in private.

Voting members present at the 2000 AGM approved the new bylaws 35 to 11. About 20 members held proxies from members not present. Ironically, CPTWE member Ray Dumont used proxies assigned to him to vote against the system. After the proxies were included, the final vote was 256 for and 36 against.

About 180 proxies were assigned to President Al Hake, thereby shading the passage of the bylaws with false hints of impropriety. Members voting by proxy could have appointed anyone intending to attend to vote for them. However, assigning proxies to board members almost guarantees that the proxy holder will be in attendance.

"I remember even some loyal TLA members were slightly disturbed by Al having all those proxies," Claire Rannie recalled. "There was an unfortunate perception that it was a bid for the Board (especially the president) to garner more power than they had a right to... I think that what disturbed me the most at that time was how ready people were to believe that introducing the proxies was some nefarious plot to grab power."

CPTWE members branded the bylaws "inappropriate," seeing no need for a small cottage organization to take what they interpreted as a closed corporate approach. A year later, Jim Dow moved and Jack Goodman seconded a motion that the TLA reconvene its bylaw committee and consider readopting the former bylaws. The motion was defeated 109 to 15.

Canadian Content

Philip Greey returned to the TLA in 1999 as a director following a 25-year absence. In his résumé, he wrote of a need for more "Canadian content" on the board, especially when dealing with the Ontario government. At the time the president and first vice president were American, as were four of the seven other directors. The nationality of board members has rarely been publically raised as an issue.

Philip's second term was cut short by his sudden death in 2000, at the age of 65, of a heart attack at the cottage. Art Avard, soon to complete his second term, agreed to fill Philip's remaining two years. His widow Lorraine sold the family's 26-foot 1927 Minett launch to a Muskoka cottager who had her restored. A 24-foot 1933 Minett-Shields runabout was on sale for $195,000 in 2009.

Wood versus Plastic

There are few classic "woodies" remaining on the lake. Their heyday was the 1930s, '40s and '50s when popular makes were Niagara-on-the-Lake Shepherds, Gravenhurst Ditchburns and Greavettes, Port Carling Seabirds and Michigan Chris-Crafts. They were displaced by low upkeep and less expensive, though easily dented, aluminum boats until rust-free fibreglass, made of glass-reinforced plastic, took the market by storm in the 1970s. Woodies were decried as money pits, taking up too much dock and winter storage space.

Some cottagers have bucked the trend. The Scovil family still cherishes its 1930s *Sal-Sam* despite or perhaps because of several costly restorations. Island 179 cottagers Barry and Sandra Smith care for a 1934 Chris-Craft and 1949 Dukes. Barry began restoring the Chris-Craft in his Oakville garage. After three years, he realized he needed "professional" help, Sandra recounted. He enlisted a retired police officer who had maintained the Toronto Harbour Police's wooden fleet. Sandra's Dukes was built in Port Carling of lapstrake construction. The interior is original but the wood work needed refurbishing, undertaken

Sandra Smith's 1949 Port Carling Dukes. *Photo: Sandra Smith*

by the lake's Hillar Lainevool and Tom Kester, while John Jerzyk added spit and polish. Both are powered by Buchanan flat head six-cylinder engines.

Island 725's Walter and Joanne Ross are also woody aficionados. Their first was crafted by B. Giesler and Sons Limited of Powassan circa1965. The same builders refinished it about 1990. The company got its start when Barney Giesler couldn't find a good fishing boat back in 1920 so he built his own and everyone wanted one. The company is operated today by Barney's descendants. Their motto is: "We don't just build them pretty, we build them pretty good." Giesler boats are constructed of western cedar planks with copper nails.

Island 847's Ernie and Helen Taylor purchased a 19-foot Chestnut freighter canoe from the post in the mid-1950s. As youngsters, their children David, Barbara and Diane made lasting friendships putt-putting around in the square-sterned canoe, powered by a six-hp motor. While family members were returning from the flea market one day, a powerboat rammed the canoe. The Taylors hauled her into the bush, Island 422's Don Barry recounted for *Times* readers.

Ten years later Island 346's Tom Kester learned about the Taylors' carcass, about to meet a "Viking funeral" end. Instead, they eagerly gave it to Tom who planned to repair it but life got in the way. Don went over to Tom's place in 2003, paddling a 1922 Old Town he had restored. The Chestnut was floating in a boathouse slip. "It was dry but in near fatal condition with dry rot cutting through the

gunwales, stems, transom and many rib ends." Two years of painstaking work in his Rochester, N.Y., basement brought it back to life.

Bill Crofut had a unique hobby – building his own energy-efficient vessels. He assembled the *Anni*, a 20-foot fantail canopied launch, named for a daughter, with a quiet, non-polluting electric motor. Another project was *The Loon Boat*, a pontoon-style craft but "no ordinary one," Bill's widow Susie said. "Bill and our daughter Erika collaborated on this venture – there are two giant loons on the sides and loons painted on the back, and an Italian-style red and black painted floor." She is powered by electric motors in each pontoon. The *Anni* and *The Loon Boat* are recharged by plugging them into solar panels mounted on the boathouse roof. Bill also constructed the *Susie*, a snub-nosed, square-sterned 1923 Hacker Craft replica.

Brad Hall has a foot in both worlds. He admires the pleasure craft of yesteryear but not their upkeep. In 1988 he had a mahogany replica of a 26-foot 1945 Greavette Sheerliner triple-cockpit runabout built in Cape Coral, Florida. A modern-day epoxy saturation technique applied at the boat yard ensures the vessel is "as tight as a drum," Brad said.

A synthetic fate also befell the wood-canvas canoe industry. The Peterborough, Lakefield, Canadian and Chestnut canoe companies predated the 1900s and were successful until the 1950s, when aluminum and later fibreglass invaded the market. The three Ontario companies folded in the 1960s, while Fredericton, New Brunswick's Chestnut obtained the Peterborough moulds and continued until 1978.

The latter generations of craft appealed to recreationists because they were less expensive, low maintenance and lighter to hoist across portages. The Temagami Canoe Company survived the sea change due to its loyal local customer base. Bill Smith opened shop in 1928. He established the first outboard motor dealership in 1930, selling Johnsons.

John Kilbridge was a Wabun camper in the 1970s and worked with caretaker Vagn Peterson repairing canoes. John and his brother Steve purchased the company in 1978. John has been the sole owner for many years, refitting centre thwarts in a weathered shed built in 1931. While Muskoka's Langford Canoes bills itself as Canada's oldest canoe company, John's predates it by 12 years.

A Mixed Bag

Some cottagers have held on to their wood-canvas canoes because they are aesthetically pleasing, quiet on the water and stay cool in the hot sun. The camps are a mixed bag. Steeped in tradition, Keewaydin still uses wood-canvas canoes in its youth program, as well as tumplines and wannigans. The fleet numbers about 140, according to Bruce Ingersoll. He commenced his Keewaydin relationship as a camper in 1976 and became director in 2006.

Wabun has some 40 wood-canvas and 25 ABS canoes, Managing Director Dick Lewis said. ABS vessels have a plastic core sandwiched between two layers of vinyl. They are nearly indestructible due to their flexibility. Wabun's ABS fleet is used for challenging whitewater

John Kilbridge's Temagami Canoe Company in 2010.
Photo: Pam Sinclair

The Old Canoe

My seams gape wide so I'm tossed aside
To rot on a lonely shore
While the leaves and mould like
a shroud enfold,
For the last of my trails are o'er;
But I float in dreams on
Northland streams
That never again I'll see,
As I lie on the marge of the old portage
With grief for company.
When the sunset gilds the timbered hills
That guard Timagami,
And the moonbeams play
on far James Bay
By the brink of the frozen sea,
In phantom guise my Spirit flies
As the dream blades dip and swing
Where the waters flow from the Long Ago
In the spell of the beck'ning spring.
Do the cow-moose call on the Montreal
When the first frost bites the air,
And the mists unfold from the red and gold
That the autumn ridges wear?
When the white falls roar as
they did of yore

On the Lady Evelyn,
Do the square-tail leap from
the black pools deep
Where the pictured rocks begin?
Oh! The fur-fleets sing on Timiskaming
As the ashen paddles bend,
And the crews carouse at Rupert House
At the sullen winter's end;
But my days are done where
the lean wolves run,
And I ripple no more the path
Where the gray geese race cross
the red moon's face
From the white wind's Arctic wrath.
Though the death fraught way
from the Saguenay
To the storied Nipigon
Once knew me well,
now a crumbling shell
I watch the years roll on,
While in memory's haze I live the days
That forever are gone from me,
As I rot on the marge of the old portage
With grief for company.

George Marsh, 1908

trips. Younger sections trip in wood-canvas. Replacement woodies were crafted on-site through the 2000s by caretaker Glen Toogood until his retirement in 2008. He now lives in town and continues to build them.

Wanapitei President Bruce Hodgins described its fleet as threefold. Advanced trippers paddle ABS vessels while middle rangers use Kevlar canoes, similar to fibreglass motorboats, because they are light but strong although they can be punctured. Wanapitei has a remnant fleet of 10 wood-canvas canoes used for flatwater trips, skill testing and leadership training.

Camp Temagami on the former Wigwasati site has rebuilt its fleet over the past 10 years

A Wabun section at the Arctic Divide in 2008.
Photo: Camp Wabun

"There is value in teaching a young person to care for and appreciate" wood-canvas, C.G. said. However, ABS canoes' lightness and durability mean campers can carry them and learn to run whitewater at a younger age. If they drop them, the consequences are less severe.

Like the actor Katharine Hepburn, the classic canoe is refined, naturally beautiful, ages gracefully and hints at royalty. (Katharine was a descendent of Britain's King John.) Like funny lady Joan Rivers, an ABS canoe is composed mostly of plastic, can take a beating and bounce back, and is flawlessly ageless.

to almost 50 wood-canvas and six ABS canoes. None of the ABS has been pressed into service in recent years, noted co-owner Scott Northey. The camp buys most of its woodies from Hugh Stewart, a Camp Temagami co-owner who operates a fabricating shop in Wakefield, Quebec.

When David and Cynthia Knudsen opened Langskib in 1971, it came with a fleet of serviceable wood-canvas canoes, mostly Peterboroughs, said Clay "C.G." Stephens. Island 86 cottagers, the Knudsens passed their directorial paddles to C.G. and his wife Jodi Browning in 2008. As the Langskib program grew, the camp began buying ABS canoes in 1975 to use on lengthy and whitewater trips. The transition was complete by about 1990.

Both Katharine and Joan's congregations worship at the altar of the Canadian Canoe Museum in Peterborough. The surrounding Kawartha Lakes were the world's canoe-building capital for more than a century. The museum is home to the largest collection of canoes and kayaks. Exhibits delve further back than Samuel de Champlain's 'duh' moment when he realized that ungainly European craft were ill-suited to Canada's inland waterways. Birchbark canoes were light yet tough, capable of carrying large loads and fashioned from the bounty of the bush.

The central role of the canoe in Temagami is well documented. An 1896 George Kelley photo of a Bear Island freight canoe, from the

Gib Cochrane with aboriginal character "Temagami Ned" Whitebear
in a Cochrane's Camp birchbark canoe now on display at the
Canadian Canoe Museum. *Photo: Carol Cochrane*

National Archives of Canada Richard Cassels Collection, forms the backbone of a fur trade exhibit. An old Cochrane's Camp birchbark canoe is on display. It hung in the dining hall for decades. A Geological Survey of Canada exhibit features an 1887 photo of Robert Bell on Lake Temagami. There's also a shot of Father Charles Paradis seated in an HBC canoe in the 1880s. Two 1940s Cochrane's Camp photos figure prominently in a canoe camp exhibit.

On the Hustings

2000 was a municipal election year. Mayor Wayne Adair was acclaimed and nine individuals vied for six council seats. The candidates were once again challenged with queries posed by the TLA and their answers were published in the fall *Times*. They commented on the draft OP, houseboat issues, spending cuts versus tax hikes and people enjoying the lake without contributing financially.

When all the ballots were counted, incumbents Biff Lowery (PAC chair), Lorie Hunter, Ike Laba and Bill Kitts were re-elected. The turnout was 56 per cent of electors compared to 54 per cent in 1997, the inaugural election year for the enlarged municipality. The average Ontario voter turnout hovers around 40 per cent.

CHAPTER 30

PLAGUED BY RESIGNATIONS

While the municipality was electing councillors the board lost two directors. Former president Sandy Navaro and Jeff Schneider, elected in 1998 and both life members, belonged to the Lake Temagami Group (LTG). Sandy died in September 2010 of Alzheimer's at the age of 68. The Schneider family purchased North Arm Island 1151 in 1961 then added Island 1173. Jeff's first cousin is Fred Reimers, former Keewaydin owner and director.

Island 770's Jeff Butler was elected at the same time. He went on to become a director of the Federation of Ontario Cottagers' Association. His daughter Katie worked as a TLA radio operator in 2003. In a 2003 *Times* retrospective, Jeff wrote that he quickly grew to respect Sandy's opinions, enjoying her and husband Ralph's company. Somehow the Navaros ended up with views dissimilar to Jeff's, or perhaps it was the other way around, he said. "I have always regretted the feeling that I had drifted to a "side" and the resulting distance that was put between me and some people I had previously had the opportunity to very much appreciate."

Despite lobbying from splinter groups, the board didn't stray from its principles: five residential and one commercial development per year, dispersed and non-cumulative; residential and commercial site plan controls;

and strict criteria to govern residential to commercial conversions. Speedy approval of the OP – way behind schedule – to replace the 1986 plan was critical. The TLA continued to promote "whole lake planning," knowing an appeal would delay approval of the cottager-friendly OP.

The final OP draft was released in May 2001. Comments were received over the summer. The TLA had submitted more than 25 documents to PAC and participated in all public sessions and workshops. The board turned its attention toward the Lot Creation and Development Study to be completed by PAC during the first five years the new plan was in effect. The board was submitting data and maps to PAC and the MNR on the implications of private lot development. Additional cottages, sleeping cabins and boathouses on existing vacant lots would have the greatest impact in Joan, Phyllis and Yates townships, due to their higher concentration of private lots. "The potential exacerbation of existing concentrations and degradation to the whole lake that could occur should be of great concern," Hilton Young said.

Al Hake, Dick Grout and Bob Campbell were acclaimed as directors in 2001. Dick and Bob were to assume office in September. Meanwhile, President Al, Dick, and Art Avard submitted their resignations. As a result, there

Grin and Bear It

The MNR moved the fall black bear hunt back to August to placate hunters after it cancelled the spring hunt in 1999. The cancellation was intended to ensure sows were around long enough to nurture their cubs. Since then, nuisance bears are believed to be an escalating problem. The TLA believes an opening after Labour Day makes more sense, putting cottagers, campers and children at less risk.

Aggressive bears caused havoc during summer 2001. A shortage of natural food and late August bear-baiting were considered responsible. Both the Times and Ottertooth. com documented incidents. One bold bruin attacked a tent occupied by a kayaker in Diamond Lake, ripping through the fly and main wall. A friend in another tent began screaming and the bear backed off.

Wanapitei, Wabun and Project CANOE campers encountered bears going through packs and trying to get into food barrels. Three cabins in Sharp Rock Inlet were broken into. Double-glazed windows, an exterior wall and a solid wood door were no obstacle. After the door was repaired, a bear returned and trashed the kitchen.

were four board vacancies. Voting members and proxy holders at the 2001 AGM resolved that for 2001 only, nominations would be received until September 15th and the AGM would reconvene in November to elect directors to the vacant posts.

The flurry of resignations was unprecedented in TLA history. It was a difficult time to be a director, caught in the crossfire between neighbours and friends turned foes, ironically over the same cause – protecting their beloved lake.

Jake and Al Hake decided to spend extended vacations in Florida and sold their Island 660 property in 2006 to David McFarlane of King Township, Ontario. He had tripped the area in the 1960s as a youth, returning in the 1970s. The family rented Gord and Doreen Lak's Island 771 cottage for several summers and then purchased South Arm Island 949 in 2003. The Hakes' Arrowhead Lodge was a real find. "My wife Susan and I are committed to maintain the authenticity of the unique log buildings," David said. He was elected to the directors' team in 2008 and was serving as treasurer in 2010.

The Smiths Step In

Barry Smith, elected a director in 1999, was installed as acting president. He and his wife Sandra purchased islands 179 and 191 in 1994. Over the preceding 20 years, Barry had canoed, camped and fished the area with family and friends. He was employed by a Canadian airline for 30 years and was experienced in conflict resolution, a skill he would need to draw on.

He was soon co-chairing the water quality committee. Regular water testing was undertaken by the MOE until 1996. Funding cutbacks by the Harris government meant it had to curtail this 'field' work. The committee made water testing bottles available at the TLA building, to be analyzed in North Bay.

Sandra dove into TLA affairs as well, helming the flea market committee in 2001 and 2002. The 2001 bazaar turned a then record $7,800 profit. She also convened a Square Island Bear Dance to celebrate the TLA's 70th anniversary. The event was a sell-out with many dancers, coached by Bill Cleminshaw, donning sashes from bygone days. Rita O'Sullivan called while musicians Hugh McKenzie, Wayne Potts, and John and Evelyn Coté kept toes a-tapping. A second dance was held at Wabikon in 2002. The TLA marked its 75th anniversary in 2006 with the release of a must-have full colour wall map.

Standstill Agreement

The final draft OP and PAC Chair Biff Lowery were subjected to a drubbing at the 2001 AGM. Concern was expressed that no funding or timetable had been established for the Lot Creation and Development Study. Biff agreed the study was necessary. He said PAC didn't yet know the impact that a land claim accord would have on the plan. He explained that an urban boundary expansion to Axe Narrows did not mean more residential lots, as development may occur only where sewerage and water infrastructure are available.

A resolution to approve the OP, subject to minor changes, was carried 121 for to 25 against. A proposed amendment that would have delayed its implementation was rejected. After the AGM a standstill agreement was circulated by the Committee for the Preservation of the

The *Chimo III* at a mid-1990s flea market. Photo: *Andy Stevens*

Temagami Wilderness Experience (CPTWE). It called for all residential lots to be created from existing private land and a delay in Crown land sales until studies determined an acceptable level of future development.

In a letter to the membership which was not an official TLA mailing, Brad Hall explained that Crown is basically the only land available in the North and Southwest arms, from where many CPTWE and LTG members hailed. Lot creation from private land only would mean most development would take place in the Hub, and the South and Northeast arms, areas already identified as over-developed.

"The agreement also negates proper municipal and provincial governance and proposes to give veto power to the dissident groups. The wording of the agreement is such that it could postpone or delay legitimate economic prospects for the municipality for years," Brad wrote. It was signed by CPTWE's Paul Schnatz, Dennis Goodman, Jack Goodman and Steven Battis, and LTG's Ann D. Navaro. It was also signed without board approval by TLA President Barry Smith and directors Bill Hand and Bruce Hodgins.

With this letter Brad enclosed proxies to approve a motion to reaffirm the AGM majority vote endorsing the final draft OP and to revoke any implied board endorsement of the standstill agreement. The proxies also appointed Director Hilton Young to act on other matters that might arise at the reconvened AGM. A question arose as to whether there could be items on the agenda other than the election of directors. A TLA lawyer replied that any

matter that could properly be brought before the earlier portion could be brought before the continued portion.

There were nine election candidates. Dennis Goodman polled them for their views on the standstill accord and heard back from six. Nominees Paul Schnatz, Steven Battis, David Kittredge, Lorie Jocius and David Knudsen supported it. The only maverick was Bob Campbell, who backed the AGM vote to accept the final OP draft.

Bob was a Toronto civil engineer who had the luck to marry Robin Johnston. Her father was a mining engineer and had flown all over the north, declaring the lake the fairest of all. In the mid-1940s the Johnstons rented a Bear Island cottage from the legendary Joe Lanoie. Two years later John Turner built them a cabin on Island 985 where they installed a septic tank, a fairly new innovation. Robin hadn't missed a summer on the lake since she was five and Bob didn't miss a summer on the lake after he started trailing his bride to be.

The Campbells purchased the Blakely property on Island 972. They installed a solar system and a composting toilet, enjoying the challenge of creating earth-friendly conveniences. The Johnston Island 985 property is still owned by family members.

Just three days before the AGM continuance, Art Avard died of a heart attack. The firm but gentle hand he played in the evolution of the local government was summarized in a *Times* eulogy co-written by Claire Rannie and Hilton: "His presence brought trust and understanding during a difficult period of amalgamation with the town of Temagami. He took as a guiding principle the establishment of good relations between the TLA and the Town." Biff Lowery called Art "the best councillor we never had."

AGM the Sequel

At the AGM part two, 345 directed election proxy ballots were received out of 555 mailed to voting members. Ray Delarosbel, Carol Lowery and Marc Shaw received the most votes. Bob Campbell, ranking fourth, was asked to complete Art's term. All of the successful candidates supported the OP and none were associated with the standstill agreement. The results were a clear vindication of the board's stand.

Ray brought a boatload of experience as a former director, PAC member, privy project supervisor, and TLA representative on two committees involved with land claim negotiations. He was the owner of North Bay's Price Signs and Carol Lowery's brother-in-law, married to Patricia, Biff Lowery's sister. Ray and Patricia bought the north end of Ogama Island in 1978.

Carol was also knowledgeable, having earlier served on the advisory board. Her father Jack Glenn was a former president. Carol's sister Pam Sinclair was a former radio operator, *Times* editor and author of *Temagami Lakes Association: An Historical Perspective.*

Island 268's Marc Shaw of Ottawa spent vacations on the lake for 30 years, mostly at his parents' Island 748 cottage. His father Duff Shaw chaired the nomination and election

committee for many years. Marc met his future wife Lynda Bailey of Island 268 on the lake. He was a senior officer in the engineering branch of the Canadian navy.

Fewer than a dozen members were present at the reconvened AGM. A quorum was achieved through 174 proxies held by Hilton. They were used to carry several motions. One revoked any TLA endorsement, or implied endorsement, of the proposed standstill agreement and expressed the TLA's opposition to it. Another recommended holding a membership vote prior to either a board member, in an official capacity, or the board as a whole, entering into agreements with other groups. A third motion recommended that the board and board members acting in an official capacity may not support any challenge of the OP with the OMB.

The strife dividing the membership and the board itself conspired to send members packing in 2002. Nearly 100 were lost, going from 663 to 569, the largest drop in TLA history. In his 2003 membership renewal letter, Tim Gooderham reached out: "The new TLA Board of Directors hopes to continue to reflect a new attitude to our members and the Lake Community, plus a renewed commitment to make things happen – to be less involved in arguments and more involved with rolling up our sleeves and trying to make things better."

Lake Collective Addresses Negotiators

The TLA was providing land claim settlement input through the public advisory committee and a smaller Lake Temagami working group, also composed of TemTOA, LaTemPRA and AYCTL spokespersons. The parties produced a "Joint Statement of Principles" in 2001, which was submitted to negotiators, the advisory committee and the municipality. It listed key recommendations: the Temagami and Cross lakes' Skyline Reserve to remain within the public domain; TFN reserve lands to be significantly smaller than proposed; traditional access to and passage through reserve lands continuing free and unabated on canoe routes, trails, scenic lookouts, etc.; a licensing system allowing non-native fishers and hunters continued use of reserve lands; no water quality impact; mainland development occurring within or adjacent to the urban neighbourhood and, if elsewhere, behind the Skyline Reserve with communal lake access; and economic opportunities not adversely affecting existing businesses.

Reuniting the Community

The Temagami community was beset with hard-hitting issues. Disputes over logging roads, old-growth forests, claim staking, access points, amalgamation, TLA bylaws, the land claim, native power struggles, and the OP had all taken their toll. Short-fused public displays of racism, elitism and anti-Americanism occasionally boiled to the surface. Some did not want to hear, let alone try to understand, the opinions of others while protecting their own interests at all cost.

Social structures sustained over decades had faltered. The boat line was the glue for 60 years. Crowds made regular visits to the village and around the lake via the passenger boats. Gregarious Captain Ted Guppy made a point of remembering hundreds of names from one year to the next so he could greet vacationers as they filed up the gangplank. Bear Island was no longer a central meeting place after the HBC pulled out and the Anglican Church burned down. The weekly square dances later ceased. The lake's only pub, drawing Bear Islanders, other lake dwellers and townies, was gone.

Bear Islanders had emerged from early roles as guides, caretakers, cooks and housekeepers to become masters of an historic domain. Their ranks included business owners, teachers, police officers, health care workers, and acclaimed journalists, poets, artists, musicians, actors and directors. A lawyer and doctor would be added to the list. The old ways were incorporated, not forgotten.

The community's more than 100-year-old struggle for justice was finally being addressed by Queen's Park and Ottawa in the early 2000s. Once a settlement is ratified, the Anishnabai will be a stronger economic driver. Orillia's Casino Rama is the only commercial gambling operation in Ontario located on a First Nation reserve. Since 2001, 65 per cent of net revenues has been split among the province's 133 other First Nations. The TFN had received more than $3.5 million by 2010. The funds have enhanced cultural, recreational, educational, health and safety services.

The Temagami Community Foundation

Island 725's Walter Ross and Deacon Island's Vicki Grant, née McKenzie, got to know each other in the 1990s through volunteer work. They hoped to find a way to bridge the lake, Bear Island and mainland communities. The seeds of the Temagami Community Foundation (TCF) were planted.

Temagami Community Foundation founders Walter Ross and Vicki Grant. *Photo: Derek Shapton for Cottage Life magazine*

The TCF set out to conquer this mean-spirited milieu and the feeling of disconnect between the mainland, Bear Island and the rest of the lake. Perhaps it envisioned a giant

hand placing everyone into the same snow globe, shaking it hard and waiting for a united community to emerge. Or, as Walter Ross put it: "The whole community has a shared history and there exist wonderful possibilities for pulling the community together."

Geographic Feature Names

Feature names include the obvious or previously described such as Grey Owl Lake and Finlayson Point Provincial Park. Others may be less evident. Aileen and Pats lakes were named for A.L. Cochrane daughters. Pat and David lakes are for Reg McConnell's children. The Anishnabai are remembered in Commanda, Petrant, Pishabo, McKenzie, Friday, Turner, Paul, and Little Donald lakes. Herbert and Price lakes recall Herbert Price, a Bear Island forest ranger. Isbister, Walsh, Edwards, Jamieson and McPherson lakes are named for Wanapitei campers.

In the 1920s Brooks Shepard mapped waterways around the Wakimika Triangle. Some of the lakes he named include one for his wife Hortense. The Ontario Geographic Names Board isn't as free and loose with names anymore and would prefer you were dead.

The first informational meeting was held at Bear Island in 2001 with about 40 people listening attentively as Walter and Vicki solicited their commitment. The TCF held its first AGM there in 2002 where 12 directors were appointed: Vicki Grant, Walter Ross,

Dick Lewis, Kay Potts, John Turner, Kim Krech, June Keevil, the late Lorne Pacey, Annette Polson, Dick Crum, Allan Marquette and Kirk Smith. It is the only community foundation in North America forged between natives and non-natives.

The TCF got off to an auspicious start with a large anonymous donation. Walter donated $25,000 in his parents' memory. His generosity was the first step in developing an endowment fund. Investment earnings generated by this fund would be used for annual grants. The TFN gave $20,000 to develop the first donor-directed fund as the Laura McKenzie Learning Centre Fund. Dick and Vicki Grant committed $150 monthly, $50 to the learning centre fund and $100 to the endowment fund. Carol Rykert gave $25,000 per year for three years to underwrite administrative costs. Office space was donated by the Temagami Station Restoration Trust and three years of meeting facilities were provided by the TFN. The TLA created memorial donations to honour deceased members.

Projects must meet obvious needs, promote dialogue, foster shared responsibility, involve volunteers and induce excitement. The TCF's main interests are environmental awareness and stewardship, community arts and culture, honouring First Nation heritage and fostering sustainable economic development. So intrigued by what Walter, Vicki and others were accomplishing, *Cottage Life* sent a reporter and photographer to trail the pair. The magazine documented their efforts to reunite the local citizenry in its June 2008 edition.

The TCF has spent more than $200,000 funding projects. One of more than 25 recipients is an annual summer art camp, bringing kids from Marten River, the lake, town and Bear Island together whose paths might otherwise never cross. The TFN provides space, councillors and snacks. The instructor is art teacher Bettina Schuller from Island 421. In its goals, the camp is a microcosm of the TCF.

The Temagami Community Foundation's 2009 champagne fish fry. Board members attending: front (l-r) Kim Kretch, Lila Cleminshaw, Victoria Calvery. Back (l-r) Kirk Smith, June Keevil, Walter Ross, Richard Lewis III, Cathy Dwyer-Smith and Pam Morgan. The fish was fried to perfection by Lance White and Millie Becker. *Photo: Pam Sinclair*

To secure the long-term sustainability of its endowment fund, the TCF launched a "Council of 100" in 2008. The inaugural $5,000 donor was Marvyn Morrison, a civil engineer who had recently moved back to Temagami from Toronto. The Morrisons are multigenerational northerners whose lineage is native and non-native. Marvyn has served on PAC, the public works committee, the Nastawgan Trails board and others.

Northern Connections

Although Walter was raised and worked as a chartered accountant in Toronto, his roots extend northward. His maternal grandfather Walter Young hopped the train to Swastika about 1907. He and his wife Grace settled in Haileybury where their daughter Margaret, Walter's mother, was born in 1912. Walter Young was a prospector in the Kirkland Lake camp. He staked the original claims to the Upper Canada mine in Gauthier Township. At the time gold had a fixed price of just U.S. $15 per ounce, to the Youngs' chagrin. They lost their home in the Great Fire of 1922 and relocated to Toronto.

Walter Ross's wife Joanne has northern ties too. Her grandfather Berkeley Stark spent the summer of 1912 or '13 as a Temagami forest ranger. Joanne still has his badge, a heavy metal shield. Berkeley married Grace Gooderham, a daughter of George Horace Gooderham whose grandfather William Gooderham was a co-founder of the Gooderham and Worts distillery dynasty. Gordon S. Gooderham, Chimo's founder, was Grace's uncle.

Walter's father Grant Ross attended Wanapitei in the 1930s. Grant and Margaret were frequent Wanapitei and Red Squirrel Lake visitors. They bought a cottage on Island 725 in 1960 from Victor Woollings' widow. Woollings Forest Products of Englehart supplied the wood used by George Angus to build the cabin in 1952.

George Angus was a World War One message runner who survived the trauma of being gassed. Tagged a "tough little Scot" by his son-in-law Murray Dickson, George hailed from Inverurie. He sloughed off the horrors of war by taking a canoe trip and was infected by Temagami fever. George apprenticed under builder George Turner. He built cabins now owned by Duff and Marinette Shaw (Island 748), Tim and Louise Richardson (795), Bobby and Marty Morrison (718), Peter and Joan Brook (721), John and Andrea Klarquist (717) and Grant and Sharron McMillen (684). He was so sure of the quality of his work, he'd say if a mouse ever invaded, he'd eat it, Walter noted.

George crafted furniture, renovated cottages and acted as caretaker. He constructed cabins on islands 721 and 723 as family abodes. His daughter Eleanor married Murray Dickson and the Island 721 cottage was passed to them. Eleanor died in the late 2000s but Murray is still a regular. George's grandchildren occupy Island 723. Rob Huff has followed in some of his great-grandfather's footsteps. He was Wabun's year-round caretaker from 2008 until fall 2010. Rob owned and was head chef at an Ontario restaurant. He became Wabun's head cook in 2007 and brought a fine dining experience to camp.

The Trickster versus the Patroller

Garden Island's Peter Healy took over property patrols in 2001. He conducts off-season checks in a universe where birds are often his sole companions. The trickster Wiskedjak of traditional lore likes to place rocks, pressure cracks and slush in his path. The rewards win out. "Never before did I appreciate some of the spectacular settings and sites many of you have in your corner of the lake. That combined with the feeling of isolation as I traveled alone made for some delightful days," he informed 2002 *Times* readers.

Peter can rhyme off common problems as quickly as a whiskey jack can snatch peanuts – fallen trees due to toothy winds or similarly-endowed beavers, overbearing bruins, windows and doors left ajar, break-ins and snow-load roof damage. One of the oddest "break-ins" was an owl flying into a window and shattering the glass. Its preserved body was inside.

Flood Fears

2002 dawned with Mother Nature pulling a few punches. Winter had not much arrived and travel was by steel boat. The ice would not be safe until the end of the month. By the time autumn 2001 had turned into winter, four times the normal amount of precipitation had fallen.

For the first time ever, the Nipissing, French and Sturgeon River watershed advisory committee met in the fall, due to rising water levels. Founded in 1979 after spring flooding in Field, it attempts to manage high spring water levels. Decisions often involve how many logs should be pulled from the Cross Lake control dam, managed by Ontario Power Generation.

The dam was opened almost fully from October through January and the outflow from Lake Nipissing was cut back, preventing French River residents from being flushed into Georgian Bay. Tim Gooderham represented Lake Temagami at the top of the watershed – "a nice place to be" – he said. He has long advocated reopening the historic Diamond Lake outlet, blocked off to accommodate the lumber industry. An MOE class environmental assessment would likely be required.

CHAPTER 31

A WATERWAY PARK

Director Hilton Young was pleased to report positive news in a spring 2002 *Times* story, exuberantly titled "Skyline Reserve/Waterway Park – Yes!!" The waterway class provincial park would encompass most of the Skyline Reserve. It included proposed aboriginal mainland settlement lands taking in about half the reserve.

Waterway parks provide canoeists with top quality recreational and historical travel experiences. The board believed this was the best route to protect the shoreline from development and logging. The park would reinforce the tenets and enhance Temagami's canoeing reputation, thereby stimulating the economy. Mining properties, high potential mining lands and private property would be excluded. A drawback for the TFN-TAA was the proposed park's management under Ontario policies.

Land claim negotiations were on track despite the ousting of TFN Chief Raymond Katt in February 2002. Raymond was elected in 2000 succeeding Jim Twain. A petition charged that he acted beyond the powers of the chief's office. In a vote of non-confidence, a simple majority ended his term. Alex Paul was elected chief in the spring and a federal court dismissed Raymond's request for an injunction to halt the election.

"We need to remain focused and remember that we are not negotiating the Teme-Augama Anishnabai adherence to the Temagami Land Use Plan," TAA Chief Doug McKenzie wrote. The waterway park was a good will concession. The TAA-TFN were not legally bound to uphold the tenets. While the land cautions were in effect, the TAA had demonstrated a willingness to lift the freeze in cases of hardship. The Anishnabai have always negotiated with amity.

The proposed park did not encompass the shoreline of Cross Lake. Ontario and native negotiators balked at including it. The TLA considers it part of a single Skyline Reserve but feared a trade-off would lead to a significant number of Crown islands coming under TAA-TFN ownership. In the park, taking in about 80 per cent of Temagami's Skyline Reserve, existing uses would be maintained subject to the Temagami Land Use Plan (TLUP).

The 290-square kilometre settlement lands would be designated an Indian reserve by the federal government and would not be subject to provincial or municipal jurisdiction. About half of the waterway park would be part of the reserve. A section of the Indian Act would be used to transfer surface rights to Ontario in order to create the park. The mineral rights of the reserve land inside the park would be held by the federal government. No mining would be permitted.

A Shiningwood Bay Townsite

By summer 2002 negotiators had agreed on the north shore of Shiningwood Bay to build a mainland community. This had long been Bear Islanders' preferred location. Other sites had been ruled out, including Finlayson park. One near Strathcona Bay just south of town would later be examined and rejected due to terrain issues. The federal government and the TLA favoured a townsite connected to town services, which would not be the case at Shiningwood Bay. Lots would be set back 100 metres from shore. The TFN would develop a site plan consistent with municipal standards.

Island 265's David Taylor of Toronto brought the concerns of 20 Shiningwood Bay cottage owners to the TLA's attention. He believed issues such as ecological damage and increased boat traffic weren't being adequately addressed. The TLA hoped that communal docks and sewerage system, and access predominantly by road would ameliorate these impacts. David was acclaimed a director in 2005.

A total of 80 acres around Austin Bay, where Ottawa had proposed a reserve in the 1880s, and a 25-acre parcel at Friday's Point were proposed for limited development. Access would be by water only and shoreline site plans undertaken. The eight square kilometres of traditional family lands, to be held as private property, could be chosen anywhere in n'Daki Menan. They would be subject to the normal MNR process for Crown land disposition. Any

portion not allocated would be added to the Shiningwood Bay townsite.

The waterway park concept was endorsed by the TLA, TemTOA, AYCTL and LaTemPRA in a joint submission to the Ontario Native Affairs Secretariat (ONAS). They recommended all existing trails, portages and roads be incorporated into the park. It could serve as a buffer around the Friday's Point and Austin Bay mainland sites, in effect creating islands of these parcels. Any roads within two kilometres should be gated. The family lands should be spread over n'Daki Menan and located further than two kilometres from the lake. The park was supported by the municipality at a later date.

Lindsay Coté of North Bay was elected TAA chief in the fall, defeating Doug McKenzie who stayed on as TFN-TAA lead negotiator. With strong artistic sensibilities, Lindsay was a musical score composer, thespian, columnist, cartoonist and lead traditional dancer at powwows.

The December 2002 deadline for a settlement came and went. A new timetable – wishful thinking as it would turn out – would end with a Bear Island signing ceremony in summer 2006. The size of the settlement lands was increased to 330 square kilometres as compensation for the TAA-TFN addressing other parties' concerns. Monetary compensation was augmented to $20 million (the same amount the TAA-TFN calculated when it had a second look at the 1993 AIP in the late 1990s). A portion would be earmarked for legal and negotiation costs.

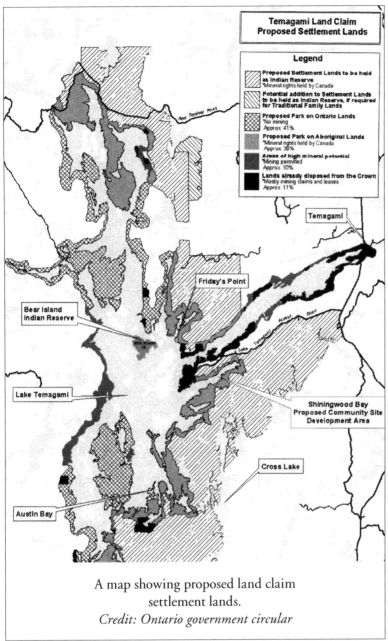

A map showing proposed land claim settlement lands.
Credit: Ontario government circular

Access to timber allocations and mining properties via reserve lands outside the park would be through TFN arrangements. The Red Squirrel Road would cross reserve land. Timber resources inside the reserve could be reopened to cutting by the TFN or the forest industry through TFN contracts. Continued use of outpost camps and hunting areas inside the reserve could be negotiated similarly or through Indian Act-issued permits, as would access to major canoe routes inside reserve lands. Holders of land use permits for private cottages and outpost camps would be offered the option of relocating outside the reserve.

On the Chopping Block

A 1999-2004 forest management plan drew criticism in 2002. The companies involved were Liskeard Lumber, the Elk Lake Planing Mill, Grant Forest Products and Goulard Lumber. The TLA observed that timber cutting in Temagami's backyard would have no obvious local benefits.

One block consigned to the chainsaw was within metres of the Spirit Rock heritage site,

Crown Land Islands Added to Proposal

A $4-million economic development package could include Crown lots on islands. Development lands would be above and beyond the settlement lands, and would conform to the OP as private property, subject to municipal taxation.

287

near the eastern edge of the Obabika Waterway Park. It was feared the towering rock pillar might be damaged from the vibrations of logging machinery. A block near Obabika Lake was adjusted when Earthroots requested it meet MOE guidelines for buffer zones between cut areas. Nine of the largest clearcuts were removed from the plan due to objections by conservation groups and the TLA. The MNR was ordered to develop size guidelines for clearcuts.

The Red Squirrel Road and extension were slated for use to reach allocations west of Diamond Lake. New roads or branches were required to reach other allocations. The board asked the MNR to make new roads temporary and winter use only, with no linkages from Elk Lake or River Valley. It requested improvements to existing logging roads to bring them to a minimum standard.

Less than half of the areas allocated for cutting were harvested because of an economic downturn in the forest products industry. The MNR proceeded instead with a large tree planting program, putting some timber plans on hold until the market improved.

Stewardship Council Steps Up

The Lake Temagami Cross Lake Focus Group became the Temagami Cross Lake Stewardship Council (TSC) in 2002. Its goal was to play an active role in decisions affecting natural resources and to assist the MNR by providing knowledge and advice. It received a $14,000 provincial grant from the Fish and Wildlife Fund, used to advance an angler's journal and subsidize a summer creel. The TSC moved from an advisory role to one of partnership with the MNR. Ontario's second lake-based stewardship council, following Lake Nipissing, could issue charitable tax receipts and access government funds.

Gaye Smith, as the first chair, kept *Times* and *Talker* readers on top. Dick Crum was vice chair and a director at large, while Lance White, Mark Johnson, Wayne Adair, Bruce Rice, Alex Paul and Jim Hasler spoke for TAFIP, LaTemPRA, the municipality, TemTOA, the TFN and Northwatch, respectively. OFAH, the MNR and the Municipality of West Nipisssing were also represented. Wayne was the secretary-treasurer.

The TSC's first major accomplishment was partnering with North Bay's Nipissing University and Sudbury's Laurentian University. Through its Laurentian liaison, a walleye netting study was undertaken. The data showed the lake supported a stressed walleye population, dominated by young fish. Mortality lowered the number of adults and few were reaching old age.

The TSC continued with the focus group's angler's journal, an online and paper-based initiative whereby anglers could record their success stories or lack thereof, so the status of the fishery could be tracked. Gaye saw it as an alternative to pricey MNR open water creel surveys. Draw prizes were introduced to entice fishers to enter their data.

The council hosted an annual trophy contest to encourage anglers to live-release. A life-like replica was the raffle prize. Other

TSC initiatives were creel surveys, inspecting walleye and trout spawning sites, water quality testing and, in partnership with OFAH, invasive species testing.

The MNR worked with the TSC to adopt a slot-size measurement regulation in 2002 to protect walleye spawners. With the financial support of Temagami Marine, the TSC distributed measuring tape decals. Gaye said walleye fishing had improved by 2008 as a result of slot fishing. However, it prompted a heated debate about the survival odds of released walleye. Loon Lodge owner and TSC director John Moskwa organized an experiment under the auspices of the MNR and TSC during winter 2004. A smaller than desired sampling pool of walleye was caught and placed in a hoop net for a few days to observe survival rates. Seven of 15 fish expired, alarming TSC and MNR representatives.

The TSC became a member of the Ontario Stewardship Program in 2005, entitling it to a stewardship coordinator shared with Lake Nipisssing and $10,000 annually in MNR administrative funding. It drew national attention in 2006 when an *Outdoor Canada* columnist interviewed Gaye.

The OP Moves Forward

After a professionally-aided review, the TLA board greenlit the draft OP. The municipality and the TFN-TAA signed a memorandum of understanding to harmonize interactions. An external relations committee was struck and the Anishnabai reviewed the draft, leading to wording changes that reflected their concerns.

After four years of work, the OP was officially adopted by Town Council during summer 2002 and forwarded to the Ministry of Municipal Affairs and Housing for review and approval. Its land base was designated a site plan control area to ensure development would be undertaken as approved by council.

One issue had not been resolved to the board's satisfaction. Always defensive of the tenets, the TLA believed they should have been built into the main body of the OP, though PAC had devoted an entire section of the preamble to them. They were also referenced frequently to explain adopted standards.

A Recipe for Success

Summer 2002 saw islanders reaching for their lemon squeezers and herb clippers, while they flipped through the TLA's latest publishing venture. *Temagami Cooks* was the brainchild of Robin Campbell, spouse of Director Bob Campbell. The cookbook was designed to bring all the lake's "neighbourhoods" together for a "whole lake" culinary adventure.

Ojibway Lodge Director Sandy Chivers, Wanapitei's Carol Hodgins and Nancey Gooderham, formerly of Chimo, gave Robin access to their published recipe books – and the fare went far beyond bannock. TLA director and teacher Carol Lowery prepared a chapter on keeping small hands engaged and the results went far beyond play dough. Mary Smellie shared her Nana's methodology for sticky brown bread. It had scored her a red ribbon in a 1997 *Cottage Life* foodie contest. Cathy Dwyer-Smith folded in some herbal wisdom. Sandra Smith, Lori Hand, Peggy Shardelow and Gloria Seaman Allen helped collect family favourites.

The paperback was sprinkled with Temagami-centric recipes like Ket-Chun-Eny pickerel batter and traditional shore lunches, plus umpteen ways to serve blueberries. It was spiced with the artwork of professional artists and Sunday painters. With Lorie Jocius's assistance, it all came together like a four-layer cake. Businesses couldn't keep enough in stock and the publication paid for itself before summer turned stale. Robin and Lorie went on to co-chair the 2003 and '04 flea market committees. The TLA made another stab at bringing members together by launching an annual welcome-back barbecue and a corn roast in 2004.

The TLA's *Temagami Cooks*, compiled and edited by Robin Johnston Campbell, featured front cover art called *Spirit* by Helen Hall

Up, Up and Away

Twenty Bear Island children didn't get much shut-eye one August Friday night. They were too antsy in anticipation of an event none of them had ever experienced, to take place first thing Saturday. They were taken on 15-minute airplane excursions. The youngsters were part of the "Young Eagles" program, an international effort to provide one million young people with the experience of flying to celebrate the 100th anniversary of the Wright brothers' first powered flight.

The flights were organized by Island 1105 cottagers Ron and Nancy Miller, along with Bear Islander Dan Mongrain. Ron and five fellow pilots donated their time, planes and fuel. Each child received a certificate signed by their pilot and an individual photo of their airplane. "The grins were huge," Peter Healy reported in the Times.

An Elder Speaks for the Founders

At the 2002 AGM the late James F. Wychgel, son of founding Timagami Association member James N. Wychgel, rose to say he was "enraged" over recent attempts to have the new bylaws amended to disenfranchise voting members not attending the AGM. He said he was "appalled" at efforts to split up the lake. "It is important that this association go back to the ideals of the founders who looked at the whole lake."

Despite James' words of wisdom, David Jones moved and Steven Battis seconded a motion that ward system elections be considered. It was inexplicably carried by the membership. The board had a planning consultant examine the ward system option and concluded members were best served by an open system to annually field enough candidates from a limited pool for an election to take place. Directors would be acclaimed three years in a row in the 2000s.

Claire Rannie's second term on the board of directors expired that summer, but she remained board and recording secretary, tasks she had taken on a couple of years earlier. She resigned as secretary in winter 2003 but stayed on as *Times* editor. Claire resigned after putting the summer 2005 edition to bed for reasons previously described, though she remained a member of the planning committee. Peter Healy briefly served as de facto editor.

Testing the Waters and Bridging the Gap

The water quality committee, co-chaired by Bob Campbell, contracted Aquapath Limited to conduct underwater chemical health mapping. Water around the old Copperfields Mine site was found to be contaminant-free and well-oxygenated. Inlet Bay near town told a different story. Colonies of anaerobic (oxygenless) bacteria were found on the bottom and can pose a problem in shallow waters. The impairment seemed to be caused by Highway 11 road salt runoff.

Bob was tragically killed in 2009 near his Toronto home while trying to rescue his beloved dogs from an oncoming train. He and his wife Robin were members of the elections committee at the time.

A separation in 2003 into Latchford north and Latchford south was the result of a bridge movement rather than a political one. The coldest January in 10 years caused the bolts holding hang poles on the Highway 11 Aubrey Cosens VC Memorial Bridge to snap. Two transport trucks barely made it across as the 40-year-old span buckled and dropped two metres. Plans were quickly implemented for the construction of a temporary Bailey bridge, which took two weeks to build in brutal -30 C temperatures.

The collapse caused major disruptions to traffic flow. Drivers were rerouted either to the west through Sudbury or to the east through Quebec. Restaurants in Temagami and the Tri-Towns laid off staff. Daily commuters between these communities, like Carol Lowery, arranged car and key exchanges, followed by a frigid march across a dam walkway. Carol's son Tom found the daily train ride to and from his New Liskeard high school cushier than his usual bus trip.

A Century at Devil's Island

Keewaydin, the oldest canoe-trip camp on the globe, celebrated 100 years at Island 1147 in 2003. The oldest alumnus attending the event was a 90-year-old 1930s guide from Temiscaming, Quebec, according to Ottertooth.com. The oldest building on Devil's Island was constructed in 1905, the same year the Frank Newton cabin was erected on Island 977. The Newton island and cabin now belong to Marilyn Corl Brinkman.

Outstanding Issues

Outstanding land claim issues were summarized in a TLA position paper distributed to all parties. It wanted OP and TLUP harmonization and enforcement policies embedded in the settlement accord, so development would be uniform and conforming. A Lot Creation and Development Study should be completed prior to aboriginal development, to be consistent with its municipal counterpart. The board was also working to ensure backcountry access stayed unrestricted.

While land issues were preoccupying the board, its landless free spirit decided it was time to retire. When Tim Gooderham was elected to the board, it never entered his mind that he would still be an administrator 26 years later. The TLA's inaugural executive secretary was granted an honourary life membership and presented with a Helen Hall painting.

Keewaydin Camp dining hall at left
and office building at right circa 1930s.
MacLean postcard photo: Reg Sinclair

Tim Gooderham in 2009.
Photo: Gerry Gooderham

A New Executive Secretary

Peter Healy commenced executive secretarial duties in October 2003. His salary was $10,800, upped to $12,000 in 2007. Since 1979 he and Trisha had spent entire summers at their cottage, which Trisha had owned with her first husband John Anderson since 1967.

Trisha and John first came to the lake with John's father John B. "Andy" Anderson, a mining engineer who was a colleague of Dr. Norman B. Keevil, and a director of the Copperfields Mine and Teck Corporation. They stayed at the director's lodge and recall eating huge breakfasts at the mine. The couple dreamed of using their meagre summer employment earnings to buy their own island. Sending $750 to the MNR for Crown land

Island 630, they were disappointed to discover that someone else had purchased the island a few hours earlier.

A local real estate agent took one look at the university students in their early 20s and decided they did not warrant any sales effort. Undaunted, the couple discovered that the late Bill Anderson's property and cottage on Garden Island had been for sale for several years, advertised only in Pennsylvania. Bill was a founder of Camp Wabun. His wife Vera did not return to the lake after his death. John and Trisha had saved about $4,500 and made the offer despite an asking price of about $17,000.

To their surprise, it was accepted and they became the proud young owners of a 1930s-era, John Turner-built cottage, albeit overgrown, leaking and thick with cobwebs. The Andersons soon met their neighbour Violet, widow of Wabun founder Dick Lewis Sr. She fed them a hearty "welcome to the island" breakfast of bacon and eggs. Did she have a hidden agenda? "We often heard her calling, "say, Jooohn! oh Jooohn!" He would obediently go over and help her open a jar or even zip up her dress. Peter would later take on this neighbourly role," Trisha recalled.

Peter is a retired King City Secondary School geography department head and served as an Aurora town councillor for nine years. Peter and Trisha's daughter Laura was a radio operator for three summers and son Andrew was elected as a director in 2009 and as president in 2010-11. Peter was the TLA property patroller and a member of PAC. He unsuccessfully ran for the board of directors in 1993 with a résumé consisting of four clipped sentences. Peter became recording secretary for board meetings. Trisha shares AGM recording duties with Robin Denninger. Three directors were acclaimed in 2003: Dick Grout, Jim Hasler and Florida's Vince Hovanec of Island 1024.

Campsites Spruced Up

The Lake Temagami Pilot Project got off to a bustling start in June 2003. Three local high school students earned credits in environmental studies and outdoor education. Supervisor Roxane Potts and crew put 74 campsites, the landings, Sand Point

and more into ship-shape. The project was a joint venture between the municipality and the TFN to address the absence of MNR maintenance. The TLA, through the TRSI, injected $5,000. The AYCTL and other donors soon came aboard. Project chair Biff Lowery explained in the *Times* that routes and campsites were heavily used by youth camps from other regions, in part due to onerous fees and canoe trip size restrictions in provincial parks.

The municipality financed another student endeavour administered by the TLA that summer. Part-time greeters ushered garbage and recycling to their appropriate resting places. The Mine Landing program, which helps to curtail the number of abusers and keep

Canoeists from all over the province enjoy Temagami's routes, including this 2010 group at the Manito Landing from a Toronto outdoor education centre. *Photo: Pam Sinclair*

garbage and disorder to a minimum, has been repeated every summer.

The pilot project resumed in 2004 when five students worked for a month at Finlayson park, the fish hatchery and on the lake. Maintenance was performed on Temagami and Cross lake campsites. Accommodation was provided by the TLA and MNR at no cost. They continued the TLA's privy project by installing 17. By 2005 the privy project had come full circle. Temagami Barge crews returned to pump out older box privies. All told, nearly 100 were built and placed.

Superfluous?

Telephone service was almost ubiquitous by 2003 prompting some members to question whether the TLA's radio service, costing about $5,000 in wages annually, was becoming redundant. Peter Healy addressed concerns in the *Times*. He noted 110 members contributed $45 each, thereby offsetting wages. Various government agencies have often subsidized wages.

Other building services, such as mail (used in 2009 by 70 members), laundry (discontinued in 2006), lending library and Internet, cost the TLA next to nothing. Some, including the flea market, are revenue generators. Publication

and product sales, especially the popular navigation chart, contribute to the profit side. The charts are also sold at outlets in the wider community. Map sales netted the TLA about $4,000 in 2009, with sales outside the TLA building accounting for about 50 per cent. The building itself is an asset, assessed in 2009 at $66,500. Outlays such as maintenance, land

Radio operator Catherine Lowery. *Photo: Pam Sinclair*

lease, hydro and insurance take a bite out of the budget, but the TLA roughly breaks even when expenditures are deducted from revenues.

Peter considered the lake's fate were it not for the radio operators. First response to a mainland fire near Friday's Point was coordinated by Tom Snyder using the VHF radio and phone to quickly summon nearby fire pump owners. Tom updated the MNR on the status of the blaze. Suppression efforts and radio communications continued after a widespread hydro blackout – caused by high-voltage power lines in Ohio going down when they contacted overgrown trees – hit eastern North America.

A Charge to Electors

2003 was a municipal election year and Wayne Adair, a 39-year Temagami resident and mayor for the past nine, was challenged by a relative newcomer to Temagami and politics. A slate of 16 candidates ran for council, including three incumbents who had served since the 1997 amalgamation election – Bill Kitts, Ike Laba and Biff Lowery. John Kilbridge was the only council hopeful to criticize the town in a *Times* section profiling candidates. He alleged that current and previous councils had only supported resource industries. "Council's style has been antagonistic toward constituent groups, including the Lake Temagami community," he said.

Ray Delarosbel was elected president by the board in 2002. He aired similar views: "The inexplicable nature of the last municipal Council to 'hear but not listen' to the lake community ratepayers is frustrating to those who wish to dialogue on important issues." He urged lake electors to vote en masse and choose candidates best representing the lake.

The municipality calculated lake residents had paid $3 million in taxes since 1998, or 33 per cent of the total bill. The lake's proportion would have been higher had TransCanada pipeline assessments been subtracted from the mainland calculation. At the 2006 AGM

Bruce Hodgins asked municipal representatives to recalculate by separating the pipeline's contribution. A pie chart was printed in the fall *Times*. The pipeline was the single largest taxpayer at 39 per cent, while the lake was second at 37 per cent and the mainland trailed at 24 per cent.

Land Claim Settlement Implementation

Board members attended an ONAS workshop in winter 2004 to review the committee structure that would handle settlement execution. It would be coordinated by a 10-year implementation committee and involve the technical transfer of land and financial compensation. The municipality would have observer status.

An aboriginal committee would develop a site plan for Shiningwood Bay prior to the transfer of land. It was to encompass about 6.5 kilometres of shoreline outside the waterway park. This process could take five years and would involve public consultation. The MNR would develop a four-year management plan for the waterway park, also with public involvement. Friday's Point and Austin Bay, 24 kilometres of shoreline along the east side of the lake and several Cross Lake islands would not be addressed until the land was transferred as an Indian reserve.

The selection, disposition and consultation process for the traditional family lands would take five years. A three-year forest management plan would involve the Local Citizens Committee, formerly the Public Advisory

Committee on forestry. The primary focus of a 10-year coordination committee would be land use and resource management, and addressing planning issues potentially affecting local organizations.

The municipality would be represented on most committees. The TLA believed implementation would require funding from Queen's Park for the municipality to effectively participate. Otherwise, the burden would be borne on taxpayers' shoulders. At the 2004 AGM, ONAS's Doug Carr said the accord was in the drafting stage and needed legal fine-tuning. Translating it into binding language would prove daunting and time-consuming.

The TAA-TFN appointed a new negotiating team in fall 2005, consisting of professional negotiator Ian Johnson, assistant negotiator and office manager Vicki Grant, and communications officer Deborah Charyna. Specialized help was sought due to the complexities of the agreement. Deborah became the first TFN municipal councillor in the 2010 election.

Help is Just a Phone Call Away

911 emergency services arrived in 2004. Affixing the civic address signs on docks so they were "visible to any approaching vessel from either direction" caused a snafu in the roadless island community. Figuring out which two of many approaches best represented left and right may have resulted in a few swollen thumbs. However, the municipality would not "assume any responsibility for injury or damage caused by the installation and/or the presence of the post on the owner's property."

Adding to carpentry woes was the notion that trees had to be cleared so that a dispatched air ambulance could "locate your property from the air" via GPS coordinates. This was a conundrum for small island owners because the helicopter requires a 60 by 60-metre flat open area to land safely. Cottagers were assured that when they made that inevitable 911 call as gangrene from post-nailing wounds set in, they would "receive emergency assistance at your door" and "telephone assistance to help you walk through any emergency situation as you wait."

Help May Be Closer than a Phone Call Away

Although 911 emergency services were working on the lake, an inability of seasonal and permanent residents to react immediately as first responders to accidents and health crises prompted Island 995's Barbara Olmsted to bring CPR and First Aid training courses to the lake in 2007. Open to members and non-members alike, four training courses were taught at the TLA building.

"One of the key benefits of First Aid training is the ability to recognize when an injury requires further medical treatment so that the appropriate steps can be taken to stabilize the casualty prior to transport," Barb wrote in the Times.

To add insult to imaginary injury, Sandy Inlet was misidentified in a 911 address notice as a "Lake Temagami access point" rather than a trail access. The municipality corrected it while noting a sign on the Red Squirrel Road was intended for 911 purposes only and not to designate a public motorized access.

Clearly, 911 is a welcomed measure, adding a layer of security. Cooperative efforts assure timely help arrives. For example, a woman suffered a cardiac event one summer. Temagami's land ambulance reached her by water taxi from the landing and paramedics stabilized her. Advanced care paramedics arrived at a Bear Island helipad via air ambulance and were brought to the patient in the TFN police boat. They treated her and she was then airlifted to hospital in Sudbury which, like New Liskeard, has a helipad. Land ambulances are permitted to use the winter ice road because it is maintained by the TFN as a public road.

A look at 2007 figures shows the magnitude of Temagami's emergency assistance, consisting of 217 medical and accident responses. Eighteen patients were met by land ambulance at the end of the access road and 20 boat trips were made to islands. One boating accident was attended to. The ambulance service also responded to calls from hikers, all-terrain vehicle operators and snowmobilers. Lakeland Airways delivered two patients to land ambulances. Ambulance destinations were New Liskeard 100 times and North Bay 27 times. Ten patients were airlifted.

CHAPTER 32

PLAN UNDER FIRE

The final draft OP was approved by the Ministry of Municipal Affairs and Housing (MMAH) in April 2004. An OMB appeal was filed by the Lake Temagami Group (LTG) the day before the 20-day public review period ended.

A two-day OMB pre-hearing was conducted in August in an attempt to preclude an expensive full-blown hearing. The TLA, the municipality and the MMAH were granted party status to defend the new plan. A negotiated settlement was reached. A major LTG concern was the conversion of youth camps to commercial tourism. The North Arm has the heaviest concentration of youth camps.

The OMB deferred that section of the plan for a public process to consider the appropriateness of draft OP policies governing such conversions. It ruled boathouses could not contain sleeping quarters. The draft allowed upper level sleeping quarters if they counted as sleep cabins. The Lot Creation and Development Study was not to rule out the concept of sub-neighbourhoods in the North and Northwest arms, as requested by the LTG.

The board viewed the Lot Creation and Development Study decision as a continuation of NIMBY politics. "The result would be more concentrated development for the balance of the lake. The TLA feels strongly that it is only fair that all areas of the lake be treated the same, and we will continue to oppose any sub neighbourhoods or special treatment for any part of the lake," recently installed president Brad Hall stated.

Brad followed in his father Standish's footsteps by attending Keewaydin in 1946 and '47. While staying with the Cattle Island Hydes, he acquired a 50-hp war surplus motor made, but never used, to push salt barges across the Rhine River. He mounted it on a 14-foot flat-bottom runabout named *Felix*, both rented from Marty Taylor's marina. Zipping around in his speed devil (a 9.8 hp was common), he was in the right place at the right time. Island 1067 lessees the Blakely family had camped there since 1931 without a motorboat or cabin. They became wind-bound for two weeks straight in 1948 and decamped in disgust, moving to Island 972. Brad roared over to the vacated island, took 10 steps, turned around and headed for Forestry Island. He met with Chief Ranger Phil Hoffman and leased the island, buying it three years later.

Arrivals to and departures from PAC were the order of the day as the committee commenced another three-year term. Outgoing lake representatives were Ray Delarosbel and Peter Healy, while incomers were Claire Rannie and Jim Leach, joining Jim Hasler and Gerry

Gooderham. Ray, 61, died of a massive heart attack in spring 2011.

The LTG went on to appeal the OP's zoning bylaw, approved by council in February 2006. It was designed to control development by implementing standards such as lot size, dwelling size and location. The LTG's earlier OP appeal had cost the TLA $10,000 and municipal taxpayers about $30,000, according to Brad. The bylaw appeal was heard in a January 2007 pre-hearing where disputed issues were identified. A long and costly appeal was averted when a few changes were made, applying to the whole lake as a single neighbourhood.

Small Acts of Kindness

As was the case in 2003, all three board aspirants were acclaimed. Carol Lowery and Marc Shaw were starting their second terms while North Bay's Margery Fryer of Island 1088 was the new kid on the block. She was also a lake representative on the TSC. Marc resigned in 2006 for personal reasons. Shortly thereafter, Marc and Linda's 17-year-old son Eric died following a life-long battle with cancer. The board did not appoint a director to complete his term.

The TLA published a list of town causes it supported in 2004, including a children's Christmas tree fund and a school snack program. The board recognized that small acts of kindness build community bridges. Director Carol Lowery, a resident whose heart beats in sync with the town's pulse, led the

board down unexplored lanes. It funded other similar programs the following year.

A TLUP Pledge Honoured

In the 1997 Temagami Land Use Plan (TLUP), Ontario pledged management plans for recreational Crown land use. In 2004 it announced a Temagami Integrated Plan (TIP). The Lady Evelyn-Smoothwater Wilderness Park, four adjoining waterway parks, eight conservation reserves and non-park Crown land would comprise its scope.

Public sessions in Elk Lake and Temagami drew polar opposite perspectives from one session in Toronto. Elk Lakers feared new regulations would restrict their all-terrain vehicle, snowmobile and motorboat access in the wilderness park. Roughly 800 people signed a petition opposing limitations. The summer-gated Liskeard Lumber Road was providing motorized access south through the park. To the relief of wilderness canoeists, the road was permanently closed at the northern park boundary in 2010. In Toronto, environmentalists fretted that more wilderness areas would be opened to motorized recreation.

As a first TIP step, Ontario Parks introduced overnight camping fees in backcountry parks. Just two wardens were hired to clear portages and clean campsites. Ontario Parks was created in 1998 and operates within the MNR.

A Keewaydin section overlooks a panoramic vista.
Photo: Keewaydin Camp

Leases, Acclamations and Fires

The TLA building's Crown land lease would expire at the end of 2004. Through the intervention of Wayne Adair, the MNR issued a three-year land use permit. After years of relationship building, the MNR generously gave the TLA a 10-year lease extension in 2008, providing time to explore relocation options outside the Skyline Reserve.

Three directors were acclaimed in 2005, the third consecutive year an election was not required. Brad Hall returned. New director Michael Harpur of Island 250 had to renege when he was appointed judge of the Ontario Court of Justice in Barrie because judges cannot serve on corporate boards. Nominations were reopened and Toronto's David Taylor of Shiningwood Bay was acclaimed.

Ontario heat records were broken in summer 2005. By mid-season there had been 30 fires on the lake. Two-thirds were started by lightning and the rest by people. The smoke and flames weren't over yet. A VHF "all stations" bulletin went out from the TLA building and neighbours with water pumps rallied at Island 315 west of High Rock, partially owned by Lorraine Greey. The blaze was started accidentally by trespassing campers. Lorraine thanked volunteers in a *Times* letter and donated to the radio service.

Five days later, a fire broke out at a mainland campsite near Slide Rock, reported by Margery Fryer via VHF radio. Volunteer firefighters could not do battle, owing to wind and heat. Trisha Healy described the MNR's response as "incredibly professional and impressive" in the *Times*. Due to dry conditions a fire crew had been stationed at Link Lake. A reconnaissance plane circled while a helicopter dropped men and equipment. Then a water bomber swooped in. The crew stayed for two days to stop the fire from spreading or reigniting. Conservation officers investigated both fires but came to inconclusive conclusions.

Scorchers

The late 1990s and early 2000s were dominated by weather extremes. June and July 1999 were the hottest in Ontario since record-keeping began in 1840 while 2001 registered record high temperatures across the province. Summer 2002 was the warmest in 63 years. Bouts of torrid heat and insufferable humidity characterized summer 2005. It was hot again in 2006 with many nights above 20 C. Putting conditions in perspective, July 1936 saw temperatures exceed 44 C in Manitoba and Ontario, claiming 1,180 lives.

Local weather abnormalities like extreme heat, microbursts and unusual break-up and freeze-up patterns make up a thin strand in the complicated web of climate change that has wrought catastrophic natural calamities around the globe.

Triumph and Tragedy

Wilderness canoe tripping carries inherent risks – a canoe capsizing during whitewater running, violent thunderstorms, whipping winds, forest fires, adverse reactions to insect stings, wildlife attacks – and the list goes on.

A harrowing scenario unfolded for a Wabun section one morning during summer 2005. It was mid-point of a James Bay trip when head staffman Pete Gwyn noticed a storm approaching. He headed his boys to an island and asked them to separate and assume a protective catcher's crouch position they had been taught. A lightning bolt hit the island and lifted camper Nate Thiel, throwing him six metres. He wasn't breathing but, within 30 seconds of the strike, Pete was performing CPR and revived him.

His next move was to report the incident to Wabun via satellite phone. Dick Lewis immediately alerted the Sioux Lookout Fire Attack Base to prepare a helicopter for an emergency evacuation. Pete gave Wabun coordinates using the phone's GPS function. Dick called them into the base and then hit the road.

Pete spotted an aircraft. Section members paddled to a nearby fish camp and found the pilot. Nate was flown to the Pickle Lake Clinic and stabilized, then flown to Thunder Bay Regional Hospital where Wabun sent his medical information electronically. Dick made contact with his parents en route to the hospital and they left immediately for Thunder Bay.

Although he was diagnosed with atrophied muscles, a fractured vertebra, burns and a ruptured disc, Nate made a full recovery. Preparedness under immense pressure turned what could have become a stain on Wabun's reputation into a textbook example of clear-thinking and competence.

The lake's canoe camps have an outstanding safety record compared to the lake as a whole. Motorboat fatalities and cottage drownings far outstrip camp deaths. Considering the tens of thousands of campers who have embarked on trips since Keewaydin and Cochrane's set up bases long ago, it's a testament to the management and staff that so few lives have been lost. There have been fatal incidents but they are extremely rare.

According to relatives of Henry and Marjorie Woodman, Cayuga never experienced the heartbreak of losing a camper. The Gardner family recalled some injuries but no fatalities when Doug Gardner owned camps Temagami and Metagami. Carol Cochrane recalled hearing about one camper death but knew no details. It is unknown if Wigwasati experienced such misfortune. There have been no camper fatalities at Langskib or Northwaters. "We have never had a serious injury," said co-director C.G. Stephens. "Plenty of cuts, twisted knees and ankles, blisters and such. We've been very fortunate." Scott Northey, a co-owner of Camp Temagami, formerly Pay's d'en Haut, also reported no deaths.

Two Keewaydin campers drowned descending La Cave Rapids on the Ottawa River in 1925. According to *The Keewaydin Way* (2004), they were given a signal to enter the rapids by a staffman before he waited to see if a first canoe finished safely. It didn't, capsizing after the second canoe was on its way. The occupants of the first canoe managed to swim to shore. Those in the second didn't.

In 1971 a Keewaydin guide carrying a canoe atop his head beside a train track was killed when he couldn't see the approach of a freight train bearing down on him. As the train roared by, its suction pulled at the canoe and the guide couldn't control it. The impact shattered the stern and a thwart fatally struck the back of his head.

Wigwasati's Homer Grafton with some campers. *Photo: John Hyde*

Wabun lost a camper in 1968 in an Albany River rapid, according to Dick Lewis. After a canoe flipped, one of its two occupants stayed with the vessel, as camp protocol dictated at the time. The other occupant swam to shore. The boy who remained with the canoe got a boot lodged between rocks and drowned. Lifejackets were not standard issue back then because they were too bulky and uncomfortable to wear while paddling in high heat.

Wanapitei experienced a pair of fatalities in 1978, said Bruce Hodgins. One happened on the Nahanni River in the Northwest Territories when a trip leader went on a sightseeing hike. He fell off a cliff over Virginia Falls. Although his knapsack was found, the body was never recovered. The other incident occurred on Quebec's Rupert River. Having run whitewater, campers were taking their canoes out of the river to bypass a dangerous falls. As an onshore boy held a bow rope, he tightened his grip instead of letting the line go slack, and slid into the water and disappeared.

The most recent deadly mishap occurred in 2005 during a swimming break on the Harricana River running into James Bay in Quebec. A camper wandered away for a solitary walk up the river and around a bend. He entered the river and his foot got wedged between rocks. The current forced him under.

Wanapitei has since enhanced its supervision guidelines. Bruce noted that none of the incidents happened while the victims were in their canoes. A website dedicated to making all types of camps safer rates four out of more than 55 in the U.S. and Canada experiencing fatalities between 2002 and 2009 as "exceptional." One of them is Wanapitei.

Many fatal accidents are attributable to human error, in contrast to the Nate Thiel rescue which is attributable to human heroics. Few occur in the vigilant modern environment of enhanced safety and lessons learned. Today lightweight personal floatation devices help protect campers. Wanapitei paddlers go the extra mile by donning helmets in rapids.

Looming in the shadows for all organizations offering physical activity is the threat of litigation. Malfunctioning equipment, reckless third-party behaviour, an insufficiently trained instructor and the like can lead to a one-way trip to the courthouse, potentially costing reputations and millions of dollars. Temagami's camps are protected by comprehensive liability insurance. Although some Ontario camps still use them, signed liability waivers don't carry much weight because of their limited value in court.

Against this backdrop, the canoe camps have excellent risk management records. Staff is annually trained and recertified in evacuation procedures, CPR and life saving, wilderness first aid and first response. Campers must pass swimming tests, and receive thorough training in safe canoemanship and water rescue. Technological advances and progress in patient care have improved outcomes.

Lot Creation Calculations

The board adopted an analytical approach to PAC's Lot Creation and Development Study. Director Dick Grout, planning committee chair, noted in a *Times* piece that past development was concentrated in the Hub and the Northeast and South arms. The proposed land claim accord, including a Shiningwood Bay townsite, and Austin Bay and Friday's Point lots, would intensify congestion.

There were about 200 lots available for severance from existing private land, 80 per cent of them in the Northeast Arm and the Hub. "This development will most likely take place sooner, rather than later, because the new OP gives preference to private land development over Crown land," Dick added. The board believed some constraints on lot creation in these parts of the lake should be considered.

Inspections and Regulations

The MOE inspected commercial and shared septic systems in 2005. Six were rated a "fail" and five a "pass." Problems were pipe leaks, improper design, age failures and unapproved alterations. Discharge to the lake was suspected at a children's camp and a provincial order was issued to construct a new system under Temiskaming Health Unit approval.

The inspections continued in 2006. There were two fails and five passes. One of the failures was a greywater treatment system at a children's camp. It was ordered to construct a new one. Steel septic tanks installed prior to 1980 are prone to rusty leaks and replacement with plastic tanks is recommended. The province did not pass proposed 2009 legislation that would have enforced private septic tank re-inspections.

New regulations were passed in the wake of the 2000 Walkerton, Ontario, tainted water tragedy. Temagami was provincially mandated to upgrade its water plant. Its one-sixth share of the total cost was $750,000. Bill Kitts, chair of the general government and finance committee, consulted with the town's accounting firm, Ontario and the TLA. They decided to fund the retrofit from municipal reserves, even though tap water is area rated and lake dwellers don't pay for this service. The board stressed that it was a one-time deal, not a precedent.

When it rains it pours. The Welcome Centre, built in 1990, was found to be contaminated with mould from various sources. Reclamation work included spore-stripping. Temporary quarters were found for municipal administration, the public library and others. Fifty per cent of the fix-ups were non-local government funded.

Going to the Birds

The TRSI conducted a loon survey in summer 2005. 100 adults but only a dozen chicks were spotted, according to Director Jim Hasler, TRSI chair. Two of the chicks met an untimely fate; one was found floating and the other choked on a fish fed to it by a parent. Data from across the country is analyzed by the Canadian Lakes Loon Survey conducted by Bird Studies Canada.

The loon survey continued in 2006 when 22 chicks and one fatality were observed. Frequent rains, a high water level, and below-normal air temperatures conspired to produce only six chick sightings in 2009. Adverse weather conditions in 2008 had led to similar

A hearty common loon greeting. *Photo: Jack Goodman*

results. Jim noted that large boat wakes can wash away loon nests. In past years the *Aubrey Cosens VC* was blamed for nest destruction by the TLA's nature guru Claire Muller.

A Green Future?

A green energy project launched by town residents was blowing in the wind by August 2005. A 60-metre wind tower was erected in the industrial park to record speed and direction for a year. Readings would gauge the town's potential for producing clean energy. The trial was run by The Renewable Energy Co-operative North (TREC North). A $158,500 grant from the Federation of Canadian Municipalities Green Fund got it off the ground. It was expanded in 2006 to the higher elevation of Friday Lake Hill, about 14 kilometres northeast of Temagami.

Wind readings at Friday Lake Hill are among Ontario's best, according to TREC North President Robin Hughes. The plan was to sell hydro to southern Ontario, but some of the wind was taken out of TREC North's sails when it learned transmission lines north of North Bay couldn't handle more electricity. The province has said northern Ontario's small population doesn't warrant a large investment to bolster capacity. The project, like another in Elk Lake, still holds promise.

A Retrospective Future?

The TLA Archives found a new home at the train station. The collection was stored at the TLA building, leaving material vulnerable to theft and temperature extremes. In a deal with the Temagami Station Restoration Trust, the collection would remain TLA property but station coordinator Claire Smerdon could use material in public programs. Archives Committee Chair Walter Kemball hoped to make it possible for people to contribute and access material online. Sadly, Walter's vision was cut short by his death in 2008.

The train station is a restored testament to bygone days, sustained by a modern era of tourism. There is a model railway with more than 27 metres of track replicating northern

Ontario in the 1930s and '40s. Books, toys, craft kits and souvenirs – some designed by local artists and manufactured onsite – are for sale.

A joint venture between Ontario Northland, the City of North Bay and the Municipality of Temagami in fall 2005 evoked the olden golden years when the T-Station platform was packed like sardines. The inaugural Dreamcatcher Express thundered into town daily for two weeks. It departed North Bay with passengers admiring fall colours while they narrowed down sightseeing options. They could cruise the lake with Leisure Island Houseboats, book a scenic flight with Lakeland Airways, chase nature in the ancient White Bear Forest, or climb the Caribou Mountain fire tower and visit an authentic aboriginal village.

Visitors were in awe of Temagami's allure. Lynn Johnson, the "For Better or Worse" syndicated cartoonist residing near North Bay,

called the Dreamcatcher Express "an amazing adventure to offer family, friends and business associates…a truly beautiful experience." That first excursion drew about 800 passengers and was still bringing dreams to life through 2010.

Temagami's beauty was captured for the big screen in a movie adapted from Bill Plumstead's 1992 novel *Loon*. Screen writers changed its name to *That Beautiful Somewhere* and Bill, a Nipissing University English professor, was the executive producer. Scenes were shot at the train station, the fire tower and a beaver pond on the tower trail. Locals, enlisted as extras, depicted an organized protest of a proposed copper mine. The cast included lead actors Jane McGregor and Roy Dupuis.

The film was released in 2006 and garnered favourable attention at film festivals. It played in select theatres in 2007 and then moved to the small screen. The *Toronto Star* awarded *That Beautiful Somewhere* two and a half stars out of five, praising its scenery and cinematography. It was nominated for a 2008 Genie Award for best original musical score. Past features using Temagami backdrops are *Silent Enemy* (1930) and *Captains of the Clouds* (1941) starring James Cagney.

The beaver pond bridge at the Caribou Mountain tower.
Photo: Gerry Gooderham

Floating Auction

2006 Flea Market Chairs Bobby Morrison, Barbara Olmsted and Heather Windrem

2008 Members of the Year Barb Olmsted, left, Bobby Morrison and Heather Windrem. *Photo: Peter Healy for the Temagami Times*

Olympic Champ in Our Midst

Barbara Olmsted, who co-owns a cottage on Island 995 west of Bear Island, won an Olympic bronze medal at the Summer Games in Los Angeles in 1984. Her father Charles Olmsted was a co-founder of the North Bay Canoe Club. The club is recognized internationally for producing five Olympians, including Barb and her younger sister Nancy. Both were members of the Canadian National Canoeing Team. Barb earned her hardware in the four-woman 500-metre flatwater kayaking event.

started a floating bidding war when they staged the auction on a George Mathias Construction barge. It was an ideal platform for auctioneers Duff Shaw and Russell Tuckerman to goad bidders into offering top dollar. Flea market revenues shattered previous records as they would again in 2007 under the same chairs. The flea market expanded again in 2008 and '09 under Chair Elodie Tichinoff. As a buy local trend caught fire, more vendors were offering preserves, cheeses, meats, herbs, art and jewelry made or grown close to home.

Temagami Public School celebrated its 100th anniversary in 2006. The first single-room schoolhouse was built on the site of the present-day Temagami Legion building. There were 28 school-aged children living in the village. Enrolment reached 350 during the 1970s, dropping to 75 in 2006. To commemorate the centennial, a reunion dinner and dance was held. The TLA donated $1,000 of 2006 flea market proceeds to the school in appreciation of flea market support from the community and its merchants.

An anniversary partnership was formed between the school and Project CANOE, Wabun, Keewaydin, Northwaters, Wanapitei, Wabikon, Canadian Adventure Camp and

Camp Temagami. Students wrote essays explaining why they wanted to go to camp and the winners scored camp sessions – plus memories for life.

"It is a great privilege and honour for us to have the camps take our students and help

The 2004 Sonadeewin 1 was the first Keewaydin girls' section to make the Hudson Bay trip. *Photo: Keewaydin Camp*

them develop different life skills, meet people from as far away as Germany and Spain and experience moments that they would not otherwise have," teacher Suzanne Daneault, campaign spearheader, informed *Times* readers. The program was so popular it is now an annual event.

Taxes and Elections

The TLA belongs to the Federation of Ontario Cottagers' Association. It grew an offshoot called the Waterfront Ratepayers after Fair Taxation to lobby Ontario to moderate

large increments in property assessments. Under pressure, the province enacted a three-year moratorium in 2006.

For the first time since 2002 the TLA elected rather than acclaimed its directors. Due to non-controversial resignations, five directors were elected for terms between one and three years. Two rookies were Toronto's Rob Corcoran of Northeast Arm Island 135 and Timmins lawyer Ted Tichinoff of Island 1058, south of Kokoko Bay.

Carol Lowery had one year remaining in her second stint when she resigned in August from the all-male board, paving the way for former director Vince Hovanec to return. He had received the next highest number of votes in the recent election, but his résumé was inadvertently omitted from the package mailed to voting members in spring. Sticking to a predetermined agenda, the board installed Vince as president in the fall. No woman has since served as a director through 2010.

Vince arrived in 1956 as a Keewaydin junior staffer. Howard "Chief" Chivers didn't blink an eye when he broke the news he had never been in a canoe. "In truth, my only strong points were a good sense of humour under the worst of circumstances or the foulest of weather, and a strong back when it came to portages. My canoe, alas, was always the slowest, at the beginning and end of the summer," he said.

His career path would prove noteworthy. He spent 20 years as a Foreign Service diplomat working overseas handling press and information assignments. Vince was witness to history in the making: assisting ABC in preparing for the 1984 Sarajevo Olympics; crisis managing the public information campaign during a 1976 Ebola outbreak; and briefing media on the 1985 Mexico City earthquakes. One memorable assignment was managing international media during the Rumble in the Jungle boxing match pitting George Foreman against Muhammad Ali. After retiring, Vince went overseas again, representing seven Balkan countries for Sprint International. He re-retired in 1998.

When he departed the lake in 1956 he took fond memories of an island girl he met at a Bear Island square dance. He dated Gloria Seaman for three years while they were in college, then the couple parted ways. During a business trip to Toronto in 1997, he returned to the lake to visit Gloria, now Gloria Allen. "Looking over the lake on that warm August day, I remarked how much it had changed in some

ways (bigger faster boats, more costly cottages, for example) but in many ways the uniqueness of the lake had been maintained. In many respects the same was true of our relationship. And we've been together since then," he said.

A photo Gloria took of a tranquil Island 976 bay was used by the Polaroid Corporation circa 1963. It was reproduced on the company's colour film package instructions as an example of a well-composed picture. An American history devotee, she went on to direct a Washington D.C. museum and has written extensively about women's needlework as it relates to pre and post-American Revolutionary times.

Member Appreciation

Peter Healy launched an ongoing Member Appreciation project in 2006, annually

Steve Drake, left, and President Rob Corcoran hold the original watercolour Steve created for membership appreciation prints.
Photo: Pam Sinclair

recognizing 40-year property-owning members. Island 1091's Steve Drake of St. Catharines was commissioned to paint a watercolour of the Elephant Rock campsite near Garden Island. In the first year, 80 members were bestowed a limited edition print titled *Tripper's Paradise.* The original was auctioned at the 2009 AGM and the flea market. The grateful owner is Peter whose $500 bid sealed the deal.

Steve was a child when he was introduced to the lake at Wabun Lodge in 1951, where he stayed with his brother and parents Tom and Shirley Drake. Property inquiries led them to Joe Lanoie. He showed them his favourite cottage site – three acres on the northeast corner of Island 1091– just north of Cayuga Island. Joe pointed out that it was bathed in sun all day and featured a quiet, sheltered bay. The Drakes had John Turner build a cottage and a bunky for the boys. They purchased a hard-top Peterborough and two 45-hp Evinrude motors from Marty Taylor, in case one broke down on the Northeast Arm during pre-Mine Road days.

Like many 1950s families, Shirley spent the summer on the lake with the children, while Tom was only able to squeeze in two weeks. The cottage became known as Cattatong, meaning "secret place," referring not to its location but to family members' unwillingness to share good fishing spots. Civilization began creeping in; indoor plumbing and electricity were added in 1967, though television has never been welcomed. Norman Keevil of nearby Island 1114 was one of the first cottagers to bring in underwater hydro cable and Tom struck a cost-cutting deal with him.

As the family grew to include grandchildren, Tom and Shirley had John Turner build a cottage in 1969 so they could enjoy some peace and quiet. With generational issues in mind, the Drakes purchased another three acres of Island 1091 in 1974 from Pennsylvanian cottagers. Bob Farr renovated and expanded the existing building, and also worked on the Drake's original cottage to accommodate the ever-expanding family.

"Cattatong is much more than the structures; it is where families talk, share laughs, tears, stories, plans, victories and defeats," Steve said. "It is a place where time slows down and you have time to smell the pine needles, where adults and children alike run to see the single or double rainbows, and occasionally northern lights. There is no doubt that the cottage is responsible for the Drake family's closeness. Today, this feeling continues to be passed on to the fourth generation. It is a priceless gift!" Steve was the 2009 Member of the Year.

TLA Fields a Candidate

2006 was a municipal election year. The province extended the term of office from three to four years, meaning 2010 would be the next. It also moved election day to October from November. The *Times* did not include its usual candidate profile. The 2003 questionnaire hadn't yielded the results the TLA hoped for. "as all candidates answered the questions to please lake residents," Director Vince Hovanec said in 2010. Further, there was no follow-up to ascertain whether successful candidates lived up to their words. It was normally the executive secretary's job to pull the election section together, but Peter Healy couldn't do it because he was on the ballot as a council hopeful.

Wayne Adair, who presided before, over and after amalgamation, chose not to run. Four candidates vied for head of council. Ike Laba, a councillor since 1998, emerged victorious. Ike moved to Temagami in 1964 as an MNR employee, retiring in 1991. A long slate of 17 candidates threw their hats in the ring. The six to emerge victorious included Claire Smerdon, returning for her second term. Councillor Biff Lowery was re-elected for a fourth term and resumed chairing PAC, a seat he had occupied since 1998. Bill Kitts also commenced his fourth term. He had been in charge of the general government and finance portfolio, but yielded it to one of three newcomers.

That newcomer was Peter Healy, an asset with his understanding of islanders' desires and past municipal experience under his belt. He had to resign just 10 months later, due to the stress of travelling up the lake or to Huntsville after meetings in town, on cold, windy fall and winter nights. Council appointed the lake's Lorie Hunter, who also has a home in town, to fill Peter's seat. She had served two terms from 1998 until 2003.

Snow bird Bill Kitts had resigned three months earlier. Applications were accepted and Barbara Pandolfo was selected as his replacement. The revolving door pattern continued. Barbara, in turn, resigned for

personal reasons in 2009 and Paul Middleton was appointed to fill the vacancy. Then Claire Smerdon had to resign in her pursuit of doctoral studies at the University of Edinburgh. Council selected applicant Sam Barnes, the first councillor from Marten River, to fill her seat.

Council adopted a site plan control bylaw in fall 2007. It mitigates negative effects of development related to new buildings, septic systems if they are being moved, and large additions. The bylaw ensures vegetation is maintained and adjacent properties are protected from construction impacts.

CHAPTER 33

BACK TO EARTH

Director Rob Corcoran, chair of the water quality committee, wrote a series of articles for the winter and summer 2007 *Times*. He explored factors affecting water quality, including historic impacts such as the Sudbury Super Stack, dredging, garbage dumping, mining and logging. Current water drinkability and key preventative measures such as properly functioning septic systems and greywater containment, and alternatives to septic systems were examined.

To keep phosphorous out of septic systems and greywater cesspools, the TLA and the Co-op grocery store sold eco-friendly cleaning and personal hygiene products. Phosphorous impairs lake trout habitat and has other environmental impacts. The TLA also began selling coliform test kits and tested water filtration systems. While some campers and cottagers still enjoyed a refreshing drink right from the lake, Rob advised against drinking untreated water, in accordance with MOE guidelines. The Ontario Department of Health made the same recommendation back at the 1964 AGM.

Boating Matters

There were more houseboats by the late 2000s than when they were first seen as a problem in the 1980s. Can-Usa's Nelson and Brenda Leudke rent out four. They are 44-foot Three Buoys with four-piece bathrooms. Ann Rice's Tamar Vacations also has four, acquired about 1999. Each accommodates six people and has a three-piece loo. Ket-Chun-Eny Lodge's Mike and Jeannie Foran have two 36-foot vessels, each sleeping six. All are equipped with grey and blackwater holding tanks, which are pumped into the resorts' septic systems. The Three Buoys fleet in town is owned by Judy Gareh. She has seven 40-foot boats, each accommodating 10 people. They have four-piece washrooms that are emptied into the town's sewerage system.

Now located on the mainland, Leisure Island is still owned by Peter and Annemarie Drenth and family. They have a 13-boat fleet, each sleeping five. There is no space for greywater containment and no showers. Portable basins are used for washing and renters are firmly instructed to empty them on land, well away from shore.

Led by Rob Corcoran, the TLA lobbied all levels of government in 2007 to enact houseboat greywater legislation. There are regulations to prevent residential greywater from entering the soil closer than 15 metres from the water's edge. "It stands to reason that all producers of wastewater on the lake should bear equal responsibility for Lake Temagami's safekeeping," Rob said. Owners strive to instil

Early morning sun dissipates fog near a Sharp Rock Inlet islet.
Photo: Adam Keevil

When Tim moved out of the TLA building, where he had spent about eight winters, and into a Temagami apartment in 2002, he purchased a 35-foot houseboat, built in 1975. She was unofficially named the *Annabelle IV.* He had the beige vessel with a "ghastly orange stripe running around her

respect for islanders' privacy. They support the radio service because you never know when a houseboater will hit a rock, run out of gas or have a toilet malfunction. Roving houseboaters have spotted and reported numerous forest fires.

Tim Gooderham once called Three Buoys houseboats "40-foot behemoths." Ironically, the former executive secretary has owned a boat that he can sleep and eat in since 1985. His first was the *Annabell Lee.* She was sold by the Gooderhams to Dick Grout's father-in-law Howard Baker in the 1940s. Reverting to Gooderham hands, she was restored by Bill and Tim. Tim replaced the *Annabell Lee* in 1986 with *Annabelle*, a 21-foot fibreglass Doral powered by a 205-hp engine. He sold the *Annabell Lee* to a Sturgeon Falls charter fisherman. She was later abandoned in a field and a Muskoka cottager had her refurbished.

Annabell Lee

Alex Gooderham, brother of Gordon S. Gooderham, had the 26-foot Annabell Lee built in Port Credit near Toronto in 1931. She was of lapstrake construction with overlapping planks acting as a shock absorber against swells. She had a long pointed bow and was powered by a six-cylinder Chrysler engine. He named her Annabell Lee for his three daughters – Ann, Jane Raybell (Wadman) and Virginia Lee (Pride).

He built "The Arc," a large boathouse on Chimo Island. Jane Wadman purchased it from Alex's estate about 1960. Jane died in 1999 and the boathouse went to her son John Wadman. Virginia Pride has had a cottage on Island 780 since 1980. Her daughter Tuz Gooderham, a North Bay physician, bought the cottage from her mother in 2007.

mid-section" painted in camouflage hues, allowing Tim to quietly meander with little notice. He stops for the night out of sight and mind of islanders. He has never moored at a campsite, staying instead in isolated bays. His vessel is equipped with an 80-gallon holding tank, which he empties at Can-Usa Vacations. Tim's three grandsons are fifth generation Lake Temagamites.

Island 1087's Angus Scully became chair of the boating committee about 2007. He parlayed his expertise as a boat safety specialist with Transport Canada into numerous articles for the *Times*. His subjects have ranged from a comprehensive history of the *Aubrey Cosens VC* to the toxic mix of boating and alcohol. Angus also provides free pleasure craft courtesy checks. He looks for mandatory safety equipment. There are no fines, just constructive criticism.

Temagami Stewardship Council Disbands

The MNR withdrew its support of the TSC and the services of an MNR biologist in 2007. The council was removed from the Ontario Stewardship Program (OSP) and lost $10,000 in annual funding. The MNR cited the council's failure to broaden its focus beyond the fishery. Although the council's main focus was improving the fishery, it was also involved in campsite cleaning, water quality testing and the annual garbage pick-up at the landings.

The OSP addresses the needs of landowners and communities in areas such as forestry, wetlands, wildlife and agriculture in an ecologically-friendly manner. The MNR tried to force the TSC to conform to this southern Ontario model, according to Gaye Smith. When the final TSC meeting was called to order in 2008 he did not stand for re-election as chair, citing the MNR's perceived contempt for public involvement and the council's refusal to submit to MNR control. No one else was willing to be nominated and the TSC disbanded.

New Editor and Marina Owner

As of summer 2007 the *Times* had a new editor. Elaine Gunnell took over from interim editor Vince Hovanec. For the first time, a permanent resident was at the helm. Elaine was the "Municipal Update" ghost writer, having succeeded artist Judy Gouin. Elaine also authored the Co-op's news for the *Temagami Talker*.

Temagami Marine – "Your First Mate since '58" – was sold by the Kitts family to André and Brenda Lamothe. Hamiltonians Bob and Betty Louks purchased the marina, then known as Northern Marine and Fuel, in 1958. Through the 1960s they made every inch of their less than one-acre property count, going from winter storage for 15 boats to 80. Bob later leased 20 acres for an expansion. Dock hand Bill Kitts rose through the ranks and married the Louks' daughter Billie. He bought the marina in the late 1970s. Expansion continued to the point where there was storage for roughly 700 boats. Three generations of

Louks were engaged in everything from waxing hulls to ordering the latest marine gadgets.

The Angele Project

2007's Angele Project was the outcome of a partnership between North Bay's Kennedy Gallery, the Temagami Station Restoration Trust and the Temagami Community Foundation. The multimedia exhibit paid tribute to Bear Island's Angele Belaney and her daughter Agnes LaLonde. It was mounted in two boxcars at the train station and drew 6,000 visitors.

Angele Belaney in traditional garb.
Photo: Carol Cochrane

The project kicked off a summer's worth of events. Donald Smith, author of an Archie

Belaney biography titled *From the Land of Shadows*, and former TAA chief Gary Potts shared tales of Archie and Angele. Bear Island square dances were recreated, Craig Macdonald made presentations, and elders' stories were retold and recorded. During the staging of the Angele Project, Agnes's son Albert LaLonde was accidentally killed while felling a red pine for a cottager. He had taken great pride as the tribute unfolded.

An arts, culture and heritage committee emerged from the enthusiasm around the

---

A Picture and a Thousand Words

Local contractor and aspiring professional photographer Gerry Gooderham, son of Bill and Nancey Gooderham, began providing scenery photos for the TLA directory in 2004. About a year later he came up with the concept of creating a lasting visual public record of the senior generation, based on candid photographs of local elders. Gerry secured a start-up grant for the Temagami Elders Project from the Temagami Community Foundation.

Getting the pixels rolling was his first challenge. Sherry Guppy was recording storytelling sessions with local elders with funding from the Ontario Arts Council. Gerry and Sherry decided to pool their efforts. Twenty of his portraits were frame-ready by winter 2009. Some of her interviews have been transcribed and published in the Temagami Talker.

Angele Project. The goal was to collaborate with the aboriginal community and showcase the area's deep-veined history. In conjunction with Community Arts Ontario, the committee staged a heritage weekend in June 2009 called the Temagami Gathering. It drew 450 people to town and Bear Island. The agenda included walking tours of the historic village, storytelling performances, poetry readings, a vintage photo display and a performance by the revived Roots and Wings theatre group. An exhibit showcased the work of local artists, including Gerry Gooderham's elder portraits.

Conservation Groups Merge

Three backcountry conservation groups – Friends of Temagami (FOT), Nastawgan Network and Friends of Chiniguchi – merged in 2007 under the FOT banner. The benefits were a larger combined membership with a stronger voice. FOT ran advocacy campaigns and canoe route maintenance programs from 1995 until 2000. Since then its volunteer base has eroded. Nastawgan Network was born in 2006 with a goal of preserving nastawgan and their ancient features, such as trail blazes still visible on trees. At the time Nastawgan Network was active and well-organized, and closely followed the TIP process. Friends of Chiniguchi had an extensive knowledge of Temagami West.

Opportunity Knocks

A number of lake businesses changed hands over the years. Brian and Margaret Youngs moved to Temagami about 1997 and Silverwater Lodge was purchased by Mike and Heather Jeschonnek. By 2005 the proprietors were George and Linda Mathias. Their daughter Holly Charyna and her husband John, whose mother is a Friday, were the managers. They drew on their Anishnabai heritage in naming the resort Deepwater Lodge.

Paul Forsythe sold Temagami Lodge about 2005 to Brian and Lesley Hoffman of southwestern Ontario. Nelson and Brenda Leudke purchased Camp Can-Usa from Dave and Joyce Harding in 1996. Mike and Jeannie Foran relocated from British Columbia and purchased Ket-Chun-Eny Lodge from Rick and Pauline Lockhart in 2007. Pauline is a daughter of long-time owner Denis St. Germaine.

Wanapitei is owned and operated by 140 shareholders and administered by a 15-member board of directors. Wanapitei Canoe is the outfitting side, co-owned by Bruce Hodgins' son Shawn. For decades the camp has morphed into a wilderness university campus for a weekend every year, as Trent faculty and alumni meet to canoe and hike. Eclectic discussion topics range from environmental history to indigenous world views.

Camp Temagami, on the former Wigwasati site, was originally called Pays d'en Haut. Its name was changed to Temagami Clearwater in 1999 when Scott Northey bought out co-founder Gord Deeks. The name was later curtailed to Temagami, in deference to the official name of Cochrane's Camp. Wabun is owned by four shareholders. Russell Tuckerman, Martin Johnson and Dick Lewis III are the grandchildren of founding directors Bill Russell, Bill Roberts and Dick Lewis Sr., respectively. Walter "Nibby" Hinchman joined the shareholders at Herbert Stokinger's invitation in the 1970s.

Youth Camps Hosting Famous People

Actor William Hurt attended Wabun in 1965 when he was 15. He called it "the seminal summer of my life" in a 2002 Maclean's magazine interview. William won a best leading role Oscar for 1985's Kiss of the Spider Woman. Long-time Wabun parent David Rasche is an actor who has performed in sit-coms, in Broadway and off-Broadway plays, and many films including the recent Coen brothers' Burn After Reading. Michael Eisner, former CEO of the Walt Disney Company, spent nine summers at Keewaydin as a camper and staffman – the one in Vermont, that is.

No Waterway Park?

A revelation by Ontario sent the board reeling. The inclusion of Indian reserve land in the proposed Skyline Reserve waterway park had encountered technical difficulties. There

was no legal precedent for such an integration of federal and provincial jurisdictions.

A deputation before Town Council by directors Hilton Young and David Taylor during summer 2007 didn't mince words: "Federal, provincial and aboriginal representatives with dedicated professional staffs have spent six years on the issues. For a problem with the provincial waterway park to surface now seems almost impossible. We at the TLA are gravely concerned about the apparent challenges of establishing a waterway provincial park and believe that the municipality should demonstrate leadership and obtain professional counsel as to how to best deal with the protection of the Skyline Reserve by a careful review of all facts and language in the documents." President Vince Hovanec noted that all options for protecting the Skyline Reserve except the waterway park were ruled out by the land claim advisory committee in 2002.

The TLA wanted mayor and council to review the land claim settlement accord prior to ratification and pursue changes where needed, before reviewing it again with the lake community. Mayor Ike Laba replied, "We concur one hundred per cent that the Municipality must be able to comment and have advance knowledge similar to the publication of the elements that were the foundation that led to the agreement."

The 2007 AGM was all about the land claim settlement. Vicki Grant, assistant negotiator for the TFN-TAA, TFN Second Chief Joe Katt, TAA Chief John McKenzie and Dan Goodwin attended. Dan was Doug Carr's successor as Ontario's head negotiator for the Ministry of Aboriginal Affairs, ONAS's replacement.

Dan was a former MNR Temagami District supervisor. He presented the accord's key elements and said the waterway park was still under discussion, among other options, including a conservation easement. Legal certainty was required that Ontario could create a park on reserve land held by the federal government. Dan also stated that having the municipality review the agreement was not a legal option.

The TLA estimated potential new mainland and island lots resulting from the settlement could number 290 or more over time, in addition to the 200 lots that could be developed from existing private land under the OP. Houseboats and day use put further pressure on the lake, as did extended family cottage use and the conversion of cottages into residences by retirees.

Vince Hovanec was given another mandate as a director. He was joined by two newcomers whose relatives had played TLA roles. Islands 1155 and 1158's Chip Kittredge was a grandson of Chessman Kittredge Sr., while Island 318's Malcolm Wilson was a son-in-law of Art Avard. Malcolm bought property on Island 725 in 1988 and relocated to Island 318 in 1999.

TIP Pledges Canoe Route Upkeep

The MNR released the Temagami Integrated Plan (TIP) in August 2007 following extensive public consultation. The 20-year plan compromised on the issue of off-season motorized access in the Lady Evelyn-Smoothwater Wilderness Park. Restrictions were applied to the core of the park and existing uses were permitted to continue in the waterway parks. It was an attempt to mollify both wilderness purists and motorized recreationists. Earthroots had hoped TIP would address high violation rates at access-control points. The MOE, under pressure from Earthroots, had earlier ordered the MNR to better monitor and improve restrictions, such as ensuring closed roads stayed that way. TIP did not incorporate enforcement policies.

For Lake Temagami, the most significant change was the resumption by the MNR of canoe route and campsite maintenance outside provincial parks. The planning team's preliminary recommendation was a user fee for Crown land camping so that funding for a maintenance program would be long term, said Andrew Healy. He was employed by the North Bay District and worked on the plan.

MNR senior bureaucrats instead decided that maintenance would be funded by the government, which wasn't an option presented during the TIP process but seemed a win-win. Funding for three students to work on backcountry maintenance, brush portages, clean campsites and install privies was provided by Ontario, the TLA, youth camps and the municipality for the 2007 season. The MNR followed up by putting crews on the ground in 2008. They cleared 170 portage trails and 382 campsites, and an additional 179 trails and 369 campsites in 2009.

My, What Big Feet You Have!

Temagami has not been immune from sightings of the legendary Sasquatch. Fishers spotted a seven-foot tall creature in 1994. In August 2005 a father and son had an intense hour of "probable" contact with "numerous" Sasquatch squatting in an abandoned mine. Filmed evidence of a Sasquatch encounter in 2006 at a Temagami area hunt camp was posted on YouTube and showed an elderly eight-foot tall beast with a broken arm picking roots from a fallen tree.

You can't make this stuff up! The Lake Temagami Monster, known as Misshepeshu in Anishnabai legends, is a humpy serpent-like critter. It has more local cred, having been eye-witnessed by cottagers and Bear Islanders alike.

The MNR formed a maintenance partnership with environmental groups, businesses, camps and the local government. Its purpose was to bring individual efforts together as a collective, pooling resources and expertise. "The role of the partnership will be crucial in establishing a long-term maintenance program, able to carry on should government coffers run dry," Andrew said. "The maintenance program did not get enough funding in its third year and was cut in half. Volunteer groups were doing the maintenance on Lake Temagami campsites before and they will be doing it again without a formal program in place," he added. In 2010 the TLA called on cottagers to adopt their favourite campsites and give them the once-over.

Access Point Planning

The TLA had made numerous submissions to the municipality and the MNR about ongoing planning for the Mine and Manito landings. They were controlled by the local government through a land use permit issued by the MNR in the late 1990s. The TLA's planning principles were outlined in the *Times*: industrial access separate from public parking and docking for safety; capital and maintenance costs partially recovered through non-resident user fees; TLUP guidelines for the Skyline Reserve applied to minimize shoreline and lake bottom impact; and consideration given to surface run-off, contaminants, shoreline rehabilitation and noise.

Recommendations were approved by the municipality and the MNR in fall 2007. The multi-year plan was available for public viewing over the winter. It proposed a third landing south of the Mine Landing for commercial and industrial users where a propane storage and distribution depot would be built. Parking would increase from 445 to 968 spaces. More docks would be added and a floating breakwall would provide sheltered docking at the Manito Landing. A high fence facing the recycling/waste transfer area would minimize visual impact.

The industrial side of the Mine Landing. It's said that if you wait five minutes at the main docks, you will reunite with five people you haven't seen for five years. *Photo: Pam Sinclair*

The TLA building would be relocated inside the land use permit area adjacent to the access road with parking for a few cars. The TLA, however, was formulating its own plan to relocate the building to a non-controversial site outside the Skyline Reserve. An engineering study of the industrial component commenced in 2010, 90 per cent funded by FedNor.

Combating Break and Enters

In response to a Barbara Olmsted *Times* letter calling for a dialogue on property protection concerns, Peter Healy arranged a meeting between the OPP, the TFN, Bear Island Police, the police services board and residents. Investigations are often stymied because the two most frequently swiped items – liquor and gas – are quickly consumed, leaving no evidence. Generators destined for pawnshops are hot targets. Police representatives suggested recording serial numbers of high-value possessions to aid recovery.

Combating break-ins over a large, sparsely populated area during winter is a challenge for the OPP. It was acknowledged that the court system often seems too lenient when sentencing convicted felons. It was not all gloom and doom on the policing front. Crime Stoppers' anonymous tip line yielded dividends. The Bear Island Police and the Temagami OPP conducted joint patrols. Constable Tom Saville trained with his OPP counterparts to strengthen communication.

The Temagami OPP Detachment, a satellite of the Temiskaming detachment, enjoyed new, spacious quarters in fall 2008. It is the only detachment in the province to have an integrated boathouse and a spectacular lake view. The old building across Lakeshore Road had presented challenges, including maintenance of the heating, water and electrical systems. The new building features upgraded telephone and information technology systems. It has two holding cells, accessed by land or water cruiser. A host of dignitaries attended the grand opening including OPP Commissioner Julian Fantino.

The new OPP building features a boathouse and dock.
Photo: Pam Sinclair

Survivor: Temagami

Canadian outdoor reality shows struck an international chord during the 2000s. *Survivorman* was a hit on the Discovery Channel. A hardened outdoorsman embarked on one-week trips into remote deserts, jungles and forests. He took no food or shelter and videographed himself. The survivorman was Les Stroud, who took his first canoe trip on the Temagami River and later lived in Temagami North in the 1990s while running a wilderness survival centre.

The show's 2005 pilot was shot in the Temagami area. Les played a winter plane crash survivor who used the shell of the plane wreck as a shelter. After six days of eating nothing but a snared rabbit, he attempted to return to civilization. The production's helicopter crew intercepted him heading away from Highway 11 and town.

Survivorman returned in fall 2008. Les and a friend played lost ruffed grouse hunters off Rabbit Lake Road. They survived by using deadfall for shelter, eating a frog unsuccessfully used as snare bait, and drinking water from rain-soaked moss. The hunters were rescued when an OPP search and rescue helicopter spotted their smoke signal. They were brought to a staging area where Scott Pourier and Kim Jones, members of the Temagami Ambulance Service and Wabun's medical team, performed a health assessment. Les Stroud completed 25 extreme survival trips all over the world before calling it quits in 2008.

Mantracker, another Canadian reality show, debuted in 2006. The premise had two people taking off into remote bush with a map, compass and a head start. Terry Grant, a tracker on horseback, tried to locate them. An episode was filmed near Temagami in fall 2009 on a route mapped by Northland Paradise's Doug Adams. The cast and crew visited Temagami Public School and attended a barbecue hosted by the municipality.

CHAPTER 34

KISS A LAKE TROUT

A municipal consultant working on the Lot Creation and Development Study was conducting research one day in 2007 on the potential of area lakes. He discovered that back in 1995, the MNR had placed a moratorium on Crown land sales on all of Ontario's naturally-producing lake trout lakes. The MNR had never officially informed the general public. Once word got out, the MNR provided the *Times* with a front page article explaining the science behind it.

MNR Biologist Chuck McGrudden wrote that only about one per cent of Ontario's lakes contain lake trout. These lakes represent roughly 20 per cent of all lake trout lakes globally. Five per cent of the province's lake trout populations have become extinct and others are threatened.

These fish have slow growth and replacement rates, and require cold, deep water where high levels of dissolved oxygen and low levels of nutrients are found. They are vulnerable to the impact of human activity, including overfishing, acidification, climate change, habitat destruction and nutrient enrichment from lakeshore development – especially septic systems. Phosphorous from septic systems triggers excessive algae growth. The death and decomposition of algae consume deepwater oxygen, thereby affecting habitat.

The bottom line of too much development is the demise of the lake trout sport fishery.

The MNR began taking a precautionary approach in the early 1980s. Some lakes with no development were classified as good trout habitat and future development was banned. A second category, under which Lake Temagami fell, consisted of lakes with good trout habitat with existing development. Limited development would be permitted in this category as long as habitat degradation did not occur. A third class consisted of lakes with existing development where trout were extinct or a small component of the fishery. Populations were deemed unsustainable and not in need of protection.

The 1995 freeze on Crown land sales, reminiscent of the land cautions, carried implications for the municipal OP and its Lot Creation and Development Study (LC&DS). The ban extended to 17 lakes within the municipality, including Temagami, Cross, Kokoko, Gull, Obabika, Cassels, Net, Jumping Caribou and Rabbit. The municipality created the OP under the misinformed impression that it would kick in when Crown lots were sold by the province and became private property. Instead, Crown land on coldwater lakes under consideration in the LC&DS would have to be shelved for the immediate future from an inventory of potential lots. A long-term ramification was the loss of prospective taxpayers.

Mayor Ike Laba led a council delegation to Queen's Park to request an exemption to the freeze. Minister of Natural Resources Donna Cansfield wasn't swayed and advised that the MNR was willing to help the municipality create lots on warmwater lakes, following consultation with the TFN. The local government began focusing the LC&DS on warmwater lakes. The goal was to develop 50 waterfront lots on Marion, Brophy and Olive lakes in the Marten River area. Consultants later identified about 80 potential lots. The municipality cited benefits of service cost increases spread among more taxpayers and local business profits.

The province produced a "Lakeshore Capacity Assessment Handbook." It prohibits lot creation on existing private land on lake trout lakes until an assessment identifies development capacity. Proposed lot development on coldwater lakes is in abeyance for three years on a case-by-case basis while dissolved oxygen levels are monitored. After the study period, private lot development may be approved if conditions are acceptable.

Testing was carried out on Net and Cassels lakes from 2007 until '09 with good results. Testing began on Lake Temagami in 2009, to be completed in 2011. The TLA believes no LC&DS is justified on any lake trout lake unless MNR policy changes. The MNR took another step to protect lake trout lakes in 2008 by reducing the daily limit from three to two for sport fishing licences. The water quality

committee, headed by Director Ted Tichinoff, proposed its own testing program in 2010. "We should not be at the mercy of someone else's data and interpretation of that data," he said.

Staycation Trend Hurts Tourism

Many factors conspired against visitors to northern Ontario in 2008 and '09. High gas prices, a strong Canadian loonie, new passport requirements, poor weather and the worst recession since the Dirty Thirties took a deep toll. Americans, who represented about 35 per cent of cottage owners, were affected the most. However, it was business as usual at youth camps, seemingly impervious to economic downturns. Enrolments were down slightly in 2010 as the recession deepened, especially in the U.S. The Co-op grocery store was sucker-punched by 2008's rainy summer. It was one of the store's two slowest years and its deficit more than doubled. The venture had lost money nine of its 12 years in business.

The Co-op board predicted in the *Times* that another summer like 2008 would "simply put an end to this business." And wouldn't you know it, the weather in 2009 was even colder and soggier. Co-op members Don Johnson and his wife Lorie Hunter made a plea for financial assistance in April 2010, saying there were no reserve funds to draw on. The TLA picked up the ball, contributing $6,000 from its own reserve funds and urging all residents to contribute. Donations topped $24,000, leaving the Co-op board very grateful and looking forward to sunnier days ahead.

Commercial Success

The Temagami Co-op grocery store partnered with Loblaws under the freshmart banner in 2008. During the depths of the recession, a TV commercial aired across Canada showing the Loblaws chain owner's son loading two carts with groceries, one with the company's no-name brands and the other with brand name products. The message that shopping for generic products can be a whole lot cheaper originated in Temagami, when former freshmart manager Don Jeremiah stacked two comparable carts, photographed them and sent the pictures to Loblaws' head brass.

The Olympic torch stops in Temagami on its 102-day cross-country journey to Vancouver for the 2010 Winter Games. *Photo: Elaine Gunnell for the Temagami Times*

Sadly, Temagami's only grocery store closed in November 2010. A notice on the doors cited "severe financial stress."

Weathering Weather Whims

It wasn't just summer weather that caused trials and tribulation. Winter 2009-10 was peculiar. High winds precluded safe ice travel until nearly the end of January. The latest freeze-ups residents had ever witnessed occurred in 2002, 2006 and 2009.

The 2009 ice was the strangest; it began to give way in places in mid-March and vanished April 15, 2010. That date matches 1946, the earliest break-up Bear Island elders can recall, according to Ottertooth.com. At the end of the 19th century, explorer A.E. Barlow with the Geological Survey of Canada observed that break-up usually occurs around May 24. A month earlier is becoming the norm.

Difficult travel conditions in 2010 led the TFN to purchase an airboat for scheduled and emergency runs. The annual March Ling Fling was cancelled for the first time, due to unsafe ice. More snowmobiles and pick-ups went through the ice than normal with no lives lost. Property patroller Peter Healy just managed to finish his winter cottage checks before the ice went out. He jokingly contemplated renting a jet ski to complete a job always done by snowmobile. Water levels were so low that he feared prop damage if attempted by boat. Peter posted photos of islands surrounded by low water and high-water bathtub rings on the TLA website. One caption read: "Lower

Breaking ice on January 6, 2007, during a late freeze-up.
Photo: Gerry Gooderham

it has been surpassed just once in modern times and only slightly – in 1979 when Field took the brunt of a flooded watershed. Many docks were submerged that year.

Sent to the Chipper

A 10-year draft forest management plan was being chopped to bits in fall 2008. A vote on its approval saw the plan turned down 6 to 4 by the Local Citizens Committee (LCC). It was the first time any Ontario LCC rejected a draft plan. There were also seven requests for issue resolution, a process that can go all the way to the MNR's upper echelon. LCC dissenters included the TLA, Friends of Temagami (FOT), Earthroots and Northwatch. They believed the plan strongly favoured the logging industry at the expense of tourism and environmental interests. This ran counter to the 1997 Temagami Land Use Plan, according to TLA representative Jim Hasler. It stresses that the forest should support economic activity. There are no Temagami sawmills but there are several businesses catering to wilderness recreation.

water levels result in larger properties – don't tell MPAC."

In 2010 Ted Tichinoff assumed the task of helping the Nipissing French and Sturgeon River watershed advisory committee determine when Cross Lake's plug needs to be pulled or put back. He questioned an Ontario Power Generation (OPG) practice in the *Times*. It generally stores water in reservoirs through the autumn and draws the water down during the winter to produce a steady flow to power-generating stations. It becomes a problem when snowfall is below normal levels because there is insufficient melt to replenish the lake. Even though OPG closed the Cross Lake control dam earlier than normal, it was not soon enough.

Polar opposite conditions presided during break-up 2009. High water and winds combined to take many a dock with them. Break-up 1991 had resulted in similar strayed moorings. The spring 2009 level was so high

LCC members took issue with cuts to buffer zones around canoe routes and hiking trails. Road building, overestimation of wood demand in a recessive housing market, lack of a climate change strategy, the cutting of 160-year-old pine, and proposed cutting near Spirit Rock and an ecosystem east of Owain Lake were critiqued. Jim noted much-maligned clearcutting was still practised on fast-growing species such as poplar and jack pine. Maximum clearcut widths were set by the distance a moose will forage into an open area. No word on how hungry the moose has to be.

After nearly four months of deliberation, the MOE rejected four requests for an individual environmental assessment. The MOE's assessment decisions had become alarmingly predictable, according to an Earthroots spokesperson cited by Jim. More than 95 per cent conducted by the MOE since 1996 resulted in plan approvals.

In a nod to the past when fire towers were manned, the MNR started testing high-tech fire detection equipment atop towers in Temagami and Atikokan in 2008. Cameras and software can recognize smoke patterns and pinpoint the location of forest fires. Data from the tower is transmitted to a central computer. If a blaze is confirmed, an immediate response follows. The Caribou Mountain tower equipment detected two fall fires in 2008 and was still proving effective in 2010.

The province shifted forest management from the MNR to the Ministry of Northern Development and Mines in 2009. Gaye Smith was highly critical, saying natural resources

are interdependent and forest management is integral to the management of all natural resources. FOT wondered if public input into forestry plans would still be considered valuable and relevant.

Complex Population Issues

By 2009 the TFN had a reserve population of 216 and an off-reserve population of 461, as a result of the 1985 Indian Act amendments. The Bear Island population had evolved from nearly all status Indians to one approaching half status. That's because the old assimilative policies were changed but not abolished in 1985, stipulating that native women who married non-natives would regain or keep their status as would their children – but not their grandchildren.

TFN members were concerned about the long-term sustainability of their First Nation on n'Daki Menan, because so many children were non-status and non-TFN members. It was a concern shared by aboriginal communities across Canada. Between 1985 and 2007 the proportion of status Indians living on reserve or Crown land had declined from 71 to 56 per cent. While aboriginal populations in Canada are increasing overall, only 18 per cent of natives reinstated as status Indians live on reserve or Crown land.

The TFN population decline on Bear Island, divisions within the community and a series of TAA-TFN political crises spurred the TFN to attempt to wrest control of its membership away from Indian and Northern

Affairs Canada (INAC) in 2007. The 1985 amendments authorized Indian bands to take control of their membership lists upon the adoption of a membership code. About 40 per cent of First Nations had established codes by 2010.

The TFN held a vote to include all descendants of traditional families (the TAA membership) in the TFN, regardless of their designation as status or non-status under the Indian Act. From an outdated and error-ridden INAC registry listing 486 eligible voters, 142 voted and 116 were in favour. However, voter turnout was below INAC's mandatory threshold. Implementation of a membership code would have brought TFN memberships to more than 1600, given all TAA members the right to vote in TFN elections and the right to live in the planned Shiningwood Bay townsite. Failure of the code's passage meant the local TFN population would continue to decline and there could be more strife.

There is another implication. The federal government recognizes the TFN only in land claim talks. Ontario has indicated it may follow Ottawa's lead by concluding the agreement and ratification with the TFN, excluding the TAA, even though the TAA negotiated the 1993 draft accord upon which the current settlement is founded. The TFN was working on another membership code in 2010 in hopes of resolving some of these complex issues.

"The internal struggles continue and are so often perpetuated by the government who ultimately decided who was, and who was not, native," said Island 1182's Peter McMillen.

"As a result, you have First Nation "status" members, both on and off reserve, which is an issue. You have non-status TAA members, both on and off reserve, which is also an issue. It's quite an internal mess, unfortunately, and pits friends and family against each other…has for years and continues to do so."

In a landmark case, the British Columbia Court of Appeal ruled the Indian Act violates the Charter of Rights and Freedoms, and ordered the federal Parliament to amend it by April 6, 2010. Ottawa extended Indian status for one more generation. More than 45,000 Canadians are entitled to register. It is a bandaid solution and problems will recur. The rusty Indian Act needs a complete overhaul.

A Colossal Compass Kerfuffle

"Indian" was the name Christopher Columbus mistakenly assigned to the people he encountered when he arrived in what he believed to be the "Indies," the medieval name for Asia. Nowadays the word is considered derogatory by the national media. According to the Toronto Star, "Indian" should only be used in a legal context, such as categorizing Canada's one million aboriginals as Indian, Inuit or Métis. What should we call those clusters of white, pipe-shaped fungi popping from the ground after a steady rain?

A Northerner for President

Torontonian Rob Corcoran was handed the president's gavel in fall 2008. Rob was raised in the north. University studies led him to southern Ontario. A brain drain is an issue northern Ontario has long grappled with as youth pursue education and employment opportunities in the Golden Horseshoe. As an avid canoeist, Lake Temagami was the logical choice for a cottage. He and his wife Sherry purchased Island 135 in 1996. Rob participated on the TLA's bylaw and water quality committees, and was elected a director in 2006. By profession he is an engineer and has worked on projects ranging from deep sea construction technology to space station robotics.

Following a three-year freeze, new Municipal Property Assessment Corporation (MPAC) assessments were mailed in fall 2008, using a four-year phase-in period. The total municipal property assessment hike was 71 per cent with islands and waterfront taking the brunt, resulting in higher tax bills. Rob labelled MPAC "flawed" because the process should not place a surcharge on a property's location unless it imposes significant servicing costs.

Inflation Hits Cottage Country

In 1950 $2,500 could get you your own private island, cabin, dock, furnishings and probably a boat or two. In 1992 you would have forked over at least $100,000 for a similar package. In 2010 a vacant 2.13-acre lot on the South Arm was going for $189,000. In the good ole days (1931) island lessees merely had to put up a structure worth $500 within a couple of years.

Major infrastructure projects were underway or planned by the town. Most related to area-rated upgrades not shared by most island and waterfront owners. The TLA struck a municipal taxation and elections committee in 2009, co-chaired by directors Rob Corcoran and Boyd Matchett. They sought an explanation of infrastructure funding sources and the reinstatement of an advisory group to help with the budgeting process.

Lake Temagami accounted for 45 per cent of municipal tax revenues of $3 million in 2009, while waterfront homes on Cassels, Rabbit and other lakes raised the total to almost 58 per cent. The rest of the municipality and the pipeline contributed 42 per cent. In the first year of amalgamation, total municipal tax revenues were $1.5 million.

CHAPTER 35

THE TENETS DODGE A SNIPER

A backdoor attack launched by a town councillor against the municipality's fundamental planning gospel – the Tenets for Temagami – was making waves in 2009.

An Ontario interest purchased a 26-acre mining patent at Ferguson Point on the Northeast Arm. The buyer asked the MNR if a 66-foot Crown shoreline reserve fronting the property could also be bought. The MNR historically reserved some of these lakefront strips to preserve aesthetics and spawning locales. Early map scales were represented by chains with one chain equalling 66 feet. The MNR made these reserves available for sale to adjacent island property owners in the late 1980s. However, the MNR had never dealt with a mainland shoreline reserve purchase request and asked the municipality in January 2009 to comment, based on its planning policies.

The TLA made its views crystal clear prior to a council vote. The Skyline Reserve was designated a special management area in the 1997 MNR Temagami Land Use Plan, where no mainland development was permitted. The MNR's 1983 land use plan also called for islands-only development. Adoption of the tenet trilogy by the Township of Temagami – no mainland development, protection of the Skyline Reserve, no new road access – was a prerequisite to the TLA entering into amalgamation talks in 1994.

The tenets later formed the cornerstone for lake development in the 2004 Official Plan. A 1995 MNR policy bans Crown land sales on naturally-producing lake trout lakes. The Ferguson Point sale would violate the intent

Where does the water end and the Skyline Reserve begin?
South Arm photo: Michael Bloomfield

and purpose of these plans and policies. The board was prepared to take legal action to protect the tenets.

The Planning Advisory Committee (PAC) and staff prepared a 16-page letter for council, raising many of the same points as the TLA's submission. With two councillors absent, council voted 3-2 in March in favour of signing and sending the letter to the MNR opposing the sale of the shoreline reserve. Biff Lowery and Lorie Hunter voted in support of the letter while Barry Graham and Wendell Gustavson voted against it. Mayor Ike Laba broke the tie. MNR agreed with the letter and refused the purchase request.

Barry Graham was the listing agent for the Ferguson Point property and a second Ferguson mining patent on some 40 acres of the North Arm's Ferguson Mountain. These mainland properties would be a realtor's dream if the option of buying the shoreline reserves was available, accompanied by a residential zoning bylaw amendment. An alleged conflict of interest was identified by the TLA but not declared by Barry.

The brouhaha had its origins in 1887 when Mattawa prospector Peter Ferguson secured mining patents on 16-acre Ferguson Island 6, nearby Ferguson Point and Ferguson Mountain. At the time, Ontario had no land tenure policies specifically for the lake.

The Ferguson family subsequently let Island 6 go by the wayside for cottage development. Three elderly southern belles from Brownsville, Texas, visited their inherited holdings in the mid-1980s to sate

their curiosity. The only activity they might have seen is on a campsite occupying part of the Ferguson Point shoreline reserve. They had no intention of staying or selling. Their descendents thought differently and decided to unload the two properties.

With the turnover of municipal councillors over time, awareness of concepts such as the tenets or the historic management of the lake can fade. The board believes the TLA must remain vigilant in keeping the tenets from getting lost in the shuffle of successive election cycles.

A practical solution for averting council decisions that ran counter to established plans and policies was proposed by the board in fall 2009. It asked the municipality to formally request Ministry of Municipal Affairs and Housing (MMAH) approval to permit councillors' remote participation in meetings via teleconferencing. If this convenience was available, perhaps more seasonal lake residents would run for council.

The province was on the verge of introducing remote council meeting participation with the passage of 2006 Municipal Act amendments but reneged. It left "cottagers out in the cold at the same time as they set the stage for massive tax increases for most cottagers in communities with a mix of waterfront and urban properties," President Rob Corcoran wrote.

Council agreed to the TLA's request and Ike Laba asked the MMAH to revisit the issue of remote attendance. He cautioned that regulations would have to ensure meetings didn't become fully remote and that in camera sessions stayed confidential. Minister Jim Watson denied Temagami's request.

The OP under the Scope

A provincially-mandated OP and zoning bylaw review commenced in 2009. Amendments must be approved by the MMAH. More than 25 issues had earlier been identified by residents, PAC and council. Another 20 arose during the review. The municipality had drafted 27 amendments by summer 2010 and hoped to call the review a wrap by year's close.

A citizens' advisory committee was established to provide input to PAC, but it would not participate in the final decision-making. Hilton Young, chair of the TLA's planning committee, was its representative. The Lake Temagami Group (LTG), which had earlier appealed aspects of the OP and zoning bylaw to the OMB, was represented by David Kittredge.

PAC lake representatives included Lorie Hunter, Claire Rannie and Dick Grout. Dick died in June 2010 following a short battle with cancer. His dedication to the TLA spanned four decades. The vacancy was filled by PAC veteran Jim Hasler. PAC's chair, replacing Biff Lowery, was Paul Middleton, a permanent resident of Temagami since 2007, with a 30-year history of vacationing there.

As part of the OP review, the TLA wanted permit and inspection processes streamlined for efficiency, and fees adjusted or eliminated, based on the size and complexity of the project. In light of council's near violation

of the tenets, no amendments should be contemplated by PAC or council that would promote development contrary to tenet-guided OP policies. Any change would be considered a breach of faith.

The TLA planning committee believed there was no justification for sub-neighbourhoods with policies unique to each in the Lake Temagami Neighbourhood, as the LTG was once again requesting. The committee again supported whole lake planning. The TLA deferred to a municipal consultant who agreed that sub-neighbourhoods could result in a concentration of development in already heavily developed parts of the lake. PAC recommended Town Council not modify the OP over this issue.

PAC and the consultant presented a revised draft OP and zoning bylaw to council in late winter 2010. Council requested a few adjustments. The plan was then re-examined by council before being released for public consultation in summer 2010. The next step would be consultation with the TFN, the citizens' advisory committee and again, the public.

PAC recommended a modification to site plan controls so they would be applied to waterfront and island lots while exempting buildings with little or no visual impact. Some town residents had wanted site plan controls abolished entirely, believing they discouraged development due to a complicated application process and a $320 fee.

PAC suggested Northeast Arm islands close to town, currently in the Urban

Neighbourhood, should be integrated into the Lake Temagami Neighbourhood. It was never an intention to connect any islanders to municipal water and sewerage systems. Rezoning the two controversial Ferguson mining properties to residential was rejected by PAC.

councillors to pursue mainland development and the potential restructuring of PAC – making it "difficult not to place the original concept of harmonious amalgamation under strain."

The Temagami waterfront and docks in 2010. *Photo: Pam Sinclair*

Council passed a resolution in spring 2010 to strike a committee to explore changes to PAC's membership composition. The lake is assigned four of eight seats. This formula was one of the key conditions the TLA and LaTemPRA insisted on before amalgamation could proceed. Rob Corcoran cited three factors – the ballooning proportion of municipal taxes paid by islanders, recent attempts by two

Staying Power

Hilton Young "retired" as a director in 2009 when his latest term ended. He still maintains a presence on several committees. Bill Gooderham, Bruce Hodgins, Jim Flosdorf and Jim Hasler are Hilton's nearest contemporaries in terms of years of altruistic volunteer service.

Bill's tenure as treasurer spanned four decades. He died in 2001, followed by his wife Nancey on December 25, 2010. The treasurer's role has been assumed by elected directors rather than an appointed official since 1998, starting with Al Hake, then Barry Smith, Grant McMillen, Cameron Crawford, Vince Hovanec, David Taylor and David McFarlane through 2010.

Bruce Hodgins was elected to the board in 1974. His final year as a director was 2003. He retired in 1996 and is a Trent University professor emeritus. Jim Flosdorf served multiple terms on the board of directors. He left the lake after 41 years at Island 588. "The Temagami of 2002 was no longer the Temagami I knew, and I just decided it was time to move on to other things. Of course, I am also no longer the person I was in 1961; time catches up," he mused.

The Sopers, Island 672 south enders, purchased Jim's island to accommodate an expanding brood. A professor emeritus of the Sage Colleges, he has made a name for himself with panoramic compositions. They are the result of blending up to 24 photographic frames into one visual statement. Jim's work is featured at a number of American galleries.

Fishing in the Dark

I like to fish these waters at dusk
As the light fades in the north
To a salmon pink
While deeper blue spreads
from east to zenith
And stars emerge
point by point;
my line runs out to the bottom
in search of silvereyed feeders
sliding in lazy schools
at the shoal's edge
to sniff the bait,
circle, return taste —
these shadows cruising the bottom
bump the line
tease it
too shrewd to get hooked
and played to the top
to lie flopping in my net
of words
Jim Flosdorf, circa 1980

Jim Hasler's relationship with the TLA commenced in 1991. He has served four terms as a director and displays longevity on the Local Citizens Committee on forestry, as a TLA representative on PAC and the earlier planning board, and as TRSI chair.

CHAPTER 36

FLAWED TFN ELECTIONS AND OTHER MATTERS

The TFN holds elections for chief and council every three years. Between June 2008 and July 2009 four elections were held. The results of all four were disputed. It all started with a tie for chief. Gary Potts triumphed over two-term incumbent Chief Alex Paul upon a coin flip by the electoral officer. Gary's nephew Peter McKenzie clinched the second chief's seat by one vote.

Due to the close results, several election appeals were filed, most aimed at the electoral officer's withholding of ballots to potentially eligible TFN members and permitting potentially non-eligible members to vote. The tribal constitution, co-authored by Gary in 1978, requires voters be residents of n'Daki Menan. The officer didn't forward the appeals to an appointed council of elders for a decision, as the constitution directs. Instead, she rejected them. At the time, there was no elders' council in place to review and rule on the appeals.

A petition requesting a community assembly, purportedly signed by voting and non-voting members, was presented to chief and council in July. Council rejected the petition, citing non-accordance with the constitution, but the community ignored council and assembled twice in late summer. Two resolutions were passed by simple majority calling for a new election and a constitutional amendment to remove some of the criteria for voter eligibility.

Councillor Roxane Ayotte, Gary's niece, quit council and ran for chief in a September election. Roxane and John McKenzie were elected chief and second chief. However, she was the sole member of the June-elected council to run. The September-elected council resolved to hold a third election to try and reunite a deeply divided community. It wanted both councils on the ballot to strengthen the next council's mandate.

Gary Potts and council referred the June election to the Federal Court of Canada for an impartial judicial review. Some TFN members interpreted his action as seeking assistance from a colonial institution symbolic of the repressive forces shaping the community's past. He defended the move, saying that finding unbiased community members to address the issues and arrive at an internal solution would be nearly impossible. It was the best way to clear the air and move forward, he added. Protesters briefly encamped outside the administrative office.

A third assembly approved the September-elected council's resolution for a third election. The same slate with one exception ran in an October election. Roxane won again and council entered the TFN office to take control under a police and elder presence. The banks and Indian and Northern Affairs Canada (INAC) had been advised to await the judicial review before making any changes. For a time Gary worked out of the band office while Roxane worked nearby in council chambers.

TFN Chief Roxane Ayotte at the 2010 TLA annual meeting.
Photo: Pam Sinclair

Gary Potts and council were charged in a February petition with exceeding their powers of office and conflict of interest. They had gone the court route without obtaining the support of the community through an assembly vote, seen as a constitutional violation. The decision to go to court was deemed a conflict of interest, because it was said to be designed to protect their interests in remaining chief and council. Gary and council countered that the petition did not have enough signatures to meet constitutional requirements and alleged some of the signatories were non-voting members.

A March assembly removed Gary et al's authority but he refused to leave office, saying the impeachment meeting was not within the constitutional framework. Police monitored as supporters of both camps crowded the TFN office when Roxane Ayotte and her council arrived once again to take power. Roxane supporters organized a multi-day sit-in.

In the spring INAC listed the TFN leadership as indeterminate pending an internal or external resolution. A Federal Court of Canada judge urged mediation. Two attempts failed. The court finally nullified the original June election results, ruling them flawed due to the absence of a council of elders to deal with appeals.

A new election was ordered. The judge also ruled that a council of elders be appointed at least one week prior to the election being called. The TFN was ordered to compensate Roxane's group for legal costs to the same extent provided to Gary Potts' group. Had Gary not asked for judicial intervention, the infighting might have dragged on indefinitely. An internal solution seemed unlikely as the parties drifted further apart and common goals were forgotten.

Roxane won a landslide victory over Gary in the fourth election held in July. Voter turn-out was at an all-time high. He sought the restorative and reflective powers of a wilderness trip. A three-member council of elders received two election appeals over signage and ballot marking. The appeals put the election results in question and the community anxiously awaited a decision. They were dismissed in December, on the grounds that neither issue had affected the results. Roxane and John McKenzie officially adopted the titles of chief and second chief when they took office in January 2010, ending a year and a half of political instability.

Gary and council had suspended joint activities with the TAA council in August 2009, thereby halting settlement negotiations. Chief Roxane Ayotte and TAA Chief John McKenzie quickly sent letters to Ontario requesting resumption. Preliminary talks to return to the table were held when TFN-TAA negotiators met with their provincial counterparts in July 2010.

"After 18 months of a trying political dispute, we are now moving forward and we are very proud of that," Roxane told 2010 AGM attendees. She said the land claim accord is 95 per cent complete and an economic development corporation has been established. The tribal constitution – "kind of what got us in trouble in the first place" – is being updated, she added.

The TFN was negotiating with Vancouver-based Northgate Minerals in summer 2010. The company is reopening the historic Young-Davidson mining property west of Matachewan in 2012. It contains four million ounces of gold and counting, as exploration continues. A claim block falls within the northern edge of n'Daki Menan. An impact-benefit agreement between the company and the TFN is mandated by the Ministry of Northern Development, Mines and Forestry.

Medical Services Upgraded

After Temagami was awarded a family health team in the mid-2000s, a larger medical centre was needed for expanded services and staff. A provincially-funded $2.3-million clinic opened in fall 2009. Dr. Stephen Goddard, Temagami's physician since 1995, was joined by a nurse practitioner, two receptionists, a family health team coordinator and in 2010 by a registered nurse. Extra examination rooms were constructed for use by allied health care workers. Telemedicine was introduced allowing patients to be seen by remote specialists. The clinic also boasts a small lab, a procedures room, a boardroom and a counselling area.

The facility replaced the Dr. Vintera Medical Clinic built in the 1980s. That centre was so small that visiting health care professionals had to schedule appointments when the physician was out. Dr. Vintera originally occupied the basement of the Spooner building in 1972 with no windows, ventilation or soundproofing. Like his predecessor Dr. Dunning of Cobalt, he made house calls, as did Dr. McGowan, a 1930s village-residing physician.

Recruiting Woes

TAFIP joined the United Walleye Club of Ontario in 2009. Founded in 2001, the club's goal is to maximize walleye fishing potential. It is affiliated with 23 partners, nine with hatcheries. It was anticipated that linking with the club would allow TAFIP to tap into the latest scientific hatching techniques and new funding sources. TAFIP was hoping to lure some younger help, the median age of volunteers being 60. TAFIP's recruiting concerns were reflective of Temagami's permanent resident population. As of 2008, 60 per cent were 55 and older.

TAFIP Vice President Claude Landry and team check nets for spring 2009 egg collection. *Photo: Doug Adams for the Temagami Times*

Like TAFIP, the TLA wasn't having much success recruiting a younger demographic. Boyd Matchett had turned down a number of board nominations following his retirement as a CEO with Cara Operations Limited, a restaurant chain and airline catering conglomerate. The time was right for Boyd in 2009. On the other side of the scale, Andrew Healy, an environmental planner with the Ministry of Transportation, was a Generation Y member when he joined the directors' team that year.

Andrew became TLA president in September 2010, the youngest ever to serve at the helm. Newcomers Peter Calverley and Gerald Kluwak joined Chip Kittredge who was commencing his second consecutive term in 2010. Female DNA has not been detected anywhere near the boardroom since 2005.

The board began honouring members who reach the grand age of 100 in 2010 with a complimentary membership. Island 731's Catherine Morrison was the first honouree. She joined the century club in 2009. Catherine may have lots of company in the decades to come.

Camp Wabun beach, a spectacular setting for the August 2009 wedding of Andrew Healy and Tawnia Robinson, who first met as staff members at Wabun. From left, Ross Burns, Laura Healy, Andrew, Tawnia, Trisha and Peter Healy. *Photo: Sarah Flotten*

Catherine Morrison with her great-grandson Ryder Morrison in 2009.
Photo: Gerry Gooderham

Finalé

More than a century ago, Temagami's deep clear waters drew those yearning for wilderness and adventure. Some strove to emulate the ways of the land's Anishnabai stewards. The thousands of cottagers who now flock to the lake seek a place less transformed by mankind's activities, where water remains pure and wildlife inhabits undisturbed forest. For 80 years, the TLA has waged a valiant battle to preserve the mainland shoreline in an unaltered state and to protect the islands against over-development. Should those from the past be watching from above, may they be smiling.

Appendix A

Acronyms and Abbreviations

Annual General Meeting (**AGM**), Agreement In Principle (**AIP**), Association of Youth Camps on the Temagami Lakes (**AYCTL**), Cassels and Adjoining Lakes Association (**CALA**), Committee on Land Use and Environment (**CLUE**), Comprehensive Planning Council (**CPC**), Committee for the Preservation of the Temagami Wilderness Experience (**CPTWE**), Friends of Temagami (**FOT**), Hudson's Bay Company (**HBC**), Indian and Northern Affairs Canada (**INAC**), Lake Temagami Permanent Residents Association (**LaTemPRA**), Lot Creation and Development Study (**LC&DS**), Lake Temagami Group (**LTG**), Municipal Advisory Group (**MAG**), Ma-Kominising Anishnawbeg (**MKA**), Ministry of Municipal Affairs and Housing (**MMAH**), Ministry of Northern Development and Mines (**MNDM**), Ministry of Natural Resources (**MNR**), Ministry of the Environment (**MOE**), Municipal Property Assessment Corporation (**MPAC**), Minister of Provincial Parliament (**MPP**), Minister of federal Parliament (**MP**), Ministry of Transportation (**MTO**), New Democratic Party (**NDP**), Ontario Federation of Anglers and Hunters (**OFAH**), Ontario Municipal Board (**OMB**), Ontario Native Affairs Secretariat (**ONAS**), Ontario Northland Boat Lines (**ONBL**), Ontario Northland Railway (**ONR**), Official Plan (**OP**), Ontario Provincial Police (**OPP**), Planning Advisory Committee (**PAC**), Public Advisory Committee (**PAC**) on forestry, later the Local Citizens Committee (**LCC**), Save Maple Mountain Committee (**SMMC**), Southwest Arm Neighbourhood Association (**SWANA**), Teme-Augama Anishnabai (**TAA**), Temagami Advisory Council (**TAC**), Temagami Area Fish Involvement Program (**TAFIP**), Temagami Community Foundation (**TCF**), Temagami Tourist Operators Association (**TemTOA**), Temagami First Nation (**TFN**), Temagami Integrated Plan (**TIP**), Temagami Land Use Plan (**TLUP**), Temiskaming and Northern Ontario Railway (**TNOR**), Temagami Region Studies Institute (**TRSI**), Temagami Stewardship Council (**TSC**), Temagami Wilderness Society (**TWS**), West Nipissing Access Group (**WNAG**), Wendaban Stewardship Authority (**WSA**).

Appendix B

Questions and Answers

In 1992's *Temagami Lakes Association: An Historical Perspective*, I mused about what the future might hold, depending on several factors I raised in the form of questions. Here they are once again, this time with the best answers I could come up with.

What direction will negotiations with the TAA take and how will the lifting of the land cautions change the face of Lake Temagami?

The Teme-Augama Anishnabai (TAA) reached an Agreement In Principle with Ontario in 1993. It ratified the draft accord but the Temagami First Nation (TFN) turned it down twice. The TFN then severed ties with the TAA. The pair made up in the late 1990s and negotiations got back on track. The TFN was now a joint negotiator. Ottawa participated because of the potential for settlement lands being designated a federal Indian reserve.

A draft agreement was reached in the early 2000s and included a Shiningwood Bay townsite, development lands and monetary compensation. Delays, including changes to both Ontario and Anishnabai negotiating teams, the accord's translation into a legally-binding contract, legal jurisdictional issues with the Indian reserve portion of a provincial waterway park and internal TFN conflicts, set ratification way behind schedule. Negotiations were suspended in 2008 but were expected to resume by 2011.

The land cautions were judicially lifted in 1995. Areas targetted for mining were soon thrown open to claim stakers. The Skyline Reserve was withdrawn from staking at the 11th hour due to media-maligned TLA lobbying. Under strict rules, the reserve was later opened to a slow stream of prospectors. The MNR banned Crown land sales on all Ontario's naturally-producing lake trout lakes in 1995. It essentially replaced the land cautions on Lake Temagami.

Will there be a stampede of city dwellers clamouring for their own Temagami experience on islands and mainland, possibly no longer managed by the Crown?

That remains to be seen. It is estimated that 300 or more lots could be created as a result of the land claim settlement. It may be an economic driver for the Municipality of Temagami, though it is still unknown how much job spin-off will result. Meanwhile, the town relies on lake dwellers' tax dollars to get by.

Will the Township of Temagami swallow the rest of the lake, or will it remain a distinct and separate entity in a spirit of cooperation with the township?

The lake and mainland areas amalgamated with the township in 1997 to become the

Municipality of Temagami, after weighing the pros and cons at length.

Will the cross-border tightening up of acid rain emission allowances ensure the continued purity of Lake Temagami and healthy fish populations, or will inadequate sewage disposal on many islands loom as just as great a threat?

The focus on acid rain pollution and other environmental issues has moved on to global warming, also known as climate change, since some parts of the globe may actually get colder, while most get warmer. Climate change is an enormous man-made calamity whose implications are still not fully comprehended. Many islanders have reduced their carbon footprint by purchasing four-stroke outboard motors, taking the canoe or kayak on short excursions, recycling, composting, using energy-efficient appliances and phosphate-free soap products, replacing old steel septic tanks, containing greywater, monitoring electricity use, etc.

Will houseboats continue to multiply, possibly at the expense of property owners' privacy?

They did but repeat customers tend to become sensitized to cottaging and camping issues.

Will the availability of telephones eventually spell an end to the need for the headquarters building and its radio communications service?

No. Though the number of calls is down from the 1980s and 1990s, the service still has core users who generously support it. It also plays a vital role in fire suppression and medical emergency response. A myriad of other member services originates at the building.

Will logging make a comeback in the Temagami forest? If so, will it be undertaken in a scientific and environmentally-sensitive manner?

A logging moratorium was in effect until the completion of the MNR's comprehensive plan. The result was the 1997 Temagami Land Use Plan (TLUP), protecting roughly 50 per cent of the area's old-growth forests. For conservationists, it fell short due to the global rarity of ancient forests.

Jim Hasler has represented the TLA on an MNR citizens' committee on forestry since 1996 and has written extensively in the *Times* of the choppiness of forest management plans. Challenges by conservation organizations have been won and lost. They won a major legal challenge in 1997 against the MNR, compelling it to rewrite management plans for Temagami and Elk Lake to bring them into compliance with provincial legislation.

Conservation groups and the TLA objected to clearcut sizes in a five-year plan, leading to the removal of the largest. The 2009-19 draft plan was rejected by a majority of forestry committee members attending a meeting. They claimed it ran counter to the intent of the TLUP, by favouring the logging industry at the expense of tourism and environmental protection.

Forestry companies did not harvest their full allocations during the 2000s. Lumber demand hovered near an historic low, due to international competition against the strength of the loonie and the crash of the U.S. housing market. Englehart's Grant Forest Products, a leading producer of oriented strand board for the housing industry, went under bankruptcy protection in 2009. Its assets were sold in 2010 to Georgia-Pacific of Atlanta, ending decades of local ownership.

And the big one – When will the TLA elect its first female president?

If you have read this book you know the answer.

Appendix C

First 10 Lake Temagami Leases

Ontario began allowing campers to lease islands on January 17, 1906. Most did not stay to build a $300 structure as required and forfeited their properties.

1. Very first lease honours go to Braeside, Ontario, lumber baron J.A. Gillies who leased Island 664 on the South Arm. Dr. George Follansbee, a Cleveland colleague of Robert Newcomb, leased the island in 1918. It was later sold to John Bricker, an unsuccessful 1944 Republican vice presidential nominee and an Ohio senator. The main cabin burned down about 1950. Dr. Ross Flett of Toronto bought the island. He had experienced Temagami in 1928 as an Algonquin Park camp counsellor, having found central Ontario overcrowded. He returned in 1949 and stayed at Chimo. Dr. Norm Flett acquired the island in the early 1970s, following his father's death.

2. E.P. Lord leased Island 496 on the Southwest Arm. His origins or length of stay are unknown. Harry Schumacher, a Buffalo real estate developer, leased the island in 1939. His cabins were designed by a Buffalo architect. Harry died on the island in the mid-1940s. He may have still been

Association president at the time. Dr. Sen. Joseph Sullivan purchased the island and became an Association executive member through the 1950s and 1960s. He sold to Richard and Dawna Armstrong in 1983.

3. Frank Newton, a printer, publisher and occasional prospector, built a small cabin on Island 977 west of Bear Island in 1905. Ohio's Frank Anderson headed north in 1910, seeking a vacation home. Frank Newton had died and his widow was ready to sign over the lease. The isle passed through Frank Anderson's daughter Marie Nibecker to her daughter Marilyn Corl Brinkman. The Newton cabin stands today with an addition. A study in contrasts is a modern cathedral-ceilinged cottage built in the mid-1980s.

4. A.S. Potter leased Island 691 southwest of Temagami Island. Who he was or where he came from is anyone's guess. The island was leased in 1931 by Professor Thomas Mylrea and his wife Cornelia of Delaware. They built a cottage which stands today. The dates of long-ago visitors are recorded on the walls. The next occupant was Ohio widow Elizabeth Cochran. She sold the island to Frank Lambert of Welland, Ontario, in 1969. Frank later bought

on nearby Island 725 and sold Island 691 to Dr. John Szasz of Woodstock, Ontario, in 1974. The Szasz family still owns the island.

5. Island 315, west of High Rock Island, was first leased by S. Ranger who left without a trace. H.M. Cochrane had the island briefly from 1920. University of Toronto Professor A.F. Coventry acquired it in 1924. The professor was a backer of Ted Guppy's Temagami Navigation Company. A.F. built a cabin, docks and a birchbark canoe. He had a dumb waiter that went into the ground as his refrigerator. An eccentric chap, he invited Philip Greey, a future TLA president, over for tea when he was about 10 years old. He greeted his guest stark naked. A.F. died in 1958 and left the island to the Crown. The Greeys purchased part of it. Lorraine Greey now owns the property.

6. H.A. Riddell leased Island 1192 on the North Arm. A small windswept isle, it was close to Sharp Rock Inlet and several canoe routes. It was also near the Lady Evelyn Hotel on Deer Island, which burned down in 1912. Island 1192 didn't see any more takers until Lockwood "Larry" Oliver Jr. patented it in 1952. He is a nephew of Brooks Shepard Sr. Larry died in 2008 and the island is now owned by his children Rexford Oliver and Lynn Oliver Garvin.

7. The first to lease Island 741 southwest of Temagami Island was B.A. Gage, possibly an associate of Robert Newcomb because it ended up in Newcomb hands. Robert built a cabin with the unusual feature of a trap door, located behind the fireplace. In 1945 three Pennsylvania couples bought the island, having earlier stayed at Chimo. Two of the couples subsequently turned over their interest to Arthur and Ruth Mayer. Following Arthur's death in 1970, Ruth sold the isle to Michael and Ellen McGrew of New York state who still own it.

8. Frank McGowan was the original lessee of Island 772 southwest of High Rock Island. It was briefly leased by Dr. Ernest Voorhis in 1920. He was a public servant and author who trekked Temagami country in the 1890s with poet Archibald Lampman. Ernest published scholarly papers about early forts and trading posts. The island was rediscovered in 1921 by brothers Steve and Philip Greey, and Alexander Gooderham. Its fate and that of Island 775 were settled by a coin flip, won by Alex who chose Island 772. Alex decided not to build and joined his brother Gordon S. Gooderham at Chimo Island. H.M. Dennehy, an insurance broker, took over the Island 772 lease in 1926. It was later acquired by the Greeys who are the current owners.

9. Frank Cobb leased Island 971 west of Bear Island. He was Robert Newcomb's law partner and a member of the Canadian Camp Fire Club of Cleveland. He kept the isle until at least the 1920s. George Turner of Bear Island bought it in the early 1950s and built an existing structure. He died before he could spend much time there. George's widow Angela sold the island to Doug and Carol Simmons in 1954. They learned about the lake on their 1953 Bermuda honeymoon. They met Brad Hall who also happened to be honeymooning. Brad invited the couple to spend two weeks the following summer at his Island 1067 cottage. They made the two-day trip from Indianapolis, Indiana. Their son Jeffrey Simmons is the current Island 971 owner.

10. Ben Bole leased Island 680 southwest of Temagami Island. He was a partner in Robert Newcomb's law practice and a member of the campfire club. Ben likely acquired the island for the Newcombs because only one lease was permitted per person. The first structure they built was a bathhouse, since converted to a sauna. Robert put up a main lodge with a loft entered through a secret trap door in the ceiling, identical to the one he built on Island 741. During the 1920s the camp was occupied by the Roscoe C. Skiles family, another Newcomb peer.

Robert's brother Adrian acquired the isle when he married. Following Adrian's death in the early 1950s, William G. Pace Jr. bought it from Adrian's widow Helen. The late Ed Loving and his wife Joan purchased the island from the Paces in the early 1970s.

Appendix D

TLA Presidents

1931-34	Robert Newcomb	1983-84	Bill Allen
1934-37	Frank Todd	1984-86	Ted Underwood
1937-40	George Cecil Ames	1986-87	Graeme Thompson
1940-44	Harry Schumacher	1987-89	Tom Romans
1944-late 40s	Harold Shannon	1989-92	Dick Grout
1950-61	Charles Earl Rodgers	1992-95	Hilton Young
1961-71	Dewey Derosier	1995-97	Sandy Navaro
1971-73	Ron Johnstone	1997-98	Art Avard
1973-74	Philip Greey	1998-99	Hilton Young
1974-75	Bill Allen	1999-2001	Al Hake
1975-77	Gordon Lak	2001-02	Barry Smith
1977-79	Tim Gooderham	2002-04	Ray Delarosbel
1979-81	Bruce Hodgins	2004-06	Brad Hall
1981-83	Jack Glenn	2006-08	Vince Hovanec
		2008-10	Rob Corcoran
		2010-	Andrew Healy

Appendix E

TLA Members Of The Year

1973	Ron Johnstone	1989	Tim Gooderham
1974	Bill Gooderham	1990	Fred Reimers
1975	Doug Buck and Jim Flosdorf	1991	Ralph McMillen
1976	Doreen Lak	1992	Sue Gooderham
1977	Gordon Lak	1993	Sandy Navaro
1978	Don and Annie Fenn	1994	Graeme Thompson
1979	Norm Flett and Ed Searle	1995	David Taylor
1981	Annie Fenn	2003	Robin Campbell, Lorie Jocius
1982	Ev Choat	2004	Gaye Smith
1983	Jeanne Underwood	2005	Duff Shaw
1984	Pamela (Glenn) Sinclair	2006	Hilton Young
1985	Ernie and Helen Taylor, David and Metta Gerstner, Jean Wilson	2007	Carol Lowery
		2008	Bobby Morrison, Barbara Olmsted, Heather Windrem
1986	Bob Richmond		
1987	Jim Dow	2009	Steve Drake
1988	Brian Back	2010	Jim Dow

The missing years are not symbolic of a dearth of worthy nominees, rather a plethora of meritorious members each deserving recognition.

Appendix F

TLA Building Staff

1979 Tom Dymond, Norman Thompson, Pam Glenn, Sue Smellie and Robert Gardner

1980 Tom Dymond, Pam Glenn, Becky Boake

1981 Pam Glenn, Becky Boake, Jane Gooderham

1982 Pam Glenn, Jane Gooderham, Sue Gooderham, handyman Bob Bangay

1983 Pam Glenn, Christine Brown, Bob Bangay

1984 Pam Glenn, Christine Brown, Bob Bangay

1985 Pam Glenn, Kelly Harding

1986 Pam Glenn, Fabian McKenzie Grant, Shana Fehrman

1987 Gord McCreary, Lee Horner

1988 Stephane Larouche, Tom Sullivan

1989 Derek Chum, Hali Denis

1990 Steve Scheleny, Nicole Mathieu

1991 Steve Scheleny, Brent Carbno

1992 Steve Scheleny, Brent Carbno

1993 Steve Scheleny, Dave Loran

1994 Doug Thompson, Steve Hope

1995 Steve Hope, Steve Wicary

1996 Steve Wicary, Doug Thompson

1997 Steve Wicary, Jennifer Wilson

1998 Doug Thompson, Laura Healy

1999 Laura Healy, Doryan Milner

2000 Laura Healy, Megan Hames

2001 Jordan Jocius, Krista Gooderham

2002 Krista Gooderham, Tom Snyder

2003 Tom Snyder, Katie Butler

2004 Lorne Brooker, Lyndsy Manderstrom

2005 Lyndsy Manderstrom, Michael MacNeil

2006 Lyndsy Manderstrom, Sarah MacLean

2007 Johanna Kilbridge, Catherine Lowery

2008 Catherine Lowery

2009 Catherine Lowery, Heather Robinson

2010 Catherine Lowery, Jessica Wert

Appendix G

Acknowledgements

Human Helpers

Christopher Allan, Nancy P. Allen, Gloria Seaman Allen, Jack Ames, Jane Anderson, Richard Armstrong, Jeff Ball, Brian Back, Audrey Bankley, Tony Bastien, Helen Bates, Donna Battersby, Denis Benson, Al Beust, Judy Beust, Michael Bloomfield, Shelley Costa Bloomfield, Pat Bonnell, William Bonsor, Margaret Brady, Marilyn Corl Brinkman, Bob Brown, David Burgess, Jack Burke, Linda Cain, Robin Campbell, Dan Carpenter Sr., Dan Carpenter Jr., Ev Choat, Elizabeth Cleminshaw, James Cleminshaw, Carol Cochrane, Louise Cochrane, Caryn Colman, Virginia Coltrin, Alf Cook, Catherine Cook, Don Cooke, Earl Cooke, Rick Cooke, Rob Corcoran, Bill Corl, Don Crawford, Susie Crofut, Barbara Currie, Pat Delarosbel, Kate Denninger, Murray Dickson, Edith Dow, Jim Dow, Steve Drake, Mike Drenth, John Eberhard, Allan C. Eustis, Gladys Farr, Robert Farr, Daniel Felix, Elizabeth Felix, Annie Fenn, Norm Flett, Jim Flosdorf, Jeannie Foran, Susan Ford, Hugh Funnell, Owen Funnell, Robert Gardner, Bob Gareh, Judy Gareh, Richard Garretson, Lynn Oliver Garvin, David Gerstner, James Kerr Gibson, Jack Glenn, Denise Gofton, Bill Gooderham, Gerry Gooderham, Nancey Gooderham, Tim Gooderham, Tuz Gooderham, Jack Goodman, Lorne Greene, Lorraine Greey, Philip Greey, Lincoln Gries, Dick Grout, Brad Hall, Frank Hartzell Jr., Jeff Hartzell, Jim Hasler, Andrew Healy, Peter Healy, Trisha Healy, Bill Hewitt, Bruce Hewitt, Roger Hill, Bruce Hodgins, Vince Hovanec, Rob Huff, Robin Hughes, Alan Hyde, John Hyde, Ted Hyde, Vivian Hylands, Bruce Ingersoll, Dan Jaeger, Ron Johnstone, Mary Kane, Adam Keevil, Harold Keevil, John Keith, William Keith, Charles King, Chessman Kittredge Jr., Ted Krofchak, Nancy Shepard Kovaleff, Ike Laba, Doreen Lak, Gordon Lak, Suzy Lake, Barbara Laronde, Margaret Lewis, Richard Lewis III, Francesco Libertini, Tom Linklater, Biff Lowery, Carol Lowery, Elaine Lowery, Andrew Lucko, Cathy Mark, Boyd Matchett, Linda Mathias, Dave McConnell, Patricia McGill, Michael McGrew, Richard McIntosh, Hugh McKenzie, Grant McMillen, Peter (Brown) McMillen, Ralph McMillen, Mary Miller, Wendy Mitchell, Peter Moes, Pamela Morgan, Sean Murray, Jean Myers, Sandy Navaro, Pearl Newcomb, Scott Northey, James Wychgel Norton, Sandy Nixon, John Oliver II, Rita O'Sullivan, Tom Pace, William Pace, Allyne S. Portmann, Gary Potts, Claire Rannie, Fred Reimers,

Lou Riopel, Larry Rodgers, Tom Romans, Walter Ross, Cheryl Ruddock, John Rykert, Liz Rykert, Bruce Saville, Daphne Schiff, Sam Scovil, Angus Scully, Fran Shannon, Peggy Shardelow, Lynn Sheeler, Jack Shepard, Jeffrey Simmons, Elizabeth Sinclair, Reg Sinclair, Susan Sleegers, George Small, Gary Smellie, Mary Smellie, Gaye Smith, Nancy Smith, Sandra Smith, Mary Soper, Frank Spitzig, Andy Stevens, Clay Stevens, John Szasz, Diane W. Taylor, Florence Thompson, Gordon Thompson, Graeme Thompson, Frank Todd, H. Arnold Todd, Russell Tuckerman, Betty Turner, George Turner, Bill Twain, Maria Twain, Jeanne Underwood, Ted Underwood, Yvette White, Malcolm Wilson, Robert Wilson, Ken Wismer, Marjorie Woodman, Alex Worman, James F. Wychgel, Dora Young, Hilton Young.

Special thanks to Trisha Healy of Island 981 and Huntsville. Trisha, a retired teacher, published author, and environmental and outdoor education consultant, commenced editing *Temagami Lakes Association: The Life and Times of a Cottage Community* manuscript in summer 2010. The best way to describe her contribution is by the numbers: four-hour phone conversations with the author to discuss chapter revisions; hundreds of email messages; thousands of hours of editing, cut and paste, dealing with punctuation and grammar rule updates, etc.; and coping with a score of eye-strain headaches. Ultimately, she helped streamline this book into what is hoped a pleasant and informative dock chair read.

Special thanks for the 1992 edition to the late H. Arnold Todd who supplied a nearly complete set of directories dating from 1956, 1930s regatta programs, personal reminiscences, even the original reward sign and boat pennant – much of it passed on to him by his father Frank Todd. And to John Hyde who had the foresight to keep correspondence between the Association and his father George Hyde. These documents helped fill in a gaping hole in the narrative concerning the 1930s and '40s. This 2011 edition would have lacked historical grounding without Robert Wilson's collection of 19th and 20th-century photographs and documents. They helped set the early scene. Brian Back and Ottertooth.com were often in the background, shining a light on both complex and minute matters. Tim Gooderham lost parts of two seasons trying to copy images from the truculent TLA Archives CD. The man has the patience of Job.

Special thanks to Stephanie Parrott for her skilled and timely typing of the manuscript.

Non-Human Help Created By Humans

Temagami Times, Temagami Experience, Temagami Talker, North Bay Nugget, Toronto Globe and Mail, Toronto Star, Bay City Times, The Temagami Experience by Bruce Hodgins and Jamie Benidickson, *The Keewaydin Way* 1983, 2004 by Brian Back, *Fort Temiskaming and the Fur Trade* by Elaine Allan Mitchell, *Wanapitei on Temagami* by Bruce Hodgins, *Moose to Moccasins* by Madeline Katt Theriault, *The Cabin* by Hap Wilson, *Islands and Lakes*

Where Souls Expand by Anne Rutzen, *Cobalt the Silver City* published by the Highway Book Shop, 1908 Temagami Steamboat and Hotel Company outfit (Michael Bloomfield), "Where the Loon Laughs" in *Forest and Stream* magazine (Robert Wilson), "A Paddler's Paradise" in the University of Toronto's *Massey's Magazine* (Peter Brook), "How We Got to Camp in Days Gone By" by the Ontario Camping Association (Carol Cochrane), "Temagami Magic" by Gordon Deeks and Richard Howard for Upper Canada College (Carol Cochrane), *Cottage Life* magazine, early Grand Trunk Railway, resort and TNOR brochures (Reg Sinclair and Michael Bloomfield), *The Masinahigan* newsletter published by the TAA, Laura McKenzie Learning Centre program, the Jack Humphrey Temagami CD Collection, TLA-temagami.org, Ottertooth.com, Temagami.ca, Temagamivacation.com, Temagamifirstnation. ca, *The Keewaydin Tattler* online, *The Wabun Way* online, Mytemagami.ca (Mike Lalonde's website to honour his father Darryl Lalonde), TLA Archives, Ontario Archives, MNR Archives, Appleby College Archives, Ontario Geographic Names Board, Cassels Brock and Blackwell LLP.

The Humanity!

The word "plan" is repeated nearly 300 times. "Committee" is mentioned about 210 times and meeting gets some 73 repeats. The word "Nemaybinagasbishing" is only attempted once.

ABOUT THE AUTHOR

Pamela (Glenn) Sinclair's family has held Island 1003 on Lake Temagami near and dear since 1905, when her Cobalt silver camp ancestors discovered a better gem. With a York University BA degree in English, she forged a career in journalism in northern Ontario, initially as editor of the *Temagami Times*. She later moved on to larger weeklies and dailies. She has also worked as a historical researcher for Trent University Emeritus History Professor Bruce W. Hodgins. Pam's 1992 book *Temagami Lakes Association: An Historical Perspective* was a Temagami bestseller.